JESUIT PEDAGOGY, 1540–1616

A READER

Edited by Cristiano Casalini and Claude Pavur, S.J.

Institute of Jesuit Sources
Boston College

No. 1 in Series: Sources for the History of Jesuit Pedagogy

Editor: Robert A. Maryks

Cover illustration: *The Education of Youth* [institutio iuventutis] *as Represented in an Emblem*. From *Imago primi sæculi Societatis Iesu* (Antwerp: Plantin, 1640), 3:468. Courtesy of the John J. Burns Library, Boston College.

Cataloging in Publication data on file.

Library of Congress Control Number: 2016932415

ISBN: 978-0-997282-30-6

INSTITUTE FOR
ADVANCED JESUIT STUDIES
BOSTON COLLEGE

In memory of the days and works of
László Lukács, S.J. (1910–98)
Editor of the Monumenta paedagogica

Table of Contents

List of Tables and Illustrations

Acknowledgments

Of the many people who have played some role in the creation of this volume, the translators/editors especially wish to thank Robert A. Maryks, who first proposed the project and carefully attended to it through all its stages of development; Paul Grendler (University of Toronto, *emeritus*) and Fr. John W. O'Malley, S.J. (Georgetown University) for their insights and helpful suggestions; Clarence H. Miller (Saint Louis University, *emeritus*), Fr. Scott Hendrickson, S.J. (Loyola Chicago), Richard Nichols, S.J. (School of Theology and Ministry at Boston College), and several anonymous experts, for their comments on the translations of various documents; Fr. James Keenan, S.J., and Daniel J. Cattolica (both of Boston College), who collaborated with us early on; and Mauro Brunello (Archivum Romanum Societatis Iesu) and Fr. Markus Pillat, S.J. (Archivio Storico del Pontificio Collegio Germanico-Ungarico) for their help with primary sources. The librarians and the personnel of Information Technology Services of Boston College also deserve gratitude for playing their usual indispensable role. One of the editors would also like to express at this time an overarching debt to his mother, Gertrude L. Pavur (1923–2016); she certainly can be listed as both a remote and a not-so-remote contributor to the making of this volume. We are particularly grateful to our director Fr. Casey Beaumier, S.J., and to all the members of the Institute for Advanced Jesuit Studies, who gave us so much support and expressed interest in our project. Perhaps the largest debt is the one we owe to the vision, the initiatives, and the care of the president of Boston College, Fr. William P. Leahy, S.J., and to all the largely hidden but essential benefactors who have worked with him to carry forward the efforts of the Institute of Jesuit Sources in its new dispensation at Boston College. May this volume be the first of many, *ad majorem Dei gloriam*.

Abbreviations

CN = *The Constitutions of the Society of Jesus and Their Complementary Norms: A Complete English Translation of the Official Latin Texts.* Edited by John W. Padberg. St. Louis: Institute of Jesuit Sources, 1996.

Constitutions, Padberg = same as CN.

Chronicon = *Vita Ignatii Loiolae et rerum Societatis Iesu historia* [The life of Ignatius Loyola and the history of the Society of Jesus], MHSI vols. 1, 3, 5, 7, 9, 11, ed. D. Fernández Zapico (Madrid, 1894–98).

Farrell = Allan P. Farrell, *The Jesuit Code of Liberal Education: Development and Scope of the* Ratio studiorum. Milwaukee: Bruce Publishing Company, 1938.

Ignatius Letters = *Ignatius of Loyola: Letters and Instructions.* Edited by Martin E. Palmer, John W. Padberg, and John L. McCarthy. St. Louis: Institute of Jesuit Sources, 2006.

MHSI = Monumenta Historica Societatis Iesu. 157 volumes. Madrid; Rome. 1894–. These are the critically edited texts of archival materials.

Monumenta ignatiana = volumes in the MHSI containing documents from or about Ignatius. There are four series: I: Epistolae et instructiones S. Ignatii (12 vols., Madrid, 1903–11); II: Exercitia Spiritualia S. Ignatii eorumque Directoria (2 vols., Madrid and Rome, 1919 and 1955); III: Sancti Ignatii Constitutiones Societatis Iesu (4 vols., Rome 1934–38); IV: Scripta de Sancto Ignatio (2 vols., Madrid, 1904; 1918).

Monumenta paedagogica = a subset of seven volumes within the 157 volumes of the MHSI, often cited in scholarly sources with the abbreviations MP or Mon. Paed. or MPSI. Though there is an early volume from 1901 entitled *Monumenta paedagogica* (= MHSI, vol. 19), these later seven works are part of a new series (indicated by the term "nova editio") in which the original sources were re-edited and supplemented with many additional documents. The volumes of this new series were all edited by Ladislaus Lukács, S.J., and published in Rome by the Institutum Historicum Societatis Iesu:

MP I ([covering the years]1540–1556) = MHSI, nova editio, 92 [published, 1965].

MP II (1557–1572) = MHSI, nova editio, 107 [1974].

MP III (1557–1572) = MHSI, nova editio, 108 [1974].

MP IV (1573–1580) = MHSI, nova editio, 124 [1981].

MP V (Ratio atque institutio studiorum Societatis Iesu, 1586 1591 1599) = MHSI, nova editio, 129 [1986].

MP VI (Collectanea de ratione studiorum Societatis Iesu: 1582–1587) = MHSI, nova editio, 140 [1992].

MP VII (Collectanea de ratione studiorum Societatis Iesu: 1588–1616) = MHSI, nova editio, 141 [1992].

Padberg = John W. Padberg, "Development of the *Ratio studiorum*," in *The Jesuit* Ratio studiorum: *400th Anniversary Perspectives*, ed. Vincent J. Duminuco (New York: Fordham University Press, 2000), 80–100.

Rib. = *The Life of Ignatius of Loyola by Pedro de Ribadeneira.* Translated by Claude Pavur. St. Louis: Institute of Jesuit Sources, 2014.

RS = *The* Ratio studiorum: *The Official Plan for Jesuit Education.* Translated by Claude Pavur. St. Louis: Institute of Jesuit Sources, 2005.

A Selective Timeline for the History of Jesuit Education[1]

1524   Ignatius of Loyola (*c*.1491–1556) returns to Spain from the Holy Land with the intention of furthering his education. At thirty-three years of age, he begins to study Latin under Jerónimo Ardévol (d.1551), a devout schoolmaster in Barcelona.

1526   Ignatius studies at the University of Alcalá, Spain.

1527   Ignatius studies at the University of Salamanca, Spain.

1528–35   Ignatius studies at the University of Paris where he cultivates a life of faith with some fellow students. He finds the "Parisian method" (*modus parisiensis*) an especially productive approach to studying, with its exercises, exams, and stages of learning.

1528–29   Ignatius reviews his Latin literary studies at the Collège Montaigu.

1529   Ignatius begins the arts (philosophy) course at the Collège Sainte-Barbe.

1533   Ignatius receives a license in arts.

1535   Ignatius receives the title of master of arts.

1540   The Society of Jesus is officially approved as a religious order. The founding charter states explicitly that the members "may [...] set up a college or colleges in universities capable of having fixed revenues, annuities, or possessions which are to be applied to the uses and needs of students" (CN #8).

1541   "Fundación de collegio" (The founding of a college) is a short list of directives for the establishment of (residential) colleges for those entering Society in need of academic training to fulfill its mission (*Monumenta paedagogica*, nova editio, 5: introduction, 2–3).

1541   **Pierre Favre, Spiritual Aspects of Studies in Jesuit Formation (Chapter 1).**

1542   The bishop in Goa, India, asks that two Jesuits in a diocesan seminary teach reading, writing, and some Latin to some boys. By 1548, the Society has taken responsibility for the seminary.

1543–56   Ignatius drafts and revises the *Constitutions*. Part 4 (discussing schools) receives contributions from Juan Alfonso de Polanco (1517–76), Diego Laínez (1512–65), and André des Freux (Frusius, 1515–56).

---

1   The texts used in this volume are printed in boldface.

1544   Jesuits are studying in their own residential colleges at universities in
            Paris, Coimbra, Padua, Leuven, Cologne, Valencia, and Alcalá.

1544–45   The "Fundación de collegio" is revised. It indicates that the particulars
            of the education and the order to be followed by every college will be
            worked out later (MHSI 63:58–59). This passage is echoed in the *Con-
            stitutions* (4.13.n2, A; CN #455), which itself looks ahead to the *Ratio
            studiorum* of 1599.

1545   *Constitutiones Collegii Patavini* (Constitutions of the college at Padua)
            are composed after it becomes obvious that more specific directives
            are needed (*Monumenta paedagogica*, nova editio, 1: introduction, 9).
            Ignatius asks Laínez to draft an outline for the college at Padua that
            might serve as an example for others. Scholastics sent to Padua in Sep-
            tember of 1546 take with them an Italian copy of these rules (*Monu-
            menta paedagogica*, nova editio, 5: introduction, 3).

1546   Jesuits have a college in Gandía, Spain, founded by the duke Francisco
            de Borja. Some non-Jesuit students are being taught.

1547   Juan Alfonso de Polanco works on the *Constitutiones Collegiorum*
            (more detailed than the *Constitutiones Collegii Patavini*) and the
            Industriae (Directives), which foreshadows the contents and structure
            of the *Constitutions* of the Society, including the material on studies.

1547   The new viceroy of the Kingdom of Sicily, Juan de Vega y Enríquez
            (1507–58), seeks to institute a general moral and civic reform there.
            He persuades the officials at Messina to write to the pope and Ignatius
            to found a college and establish a permanent residence there.

**1547   Juan Alfonso de Polanco, The Importance of Humanistic Studies in
            Jesuit Formation (Chapter 2).**

1548   The college in Messina is opened as the first Jesuit teaching college
            primarily for non-Jesuits.

1548   Nadal, rector at Messina, and Andrés de Oviedo, rector at Gandía,
            ask Ignatius for rules for organizing their respective schools. Ignatius
            answers that they should write them up and send them to Rome for
            approval. Nadal's document becomes the essential core of all later
            plans for Jesuit education. It seems to have been used for the school
            in Palermo (1549); soon requested by Antonio Araoz, the provincial
            in Spain; and later given important attention and use by Ignatius in
            Rome (*Monumenta paedagogica*, nova editio, 5: introduction, 4).

1548   Juan Alfonso de Polanco, Directives on Academic Progress (Chapter 3).

1548   **Jerónimo Nadal, Constitutions of the College at Messina (Chapter 8).**

1549–50   Statutes of the University of Gandía are drawn up by Andrés de Oviedo (rector at Gandía), Antonio Araoz (provincial of Spain), Diego Mirón (rector at Valencia), and Francisco de Rojas (superior at the residence in Saragossa). They use the constitutions of the university in Valencia, adapting them to the "Parisian style."

1549   **Diego Laínez, Studying Philosophy (Chapter 28).**

1550   The Society's *Constitutions* appear for the first time. Part 4 is entitled "The Learning and Other Means of Helping Their Neighbor That Are to Be Imparted to Those Who Are Retained in the Society." It calls for a formal universal plan of studies (*Constitutions* 4.13.n2, A; CN #455).

1551   Jean Pelletier (d.1564) and fourteen Jesuits open the Roman College, which Ignatius wanted to make "the center and model of the Society's educational work" (Farrell, 69), both for Jesuits and for others. The tablet on the front door reads: "School of Grammar, Humanistic Studies, and Christian Doctrine, Free."

1551   Using his earlier *Constitutiones collegiorum*, Polanco composes *Regulae rectoris Collegii Romani* (Rules for the rector of the Roman College), and it is sent out to provincials and rectors of Jesuit colleges.

1551   **Juan Alfonso de Polanco, Rules for the Rector of the Roman College (Chapter 9).**

1551   Hannibal de Coudret (1525–99), at the instruction of Rector Jerónimo Nadal (1507–80) writes up and sends to Rome the plan for the school at Messina. Polanco entitles the document *Ratio studiorum Collegii Messanensis* (Plan of studies for the college in Messina). This is followed (perhaps in early 1552) by Nadal's *De studiis Societatis* (On the Society's studies) which looks to a full university program (Farrell, 54).

1551   Ignatius states to various college rectors that "no rule of studies was to be considered fixed or final until a program applicable to all the schools could be drafted and approved" (October 31, 1551, cited in Farrell, 47 [MHSI 28:703–6]).

1551   On December 1, Ignatius writes to the Spanish provincial Antonio Araoz (1515–73) a letter that has been called "in many points a remarkable epitome of Ignatius's spirit in the work of education" (Ignatius, *Letters*, 360).

1551   **Ignatius's View of the Society's Involvement in Studies (Chapter 4).**

1552   The German College is established through the efforts of Cardinal Giovanni Morone (1509–80) working with Ignatius to care for the future of the church in Germany. The college is put under the direction of the Society, whose Roman College soon (1553) begins to offer the higher courses in philosophy and theology, partly for the sake of these students.

1553   *Regulae de scholis* (Rules concerning classes) makes Nadal's organization of studies "universal in the Society" and "truly the nucleus of the entire plan of studies" (*Monumenta paedagogica*, nova editio, 1: introduction, 17).

1553   Jerónimo Nadal is chosen as a "commissary" or representative to organize and direct the rapidly expanding educational work (Farrell, 188–216). He had power to "collate and communicate the existing legislation of the Society, to found and organize colleges, approve and revise local customs, and in general to direct the manifold undertakings of the Order" (Farrell, 221).

1553   Ignatius, The Aim and State of the Roman College (Chapter 6).

1553   Juan Alfonso de Polanco, Considerations Regarding the Multiplication of Colleges (Chapter 5).

1554   Ignatius, Teaching Composition (Chapter 23).

1555   The Royal College of the Arts in Coimbra is entrusted to the Society and operates in connection with the university there.

1556   Pope Paul IV (r.1555–59) grants the Roman College the right to confer philosophy and theology degrees, thereby raising it to the level of a university.

1556   In a letter of February 14 to Philip II the king of Spain (1527–98), Pedro de Ribadeneyra (1526–1611) expresses the idea that the Society has involved itself in teaching because "all the welfare of Christianity and of all the world depends upon the sound education of the young" (*Monumenta paedagogica*, nova editio, 1:475).

1556   Pedro de Ribadeneyra, The Origin of the Colleges (Chapter 7).

1556   Ignatius of Loyola dies on July 31. He had opened or accepted forty-six colleges (*Monumenta paedagogica*, nova editio, 2: introduction, 43).

1558   *Ratio studiorum* of the Roman College, composed by the teachers there at the request of Superior General Diego Laínez.

1559   Lorenzo Maggio, Report on the Boarders of the German College (Chapter 10).

1560   Diego Laínez, through a letter to Jesuit superiors drafted by Juan Alfonso de Polanco, makes teaching a standard part of the formation and apostolic activity of Jesuits (MHSI 50:165–67).

1561   Ortensio Androzzi, Comments on the Effectiveness of the German College (Chapter 11).

1562–63 Nadal writes *Ordo studiorum Germanicus* for the schools in Germany, adapting the rules for the Roman College.

1563   Diego de Ledesma (1519–75), prefect of studies at the Roman College, asks Superior General Laínez that Nadal write a document covering in detail the entire educational plan and method for each class.

1562–75 "Painstaking examination and revision of every element contained in [the early formulas used for school organization]" (Farrell, 153).

1564   The faculty of the Roman College issue a revision of the rules they had completed in 1558. The distribution of prizes at Rome in this year was not the first such event, but it had a wide impact, through the rules composed by Pedro Juan Perpinyá, an outstanding teacher of rhetoric. The first Marian sodality is created, accepting the best students; similar sodalities are eventually created in other Jesuit schools (*Monumenta paedagogica*, nova editio, 2: introduction, 21).

1564   Diego de Ledesma, Studies and Morals at the Roman College (Chapter 14).

1564   Benet Perera, Best Practices in Humanistic Studies (Chapter 17).

1564   Giuseppe Cortesono, Spiritual and Academic Progress (Chapter 18).

1564   Benet Perera, Teaching Philosophy (Chapter 29).

1564–65 Diego de Ledesma, The Plan and Order of Studies at the Roman College (Chapter 15).

1565   Earliest reference to the *Summa sapientia* in the documents of the Second General Congregation (Farrell, 221–22). Named after the opening words, it was a collection of rules and guidelines written in service of formulating a comprehensive educational plan.

1565   Pedro Juan Perpinyá, Refined Education (Chapter 19).

1565   Pedro Juan Perpinyá, How to Teach Children Latin and Greek (Chapter 24).

1567   Ludovico Gagliardi, Report on the German College (Chapter 12).

1567–70 Giuseppe Cortesono, Constitutions for the German College (Chapter 13).

1568   *De arte rhetorica* of Cipriano Soares (1524–93) is published. It becomes the standard manual of rhetoric in Jesuit schools.

1569   Ledesma's *De ratione et ordine studiorum collegii* is issued by Superior General Francisco de Borja (1510–72). It is a universal plan of Jesuit studies that becomes known as the *Ratio Borgiana*.

1570   Ludovico Gagliardi, Difficulties in the Governance of the Roman Seminary (Chapter 16).

1572   Pedro de Ribadeneyra's *Life of Ignatius of Loyola* is published. It describes the Society's Institute, gives an extended reflection on "Why the Society Has Colleges for Educating Youth" (Rib., nos. 351–87), and surveys the openings of many of the early educational works of the Society.

1573   The Third General Congregation proposes that the *Summa sapientia* be examined, revised, and made normative for the entire Society.

1573   Juan Maldonado, Teaching Theology (Chapter 30).

1574   Diego de Ledesma, Specificity in Doctrinal Content (Chapter 21).

1575   Publication of the Latin grammar of Manuel Álvares (1526–82), *De institutione grammatica libri tres* (Three books on the teaching of grammar), the Latin grammar prescribed in the *Ratio studiorum* of 1599 (RS #46).

1575   Juan Bonifacio (1538–1606) publishes the earliest Jesuit educational tract, *Christiani pueri institutio adolescentiaeque perfugium* (The education of the Christian child and a shelter for adolescence [Salamanca: Mathias Gastius, 1575]). To Bonifacio is attributed the motto often used in connection with the Jesuit investment in education of young people, "*Puerilis institutio est renovatio mundi*" (The education of the youth is the renewal of the world" [*Monumenta paedagogica*, nova editio, 3:402n]).

1577   Superior General Mercurian codifies instructions and rules for particular officials involved in running schools.

1581   Superior General Claudio Acquaviva (1543–1615; in office, 1581–1615), very soon after his election, appoints a committee of twelve to compose "a formula of studies."

1581–94 Christopher Clavius, Teaching Mathematics in Jesuit Colleges (Chapter 26).

1584   Acquaviva appoints an entirely new committee of six to carry on this work.

1584–90 Fulvio Cardulo, The Promotion of Humanistic Studies (Chapter 20).

Editorial Note

The following translations are based on a selection of the documents from the *Monumenta paedagogica* series (seven volumes, edited by László Lukács), a subset of the volumes of the Monumenta Historica Societatis Iesu. There is in addition one item taken from the letters of Saint Ignatius also edited in the MHSI. The specific sources are noted immediately under the introductory synopses for the individual items. All of the translations are original, except where noted.

We have followed Lukács's ascription of the documents, many of which have come down to us without any indication of authorship. Often the titles attributed to the documents are either Lukács's or our own; they are merely a convenient way to suggest the contents. We have also relied on Lukács's transcription, correcting it only where we found evident typographical errors or misleading punctuation.

Introduction

Prelude

The period stretching from 1543 through early 1548 was decisive for the origins of Jesuit education.[1] After Francis Xavier (1506–52) had acceded to an episcopal request in Goa, India, that the Society manage a seminary there, Jesuits were teaching some seminarians a mere three years after the official founding of the Society in 1540. Jesuits were soon given full administrative powers of that institution in 1547.[2] In 1546, at the Jesuit college in the University of Gandía, Spain, some Jesuits were teaching a few non-Jesuits.[3] But the school founded in 1548 at Messina is known as the *protocollegium*: it was the first school (1) founded and run directly by the Society, and (2) aimed primarily at educating extern (i.e., lay or non-Jesuit) students.[4] From these beginnings, there developed over the following centuries a vast Jesuit educational network embracing millions of students. By the time of the Society's suppression in 1773, Jesuits had gained a reputation as the leading schoolmasters of Catholic Europe and of other parts of the world where they had

---

1 An extensive literature covers this topic. See Allan P. Farrell, *The Jesuit Code of Liberal Education: Development and Scope of the* Ratio Studiorum (Milwaukee: Bruce Publishing Company, 1938); George E. Ganss, *Saint Ignatius's Idea of a Jesuit University* (Milwaukee: Marquette University Press, 1954); László Lukács, "De origine collegiorum externorum deque controversiis circa eorum paupertatem obortis," *Archivum historicum Societatis Iesu* 29 (1960): 189–245; 30 (1961): 1–89; Gabriel Codina Mir, *Aux sources de la pédagogie des jésuites: Le "Modus Parisiensis"* (Rome: Institutum Historicum Societatis Iesu, 1968); John W. O'Malley, *The First Jesuits* (Cambridge, MA: Harvard University Press, 1993); Robert Bireley, *The Refashioning of Catholicism 1450–1700: A Reassessment of the Counter Reformation* (Washington, DC: Catholic University of America Press, 1999). And, more recently, John W. O'Malley, "How the First Jesuits Became Involved in Education," in *The Jesuit Ratio studiorum: 400th Anniversary Perspectives*, ed. Vincent J. Duminuco, S.J. (New York: Fordham University Press, 2000), 56–74, then reprinted in O'Malley, *Saints or Devils Incarnate? Studies in Jesuit History* (Leiden: Brill, 2013), 199–216; Macau Ricci Institute, ed., *Education for New Times: Revisiting Pedagogical Models in the Jesuit Tradition: International Symposium Organised by the Macau Ricci Institute, Macao, 25th–27th November 2009* (Macau: Macau Ricci Institute, 2014); Paul F. Grendler, "Jesuit Schools in Europe: A Historiographical Essay," *Journal of Jesuit Studies* 1, no. 1 (2014): 7–25.

2 For details about the seminary in Goa, see Ignacio Arellano and Carlos Mata Induráin, eds., *St. Francis Xavier and the Jesuit Missionary Enterprise: Assimilations between Cultures / San Francisco Javier y la empresa misionera jesuita: Asimilaciones entre culturas* (Pamplona: Servicio de Publicaciones de la Universidad de Navarra [BIADIG, Biblioteca Áurea Digital-Publicaciones digitales del GRISO], 2012), 9–21.

3 László Lukács, "De origine collegiorum," 197–99. This school had been founded by Duke Francisco de Borja, who had invited Jesuits to come to it. It was a modest undertaking, but it received formal status as a university in 1547 through a bull issued by Paul III (r.1534–49).

4 See Codina Mir, *Aux sources*, 263.

established a missionary presence.[5] After the restoration of the Society in 1814, they again taught millions of students and continue to do so today.

During the days of the rise of Jesuit education, there were two major kinds of educational institution in Europe.[6] The first was universities. Born as corporations of students or masters in the Middle Ages, they offered a professional education in which students would often apply themselves first to a course in (philosophical) "arts" before proceeding to one of the major courses of theology, law, and medicine.[7] The teaching was based on Scholastic methods which employed the threefold pedagogical device of *lectio* (lesson), *repetitio* (repeating), and *disputatio* (disputing). Students usually graduated with a bachelor of arts degree after some years studying the subjects of the *trivium* (grammar, logic or dialectic, rhetoric) and *quadrivium* (arithmetic, geometry, music, astronomy). They would attain a master of arts degree after three and a half years of philosophical studies based on Aristotle's works, moving from logic to natural philosophy (*On Physics, On the Heavens, Short Treatises on Nature, Meteorology, On the Soul*) and then to ethics and metaphysics.

After the arts course, students could remain in those studies or pursue one of the other major faculties in order to earn a doctorate, typically in seven or eight years. Law was divided into civil law and canon law, relying on the *Corpus juris civilis* (Body of civil law) and on a set of works such as the *Decretum Gratiani*, which were to be assembled and codified in the *Corpus juris canonici* (Body of canon law) only in 1582. Theology was commonly based on the *Sentences* of Peter Lombard (1100–60) and the *Summa* of Thomas Aquinas (1225–74). Among medical faculties, Avicenna's *Canon* held sway as the major text until it was replaced by Galen's authority in the wake of that author's renaissance at the beginning of the sixteenth century.[8]

5　In 1623, the famous English philosopher Francis Bacon (1561–1626) commented in the Latin (and expanded) version of his *The Advancement of Learning*: "As for what concerns pedagogy, the shortest way to put it is 'Consult the schools of the Jesuits': for nothing better than these has appeared" (Ad paedagogicam quod attinet, brevissimum foret dictu, consule scholas Jesuitarum: nihil enim, quod in usum venit, his melius [*De dignitate et augmentis scientiarum* (London: J. Haviland, 1623), originally published as *The Two Bookes of F. B. Of the Proficience and Advancement of Learning, Divine and Humane* (London: H. Tomes, 1605)], book 6, chapter 4).

6　For a broader survey of the educational scenario in the sixteenth century, particularly in Italy, see Paul F. Grendler, *Schooling in Renaissance Italy: Literacy and Learning, 1300–1600* (Baltimore: Johns Hopkins University Press, 1989); and Grendler, *The Universities of the Italian Renaissance* (Baltimore: Johns Hopkins University Press, 2002).

7　See Jacques Verger, *Les universités au Moyen Âge* (Paris: Presses universitaires de France, 1973) and Hilde de Ridder-Symoens, ed., *A History of Universities*, vol. 1, *Universities in the Middle Ages* (Cambridge: Cambridge University Press 1992).

8　Avicenna (Latin form of Ibn Sina, *c.*980–1037) was the author of a famous medical text known as the *Canon of Medicine*, a large encyclopaedia of medical knowledge. Galen (Aelius Galenus or Claudius Galenus, 129–*c.*200/*c.*216) was also a great medical authority in the

At the beginning of the sixteenth century, universities had evolved an organizational structure based on a system of colleges. There, classes were given to boarding students. The colleges' scope varied: they could be simple boarding houses, boarding houses managed by a pedagogue, boarding houses where "repetitions" (i.e., reviews) were conducted for students who attended their classes elsewhere, and finally boarding houses provided with masters and *repetitores* (reviewers or review-tutors) who actually gave their classes there. Indeed, Ignatius of Loyola (*c*.1491–1556) and his first companions met in a Parisian college of the last kind. Colleges were sometimes funded and could host students for free, but the majority of them also (or sometimes exclusively) accepted paying students.

Two different pedagogies were in vogue: the one of Bologna, also called *mos italicus* (the Italian mode or manner or approach), focused on the lecture or "reading" of the master, and the one of Paris, called *modus parisiensis*, focused on advancing students' learning. These methods concerned mostly practical issues of the organization of the lessons and the structure of the university as an institution; they were not representative of a comprehensive articulated philosophy of education. The professional goals of universities probably made it unnecessary for them to develop a full-fledged and consistent system of thought about the individuals they were forming or about the means by which that formation should best be achieved.

The second major kind of educational institution was the humanistic or literary school. These started to proliferate during the fifteenth century, especially in the Italian peninsula. They would usually consist of a small gathering of students studying grammar, rhetoric, and humanistic studies under a renowned master.[9] The textbooks were the writings of the Greek and Latin authors whom the master considered the most eloquent. Quintilian's (*c*.35–*c*.100) expression for the perfect orator—*vir bonus dicendi peritus* (a good man skilled in speaking)—was often quoted as the motto for humanistic education. It directly joins good expression with good character. Communicational abilities necessarily entailed moral considerations.[10] So humanistic schools aimed to form their stu-

---

Middle Ages. His texts were rediscovered in the early sixteenth century, influencing the anatomist Andreas Vesalius (1514–64), among others.

9   The present text uses the phrase "humanistic studies" where some might prefer "humanities" as a translation for *studia humanitatis*. Contemporary usage of the term "humanities" suggests a broader range, one that includes theology and philosophy, in contrast to the curricular practice of the Renaissance. In fact, the "more humane letters" (*litterae humaniores*) were explicitly contrasted with the "studia divina" (divinity studies). See also on this topic Anthony Grafton and Lisa Jardine, *From Humanism to Humanities: Education and the Liberal Arts in Fifteenth- and Sixteenth-Century Europe* (Cambridge, MA: Harvard University Press, 1989).

10 The connection of character and speech was a widespread ancient belief. See Seneca the Younger, *Epistulae*, 114, which cites a Greek proverb, "The way a person lives fits the way he talks." The ancient Greek rhetorician Isocrates wrote in the fourth century BCE that

dents' characters by developing their powers of eloquence rather than sharpening their intellectual abilities by cultivating their powers of disputation. This is made clear by the titles of the Latin textbooks that humanists such as Lorenzo Valla (1407–57), Erasmus (1467–1536), and Juan Luís Vives (1493–1540) produced: *colloquia, elegantiae,* and *elegantiolae.* These were anthologies of classical texts that introduced the students to Latin by means of good moral examples.[11] And even apart from such examples, the very acquisition of what was considered the most rational languages from the most accomplished cultures was directly connected with the formation of an upright character and therefore a good citizen.[12]

Cicero (106–43 BCE) and Seneca (*c.*4 BCE–65 CE) were the princes of eloquence. The core of the advanced humanistic education was based on their texts. Unlike the university professionals, the humanists thought very carefully and produced a great deal of writing about pedagogy. The need for a comprehensive and consistent philosophy of education lay the heart of the relationship between humanists and their ancient authorities, such as Cicero and Quintilian. Most of the masters who ran a school wrote or published a book about their methods for educating youth. Vittorino da Feltre (1373/78–1446/47) and Guarino Guarini (1374–1460) were among them.[13]

The smaller enrollment of the humanistic schools helped them to foster a major concern for the individuals' talents. As Jesuit historian John W. O'Malley argues, "rather than placing first importance on the development of professional and technical skills, it put in first place the human development of the student— physical, moral, religious, and cultural."[14] Humanistic masters were sometimes hired as preceptors for noble youths. When the teachers opened a school, students would have to pay to be admitted, though communities sometimes sponsored them.

Jesuits mostly chose to run the second kind of institution, that is, the humanistic school rather than profession-oriented Scholastic institutions of the universities. Even when Jesuits did run a university or set up their largest colleges, they would mix the two forms, keeping the humanistic studies as the basis of the curriculum. The fully evolved educational scheme comprised three major

---

"discourse which is true and lawful and just is the outward image of a good and faithful soul" (Isocrates, *Antidosis*, section 255, trans. George Norlin, *Isocrates in Three Volumes* [Cambridge, MA: Harvard University Press, 1982], 2:327).

11 See Craig W. Kallendorf, ed. and trans., *Humanist Educational Treatises* (Cambridge, MA: Harvard University Press, 1999).

12 See Eugenio Garin, *L'educazione in Europa 1400–1600* (Laterza: Bari, 1957), 137–52. And Grendler, *Schooling in Renaissance Italy,* in part. 111–41.

13 Guarino's school was actually a *contubernium,* where the master and his students shared housing, dining, and lessons. Grendler, *Schooling in Renaissance Italy,* 123.

14 John W. O'Malley, "Jesuit Schools and the Humanities Yesterday and Today," *Studies in the Spirituality of Jesuits* 47, no. 1 (2015): 1–34, here 11.

successive stages: Letters (i.e., what we are calling humanistic studies, covering grammar, language, literature, "humanity" or culture, and rhetoric), philosophy (corresponding to the arts programs), and theology. These stages can roughly be mapped on to contemporary divisions of high school (humanistic studies), college (philosophy), and graduate school (theology).[15]

A few helpful points can be highlighted here. First, a major reason—though not the only one—for the success of Jesuit education was that it was free of charge. This was unusual at the time. Most pre-university schools and teachers in the sixteenth, seventeenth, and eighteenth centuries charged fees. Second, Jesuit schools taught a Latin curriculum, which meant learning to read, write, and speak Latin using classical texts. They did not normally teach beginning vernacular reading and writing, what some call the ABCs or the rudiments. So boys had to know how to read and write a little before entering a Jesuit school. Third, historians have often described Jesuit schools as being elitist and catering to the upper classes. They certainly did teach many noble and wealthy students. But because the schools were free, they also taught boys from the middle ranks of society and many poor ones. The threshold of basic literacy was not impossible for poor boys to surmount. The only real discrimination was the strict limitation of admission to males. Very few schools of that day did otherwise. The education of females was usually left to family circles and convents.

Why the Jesuits Became Involved in Education

Historians of the Society of Jesus generally agree that Ignatius and his earliest companions did not intend that education would be a major ministry for their order. In fact, they originally excluded formal teaching in the Society as an option.[16] They wanted to be missionaries. This was their goal when they left Paris in late 1536 and reached Ignatius in Venice in January 1537 in order to embark for Jerusalem, where they hoped to proselytize among Muslims. Impeded in their attempt because of the Third Ottoman–Venetian War (1537–40), they proceeded to Rome to discern their future as a group. The best expression of their intentions can be found in the essential defining document known as the *Formula of the Institute*. This was the original formal expression of the basic elements of what the founders of the Society would later refer to as their "Institute," that is, the idea of what they were instituting or establishing with their new association—their way of living, their self-concept, what they intended to be doing, and how they intended to be proceeding and governing

---

15 A case can be made that the first two years of college (in the educational program usually followed in the United States) should parallel the last part of the stage devoted to letters.

16 In 1541, the first Jesuits addressed this issue in some early documents with the following statement: "No estudios ni lectiones en la Compañía." See *Historia Societatis Jesu*, 1:47. Quoted in László Lukács, "De origine collegiorum," 197–99.

themselves.[17] This *Formula* did not mention schooling as one of the major ministries or intentions of the Society.

O'Malley highlights three factors in Ignatius's spirituality that help explain why he decided the Society should operate schools. First, there was the primacy of personal spiritual experience. Second, there was Ignatius's own experience of "reconciliation with the world." Third, Ignatius saw social institutions as powerful means to help souls.[18] Moreover, both Ignatius's inclination towards study and his familiarity with the university environment help us understand why, as soon as the Society became involved in education, he insisted that the foundation of colleges that included schools should be given precedence over professed houses.[19] The Jesuits seemed to accept the ministry of education as their own easily, even with enthusiasm. Some criticisms about the Society's commitment to education were eventually raised. But they all focused on the excessive and supposedly ungoverned growth of colleges, not on the educational mission itself. This can be explained only if the academic dimensions were present in the Jesuit mindset from the beginning.

Indeed, this mindset must be understood in order to grasp the character of the Society. The generally accepted interpretation of the Society's relationship with education should be qualified by a few important considerations. First, the order was born in a university environment. All of the first ten Jesuits obtained degrees that made them masters of arts; that is, they all shared *a teaching credential*. To be a "master" meant that one could have "apprentices." A master's degree was a license to teach. This educational qualification was part of their professional persona, even before all but three of the ten (Pierre Favre [1506–46], Claude le Jay [1504–52], and Paschase Broët [1500–62]) formally had a priestly persona through ordination. Since they all not only pursued but also achieved this degree, we can very reasonably assume that they believed that education was a great and worthy good, one fully consonant with the Christian spiritual lives they hoped to live. Such a mentality would help explain why, when Ignatius agreed to commit the Society to educational work, there was no complaint from the others—a fact that historian Paul F. Grendler sees as "unusual."[20]

---

17 For the two important versions of the *Formula of the Institute* (from 1540 and 1550), see John W. Padberg, ed., *The Constitutions of the Society of Jesus and Their Complementary Notes* (St. Louis: Institute of Jesuit Sources, 1996), 3–14. The important concept of the "institute" of the Society grew to encompass the major documents that defined the order. See Saint Ignatius of Loyola, *The Constitutions of the Society of Jesus*, translated with an introduction and commentary by George E. Ganss (St. Louis: Institute of Jesuit Sources, 1970), 43–44.

18 John W. O'Malley, "How the Jesuits Got Involved in Education," in *Saints or Devils Incarnate? Studies in Jesuit History* (Leiden: Brill, 2013), 199–217.

19 A professed house was a Jesuit residence totally dependent on alms.

20 Paul F. Grendler, "The Culture of the Jesuit Teacher 1548–1773," *Journal of Jesuit Studies* 3, no. 1 (2016): 17–41, here 24.

Second, the *Formula of the Institute* radically committed the membership of the Society to activities for which education was not only an essential prerequisite but a presumed mode of apostolic action. The two essential governing aims of the Society are expressed in the *Formula* as (1) the progress of souls in Christian life and doctrine, and (2) the defense and propagation of the faith. But how could one possibly teach doctrine without education? How could one possibly defend and competently explain the faith without the same? Thus the *Formula* itself mentions lectures and teaching and the education of children and unlettered persons in Christianity. So Jesuits themselves had to have the education to perform these tasks. But the very achievement of the task was in itself a kind of educative act: progress in doctrine has to mean learning it and understanding it better; defending and propagating the faith likewise involves the minister in an educational project: good defense, good explanation require well-considered argumentation. The Society at its core presupposed and embraced an educational apostolic project. In this way, even granting that a network of schools was not envisioned, it was at its core a "learning and teaching order."

And the Society knew it. Ignatius was already sending young Jesuit aspirants to the University of Paris in 1540. One of the very first documents of the Society is entitled *Fundación de collegio* (The founding of a college), drawn up in 1541.[21] The reference is to residential colleges, not to teaching institutions, but it was not long before the university lectures were being reviewed, supplemented, and expanded in these Jesuit colleges. In fact, even in the 1540 version of the *Formula of the Institute*, there is a substantial paragraph on how the new order, though pledged to poverty, had the right to found and govern colleges for its new members capable of receiving certain kinds of income and having properties.[22] And these colleges, though admittedly residential in nature, are not conceived apart from the typical pattern of the times, where at minimum there would be cooperative learning among the residents (as in mutual review). The *Formula* directly suggests more structure and purpose than a simple dormitory might be imagined to have:

> The general or the Society retains the full government or superintendency over the aforementioned colleges and students; and this pertains to the choice of the rectors or governors and of the scholastics [i.e., Jesuits in studies]; the admission, dismissal, reception, and exclusion of the same; the enactment of statutes; the arrangement, instruction, edification, and correction of the scholastics [...].[23]

If someone should object that in this document the teaching of children and unlettered persons is really aimed at cultivating humility, as the *Formula*

---

21 MHSI 63:48–67.
22 Padberg, *Constitutions*, 10–12.
23 Ibid., 11.

certainly makes clear, it should also be added that the increase of Jesuit learning is also presupposed as a key reason that superiors should be very careful to see that the members engage in this humble act "since in our own members there is danger that *as one becomes more learned* he may tend to decline this occupation." Becoming more learned is expected. Even though that kind of lowly education of children looks less prestigious, the *Formula* goes on to say, it should be considered crucial because "the edifice of faith cannot arise among our fellow men without a foundation."[24]

The question of when the Jesuits became involved in education might therefore best be reformulated to: "When did the Jesuits become involved in *studia* [studies]?" The Society did not typically speak of "Jesuit education," after all, but of the *studia Societatis* (the studies of the Society). That phrase embraced both Jesuits and non-Jesuits, both the learning and the teaching. The answer to this newly formulated question is that Jesuits were deeply and essentially invested in *studia* from the very beginning—and from even before that. Ignatius wished to acquire learning and embark on a university course of study when he undertook Latin lessons at Barcelona in 1524–26. What learning had he perhaps absorbed from Dominican and other preachers and spiritual directors or confessors at Manresa? What inspired him to write a book of spiritual exercises rather than remain "unpublished," as it were, sticking to his winning conversational arts and charismatic influence? Before Manresa, he had not only been awakened spiritually but also educated by the learning found in the reading he did on his conversion bed, with books that were not without scholarly and intellectual aspects. The *Life of Christ* of Ludolph of Saxony (*c*.1295–1378) has been called "profound and scholarly."[25] The other work Ignatius is known to have read during his conversion is *The Golden Legend* by Jacobus de Voragine (alternate forms: Jacobus Varagine, Giacomo da Varazze, Jacopo da Varazze; *c*.1230–98). Its opening shows it to be more than a mere collection of edifying and fanciful stories: "The whole time-span of this present life comprises four distinct periods: the time of deviation or turning from the right way, the time of renewal or of being called back, the time of reconciliation, and the time of pilgrimage."[26] Thus we might say that the roots of the *studia Societatis* lie in the disposition and earliest choices of Ignatius himself.[27]

---

24 Ibid., 9. Emphasis added.
25 George Ganss, ed., *Ignatius of Loyola: The* Spiritual Exercises *and Selected Works* (New York: Paulist Press, 1991), 19.
26 Jacobus de Voragine, *The Golden Legend: Readings on the Saints*, trans. William Granger Ryan (Princeton: Princeton University Press, 1993), 3.
27 For the larger relevant cultural background that likely shaped Ignatius's dispositions, even beyond the long-standing connections of Christianity and religious life with education, one should explore the areas of courtly diplomacy, the training of courtiers, and also the connections of knighthood and literacy. See Martin Aurell, *Le chevalier lettré: Savoir et conduite de l'aristocratie aux XIIe et XIIIe siècles* (Paris: Librairie Arthème Fayard, 2011).

The documents translated in this Reader confirm that the Jesuit move towards education started as early as 1540. Although the Society did not initially take on the direction of classes, Ignatius established Jesuit colleges in cities where a renowned university, such as Padua and Paris, already existed. Young men who wished to enter the Society were sent to these colleges in order to receive the best education possible. At the beginning, these colleges were intended above all to provide housing for young future Jesuits studying at the university. But the letters of Favre and Ignatius himself to these students reveal an underlying philosophy of education, and they indicate that a better-educated Jesuit was chosen from among them to help other Jesuits attending university classes. This person acted as a kind of learned tutor helping the others to understand the university lectures, review what they had learned in class, and talk to teachers in order to win their favor and guidance.

This kind of residential Jesuit college was not an educational novelty. It was similar to the student colleges that constituted much of the University of Paris in the sixteenth century. At Paris, many students, including the first Jesuits when they were there in the 1520s and 1530s, lived in colleges where they prayed together, studied together, and learned together, both by attending lectures in the larger university beyond their doors and from teachers and tutors inside the college.

From this early and modest beginning, Jesuit teaching accelerated in the decisive three-year period between 1545 and 1547, when the possibility of setting up a structured college for young Jesuits in formation was discussed by Ignatius and other Jesuits. Other events, mentioned at the start of this essay, started a direction of apostolic thought: Jesuits were invited to manage the seminary in Goa, India; and in Europe, Francisco de Borja (1510–72), duke of Gandía, soon to become a Jesuit, begged Ignatius to open a college in his domain; he obtained his wish in 1546. This Jesuit college taught humanities and philosophy to a few young Jesuits plus a few boys, some of them from families that had converted from Islam (known as *moriscos*). Then the real beginning of what would soon become the Jesuit educational network took place at Messina, Sicily. Reforms begun by the new viceroy of Sicily, Juan de Vega (1507–58), led to his and the Messina senate's requests to the Society and Pope Paul III (r.1534–49) that Jesuits open a school there to teach lay students. In light of what has been said above about the Society's native mentality and institute, it is not surprising that Jesuits were seen as suitable for such an enterprise, even if they had done very little formal teaching to this point.

But beyond such considerations, the way the Jesuits performed their ministries, particularly those "of the Word," was eminently appreciated by members of society to whom those ministries were addressed. Preaching, hearing confessions, giving the Exercises, and especially teaching Christian doctrine were activities that implied pedagogical skills. The request from the senate of Messina that was delivered to the viceroy of Sicily on December 17, 1547, expressed this appreciation. The senators reported that they needed to improve their city as a Christian republic by means of "exemplary men in life and letters, who might teach, preach, perform and give Christian exercises."[28] They also wanted formal education, because they asked for ten Jesuits known to be "very learned" to teach theology, cases of conscience, arts (meaning philosophy), grammar, and rhetoric. This part of the request was so precisely stated as to suggest that Jerónimo Doménech (1516–92), a Jesuit whom Ignatius had sent to Sicily and who had become Vega's confessor, had been exercising influence behind the scenes. Whatever the circumstances, the plea demonstrates two major points. First, the citizens of Messina appreciated the activities pertaining to Christian doctrine that the Jesuits performed in the city as a "common good" for the Christian republic and, second, whatever his role in the plea, Doménech's efforts reveal that the Jesuits were mentally prepared to undertake the ministry of formal education.[29]

What kind of schools did the Jesuits open? What educational traditions did they follow when they became involved in education? A document written by Juan Alfonso de Polanco (1517–76) helps answer this question and some of their motivations in this ministry. It is a list of the practical and spiritual benefits that the Society, its students, and the locality receive through an education that furthers the common good of a Christian republic. The underlying educational ideal was clearly humanistic. As O'Malley remarks, this list "could [have been] written by Erasmus himself."[30] It does not mention any of the purposes that some contemporaries and subsequent historians mistakenly assigned to the Jesuit commitment to education. Polanco did not refer to the Protestant Reformation nor did he mention any special commitment to educating the upper classes. What received attention was the common good of the local society, in line with the civic orientation of Renaissance humanism.

Just as the purpose of education was grounded in humanist values, so were the schools that the Jesuits would open. The school in Messina was a humanistic school, because the curriculum focused on the *studia humanitatis* (humanistic studies). Although the Jesuits had both the university and humanistic school as possible models, they overwhelmingly preferred the latter. And even their most important educational institution, the Roman College, only added philosophy and theology to humanistic studies. It did not offer classes in law or medicine, the disciplines that characterized a full-fledged university.

28 *Epistolae mixtae*, 1:451.
29 For an early narrative of the opening of the school in Messina, see Pedro de Ribadeneira, *The Life of Ignatius of Loyola*, trans. Claude Pavur (St. Louis: Institute of Jesuit Sources, 2014), 204–5.
30 John O'Malley, "Jesuit Schools and the Humanities," 19–20. Erasmus of Rotterdam (1467–1536) was the great champion of humanistic education, especially in northern Europe.

From Messina to a Worldwide Network of Schools

The reaction of Ignatius to the request of Messina's senate leaves no doubt about how seriously he committed the Society to the venture of "teaching publicly"— teaching in classes open to anyone, including lay students. In March 1548, he sent to Messina ten talented Jesuits in order to found the college and the school. Once in Sicily, Jerónimo Nadal (1507–80) became their superior. The school opened in the spring of 1548, quickly closed because of the heat, then formally opened in October. It made a far more impressive impact than the earlier involvements in Gandía and Goa had. Shortly thereafter, the officials of the city of Palermo, also encouraged by the viceroy of Sicily and his wife, asked Ignatius to establish a Jesuit school there. Schools at Tivoli, Naples, Venice, Ferrara, Florence, Padua, Vienna, Lisbon, Monreale, and elsewhere followed in the next five years. Most importantly, in 1551, the Roman College opened in Rome.

Historian Allan Farrell lists thirty-three schools functioning a mere five years later at the time of Ignatius's death (July 31, 1556), and six more approved by Ignatius that opened after his death.[31] O'Malley remarks that these numbers are "an astounding revelation."[32] Another astonishing point was their high enrollments: in 1556, school sizes ranged from sixty students in Venice to eight hundred in Billom (France) and nine hundred in Coimbra. More than one hundred students were attending the schools at Bologna, Naples, and Perugia, while around three hundred were attending in Palermo, Córdoba, and Vienna. In Vienna and other places where the Reformation had spread, Protestant students were admitted to the Jesuit colleges. Although their colleges were not created to fight Protestantism, the Jesuits soon realized how powerful the instrument of education was for winning back people who had been "alienated from the Catholic faith."[33]

Could this evolution in the Society simply have been the result of Ignatius's change of mind and inspiration?[34] Certainly there were other relevant factors. The Society would have in these schools the opportunity to present "in living form" an appealing image of its own Institute to young people at a critical time in their lives, and it would thus be able to discover new vocations (even though direct recruitment was disallowed). Even more importantly, the Society needed to fund the schooling of many of the young people who were joining the Society without the requisite training. In almost every case, Ignatius made some

---

31 Farrell, *Jesuit Code*, 431–35.
32 John W. O'Malley, *The First Jesuits* (Cambridge, MA: Harvard University Press, 1993), 205.
33 *Chronicon*, 2:460.
34 This could apparently be justified by a mere comparison between Ignatius's denial of teaching in 1541 and a letter he wrote in 1554, answering Peter Canisius (1521–97) about how the Society might best help Germany: he pointed out just one thing, that is, "colleges." Quoted in Lukács, "De origine collegiorum" (1960): 234–35.

support of Jesuit students a formal precondition for the Society's sponsorship of a college.[35]

In any case, the speedy journey that transformed the Society into a teaching order with a network of schools can be recapitulated under these four headings: (1) The first Jesuits were a gathering of university students seeking a teaching credential. (2) There was some tutoring of young Jesuits in formation in the very first colleges of the Society even though formal teaching was not yet a ministry of the Society. (3) The Jesuits began to teach a small number of students, sometimes Jesuits in training, at Goa and Gandía. (4) The Jesuits founded the college and school in Messina in 1548, and more than thirty colleges with schools for external students in the next eight years.

After Ignatius's death, the number of Jesuit colleges increased at a relentless rate. As Grendler points out, Ignatius's successor, Diego Laínez (1512–65), and his lieutenants, Polanco and Nadal, continued the policy of opening as many new schools as possible "as quickly as possible."[36] Yet, not every venture was a success; some of schools had to close because of a lack of funding, not enough students, or unqualified teachers. As early as 1553, the Society found itself short of personnel, and some criticisms were raised by the families of the students about the quality of the Jesuit pedagogues. In the so-called *Constitutions for the German College*, the former rector Giuseppe Cortesono (1537–71) lamented that the Society was heading to ruin by taking on too many schools.[37] Nonetheless, despite these concerns, the failure of some schools, and an almost chronic shortage of teachers, the first Jesuits never changed their minds about making the Society ever more committed to formal education.

In 1560, Polanco dispatched on behalf of Superior General Laínez a crucial letter to all the superiors of the Society, telling them that the ministry of the schools was to be considered the primary base for other ministries, and that every Jesuit must ordinarily "bear part of the burden of the schools."[38] In Laínez's mind, every Jesuit, except for the temporal coadjutors, was expected to teach.[39] Even the

---

35 Farrell, *Jesuit Code*, 134–35. The presence of Jesuit scholastics in the Society's colleges was considered legally necessary by many until the Sixth General Congregation declared otherwise in 1608. There had been a concern that the Society's founding papal charters permitted revenues only for institutions that included scholastics in formation. See Ganss, *Ignatius of Loyola*, 480n35, and also Ganss, "The Origin of Jesuit Colleges for Externs and the Controversies about Their Poverty, 1539–1608," *Woodstock Letters* 91 (April 1962): 123–66, reprinted in Thomas H. Clancy, *An Introduction to Jesuit Life: The Constitutions and History through 435 Years* (St. Louis: Institute of Jesuit Sources, 1976), 283–326.

36 Grendler, "Culture of the Jesuit Teacher 1540–1773," 22.

37 See Chapter 13 in this Reader.

38 *Monumenta paedagogica*, nova editio, 3:305–6.

39 Temporal coadjutors, frequently referred to as "brothers" or "lay [i.e., non-clerical] brothers," were non-ordained members of the Society who primarily assisted it in temporal matters (shopping, cooking, carpentry, tailoring, painting, construction, and so forth).

scholastics who had yet to complete their own studies would teach classes in Latin grammar, the humanities, and/or rhetoric, disciplines that they had already mastered. This measure was aimed at fixing the problem of the shortage of teachers. Over time, it provided a supply of teachers that fueled the enormous expansion of Jesuit education which reached its greatest dimensions in the seventeenth century. At the time of the suppression of the Society in 1773, the worldwide Jesuit network of schools numbered about eight hundred institutions.

Although the *Constitutions* of the Society of Jesus, written by Ignatius of Loyola in collaboration with Polanco, envisioned Jesuit education as a seamless whole beginning with Latin grammar and culminating in Scholastic theology, in practice Jesuit schools were divided into a lower school and an upper school. The lower-school curriculum, found in almost every school, was humanistic: it consisted of classes in Latin grammar, the humanities, and rhetoric based on the ancient Latin and Greek classics. The complete upper-school curriculum found in the larger colleges consisted of classes in logic, natural philosophy, and metaphysics, usually mathematics, and two classes of Scholastic theology. The most important and largest Jesuit schools like the Roman College also offered courses in moral philosophy, Hebrew, and/or biblical studies. Classes in cases of conscience (a form of practical moral theology) were not part of the regular Jesuit curriculum because they were service courses intended to help educate local clergymen in confessional matters. Cases of conscience lectures often met only two or three days a week, instead of the five or five and a half days of the courses in the regular curriculum. Many colleges, even those with only a small lower school, taught cases of conscience.

The Jesuits believed that the humanities were particularly important, both for their content and for the public favor that they won. Iacobus Pontanus (Jakob Spanmüller, 1542–1626) strongly defended the teaching of humane letters as of crucial importance to the Society. The humanities were widely praised and had a strong appeal for the public, he claimed. He held that "even if they do not rival the other [disciplines] in rank, nevertheless, they are preeminent in richness and impact," and that "the rest of the studies are chilly without the humanities; in a certain way they are mute and dead. These humanistic studies are their life, spirit, movement, blood, and bone."[40] The humanities attracted the public. They were "the portal through which we enter the biggest cities"; and through them "we acquire the friendship of great princes."[41]

---

40 See Chapter 25 in this Reader.
41 This thought moved Pontanus to work on providing Jesuit textbooks that could spread all over Europe. In his masterpiece, after discarding all the other kinds of Latin textbooks at his time, Pontanus states that "nihil adolescentibus utilius, nihil iucundius Dialogis, nihil etiam, pueris praesertim, perinde necessarium" [For adolescents, nothing is more helpful, nothing more pleasant than dialogues, and there is nothing quite so necessary, especially for boys]. *Iacobi Pontani de Societate Iesu progymnasmatum Latinitatis sive dialogorum volumen primum*

Types of Schools

The Jesuits had several different kinds of schools with respect to structure and the composition of the student body. The most common was the school open to both Jesuits and external students. Another kind of school was the university. The Jesuits founded their own universities or taught humanities, logic, natural philosophy, metaphysics, cases of conscience, and Scholastic theology in lay or civic universities in which lay professors taught law and medicine.

Another typical Jesuit educational structure was the boarding school for nobles, that is, a school limited to boys and youths of nobility. The boarders attended academic classes in the Jesuit school of the town, but they also received, from lay teachers in the teachers' own quarters, instruction in vernacular languages, horsemanship, fencing, music, even dancing—all useful for future careers in princely courts. The academic classes of the regular Jesuit curriculum were free. But the boarders paid high fees for the classes in other subjects and for room and board. Some of the boarding schools for nobles acquired a very fine reputation.[42]

Finally, for those studying for the priesthood, the Jesuits often supervised residences like the Roman Seminary, the seminary for the diocese of Rome. Although the seminarians attended classes at the Roman College, Jesuits living in the Roman Seminary provided supervision, moral guidance, and sometimes tutorial assistance.[43]

---

cum adnotationibus. De rebus litterariis. Ad usum scholarum humaniorum Societatis Iesu [Progymnasmata of Latin or the first volume of dialogues with notes. Concerning literary matters. By Jacobus Pontanus, S.J. For the use of the Society of Jesus's classes in humanistic studies] (Ingolstadt: Sartorium, 1589), c.17^r. The Progymnasmata were aimed at the cultivation of correct speech; they had to compete with Erasmus's works on the same subject ("Comparentur libri mei non dico cum Roterodami codice, qui non modio, aut trimodio, vero ipsum propemodum horreo demensas largitur facetias, sed cum aliorum Dialogis: iudicabor ego pro rata portione nimium parcus fuisse" [I do not say compare my books with the Erasmus's tome, which lavishes it with witty sayings scooped out not by the bushel or by the triple-bushel, but almost by the barnful, but I say compare them with the dialogues of others (or) I will be judged to have been proportionately all too sparing] (ibid., c.25^r). This volume of Progymnasmata eventually spread throughout Europe and was even adopted by Protestant schools. See Barbara Mahlmann-Bauer, "Catholic and Protestant Textbooks in Elementary Latin Conversation: Manuals of Religious Combat or Guide to Avoiding Conflicts?," in Scholarly Knowledge: Textbooks in Early Modern Europe, ed. Emidio Campi, Simone de Angelis, Anja-Silvia Goeing, and Anthony T. Grafton (Geneva: Droz, 2008), 341–90.

42 Gian Paolo Brizzi, La formazione della classe dirigente nel Sei-Settecento: I seminaria nobilium nell'Italia centro-settentrionale (Bologna: Il mulino, 1976); Simona Negruzzo, Collegij a forma di seminario: Il sistema di formazione teologica nello stato di Milano in età spagnola (Brescia: La Scuola, 2001). And Alba Mora, ed., Il Collegio dei Nobili di Parma: La formazione della classe dirigente (secoli XVII–XIX)—Atti del Convegno nazionale. Fornovo, Sala Baganza, Fontevivo. 22–24 maggio 2008 (Parma: MUP, 2013).

43 A detailed history of the early life of the Roman Seminary can be found in Luca Testa, Fondazione e sviluppo del Seminario Romano 1565–1608 (Rome: Pontificia Università Gregoriana, 2002).

Several of the most important and typical Jesuit educational institutions merit special attention. The most important Jesuit school was the Roman College founded by Ignatius in 1551.[44] He intended to make it the most renowned institution of the Society of Jesus. Its beginnings were very modest, with little financial support. A room was rented and a sign hung over its door: "School of Grammar, Humanities, and Christian Doctrine, Free." The sign expressed the core of all Jesuit education: free education in humane letters and Christian doctrine. In a few decades, the Roman College expanded to teach both a comprehensive lower- and upper-school curriculum, including Hebrew and different kinds of theological subjects. Most importantly, Ignatius and the superior generals who succeeded him sent their most talented young Jesuits to study at the Roman College, where the ablest Jesuit scholars had been given teaching positions. A very great number of the most renowned Jesuit scholars, including the rhetorician Pedro Juan Perpinyá (1530–66), the historian Juan de Mariana (1536–1624), the theologians Francisco de Toledo (1515–82) and Francisco Suárez (1548–1617), and the great mathematician and astronomer Christopher Clavius (1538–1612), attended the Roman College, taught there, or did both. Its regulations, procedures, textbooks written by its teachers, and the views expressed by its theologians were held up as models for all the other Jesuit schools and teachers. The Roman College thus carried a special aura as the center of Jesuit education located in the heart of the Catholic universe. Many Jesuit schools had difficulty implementing the entire curriculum of the *Ratio studiorum*, officially adopted in 1599, but the Roman College did not.

A different kind of institution was the German College, later called the German and Hungarian College when it added Hungarian clerical students as well.[45] The Jesuits opened it in 1552 at the request of their eminent supporters, such as the cardinals Giovanni Morone (1509–80) and Marcello Cervini (1501–55), who sought an institution which might educate future German priests who would return to their native land to lead the Catholic Church in German lands. The German College had even more difficulty at the beginning than the Roman College because it failed to attract a substantial number of German students and it received very little financial support from the German bishops. These difficulties partly changed the nature of this institution, because Laínez was forced to allow it to admit paying boarding students, most of them boys and youths from wealthy north-Italian noble families. Laínez's action saved the German College

---

44 The main reference book for the history of the Roman College is still Ricardo García Villoslada, *Storia del Collegio Romano dal suo inizio (1551) alla soppressione della Compagnia di Gesù (1773)* (Rome: Pontificia Università Gregoriana, 1954).

45 For a history of the German College see Peter Schmidt, *Das Collegium Germanicum in Rom und die Germaniker: Zur Funktion eines römischen Ausländerseminars (1552–1914)* (Tübingen: Max Niemeyer, 1984). See also Francesco C. Cesareo, "The Collegium Germanicum and the Ignatian Vision of Education," *Sixteenth Century Journal* 24, no. 4 (1993): 829–41.

but gave rise to the difficult task of dealing with a hybrid body of students, as the documents in this Reader reveal.

The German College did not offer lessons; rather, its boarders attended classes at the Roman College. The lay boarders were expected to pay for meals and accommodation. They could have servants living with them, and Jesuit chaperons who lived in the college accompanied them back and forth between the German College and the Roman College. However, the German College was more than a residence. It offered tutoring by young Jesuit students inside the walls of the college. Students lived in dormitories where they studied, reviewed lessons, discussed, and engaged in practice disputations according to the direction of a Jesuit prefect who lived in the college. They also enjoyed recreation activities both indoors and outdoors, over which the prefects were expected to watch, so that students might improve their spirituality, behavior, and physical health.

Thanks to the financial support of Pope Gregory XIII (r.1572–85) and the favorable reputation the German College gained all over German-speaking northern Europe, the number of young German clerical students steadily increased. It became the model for other national colleges of clerical students that the Society of Jesus opened in Rome by the end of the sixteenth century, including the Anglican, Maronite, and Greek colleges. Each was a boarding residence whose students attended classes at the Roman College.

The most common kind of Jesuit school was a city or town day school open to all, especially to lay students, and free of charge. City governments and princes most often wanted this kind of Jesuit school, and the Jesuits provided them. There were hundreds of them across Europe by the seventeenth century in Europe and in some mission lands. Almost all of the students were lay students from the town. A handful of young Jesuits living in the college might also attend class. The school at Messina was the first of this type. A few of these city or town colleges, especially if they enjoyed strong financial support from a prince, city government, and/or individual donors, also hosted small boarding schools for noble boys. Young Jesuits who had not yet studied theology taught the lower-school courses, while Jesuit priests who had completed their philosophy and theology studies taught the upper-school classes.

The Society also operated for diocesan clergy seminaries that had been mandated by the Council of Trent in 1564. The first and most important of these was that of Rome, which the Jesuits undertook on the order of Pope Pius IV (r.1559–65) and ran until the suppression of the order in 1773. As an institution, the Roman Seminary worked like the German College: the seminarians lived in a boarding residence and attended classes at the Roman College. The difference was that the seminarians came from the diocese of Rome. In addition, the two institutions differed insofar as the Jesuits had no control over admission and dismissal from the seminary. It was extremely difficult to supervise the students, some of whom were troublemakers, without being able to dismiss the worst ones. The difficulties the Society had with the Roman Seminary taught them that they had to be very cautious in accepting governance of episcopal seminaries. In 1565, the same year that the Jesuits opened the Roman Seminary, the Second General Congregation of the Society banned the acceptance of episcopal seminaries unless a general had very strong reasons for doing so.[46]

Finally, there were the schools the Jesuits ran in foreign missions. These often taught basic literacy, the rudiments of Latin grammar, and elementary Latin reading.

Towards a Plan of Studies

The rapid and wide increase of schools challenged the Jesuits to offer an education of quality. A typical concern of the early Jesuits who served as rectors, teachers, and prefects of studies was finding a way to manage the many different types of challenges that arose. They therefore felt the need to create a consistent and effective set of rules for guidance. They also wanted to offer a standard education that was recognizably consonant with the Institute of the Society. Hence it is not surprising that the generals and their collaborators started to formulate rules that might be applicable in all Jesuit schools.

The Jesuits produced a large amount of documentation as they slowly moved towards the definitive edition of the *Ratio studiorum*, the authorized complete plan of studies the Society of Jesus promulgated in 1599. The *Ratio studiorum* has often been judged to be one of the most influential documents in Western education and certainly a hallmark of the Society of Jesus. However, the *Ratio studiorum* can be deceptive because it might seem to imply that most Jesuit schools offered classes in all the disciplines that it outlines.[47] As noted earlier, many Jesuit schools taught only lower-school classes. Furthermore, the *Ratio* does not offer an explicit philosophy of education. It assumes without comment that the Renaissance humanistic pedagogical program and the intellectual goals of contemporary universities were good and worth pursuing. The official edition of the *Ratio* seems primarily intended for the education of the Jesuits themselves, although external students were taught the same program. Finally, although the *Ratio studiorum* was intended to be applied universally, many schools were allowed to keep some local practices which might differ from its prescriptions.

The *Ratio studiorum* was the product of a long process in which many Jesuits discussed, reviewed, and perfected its outline over a period of about fifty years.

---

46 On this issue, see Kathleen M. Comerford, "Teaching Priests to be Pastors: A Comparison between Jesuit Schools and Diocesan Seminaries in 17th-Century Italy," *Archivum historicum Societatis Iesu* 72 (2003): 297–322.

47 See Gian Paolo Brizzi, "Per un'archeologia della *Ratio*: Dalla 'pedagogia' al 'governo,'" in *La* Ratio studiorum: *Modelli culturali e pratiche educative dei gesuiti in Italia tra Cinque e Seicento*, ed. Gian Paolo Brizzi (Rome: Bulzoni, 1981), 11–42.

Even before a formal decision to prepare it was taken, Jesuit schools had the *Constitutions* to provide some specific instructions on schools and on the education of young Jesuits, as well as documents written by early Jesuits like Nadal who directed the first school at Messina for several years and wrote up a plan for it. The final *Ratio* stands upon a long career in running schools and on the comparison of a very wide range of experiences and insights that were frequently encapsulated in the various plans that were sketched out and circulated.

Rules about how to govern colleges were set down as soon as Ignatius was asked for them by some early Jesuits including Simão Rodrigues (January 18, 1543), Martín Santa Cruz (June, 1544), and le Jay (1545).[48] They especially needed rules for the schools for Jesuit scholastics in Portugal and Germany. Ignatius entrusted Laínez with writing the *Capituli et ordinationi delli nostri scolari de Padova* (The chapters and ordinances of our scholastics in Padua). He expected that these would be diffused to other provinces as an example.

In 1548, Polanco drafted two documents on Jesuit education that echoed Laínez's words concerning the organization of the education of Jesuit scholastics. The first, entitled *12 industrias, con que se ha da ayudar la Compañía, para que meior proceda para su fin* (Twelve directives by which the Society can help itself better proceed towards its goal) devoted a chapter on how to improve the education of scholastics in spirituality and letters. The second, entitled *Constitutiones que en los collegios de la Compañía de Jesús se deven observar para el bien proceder dellos a honor y gloria divina* (Constitutions that the Society of Jesus should be sure are observed in the colleges for their better progress towards the honor and glory of God) was a more detailed elaboration of the *Capituli* of Padua by Laínez. Because Polanco wrote in a period of evolution in Jesuit education, when the teaching of lay students was suddenly more of a pressing question, the latter was left as a draft and never disseminated. The fourth part of the *Constitutions*, soon to appear in 1551, was also already an object of attention for Polanco.

In 1548, the school at Messina provided the first set of rules for Jesuit schools. Although Nadal's *Constitutions* for the Messina school was not sent to other provinces of the Society, they enjoyed great prestige and had a lasting impact on the shaping of Jesuit education. The Palermo school adopted the same rules; the Roman College partly reproduced them, as did the *Constitutions* of the Society.

Polanco's 1551 instructions for the rector of the Roman College marked a step forward in the development of a universal code for Jesuit education because of the importance of that institution. Polanco wrote them with Jesuit scholastics in mind; nevertheless, he addressed two chapters on the education of lay students, which had become important in this new ministry for the Society.

In 1552, Ignatius had a set of rules sent to all the provinces. Drafted by Nadal for the Roman College, they concerned teaching in the lower school. These were

48 Simão Rodrigues (1510–79) and Martín Santa Cruz (?–1548).

the first regulations to be diffused as an example for all Jesuit schools. Nadal brought copies of them when he visited Jesuit colleges in Spain and Portugal in 1553 and 1554. He explained how to apply them.

The centrality of the Roman College to the Jesuit network of schools was further confirmed after Ignatius's death. Diego de Ledesma (1524–75), prefect of studies at the Roman College, was a tireless proponent of the idea of preparing a complete set of rules for the college which might be adopted everywhere.[49] Between 1559 and 1565, he engaged the Roman College teachers in a collective examination of their teaching in order to prepare an *ordo studiorum*, which was to include both the lower and the higher disciplines. Laínez ratified Ledesma's commitment by ordering the Roman College to compose such an *ordo*, but his death in 1565 prevented him from seeing the project to completion.

Francisco de Borja, superior general of the Society from 1565 to 1572, confirmed Laínez's order, and by the end of 1565, the first part, concerning the lower disciplines and the instructions for the prefects of studies, teachers, and students, were finished. This material, mostly compiled by Ledesma, was sent to the provinces in 1569, and it came to be known as the *Ratio Borgiana*. However, it was a preliminary *ratio* that did not contain any rules for the higher disciplines, particularly for the content of the teaching of theology. Doing this would have involved the Society in a long and complicated debate.

Only after the 1581 election of Claudio Acquaviva (1543–1615) as the fifth superior general of the Society do we see the project of preparing a complete *Ratio studiorum* officially revived. He thought that a fully developed plan of studies would be a pillar in his program of centralization and standardization. As soon as he was elected, Acquaviva appointed a commission of twelve to draw up the plan. For some unknown reason, nothing seemed to result from this group, so, in 1583, he replaced it with a committee of six fathers who were called to Rome to prepare two parts of the *Ratio studiorum*. The first, called the *pars speculativa* (speculative part) or *delectus opinionum* (a choice of opinions), dealt with the issue of describing a sound and orthodox theology to be taught in the Jesuit colleges. The second, called the *pars practica* (practical part), was to provide instructions and rules for the governance of the school.

A sketch of the work was completed by the end of 1584, but several criticisms and necessary changes prevented Acquaviva from issuing it as an official draft. A version of this *Ratio* was finally released and sent to the provinces in 1586 for review only, in order to get suggestions for improvement. The provinces examined it meticulously and raised harsh criticisms, especially of the *delectus*

---

49 See Christoph Sander, "The War of the Roses: The Debate between Diego Ledesma and Benet Perera about the Philosophy Course at the Jesuit College in Rome," *Quaestio* 14, no. 1 (2014): 31–50. Sander argues that Ledesma's commitment to this task was linked to a conflict between him and Benet Perera, which was actually based on their different ideas for philosophical pedagogy. Sander provides an exhaustive and up-to-date bibliography on this issue.

opinionum. A commission led by Stefano Tucci (1541–97) was charged with producing a revised trial version, which was finally released in 1591. The printed version contained only the practical rules, since the *delectus opinionum* was to be sent later in a manuscript form. The 1591 version was sent to all the provinces to be tested for three years.

Crucial for the final version of the *Ratio studiorum* was the general congregation summoned in 1592, where issues pertaining to its content were debated. The project of a *delectus opinionum* was finally abandoned, while a new commission was entrusted with a final revision of the practical part. This was eventually approved, printed, and promulgated in 1599.

The Society of Jesus finally had its definitive plan of studies, even though one should keep in mind that very few Jesuit schools implemented its full program. A few changes were incorporated into an edition published in 1616, the version that remained in force until the suppression of the Society in 1773. After its restoration in 1814, the Society realized the need for an update, particularly to incorporate modern vernacular literature and also mathematics and the sciences. Superior General Jan Roothaan (1785–1853) nevertheless made it quite clear, in his cover letter for a non-binding revision issued in 1832, that the original plan retained its force and place of honor.[50] Even as late as 1957, General Congregation 30 wrote that "all should know well and greatly esteem the *Ratio studiorum* and its method and rules should be carefully observed in the education of our young men."[51] Thus this sixteenth-century plan rode the entire course of modernity, stretching all the way from the seminal experiences of Ignatius and the founders of the Society (1520s and 1530s) into the second half of the twentieth century. It lived on especially in the formation plans for Jesuit scholastics, which, until about 1965 and shortly thereafter, followed the broad lines of the old schema: letters, philosophy, and theology.

Life in the Jesuit School

The Jesuit college was a highly organized institution with a precise division of labor. The provincial superior (i.e., the superior of all colleges and all Jesuits in the geographical area known as a province) had ultimate responsibility for all the schools in his domain. Despite the influence of the Parisian tradition on the organization of a Jesuit school, the headmaster was called "rector," an Italian

50 For the text of this letter, see Georg Michael Pachtler, *Ratio studiorum et institutiones scholasticae Societatis Jesu per Germaniam olim vigentes collectae concinnatae dilucidatae*, ed. Karl Kehrbach. Tomus 2. *Ratio studiorum ann. 1586, 1599, 1832*. Monumenta Germaniae paedagogica 5 (Berlin: A. Hofmann, 1887), 228–33.
51 John W. Padberg, Martin D. O'Keefe, and John L. McCarthy, *For Matters of Greater Moment: The First Thirty Jesuit General Congregations—A Brief History and a Translation of the Decrees* (St. Louis: Institute of Jesuit Sources, 1994), 678.

TABLE 1.   Class schedule agreed upon by the Jesuit fathers in the Rhineland, 1586.

Hour	Third (Lower) Grammar Class	Hour	Class of Humanities
6 AM	½ hr. parts of Latin speech; ½ hr. exercise in Latin declension and conjugation; ½ hr. instruction in reading Greek	6 AM	Prelection and repetition of a poet ½ hr. alternate days: poetical theme composed extemporaneously and corrected
9 AM	½ hr. alternate days: Cicero and compendium of catechism, e.g., Our Father, Hail Mary, Apostles' Creed, Ten Commandments, Commandments of the church, sacraments, etc.; ½ hr. declension of nouns, conjugation of verb	9 AM	First two months: prosody; rest of the year: history
1 PM	Same schedule as for six o'clock period	1 PM	Greek
3 PM	Same schedule as for six and one o'clock periods; but at middle or end of the year include intransitive forms ½ hr. Latin theme or conversation	3 PM	Cicero: towards end of the year study of Cipriano Soares's *Rhetoric*, and an oration; ½ hr. extemporaneous Latin writing
	Second (Middle) Grammar Class		**Class of Rhetoric**
6 AM	½ hr. genders and declensions; ½ hr. review, and exercise in declensions and conjugations; ½ hr. extemporaneous theme	6 AM	rhetoric; ½ hr. correction of compositions
9 AM	½ hr. Cicero; review in the form of a contest; brief theme proposed at end of hour to be prepared for one o'clock period	9 AM	Greek
1 PM	½ hr. correction of themes ½ hr. preterites and supines	1 PM	history: but a poet on Tuesdays and Thursdays
3 PM	½ hr. same as for six o'clock period ½ hr. same as for six o'clock period Intransitive in middle of year ½ hr. Greek	3 PM	an oration of Cicero; ½ hr. extemporaneous writing based on Cicero or sometimes a poet where a philosophical [...] is not [...] in the last three months, dialectic can be taught
	First (Highest) Grammar Class		**Classes in Philosophy**
6 AM	½ hr. explanation and review of syntax ½ hr. theme proposed based on previous prelections and reviews	6 AM	Aristotle; ½ hr. review
9 AM	Greek	9 AM	ethics and mathematics on alternate days

TABLE 1.   Class schedule agreed upon by the Jesuit fathers in the Rhineland, 1586
            (*continued*).

Hour	Third (Lower) Grammar Class	Hour	Class of Humanities
1 PM	theme dictated in morning corrected Explanation of prosody or the principles of the scansion of verses and reading of some rather easy poet; at end of the period, oral exercise by way of contest on meanings of words, phrases, content of the author	1 AM	review
3 PM	½ hr. Cicero with phrases excerpted from the reading; ½ hr. exercises in declining, conjugating, and so forth; ½ hr. extemporaneous writing based sometimes on phrases of the Ciceronian lesson, sometimes on phrases from material taken earlier	3 PM	same order as for 6 o'clock period
			Theology
		6 AM	Scholastic theology
		9 AM	the same
		1 PM	controversies and cases of conscience
		2 PM	scripture ½ hr. after the second [hour], Hebrew

term, instead of "principalis" (the principal). Nevertheless, he was nominated, not elected, as was the case in Paris. The rector of the college governed the school of the college (which, as has been noted, could be primarily residential). A prefect of studies, who did not teach himself, oversaw the instruction of the teachers and was the most important person in the school. He largely filled the role of a principal in American middle schools and high schools, or the role of the academic provost in American universities and colleges.

Colleges with boarding students, such as the German College for example, were provided with other kinds of prefects. The prefect of spirituality supervised the spiritual improvement of the students, and he often worked with the confessor of the college. The prefect of recreation and the prefect of the schoolyard patrolled communal extracurricular activities, while the prefect of the dormitory was usually a Jesuit scholastic who tutored the students of his dorm. Students were indeed grouped in dormitories, which was the place where they would spend most of their school time.

Jesuit temporal coadjutors were entrusted with the functioning of the college as a residence: one kept watch at the door as a receptionist, one was a janitor, one a cook, one a tailor, one a laundryman. Some of them were painters, carpenters,

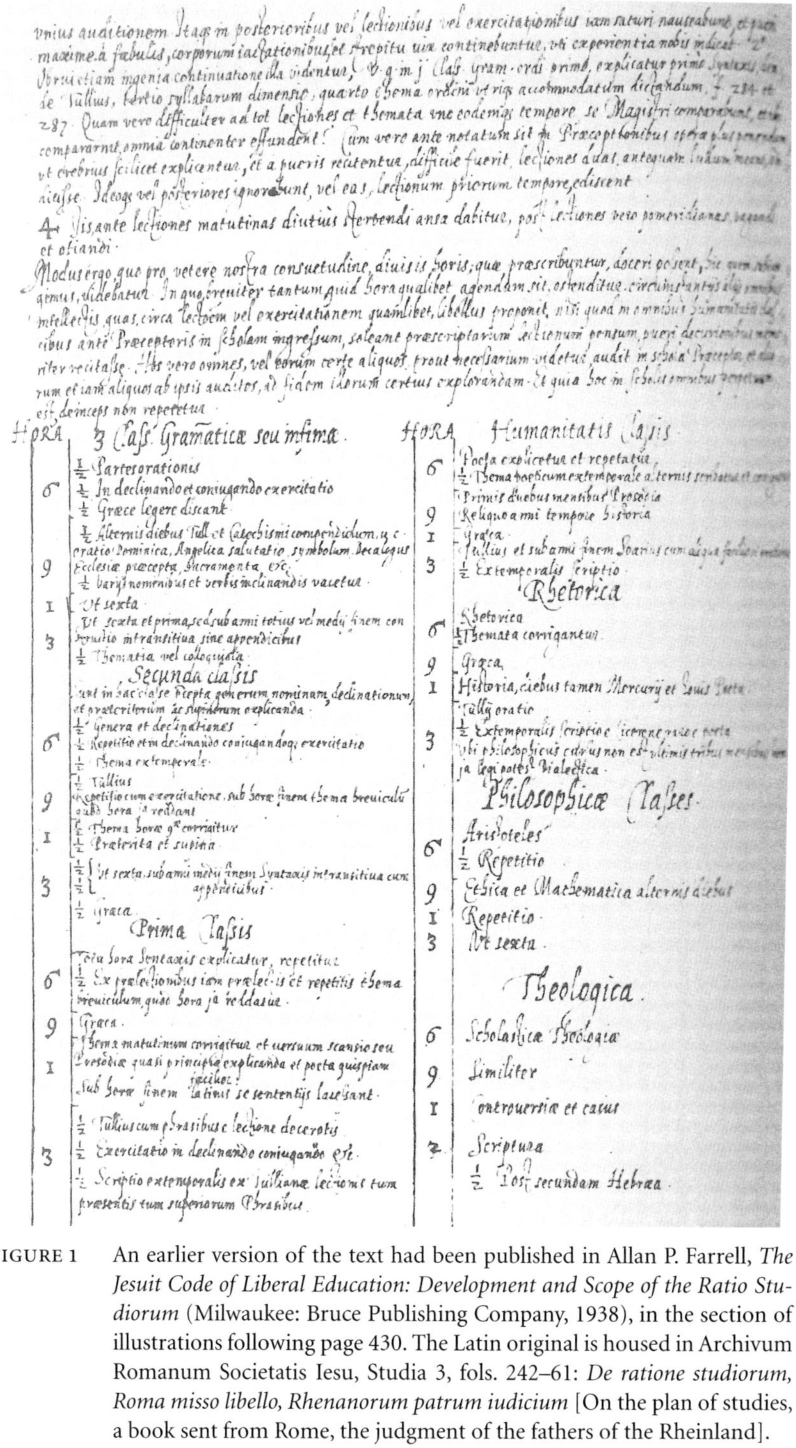

FIGURE 1 An earlier version of the text had been published in Allan P. Farrell, *The Jesuit Code of Liberal Education: Development and Scope of the Ratio Studiorum* (Milwaukee: Bruce Publishing Company, 1938), in the section of illustrations following page 430. The Latin original is housed in Archivum Romanum Societatis Iesu, Studia 3, fols. 242–61: *De ratione studiorum, Roma misso libello, Rhenanorum patrum iudicium* [On the plan of studies, a book sent from Rome, the judgment of the fathers of the Rheinland].

or masons. While the physician was usually hired on demand, a temporal coadjutor might serve as nurse or infirmarian. An accountant had the responsibility of managing food and other supplies for the college, while Jesuit wine-growers are often listed in the catalogs of the Society as taking care of the vineyards that many of the colleges owned.

As concerns the teaching staff, we can turn to the historian of Renaissance education Paul Grendler for a clear outline of the shape of a typical teaching career for a Jesuit. After two years of novitiate training, young Jesuits were usually sent as scholastics to study or review language, composition, literature, and rhetoric (what we are calling "humanistic studies"). If already well prepared in these subjects, they were immediately admitted to three years of philosophical studies during which time they studied Aristotelian logic, natural philosophy, and metaphysics. After finishing philosophical studies, young Jesuits were usually required to teach grammar, the humanities, and/or rhetoric in a lower school in their province. Most of them spent three to five years doing this. After finishing this teaching, they studied Scholastic theology in a major school in the province. Jesuit theology followed the tradition of St. Thomas Aquinas with a few differences. The study of Scholastic theology included some study of moral theology and sometimes biblical studies:

> Some Jesuits spent most of the rest of their lives teaching the philosophical trio. Others taught the philosophical trio for a few years, then taught theology. After that a Jesuit alternated. He taught philosophy for five or six years, then theology for five or six years, then went back to philosophy. A handful of Jesuits, considered the leading scholars, taught theology for the rest of their lives.[52]

A student attending a large Jesuit school benefited from a teaching staff committed to his academic advancement. If he attended a Jesuit boarding school, he had even more help. The prefect of his dormitory, usually a Jesuit scholastic, was often entrusted with the task of being a *repetitor*, that is, someone who reviewed the lessons of the teachers for the students of a class. Moreover, Jesuits required of their teachers that they should be "not only scholarly but also diligent pedagogues," as Polanco wrote in 1553. This meant that the teachers were not only well prepared in the discipline they had to teach but also shared a common pedagogical culture whose focus was the improvement of every student in both spirituality and letters.

It has often been pointed out, even by the first Jesuits, that their educational method was derived from the *modus parisiensis* (the Parisian method), essentially defined as "an organized plan for the progress of the student through increasingly complex materials and a codification of pedagogical techniques designed to elicit

---

52 Grendler, "Culture of the Jesuit Teacher 1548–1773," 24.

active response from the learner."[53] The Jesuits perfected the Parisian method with some techniques that they found in the humanistic tradition. Lectures were delivered in the Parisian tradition and complemented by a full array of drills, repetitions, and disputations intended to help students master the material. Students were divided into classes that followed a plan of progression in which permission to advance was achieved through competent performance in examinations. It is important to note that a class represented a unit of work rather than a period of time. That is, students advanced to the next class not annually or semi-annually, but only when they had mastered the contents of the previous class.

When the class was very large, Jesuit teachers divided it into *decuriae* (decuries), groups of ten led by a superior student who supervised the other nine students of his decury and assisted the teacher.[54] The furniture in the Jesuit classroom was arranged for pedagogical purposes; it also expressed the hierarchy of the classroom. The teacher sat in a raised chair. Decurions sat in small chairs in the front reserved for the best students; the rest of the students sat in rows of benches. A lesson was organized according to the Parisian trio of *lectio* (lecture), *repetitio* (review and memorization), and *disputatio* or *exercitatio* (exercising). The first element—the lecture—was divided in turn into the three moments of *praelectio* (introduction to reading, or the "lesson"), *lectio* (reading), and *explanatio* (explanation), whose focus was the text of the authority in the field. It is important to note that the activity of a student during the lecture was mostly that of taking notes. Memorizing the contents of the lessons was crucial and textbooks were scarce, although the Jesuit schools did make increasing use of textbooks such as grammar manuals as the years passed, so the ability to take serviceable notes was extremely important.[55]

Taking notes also enabled students to do their own daily homework, which in the lower humanities school might consist of a writing a short composition or a speech to deliver orally in class. Jesuit schools encouraged what they called "emulation," which really was spirited rivalry between students. For example, teachers commonly required students to correct each other's homework, and they awarded or penalized the correctors according to their ability to note mistakes. Students were awarded positive and negative points on many aspects of their academic performance. Designated students called "censors" kept track of each student's positive and negative points on large sheets of paper. At the end of the month, students were rewarded or penalized. The best were named emperor, or prince, and were given chairs in the front of the classroom. The worst students might be called "asses" and have a picture of an ass attached to their necks until

---

53 O'Malley, *First Jesuits*, 217.
54 The system of decuries was introduced in 1558 in Sicily. See *Monumenta paedagogica*, nova editio, 2:35.
55 A very interesting overview on this issue is provided by Paul Nelles, "*Libros de papel, libri bianchi, libri papyracei*: Note-taking Techniques and the Role of Student Notebooks in the Early Jesuit Colleges," *Archivum historicum Societatis Iesu* 76 (2007): 75–112.

they improved. The student who wrote a good composition or gave an excellent oral presentation might be granted the honor of delivering it publicly in the presence of dignitaries, special guests, and families of students. The introduction of prizes, strongly endorsed by Perpinyá, was another effective means of stimulating high academic achievement from all students.[56]

It should be noted that the philosophy of education that lay behind this culture of competition was quite different from that of medieval universities. In the view of the Jesuits, the fame that winning scholastic disputations brought with it pushed both students and professors towards subtleties and dialectical techniques which had no educational goal. Like the humanists, the Jesuits repeatedly criticized this even though they made use of dialectical disputations. For the Jesuits, competition was intended as a pedagogical instrument that fostered an active engagement on the part of the learner. Students were expected to create something on their own, even though it was based on the imitation of exemplary authorities such as Cicero.

The Jesuits cultivated school theater as a means of teaching poise and self-confidence to students because they were required to impersonate characters on a stage.[57] The professor of rhetoric, who usually had charge of the theater, or the students themselves might write plays. Jesuit schools became famous for their tragedies and comedies; at the same time, successful plays performed publicly helped promote the schools.[58] In addition, staging a play required students to learn something of the arts so that they might perform with musical instruments and dance.[59] An elaborate technology was developed, including theatrical machines, sound effects, and so forth. The Jesuit plays staged at the Roman and the German Colleges contributed much to Italian Baroque theater.

---

56 *Monumenta paedagogica*, nova editio, 2:636.

57 Self-awareness was a key feature of Jesuit education, deriving from Ignatius's spirituality. An insight into the modernity of this aspect of Ignatius's psychology is provided by Moshe Sluhovsky, "Loyola's *Spiritual Exercises* and the Modern Self," in *A Companion to Ignatius of Loyola: Life, Writing, Spirituality, Influence*, ed. Robert A. Maryks (Leiden: Brill, 2014), 216–31.

58 It is well known that Jesuit colleges were often the most renowned stages for plays in the cities where they were operating. An increasing amount of literature has been devoted to this branch of Jesuit studies. Insights on the pedagogic concerns of the Jesuit theater are provided by Nigel Griffin, "Miguel Venegas and the Sixteenth-Century Jesuit School Drama," *Modern Language Review* 68, no. 4 (1973): 796–806. More recently, Giovanna Zanlonghi, *Teatri di formazione: Actio, parola e immagine nella scena gesuitica del Sei–Settecento a Milano* (Milan: Vita e Pensiero, 2002); Luana Salvarani, "Venegas e gli altri: Il teatro nella prassi pedagogica gesuita del Cinquecento," *Educazione: Giornale di pedagogia critica* 1, no. 1 (2012): 5–22; and Jan Bloemendal and Howard B. Norland, eds., *Neo-Latin Drama in Early Modern Europe* (Leiden: Brill, 2013).

59 See, e.g., Judith Rock, *Terpsichore at Louis-le-Grand: Baroque Dance on the Jesuit Stage in Paris* (St. Louis: Institute of Jesuit Sources, 1996); and Alessandro Arcangeli, "The Ballroom and the Stage: The Dance Repertoire of the Society of Jesus," in *I Gesuiti e la Ratio studiorum*, ed. Manfred Hinz et al. (Rome: Bulzoni, 2004), 67–73.

When a school had some outdoor space in a courtyard or plaza, students played games and sports outside. Some Jesuit colleges with schools, especially wealthy colleges hosting noble boarding schools, owned properties in the countryside. They were able to give their students country outings in the spring and summer. The Jesuits agreed with the humanists that a *mens sana in corpore sano* (a sound mind in a sound body) was important. Jesuit schools pursued the ideal of educating the whole person.[60]

In the Jesuit philosophy of education, learning and spirituality were united. Mastering curricular content was in itself insufficient, even less than half of what the Society was aiming for in its schools. It insisted on the concept of the joining of letters and morals, the Renaissance humanist ideal of *docta pietas* (learned piety), in which perfection of learning, maturity of character, the enlightenment of the spirit, and religious commitment were combined. Hence, devotional and spiritual activities were very important in Jesuit schools. Classes teaching Christian doctrine were part of the curriculum. Students were required to attend Mass, confess regularly, and hear sermons. This was particularly true on saints' days. Classes were suspended and the students attended Mass, heard sermons, and participated in devotional activities honoring the saint. Many students joined Marian congregations and participated in their programs of devotional and charitable activities. The schedules of boarding schools were particularly well organized to ensure the students participated in alternating academic, religious, and recreational activities. When students returned to their dormitories, they had periods in which they rested, reviewed their lessons, did homework, recreated, and attended to their spiritual lives with the assistance of resident Jesuit priests.

This Anthology of Readings: Rationale, Criteria, and Structure

On January 27, 1965, László Lukács, S.J. (1900–98) received permission from Paolo Dezza, S.J. (1901–99), delegate of the general, to publish the first volume of the new version of the *Monumenta paedagogica*.[61] Nine years had passed since Lukács was commissioned to "adorn" the *Ratio studiorum* with the publication of documents that might illustrate such an important text, whose rich and colorful background was regrettably still buried under its "merely juridical" prose. Lukács first looked at the *Monumenta paedagogica*, a single volume that had appeared in 1901 as a spin-off of the *Monumenta historica Societatis Iesu*.[62] But

---

60 The phrase "mens sana in corpore sano" is taken from Juvenal, *Satires*, 10.356. For the Jesuit innovations concerning the place of physical exercise in schools, see François de Dainville, *Les jésuites et l' éducation de la société française: La naissance de l'humanisme moderne* (Paris: Beauchesne & fils, 1940), 518–25.

61 The first volume was printed in the same year. The other six volumes of the *Monumenta paedagogica* were published between 1974 and 1992.

62 At the end of the nineteenth century, José María Vélez (1843–1902) began publishing the *Monumenta historica Societatis Iesu* series in Madrid. He and some of his colleagues had

he felt truly dissatisfied with the uncritical method the editors had followed in selecting, introducing, and annotating the documents.

Most of the documents had already been published elsewhere; the editors had followed neither a chronological order nor scrupulous editorial rules. The authors of the documents were often unknown, and several kinds of sources had been completely neglected. The result was little more than an illustration of what the historical process of preparing the *Ratio studiorum* had involved. Lukács's meticulous research in the archives led him to conclude that a range of sources was worthy of being edited and published, and that one volume was not sufficient to contain the whole matter. He therefore decided to discard most of the criteria that had guided his predecessors. The seven volumes of the new version of the *Monumenta paedagogica* were published between 1965 and 1992. Since then, they have been recognized as the essential collection of sources for anyone wishing to study Jesuit education.

The first virtue of Lukács's significant collection was that the story of the preparation of the *Ratio studiorum* from the Jesuits' point of view could now be said to be definitively uncovered. The first four volumes include a multitude of documents describing Jesuit thinking about education between 1540 and 1580. Volume 5 is devoted to the different editions of the *Ratio*. Volumes 6 and 7 report almost all the remarks that assistancies, provinces, colleges, and individual Jesuits had relentlessly discussed and sent to Rome from 1582 until the official publication of the *Ratio* (1599) and beyond (1616). A large majority of these documents are suggestions for perfecting particular rules, or textbooks, or school timetables proposed for insertion into the *Ratio*. The strict chronological order that Lukács followed turned this collection of documents into a grand saga of the story of the Jesuit plan of studies that has long been considered the hallmark of the Society of Jesus.

However, the opulence of Lukács's work transcends the boundaries of the strict editorial production of the *Ratio*, which was intended to provide superiors and teachers of the Society with rules about their offices and duties. The full range of pedagogical documents reveals a constant and firm attitude of the early Jesuits towards the ministry of education and reflection on it.[63] O'Malley

---

been entrusted by Superior General Luis Martín (1846–1906) to publish the most important documents pertaining to the history of the order. The following superior general, Włodzimierz Ledóchowski (1866–1942), established the Institutum Historicum Societatis Iesu in Rome, which undertook the task of editing the series. See Robert Danieluk, S.J., "Monumenta Historica Societatis Iesu: Uno sguardo di insieme sulla collana," *Archivum historicum Societatis Iesu* 81 (2012): 249–90.

63 A broad literature about Jesuit education has primarily focused on the *Ratio studiorum*. On the other hand, historiography has dealt with the history of the Jesuit colleges, providing a remarkable counterpoint to the "ideal" education which was profiled by the dictate of the *Ratio*. In contrast, few studies have been devoted to looking at the two sides of the Jesuit educational coin, so that a fuller view of Jesuit pedagogy might emerge from the large number of sources that are still available. Noteworthy efforts in this direction were

remarks that the large quantity of the documents the early Jesuits wrote concerning their educational enterprise makes it difficult "to find the forest amidst the trees."[64] We have tried to let the early Jesuit ideas about education emerge from the trees. This statement can be considered as the starting point for the selection of documents we have translated from Lukács's collection. We had to first answer some key questions and, second, set consistent criteria.

The first question we had to face was the most general one: Was there a specific Jesuit concept of education? After all, the documents collected in the *Monumenta paedagogica* were written by dozens of Jesuits over a period of about seventy years. Yet the Jesuits were basically a gathering of people who shared the same formation and the same mission. They could dissent from one another about this or that particular aspect of pedagogy—as happened, for example, between Perpinyá and Ledesma about the teaching of the lower disciplines—but they definitely shared a common culture of teaching.

A set of characteristics, which we might call a sort of discordant harmony, is traceable throughout the volumes Lukács edited. First of all, this harmony can be found in the fundamental humanistic philosophy of education that provided the Jesuits with the core values for their pedagogy. Every Jesuit knew that the focus of the school was on the students, according to the motto of the Roman poet Juvenal: *Maxima debetur puero reverentia* (Students deserve the greatest respect).[65] Everyone knew that the first goal of an education was to form the upright character of a learned man who was to fulfill tasks for the common good. They knew that, in order to accomplish this mission, they had to educate students' minds, spirits, and bodies at the same time. This required the active participation of the students, who had to be moved towards their final goal by means of the example of the teachers, rather than their words alone. Every Jesuit teacher knew that he was called to give far more than lessons: he was above all an educator, a "formator," one who helped along the growth and maturation of souls. He should be easily approachable, helpful, and wise. Wisdom was especially needed to discern the talent of each student and work on his skills so that this talent might emerge through a sound education. Finally, every Jesuit knew that in order to attain such an education, he had to strive continuously to perfect his pedagogy by means of what could be gathered from the order's experiences of running schools. Writing about education was actually a part of a teacher's job, as was the case with renowned pedagogical humanists such as Vittorino da Feltre (1373/78–1446/47),

---

made in the past by a few scholars such as François Charmot, *La pédagogie des jésuites: Ses principes—Son actualité* (Paris: Spes, 1943); John W. Donohue, *Jesuit Education: An Essay on the Foundation of Its Idea* (New York: Fordham University Press, 1963); and more recently, Javier Vergara and Ana Costa París, "La identidad pedagógica de la Compañía de Jesús en el siglo XVI," *History of Education and Children's Literature* 8, no. 2 (2013): 11–31.

64 O'Malley, *First Jesuits*, 225.

65 Juvenal, *Satires*, 14.47.

Guarino Guarini (1374–1460), Erasmus (1466–1536), Johannes Sturm (1507–89), and Juan Luís Vives (1492–1540).[66]

The second key question was whether there was a distinctively Jesuit link between this basic philosophy of education and the pedagogical techniques the documents described. Exercising, talent, an orientation to creative activity ("activism"), efficiency, and gentleness were the links between the Jesuit philosophy of education and their pedagogy. Even those Jesuits who complained about the difficulties of governing such turbulent populations of students as those of the German College and the Roman Seminary were aware that the distinctiveness of their method was based on these values. Exercising students (i.e., having them learn Latin grammar, write compositions, and practice orating) was often considered more important than delivering a lecture. In addition, despite a long tradition, the Jesuits did not like the practice of dictating in class because they felt it wasted precious time for exercising. The origins of such important Jesuit textbooks as the *Rhetoric* (1568) of Cipriano Soares (1524–93), the *Grammar* (1572) of Manuel Álvares's (1526–82), and the *Cursus conimbricensis* (an entire course of philosophy composed by the Jesuits of Coimbra and published between 1592 and 1606) give witness to this dissatisfaction.[67] Exercising was part of a broader activism the Jesuits followed in writing about pedagogy: they were all well aware that education was more than transmitting the contents of a discipline through a lecture, or moral values through discipline and punishments.[68] Exemplarity was

---

66 On the relation between the Jesuits and Vives see Paul F. Grendler, "The Attitudes of the Jesuits towards Juan Luis Vives," in *Neo-Latin and the Humanities: Essays in Honour of Charles E. Fantazzi*, ed. Luc Deitz, Timothy Kirchner, and Jonathan Reid (Toronto: Centre for Reformation and Renaissance Studies, 2014), 123–43. Contrary to their attitudes towards Erasmus, the Jesuits did always seem particularly inclined towards Vives and his pedagogy. For instance, Antonio Possevino (1533–1611), who disparaged Erasmus as a precursor of Luther, considered Vives an authority in his *De cultura ingeniorum*, borrowing several ideas from Vives's *De disciplinis* (1531). See Foster Watson's introduction to *Vives: On Education—A Translation of the* De tradendis disciplinis *Together with an Introduction by Foster Watson* (Cambridge: Cambridge University Press, 1913), xvii–clvii; and also Valerio Del Nero, *The De disciplinis as a Humanistic Text*, in *A Companion to Juan Luis Vives*, ed. Charles Fantazzi (Leiden: Brill, 2008), 177–226. As for the Jesuit attitude towards Erasmus, see O'Malley, *First Jesuits*, 260–64 and Paul F. Grendler, "The Attitudes of the Jesuits towards Erasmus," in *Collaboration, Conflict, and Continuity in Reformation: Essays in Honour of James M. Estes on His Eighty Birthday*, ed. Konrad Eisenbichler and Martin E. James (Toronto: Centre for Reformation and Renaissance Studies, 2014), 363–85.

67 See Charles B. Schmitt, "The Rise of the Philosophical Textbook," in *The Cambridge History of Renaissance Philosophy*, ed. Charles B. Schmitt, Quentin Skinner, Eckhard Kessler, and Jill Kraye (Cambridge: Cambridge University Press, 1988), 792–804.

68 This attitude was rooted in Jesuit mentality as a distinctive trait of the Society among the religious orders of the sixteenth century. See Paolo Prodi and Carla Penuti, eds., *Disciplina dell'anima, disciplina del corpo e disciplina della società tra medioevo ed età moderna* (Bologna: Il Mulino, 1994).

the corollary of this activism: the teacher was asked to be a human model for his own students. The Jesuit philosopher and teacher Benet Perera (1535–1610) wrote that

> the teacher should be the sort of person whom the student trusts because of his learning and practice, understands because of his skillful fluency in teaching, loves for his enthusiasm and diligence, respects for the integrity of his life, and, when the occasion arises, feels he can approach freely for advice because of his humanity and personal warmth.[69]

When the Jesuits wrote about pedagogy, they focused on their students' talents. A Jesuit college was a perfect stage for gifted scholars: public recognition was at hand for everyone who excelled. Yet the Jesuits paid attention to their students' differences; they tried to adapt their pedagogical techniques to the qualities of each one. A large majority of the documents collected by Lukács refer to the concept of talent (*ingenium*). It meant both the different expectations they had about the ability to learn of every student, and the different gifts every mind was endowed with. Adapting pedagogy to human differences became a distinctive trait of Jesuit education.

In terms of efficiency, the purpose of every Jesuit who wrote about education was to perfect a system, the goal of which was to provide the best education possible as quickly as possible. Every pedagogical technique, every proposal for a new timetable or a new arrangement of the classes, was intended to improve the efficiency of their system of education.

Finally, gentleness was another distinctive trait of Jesuit pedagogy. This was a shared general tenet of the Jesuit mentality. Where school life was concerned, gentleness was widely considered to be the lodestar for governing, correcting, punishing, or even expelling students. It led superiors, teachers, and prefects to watch over both the behavior of students and the humanly sustainable balance of daily life. Rectors and prefects of studies were expected to take care to have students have a healthy alternation of study and rest, work, and leisure. In his proposals for the constitutions of the German College, Giuseppe Cortesono devoted a chapter to this subject, "How to Keep the College Happy," because he found it to be extremely useful for student improvement.

These basic characteristics might be said to be widely shared in the *Monumenta paedagogica*. They have guided our selection of material for this Reader. But before taking up the question of its organization, we must make a few preliminary comments.

69　See Chapter 17 in this Reader. See also Paul R. Blum, "Benedictus Pererius: Renaissance Culture at the Origins of Jesuit Science," *Science and Education* 15, no. 2 (2006): 279–304 and Paul Gilbert, "La preparazione della *Ratio studiorum* e l'insegnamento di filosofia di Benet Perera," *Quaestio* 14 (2014): 3–30.

The *Monumenta paedagogica* offers a large collection of documents written from the inception of the Society of Jesus to the final edition of the *Ratio studiorum*. Many documents are related to that edition. Since the English reader already has a translation of the *Ratio studiorum* available,[70] we decided to omit those documents which are too directly linked to it, or whose contents are clearly reflected in it. Similarly, we preferred to translate readable, discursive texts rather than mere sets of rules.

The Reader respects the time range of the *Monumenta*, even though Lukács's selection is no doubt incomplete and the Jesuits did not stop thinking about education in 1616. We are also aware of the fact that many other documents, such as introductions or prefaces of early Jesuit books, and sources not edited by Lukács, might be related to aspects of education that our selection does not cover.

Finally, our translation relies on Lukács's transcription, which is philologically accurate, but sometimes—especially in the documents written in Italian—misleading because of the condition of the original document, or a mistake in solving one of the many contractions of words that were very frequently used in sixteenth-century handwriting. When a comparison with the original source was possible, we undertook that review.

Our choices try to show how the fundamental tenets of Jesuit pedagogy were applied in four major areas of education as they can be seen in Lukács's selection of documents:

First, inspirations. The Jesuits always kept in mind the principle of adapting the means to the goals in every endeavor. They applied this to education even when Jesuit colleges were not yet offering formal teaching. The first set of documents presents letters from some of the most representative early Jesuits dealing with the aims of studying, teaching, and operating schools. This section aims to show what the Jesuits expected from the process of learning, and how they thought they could improve on it.

Second, administration. Once they decided to run schools, the Jesuits kept adjusting their pedagogy on the basis of their experience governing them. This section collects a range of the rules the Jesuits put forward for the major educational institutions they ran, starting with the school at Messina and ending with the Roman Seminary. The documents show a particular Jesuit interest in drafting instructions for guiding both the spiritual and the intellectual life of the students, and, in so doing, perfecting the art of governing schools. Documents in this section also provide the reader with insight into the daily life of Jesuit schools, where frustration, difficulties, troubles, and even dissent among the teaching staff were not rare.

---

70 *The* Ratio Studiorum: *The Official Plan for Jesuit Education*, trans. and ed. Claude Pavur, S.J. (St. Louis: Institute of Jesuit Sources, 2005).

Third, formation. The third section of the Reader collects some treatises explicitly devoted to the issue of educating students as whole persons. This section offers an insight into what the Jesuits meant by the ancient pedagogical ideal of *humanitas*, and the means they thought necessary to attain it. As part of this general landscape of values, the role of freedom of inquiry and instruction also became a matter of strong disagreement within the Society, because, as an organization, it necessarily sought a certain amount of unanimity and tried to avoid centrifugal tendencies. Two documents, from Ledesma, prefect of studies at the Roman College, and Acquaviva, deal with this issue. They are important in order to show the kind of mentality that Jesuit teachers sought to present to their students as an example for life.

Fourth, practical issues about teaching. Jesuit schools offered a wide range of subjects. Because of their commitment to pedagogy, every discipline was made the object of debate about how to perfect the transmission of its content to students. This section offers one or more documents for each discipline that could be taught in a Jesuit school. The Jesuits who wrote them provided reasoned pedagogical techniques, syllabi, bibliographies, and even tips for the teacher to help him to get his students interested in the discipline he taught.

We now invite the reader to follow the early Jesuits as they pondered, experimented with, and realized the principles and plans that guided the development one of the most important international systems of education that the world has yet seen.

Part 1:
Inspirations

A. *Parisiis in æde Virginis qui mons martyrum dicitur omnes focij Christi corpus suscipiunt et prima vota nuncupant . Lib. 2. c. 4 .*

B. *Quòd adolescentes ad pietatis studium adhortetur virgis cædere parant;sed collegij Rector demum procumbens in genua veniam petit. Lib. 2. c. 3.*

C. *Vt lasciuum iuuenem a turpitudine reuocet in gelidam aquam immersus sese macerat atque affligit. Lib. 3. c. 2.*

FIGURE 2   An engraving by Karel van Mallery (1571–c.1635) depicts Ignatius and his first companions taking vows at Montmartre. On the right, the author depicts the famous episode of Ignatius's life at the Collège Sainte-Barbe: he had to be punished according to an old custom of the University of Paris because he had drawn a couple of students away from their studies. In this apologetic print, Diego de Gouveia, the principal of the Collège Sainte-Barbe, is depicted as kneeling in front of Ignatius and begging pardon.

Originally printed in Pedro de Ribadeneyra, *Vita Beati Patris Ignatii Loyolae religionis Societatis Iesu fundatoris* [Life of Blessed Father Ignatius, founder of the Society of Jesus] (Antwerp: Plantin, 1610).

CHAPTER 1

Spiritual Aspects of Studies in Jesuit Formation (1541)

Pierre Favre

In 1540, Ignatius of Loyola (c.1491–1556) sent to Paris some young men who wanted to enter the Society but did not have an adequate academic background.[1] In a letter to Simão Rodrigues (1510–79), written in 1542, Ignatius explained the criteria he used when he was deciding to send such individuals to studies: the candidates should be talented, firm, trustworthy, and humble.[2]

Pierre Favre, the first companion of Ignatius at the Collège Sainte-Barbe and the first of Ignatius's circle to become a master of arts, wrote a letter to the Jesuit students at Paris in 1541. A contemplative character, Favre always combined his commitment to teaching with giving the Exercises. He urged his fellows in Paris to remember that fervor in learning must not be allowed to cause a diminishment of spiritual fervor. He wrote this letter from Ratisbon, where Pope Paul III (r.1534–49) had sent him to assist at the famous Diet, the last effort at reconciliation between Catholics and Protestants before the Council of Trent. His journal notes of 1540 to 1546 (the Memoriale*) reveal that in Ratisbon Favre was particularly active in giving the Exercises and concerned about his spiritual progress.[3] The following letter reflects his attention to spiritual matters as well as an awareness of his audience's university life and spiritual culture.*

Pierre Favre (born April 13, 1506, Villaret in Savoy, France—died August 1, 1546, Rome). One of the original founders of the Society of Jesus, Favre was a roommate of Francis Xavier (1506–52) at the University of Paris when Ignatius joined them during his studies there. He had a talent for friendship as well as impressive abilities in spiritual direction and in giving the Exercises. He preached, traveled, opened communities, and taught. The Jesuit pope Francis (r.2013–) declared him a saint on December 17, 2013.

Source: *Monumenta paedagogica,* nova editio, 1:355–57 (original: Spanish)

[...] Our Redeemer Jesus Christ give all of you all the grace you need to enable you to carry forward your studies to your intended goal, without relaxing the bow of your intentions; so that in the end you might be able to delight in the Lord over the triumph you will win, if you do not extinguish the spirit of a holy thinking and feeling [*el espíritu del santo sentir*] with the spirit of knowing [*el espíritu del saber*].

---

1 See Juan Alfonso de Polanco, *Chronicon,* in *Monumenta paedagogica,* nova editio, 2:497–98.
2 *Monumenta ignatiana,* series prima, 1:208.
3 Edmond C. Murphy and Martin E. Palmer, trans., *The Spiritual Writings of Pierre Favre* (St. Louis: Institute of Jesuit Sources, 1996), 76–77.

This desire of mine and of the entire Society will be easily accomplished, with Christ as our leader, provided that the supreme instructor and the final printer of the letters is always your *repetitor*. This is the Holy Spirit, in whom whatever is known is known well, and without whom, whoever knows anything does not yet know in the way he should know it [1 Cor. 8:2]. So even the very words of Christ, our highest teacher, uttered by his own mouth, have need of this *repetitor*, according to that saying: The Holy Spirit will supply you with everything I have told you [John 14:26]. And he did not merely say he will supply, but first of all, he will teach. If therefore Christ, our teacher, our light and peace, who is the way, the truth, and our life [John 14:6] desires us to keep his spirit not only through the feeling of the will and the heart, but also by means of the knowledge of understanding; how much more necessary will this be for the other subjects dictated through the mouth of instructors that are inferior to Christ Our Lord? You already know an example of this, namely Saint Thomas, who was eager not only to review in prayer his lessons in whatever science or area of learning he was studying, but even to go over them with his inmost teacher before going to hear them with other instructors. Finally, what I am asking of you in the Lord is that you always prepare your lessons through so great a teacher and later review them with him as well.

I delight greatly in the Lord that you have such an advantage on us, I mean at least for myself, which is to say that before starting to study, you already have a fixed goal to which you are directing your studies on a straight line of ordered intentions. In this way, already grasping the principle on which all wisdom depends as the sole reason for which you have begun your studies, and also grasping the truth of the means, you know where you are finally going to stop after your studies. And that is why you cannot fail to be at peace, not only when you arrive at the end of your studies but also in the very midst of them (though in a different fashion), just as you were when you began them in all tranquility.

The reason for all of this benefit to you is that, since you are shooting straight, and by Christ who is the life in which you finally enjoy perfect calm [cf. Mt. 11:29], and since you have already arrived, at the start, by the right road that is Christ, it is necessary that even in the truth of the means, that is, in your studies, you are also enjoying a restfulness, working through that very same mediator of ours who is the truth that has gone out from the Father and has returned to the Father by the straightest line.

Therefore you have reasons to give thanks to God Our Lord, and we no less than you, even though (as I already started to say) we had not had the same opportunities for real study, and that was because we thought it enough for us to be taught the beginnings and the ends of letters and at the same time what kind of means they are in themselves. And since I did not first have a true understanding of the right place to start, nor a true understanding of the real goal to which the anchor of my intentions needed to be fixed, I could not proceed in anything other than a haphazard and disturbed manner. I did not know how to grasp through the truth of letters the good that they teach, since I rather took the means for the end and the end for the means.

We also had another great inconvenience (I am speaking of myself, at least), and this was that I did not think that the cross merited a place either at the beginning, or in the middle, or at the end. You know that its main place is in the middle, as it holds the place of our mediator Jesus Christ. And this is no small advantage that you have over me, being familiar with the cross; in addition to knowing and understanding the manner in which our Lord, the crucified Jesus Christ, proceeds. We owe him so much: some, because he did not allow them to enter the sea of many deceptions; others, because he rescued them from those deceptions by his grace and mercy, in such a way as not only to redeem the time but also so that they could speedily learn what they would never find by indirect paths, that is, Jesus Christ crucified. He is the one whom we preach, holding him up for imitation in this life, not as glorious and powerful in ruling over this fleshly life, but in how he can appear to be foolishness to the gentiles and those living [as they do], and to the Jews a scandal, but to those who are good, the power of God and the wisdom of God [cf. 1 Cor. 1:23] […].

CHAPTER 2

The Importance of Humanistic Studies in Jesuit Formation (1547)

Juan Alfonso de Polanco

Answering Diego Laínez's request for the best scholastics who had been studying at Padua for at least two years, Juan Alfonso de Polanco engages his argument that extending humanistic studies is harmful for the most talented Jesuits. Polanco concedes that they should not be allowed to grow old in these studies, but there are many reasons (drawn from authorities, tradition, and finally reason) that speak against Laínez's position.

This letter is written on two tracks: that of the general rule for all of the Jesuits and that applicable to a particular case (Pedro de Ribadeneyra [1526–1611]). Laínez must have requested that Ribadeneyra, who already seemed adequately prepared, be missioned elsewhere. In his refusal, Polanco appeals to Ignatius's authority about the importance of humanistic studies for the training of younger Jesuits. Mastery of the communication arts was essential for preaching and for many other kinds of interactions as well, including the higher studies of philosophy and theology. Polanco argues that one needs to work hard at the right age and to spend more than two years in the exercises of disputations and compositions.

Juan Alfonso de Polanco (born December 24, 1517, Burgos—entered the Society 1541, Rome—died December 20, Rome, 1576). A prolific and influential secretary of the order for twenty-six years, Polanco helped Ignatius turn the Society into a teaching order, particularly through his substantial contributions to part 4 of the Constitutions, *which concerns the colleges and the spiritual and academic formation of students. His effective organizational mind inspired the march towards the creation of a worldwide network of colleges. Polanco is known also for the many letters he wrote for Ignatius "on commission" and for his extensive* Chronicon, *the first detailed chronicle of the early Society.*

Source: *Monumenta paedagogica,* nova editio, 2:366–73 (original: Spanish)

Rome, May 21, 1547

May the grace and peace of Jesus Christ Our Lord be always in our souls and grow there. Amen.

Your Reverence's letter to me was no small favor: writing to me as you do in the midst of the articles and your other tasks, you give me even more cause to be grateful for the testimony of your memory of me.[1] This makes me hope for a remembrance in your prayers, for which I have so much need and of which I take assurance from the same charity which prompts you to remember to write me. I look forward eagerly to the summary you promise when there is a lull in your occupations assumed for the common good, and I will receive it as a great kindness.[2] For it, and for so many others received from Your Reverence, may you be rewarded by him who does so with generosity for the sake of his poor, for whose service all is done and received.

With regard to Ludovico, Pedro de Ribadeneyra, and Fulvio, I have laid your views and those of Master Claude [le Jay] before our Father Master Ignatius.[3] He has given me no definite answer about these individuals. It may be that he will make a more definite decision before the end of the summer: new factors might emerge that could affect the deliberation.

With respect to Pedro: I know and can see that Father Master Ignatius has for him—over and above his charity towards everyone and his special charity towards those of the Society—a very particular love.[4] He is anxious for him to have every possible advantage for his progress in studies and everything else, being confident that God Our Lord will make use of him. So far, however, he has not indicated to me much inclination either way as to changing him or keeping him where he is. He may be waiting for some further development before reaching a decision about him.

I now turn to Your Reverence's general observation that for a mind to nourish itself excessively on the humanistic studies tends to render it so dainty and spoiled that it loses the ability and inclination for profounder matters, particularly

---

1 Polanco refers to the work Laínez was doing at the Council of Trent. Diego Laínez (1512–65), Alfonso Salmerón (1515–85), and Claude le Jay (1504–52) had been appointed as papal theologians. Laínez had been there since May 18, 1546.

2 Laínez actually sent a report to Ignatius on June 16, 1547. See *Monumenta ignatiana*, series quarta: *Fontes narrativi*, 1:54–145. The letter was sent from Bologna, where the council had been moved temporarily.

3 Louis du Coudret (*c.*1523–72), Pedro de Ribadeneyra (1526–1611), and Fulvio Cardulo (1528–91). Cardulo and Ribadeneyra were sent to study at Padua together, along with Claude du Coudret (dates uncertain), younger brother of Louis. See *Monumenta paedagogica*, nova editio, 1:7. It is possible that Polanco might have confused the Coudret brothers in this letter.

4 Ribadeneyra himself was well aware of Ignatius's particular affection. In a letter to his mother (1553), he reported that Ignatius had called him to Rome "because of that special affection and love his reverend paternity holds me in." *Ribadeneyra*, 1:104.

when the latter have to be sought in authors whose style offers no allurement. On the matter of excess I agree with Your Reverence, because of your own authority as well as because of the instances we have of men who, once entering higher studies, found themselves exhausted by even slight exertions. Such people really are spoiled: they get used to studying only things easy and appetizing and end up afraid or reluctant to deal with anything showing the opposite qualities, as do the difficult and bland topics that we find in philosophy and Scholastic theology. However, while in agreement about spending excessive time on these studies, I would not consider it excessive (again, as a general observation) to spend as much time on them as is needed to master humanistic studies, particularly the languages, in the case of students of the proper age and ability. My reasons are as follows:

First. There is the authority of those, both ancient and modern, who urge the study of languages as essential for scripture. Moreover, I confess myself particularly impressed by the fact that Father Master Ignatius thinks the same as I on this matter. He is very set on wanting the Society's members to be good Latinists;[5] and, over and beyond whatever human prudence and experience he possesses, it is my belief that God inspires him with particular inclinations and convictions of this sort, since it is the wont of divine Providence to bestow upon those charged with governance a special influx of his grace for the general good of those governed.

Second. We have the example of ancient authors, such as Jerome, Augustine, and other Greek and Latin [church] fathers, whose humanistic studies certainly did not dull the edge of their minds for penetrating deeply into the knowledge of things—to say nothing of the Platos and Aristotles and other philosophers.[6]

Third. There is the common practice. In not overly lofty matters of this sort (and barring deception or violence on the part of the sensual appetites), there will not be universal error. But from ancient times to the present day, the commonest practice has been to begin with humanistic studies—except for certain periods when in places of learning barbarism reigned in the writings no less than in the writers; except for these periods, we find in Greece and Italy (and I assume in other places as well) the practice of proceeding from a solid foundation in humanistic studies to the other disciplines.

---

5 Ignatius's purpose was to provide the Society with especially good preachers; they were to study the Greek and Latin orators and the classical treatises on rhetoric so as to avoid any rough and dry Scholastic style in preaching. See O'Malley, *The First Jesuits*, 100.

6 In the sixteenth century, both Plato and Aristotle were considered magnificent examples of eloquent philosophers. A Ciceronian description of Aristotle was often cited: "flumen orationis aureum fundens" [pouring forth a golden river of speech] (Cicero, *Academica*, 2.119).

Fourth. Experience shows us that because of their inarticulateness many highly learned men keep their learning to themselves and fail to reach the goal at which they should chiefly have been aiming with it, that is, the help of their neighbor. There are others who communicate their learning, but lack the influence and success they might have if their powers of expression matched their knowledge or if they could put an outward luster on their ideas that matched the interior light of their insight. This I think can be seen even in the Scholastic doctors: if they could trade a portion of their subtle and learned arguments for a certain skill in expounding the rest, they might achieve more widespread good with the latter than they now do with them all.

Fifth. A fifth motive for establishing a foundation in humanistic studies is a whole series of rational considerations which occur to me:

> The first is that, just as one needs to embark upon physical exertions gradually, beginning with lighter exercises until becoming more used to the toil, so it would seem that before the mind launches into toilsome subjects like philosophy and Scholastic theology, it needs to acquire the habits of work. It should do this on less difficult and forbidding subjects, such as humanistic studies: these are more proportioned to a mind that lacks training and strength; they open it up and render it capable of entering upon weightier matters.

> The second reason for thinking that time dedicated to acquiring this instrument of humanistic studies is well spent is that as a person advances in years and his head fills up with larger impressions of reality, it is unlikely that he will have much success with language studies. Experience and reason seem to me to prove this. His memory is no longer empty as it was in early years, no longer as ready to receive impressions of even petty matters.[7] He cannot apply himself to the study of conjugations and other elementary matters in the same way as can those who have had no dealings with more important matters. Such matters incline the mind, once it is habituated to large and noble operations, to scorn lowering itself to petty ones—as if someone used to administering and ruling the affairs of a kingdom were to be busied with those of a village.

---

7   In ancient psychology and medicine, memory was a mental power thought to retain the sensible "impressions" (*species*) that the object sent to the subject in order to be perceived by him. The same went for the intellective cognitions (called *species*, as well), which memory was supposed to retain. Since children's memory was less encumbered by notions, they were supposed to learn things that pertained to memory, such as languages, more easily than adults. See Leen Spruit, Species intelligibilis: *From Perception to Knowledge: 2. Renaissance Controversies, Later Scholasticism, and the Elimination of the Intelligible Species in Modern Philosophy* (Leiden: Brill, 1995).

The third is that languages are without doubt useful for understanding scripture, so that the time spent until they are mastered is well employed.

The fourth is that, besides their importance for understanding all the natural, acquired, and infused gifts of God, languages, especially Latin, are essential if one wishes to communicate to others what God has given to him.

The fifth is that the times we live in are so fastidious in this regard that, with so many people wanting to know languages, anyone who does not will not have much influence on them.

The sixth is that this subject seems particularly necessary in our Society, not only for dealing with people of different languages through conversations and letters, but also for being equipped to preach and speak successfully to ordinary people: humanistic studies are more on their level and so are helpful in dealing with them.

The seventh is that, even during the time when they are studying subjects they will use in the future, such as history, geography, figures of speech, and rules of rhetoric, I have no doubt that these "work together unto good for those who love God" [Rom. 8:28], and that more than a little.

The eighth is that there is in fact opportunity to exercise their wits and powers when they engage in rhetorical disputations (for those expert at it) or in original compositions, whether in verses or in prose pieces, in speeches or in letters.

The ninth is my conviction that it is essential to master a language once and for all if one is to possess it later on and make proper use of it. The only way to get this mastery is to give the required time and effort once and for all. Many people carry the rock of Sisyphus to the top of the slope and then leave it there and go back to the bottom. I know something about this by personal experience. I began Greek three different times; I bore the weight and trouble of the grammar and was just beginning to have a fair understanding of the authors. But I never got to the point where I could say I really possessed the language and had sufficient training and practice, and as a result it all did me little good. With Hebrew it was even worse: I never had all that much to forget, but now seem to have been completely relieved even of that. All this was because I did not make the effort once and for all to master the language; otherwise it would not have left me so easily.

In addition to this, the objections we mentioned at the beginning can be solved: it can be argued that not everybody who stays with the study of Latin and Greek long enough to master them thereby falls into the disadvantage of inability or reluctance to take on deeper subjects. A certain inclination may be left in the mind and the will, but certainly no unshakable habit having the force of nature, especially in a person who does not grow old in these studies, provided he stops them when he has reached the goal that I mentioned. And assuming a moral probability that this inclination produces in many persons an apathy towards higher studies, a good will can overcome the inclination. Many people overcome it for worldly designs and make themselves study subjects for which they have no personal taste.

So it would appear that any members of the Society who are somewhat so inclined could overcome this with a similar effort of the will for the love of God. For this they would have three aids which worldly people lack. One is their purpose in taking up humanistic studies and everything else: solely the greater service of God and the help of our neighbor. A second is obedience, which will not allow them to dawdle over language studies even if they want to. A third is God's grace, which, given the two preceding dispositions, can rightly be expected to be more abundant. So far my general considerations.

Returning to Pedro de Ribadeneyra, there are additional reasons for keeping him at these studies a little longer. First, it will not hurt him to know more Latin, although he is well along in it, by seeing more authors, getting more practice, and, as I said, mastering the language more thoroughly. Second, I assume there will be plenty for him to learn in rhetoric, history, etc. Third, he only began Greek a short while ago, and in what little is left of this year would not be able to get very far in it. If he stays another year, I anticipate that with his ability he will turn out a fine Greek scholar. Fourth, I think what he learns will equip him for any other subjects he may take up, and keep him from being easily daunted by difficulties he meets with. Fifth, I suspect that the prior [of the Trinità][8] may somewhat resent our removing the better students, or at least the more promising ones. Sixth, I do not see at present where else he could go. Master Ignatius does not think it would be good for him to be sent to Spain. The duke of Gandía[9] and others wrote asking that students be sent there, and our father replied that it would be better if they provide them from there, and they agreed. Hence, it

---

8   Andrea Lippomano (dates uncertain), prior of the community at the Church of the Holy Trinity in Venice, was an old acquaintance of Ignatius. He had hosted Ignatius in Venice, letting him use the library and giving him a place for reflection. Lippomano offered to the Society a building in Padua owned by his community in order to open a college there (1545). See Polanco, *Chronicon*, in *Monumenta paedagogica*, nova editio, 2:501. Moreover, Ignatius asked Lippomano for advice in 1549 about censoring or emending ancient texts of humanities, which, according to Ignatius, contain, nevertheless, "very useful" and "honorable" things. See *Monumenta paedagogica*, nova editio, 2:389–90.

9   Francisco de Borja (1510–72), who as a layman had founded the college of Gandía in 1545 for the training of Jesuits. In 1546, the year Borja entered the Society, it became the first Jesuit educational institution to accept lay students, two years before the college in Messina was opened primarily for non-Jesuits. Many date the beginning of the Jesuit educational apostolate from the Sicilian school because of this distinction in the original intention.

might not be a good idea for us to send anyone there now, to say nothing of the difficulty of travel and so on. In Paris, there are no accommodations either at the moment. If we wait a year, I am sure there will be more opportunity.

But an end to arguments: there is no use multiplying them until Your Reverence tires of listening to them, even if my letter reaches you in a moment of leisure.

If the articles are still going on, there is no urgency about reading this; it will keep for reading until after the feast—although it would have been better to mention this at the beginning of the letter.

No more for the present, except humbly to commend myself to the prayers of Your Reverence and of all my reverend fathers in Christ there, as well as of everyone else in the house.

May Jesus Christ increase his grace in all, so that in all the honor and service of his Divine Majesty may increase continually.

CHAPTER 3

Directives on Academic Progress (1548)

Juan Alfonso de Polanco

Before it started founding its own schools, the Society sent applicants in need of more education to Jesuit houses in a university city for studies. These collegia *were intended at first to be purely residential institutions. The prestige of the University of Paris made the residential college there the most desirable one. In 1542, Ignatius wrote to Simão Rodrigues about criteria to be used to send scholastics there (Letter 42, 1:206–10).[1] Polanco's* Directives *(Industriae) of 1548 went further, including some points that would recur in later Jesuit documents: effective training requires keeping students in sufficient comfort, healthy and refreshed enough to sustain their academic focus, protected from the distractions of other tasks or religious duties, and equipped with techniques to get the most from their studies.*

Juan Alfonso de Polanco (born December 24, 1517, Burgos—entered the Society 1541, Rome—died December 20, Rome, 1576). A prolific and influential secretary of the order for twenty-six years, Polanco helped Ignatius turn the Society into a teaching order, particularly through his substantial contributions to part 4 of the Constitutions, *which concerns the colleges and the spiritual and academic formation of students. His effective organizational mind inspired the march towards the creation of a worldwide network of colleges. Polanco is known also for the many letters he wrote for Ignatius "on commission" and for his extensive* Chronicon, *the first detailed chronicle of the early Society.*

Source: *Monumenta paedagogica*, nova editio, 1:28–37 (original: Spanish)

Directives to Help the Society Attain Its Intended Goal
Fourth Set of Directives: For Academic Progress

Those who are sent to study—We now need to consider what concerns the assignment to studies as well as getting the most from them. But to see what needs to be done here, we have to note that three sorts of individuals are sent: some who, thanks to their age, talent, and so forth, show promise of making great progress and becoming truly learned; others who do not show this promise but are able to do well enough to help themselves and others in confessions, and so forth; a third category could be added for those who are sent in order to relieve others of corporal or spiritual ministries such as confessing, serving, and so forth. It

---

1 See *Ignatius of Loyola: Letters and Instructions*, ed. Martin E. Palmer, John W. Padberg, and John L. McCarthy (St. Louis: Institute of Jesuit Sources, 2006), 77–80.

should also be noted that, among these, some go to study at their own expense, others at the expense of the Society, and they are firm in their obedience; others have the intention, but no vow nor such resolution.[2] In addition, some places certainly have more resources for studies than others do.

1. *The most promising should be sent to the best places.* Granting this, it first of all seems that the most promising students should be sent to the best universities, where there are more academic resources, provided that the individuals are not already so advanced that it is enough for them to have a place for reflection, without much help from teachers and exercises, and so forth.

2. *Those who have the vow and live on the Society's expenses*—It seems that those who have vows and are firmly committed to the Society should be sent where they are maintained at the expense of the Society, that is, to the colleges. Those who do not have vows or are not inclined to make them could be sent to studies at their own expense if they wish, and they could join our companions, but not on the Society's financing, as we have said, so that they may not pursue another way of life and follow other plans after they have gotten educational support and credentials in our Society.

3. *They should be tested in life, and so forth*—It seems that before being sent to studies, they should manifest some mortification of "the old man" [Eph. 4:22; Col. 3:9] and some taste for spiritual things, and it seems that they should be inclined towards studies as means for divine service, not for any other design having to do with particular interests, honor, or investments. The studies would not contribute to the ends that the Society is hoping for, that is, God's glory and the help of souls and of the students themselves.

4. *They should travel without hindrance*—Taking notice of the provisions, both temporal and educational, in the places where they are sent, they should be granted permission to travel with benefit of traveling expenses if these are available; and they should go in a manner in which they do less damage to their health, even if this delays them.

5. *Relieving them from temporal concerns*—Once they have arrived, it is not to their benefit that they should have to worry about necessities like food, clothes, books, and so forth. In the third set of directives, we have said that we should take some charge of these and of other worldly material concerns so that they should think as little as possible about them. And in order to lighten their load in everyday circumstances and in the extraordinary ones of illnesses, it seems advisable to employ some individuals of good will more

---

2   The order's *Constitutions* would restrict the scholastics eligible for the Jesuit colleges: "Only those are admitted as approved scholastics who have undergone their probation in the houses or in the colleges themselves and who, after two years of experiences and probation and after pronouncing their vows along with the promise to enter the Society, are received to live and die in it, for the glory of God our Lord." Padberg, *Constitutions*, 139.

than those who have literary talent; because otherwise there are many occasions to interrupt study and turn away from it. An exception would be if on an occasion the students would contribute to providing care in some respect; when there is another who has the main responsibility, the assistance is not as much distraction.

6. *They should not be distracted by associations, and so forth*—They should not be distracted from their studies by disreputable study companions, nor by anxiety about work.

7. *They should not practice too many devotions*—Meditations and devotions should not be so extensive as to diminish their academic progress, partly through spending long periods of time on them, partly through putting so much of their heart into them, and partly by wearing themselves out in that direction.

8. *They should not be too much in touch with their neighbor*—They should not be in touch with their neighbor so much during their study, which allows them to learn what enables to serve him in the long run. This also goes for confessing, as it does for preaching or for giving Exercises or for conversing. And as they are not ordained, it seems that they should not become involved in these practices until they complete their study. Nevertheless, if someone is advanced [in his studies], he should not lose the opportunity to give Exercises to and confess someone, and so forth. And if it happens that someone who has completed the studies can take care of the neighbor, or if he is one who is more of a helper than a student, he may take up this task, thus relieving his companions. They will also endeavor to attract others to their way of life by means of their example and good conversation.

9. *Taking rest*—They should not pull the bowstring too tight, neither in studying nor in any other exercise without occasionally taking a break from the work, because a mind moderately refreshed will last a long while in study, avoid illnesses, and so forth. Up to now it has helped avoid difficulties.[3]

10. *Good intention*—But after avoiding such pitfalls, they should take other advantages as the fragrance of one's disposition towards God,[4] as is purely seeking in study his greater praise and glory in the help of souls and being deeply persuaded that this occupation of study, even if it appears in itself remote, when

---

3   Alternating hard work and rest was a distinctive aspect of Jesuit pedagogy in the sixteenth century. See Cristiano Casalini, "Active Leisure: The Body in Sixteenth-Century Jesuit Culture," *Journal of Jesuit Studies* 1, no. 3 (2014): 400–18.

4   The Spanish version of this phrase is "como canela de la dispositión para con Dios," which is literally, "as the cinnamon of the disposition towards God." Cinnamon was known for its appealing fragrance from biblical times and it was an ingredient in the holy anointing oil (Ex. 30:23). Ignatius and others would occasionally evoke the imagery of "pleasing odor" as in Eph. 5:2: "And walk in love, as Christ loved us and gave himself up for us, a fragrant offering and sacrifice to God" (RSV; Vulgate: "in odorem suavitatis").

taken up with such an end is very holy and acceptable to His Divine Majesty. Because the study holds hope not only of future usefulness but also of a present one: when we experience a dying in it, it is an act most pleasing to God and so forth, no less than in preaching, and so forth, in the time of study.[5]

11. *Moderated devotions*—As too many devotions hinder studying, so some moderated devotions help them, particularly those that are aimed at the purity of conscience, as happens in the examen and confessing and communicating every week. Furthermore, one should attend Mass every day and sometimes make short prayers that are mixed with the study. And, if the superior considers it expedient, they will devote some hour to meditation and to some more extended prayer.

12. *Good teachers*—They should have good teachers as far as possible, and they should make an effort to take care of their students and see that the students faithfully attend class, and so forth.

13. *Good humanity*—Those who lack the Latin proficiency to understand, speak, and write well should learn it, quite without question. Concerning Greek and the other parts of humanistic studies, such as rhetoric, poetry and history, and cosmography, those who have more time and ability can take them. And, generally speaking, look to the quality rather than to the quantity of the authors.

14. As for those who do not give hope of becoming learned on account of age or poor health or talent but are quite able to assist their neighbor: with a short course in arts these could take the theology most necessary for their own benefit and that of others and for the practice of the priesthood, covering the virtues and vices, the passions, the sacraments, some summary for cases of conscience, scripture (chiefly the New Testament with some good commentator), something from the holy doctors, and other spiritual books, following the best authors, without concern for how many of them are studied.

15. Those who are more capable should fully study the arts and what is read in them, as well as the safest Scholastic theology, that is, the theology of Saint Thomas, approved by the Holy See. They should not swear by the words of the master so that there is no room for other opinions that are more valid in certain respects, even the holy doctor is followed in part.[6] They should endeavor to cover the Old and the New Testaments using only a few good commentators, especially taking into account those who explain the linguistic difficulties that arise from translations and foreign phrases. For the remainder, what has been said in points 13 and 14 touches them as well.

---

5   Polanco argues that studies are intrinsically worthy in the sight of God. Unlike Pierre Favre, who in the letter above was addressing scholastics (Chapter 1), he wanted Jesuits eager to perform charitable works to realize the spiritual importance of studying.

6   "To swear by the words of the master" (*iurare in verba magistri*) is a phrase found in Horace, *Epist.* I.1.14.

16. *Concentrate on the more necessary content*—Similarly, it is a reasonable approach to concentrate with great diligence on the more useful content, and also on that which deals with heretics and on that which is very important for preaching, confessing, and so forth.

17. *They should study for an appropriate time*—They should study for an appropriate length of time in every subject, adequate for them to get the intended result, not skipping anything to shorten the time; and they should not interrupt their study easily except for a good reason.

18. *They should do exercises*—They should not fail to perform their academic exercises, neither at home nor outside. Those in humanistic studies should practice speaking Latin, reviewing and disputing, and above all exercising their skills in composition. But very special care should be taken with epistolary composition because, although the style of orations of Demosthenes and Cicero is very helpful for preaching—if one uses discretion to discern what is appropriate—the main application of a good knowledge of Latin consists in the dictation and composition of letters. The students of arts and theology also, in addition to hearing and reviewing the classes, need to practice disputation often, keeping all modesty and charity, being diligent, and they need to hold to their conclusions, and so forth.

19. *The rector should be careful*—It is necessary for the rector to know how everyone is performing his duty, to be able to critique or approve or if necessary punish; and, as he wishes, to help the individual to do his duty better.

20. *They should make abstracts*—All students, especially those of arts and theology, ought to get used to making abstracts of the course material; and if someone cannot do it on his own, he should get help from others who have done it better, because this way one can understand more effectively the course content and fix it more firmly in memory.[7] When memory fades, he can fall back on the abstract. And for those who have spiritual duties and additionally need to study sermons or lessons, they would do it more efficiently and in less time if they had an ordered collection of these abstracts of their studies. And after this, those that are most highly valued could be gathered, or a new collection composed, and a book or books could be put together from this with an index to find the contents.

21. *Turning in their compositions and supervising*—Take notice of what they read and hear. Those in humanistic studies should occasionally submit their compositions, perhaps every year or every six months, so that their improvement is seen. And similarly the students of arts and theology should

---

7   One might find the same concept about the importance of note-taking in *Constitutions*, part 4, chapter 6. See Paul Nelles, "*Libros de papel, libri bianchi, libri papyracei*: Note-Taking Techniques and the Role of Student Notebooks in the Early Jesuit Colleges," *Archivum historicum Societatis Iesu* 151 (2007): 75–112, here 84–85.

send their conclusions to Rome directly or to the provincial prefect (but for the present, to Rome).

22. *Someone should be in charge of this*—Although there is a rector there with oversight, it seems that there ought to be an individual there in Rome to take special charge of examining students' compositions and conclusions in detail, and so forth, as a basis for being able to make good judgments (by being informed about people) about extending or shortening the period of study, or directing it differently, and so forth.[8]

23. *Practice teaching*—After they have advanced, it seems good that they should also have to practice teaching classes among themselves, perhaps when someone is coming to the end of the period of study, so that he would undertake to teach a class. This would help him understand and practice how teaching is done, and he would also be able to assist others. In preaching, if it seems feasible, they could do the same.

24. *Moderate recreation*—Eating, sleeping, and taking adequate rest helps advance learning, because it makes one not only understand things better but also continue and persevere in studies. So an approach should be followed that does not neglect this.

25. *Not letting them grow old [in studies]*—When they have studied a sufficient amount, it is not necessary to let them feed too much on studies or grow old in them. The rector could be informed about those who have finished their courses. And they themselves should put into writing something to show their intention and their spiritual disposition.[9]

26. Concerning all that has been said and remains to be said, it will help to have from every place that admits students information sent about their character and qualities, together with their names and their record, what has been noteworthy about their progress or the opposite, and about their studies and life, in order to see how they have to be helped and if there are appropriate grounds for transferral or dismissal, and so forth.

---

8 Ignatius himself sometimes did this, as one can infer by reading the letter translated below (to Pierre Le Gillon [*c*.1520–*c*.1565], March 17, 1554).

9 This practice would later become customary for the Society: superiors were to fill out catalog entries for the members of each college and each professed house, reporting their attitudes, academic achievement, and employability. See Marina Massimi, "Engenho e temperamentos nos catálogos e no pensamento da Companhia de Jesus nos séculos XVII e XVIII," *Revista latinoamericana de psicopatología fundamental* 11 (2008): 675–87; and, recently, Lidiane Ferreira Panazzolo and Marina Massimi, "Categorias antropologicas nos Catalogos Trienais da Companhia de Jesus," *IHS: Antiguos jesuitas en Iberoamérica* 1 (2015): 21–45.

CHAPTER 4

The Society's Involvement in Studies (1551)

Ignatius of Loyola and Juan Alfonso de Polanco

In December 1551, Ignatius had his secretary Juan Alfonso de Polanco write to Antonio Araoz (1515–73), the provincial of Spain, about the Society's rapidly developing educational apostolate. What resulted was a concentrated epitome of the early Society's thinking about this enterprise. Polanco swiftly covered issues of "method" (founding, administration, faculty, structure, content), and "advantages," both for the Society and for the external students and the local civil society. It is apparent that Ignatius, even at this very early date, had a particular idea that he wanted to be replicated in new localities in light of the experience gained elsewhere.

Ignatius of Loyola (born c.1491, Guipúzcoa, Spain—co-founded the Society in 1540, Rome—died 1556, Rome). Chief founder of the Jesuit order, Ignatius was a great supporter and administrator of "Jesuit studies" from the Society's earliest days. Of course he himself had made his own substantial investment in studies in Barcelona, Alcalá, Salamanca, and Paris (a period covering 1524–34). The Society itself was uniquely tied to the University of Paris, where all of the founders were students. Though Ignatius did not at first intend the Society to run its own schools, he soon saw the great apostolic promise of this work. He was happy to open as many colleges as feasible, showing a special enthusiasm for the Roman College. Ignatius is often listed as one of the great figures in the history of education.

Juan Alfonso de Polanco (born December 24, 1517, Burgos—entered the Society in 1541, Rome—died December 20, Rome, 1576). A prolific and influential secretary of the order for twenty-six years, Polanco helped Ignatius turn the Society into a teaching order, particularly through his substantial contributions to part 4 of the Constitutions, *which concerns the colleges and the spiritual and academic formation of students. His effective organizational mind inspired the march towards the creation of a worldwide educational network. Polanco is especially known for the many letters he wrote for Ignatius "on commission" and for his extensive* Chronicon, *the first detailed account of the early Society's history.*

Sources: (1) *Cartas de san Ignacio de Loyola, fundador de la Compañía de Jesús* (Madrid: Aguado, 1875), 2:386–87. Ignatius's cover letter is newly translated here from the Spanish original. (2) MHSI 29 (*Epistolae Ignatianae* 4), letter 2226, 5–9. This translation of Polanco's letter is slightly adapted from *Ignatius of Loyola: Letters and Instructions*, trans. Martin E. Palmer, ed. John W. Padberg and John L. McCarthy (St. Louis: Institute of Jesuit Sources, 2006), 360–63.

Rome, December 1, 1551

The supreme grace and eternal love of Christ Our Lord be always to our constant favor and help.

I have instructed Master Polanco to write to you about the pattern for founding colleges that is in place here, and about the advantages that our experience shows us to be accruing from them. I have wanted to entrust to you the task of seeing that (wherever possible) this manner of teaching is introduced in the colleges of the Society; and if we do not go beyond a humanistic program, it would not take much to establish this in a college. It would be very advantageous to have a couple of priests to hear confession and teach Christian doctrine, even if there were no preachers, and all the more so if there are some who have the talent to preach or give public exhortations. In Oñate, Burgos, and Medina del Campo, it seems that it would be less trouble than in Salamanca, Alcalá and Valencia, and Coimbra; but even in these universities, I would be happy if this way of proceeding could be introduced.[1]

I leave the other matters to Master Polanco. I only entrust myself deeply to your prayers, and I ask that God our Lord give us his grace always to know his most holy will and to accomplish it completely.

Written below this text: =JHS= To my brother in our Lord, Doctor Araoz, provincial in Spain, of the Society of Jesus, in Valladolid or wherever he is.

IHS

The Peace of Christ!

Seeing that in your region as well as here in our own, God Our Lord is moving his servants to start various colleges of this Society, it has seemed to our father that it would be a good idea to give an account of the method and advantages which have been found through experience in the colleges here [in Italy], those of the colleges there being already well known; his intention is that this be carefully studied and, so far as the matter is in our power, nothing be left undone for God's greater service and the aid of our neighbors.

The manner or method employed in founding a college is this. A city (such as Messina and Palermo in Sicily),[2] or a ruler (such as the king of [the] Romans and the dukes of Ferrara and Florence),[3] a private individual (such as the prior of

---

1   The reason for this was that Salamanca, Alcalá, Valencia, and Coimbra had universities known for solid pedagogy.

2   Messina's city officials formally asked Ignatius on December 19, 1547, to send Jesuit scholastics and teachers for classes there. Another similar request came one year later from Palermo.

3   Ferdinand I (1503–64) was at this time king of the Romans. The duke of Ferrara was Ercole II D'Este (1508–59). Cosimo I de' Medici (1519–74) was the duke of Florence.

the Trinità in Venice and Padua),[4] or group of people (as in Naples, Bologna, and elsewhere) furnish an annual sum of money—some of them in perpetuity from the beginning, others not until they have come to know and verify the advantages of this work. A suitable building is procured and two or three priests of more solid learning are sent, the rest being students of our own who, in addition to advancing their own education, can aid that of others and, through their good example, personal contact, and learning, also assist them in virtue and spiritual progress.

The procedure in such places is this. At the beginning, three or four teachers in humane letters are appointed. One starts off with the elements of grammar, accommodating himself to beginners; another is assigned to those on an intermediate level; another for those advanced in grammar; and another for the more advanced humanities students in Latin, Greek, and—where there is a readiness for it—Hebrew. When the school has been announced, all who so desire are admitted free and without receipt of any money or gratuity—that is, all who know how to read and write and are beginning Latin grammar. However, if they are young boys they must have the approval of their parents or guardians and they must observe certain conditions, as follows:

They must be under obedience to their teachers regarding which subjects they study and for how long.

They must go to confession at least once a month.

Every Sunday they must attend the class on Christian doctrine given in the college, as well as the sermon when there is one in the church.

They must observe decorum in their speech and in all other matters, and be orderly. Where they are not or fail to behave as they ought, in the case of young boys for whom words do not suffice, there should be a hired extern corrector to punish them and keep them in awe; none of our own men is to lay a hand on anyone.

The names of all these pupils are registered. Care is taken not only to provide various kinds of classes but also to have them exercise themselves in debating, writing compositions, and speaking Latin all the time, in such a way that they will make great progress in letters along with the virtues.

When there are a fair number of students already grounded in humane letters, a person is appointed to inaugurate the arts course [namely philosophy]; and when there are a number of students well grounded in arts, a lecturer is appointed to teach theology—following the method of Paris, with frequent exercises. From then on, the whole arrangement is continued. For experience has shown that it is inadvisable to begin by teaching arts or theology: lacking a foundation, the students make no progress. This plan applies where there is a readiness for more than humane letters. This does not exist everywhere; in such places it is sufficient to teach languages and humane letters.

---

4   Andrea Lippomano (dates uncertain). For his sponsorship of the college at Padua in 1542, see Ribadeneyra, *Life of Ignatius*, book 3, chapter 6.

Beyond this, the priests in the colleges will aid in hearing confessions, preaching, and all other spiritual matters; moreover, in this work the young men sometimes have grace that equals or exceeds that of the priests, God Our Lord being greatly served thereby.

So much for the method. Now I shall mention the advantages which experience has shown to accrue from this kind of college for the Society itself, for the extern students, and for the people or territory where the college is situated (although this can in part be gathered from what has already been said).

The advantages for our own men are these:

1. First of all, those who teach make progress themselves and learn a great deal by teaching others, acquiring greater confidence and mastery in their learning.

2. Our own scholastics who attend the classes will benefit from the care, continuity, and diligence which the teachers devote to their office.

3. They not only advance in learning but also acquire facility in preaching and teaching Christian doctrine, get practice in the other means they will later use for helping their neighbors, and grow in confidence through seeing the fruit which God Our Lord allows them to see.

4. Although no one may urge the students, particularly young boys, to enter the Society, nevertheless, through good example and personal contact, as well as the Latin declamations on the virtues held on Sundays, young men are spontaneously attracted, and many laborers can be won for the vineyard of Christ Our Lord. So much for the advantages to the Society itself.

The benefits for the extern students who come to take advantage of the classes are the following:

5. They are given a quite adequate grounding in letters through the great care which is taken to ensure that everyone learns by means of classes, debates, and compositions, so that they are seen to profit greatly in learning.

6. Persons who are poor and unable to pay the ordinary teachers, much less private tutors at home, here obtain gratis an education which they could hardly succeed in obtaining at great expense.

7. They profit in spiritual matters through learning Christian doctrine and hearing in the sermons and regular exhortations what they need for their eternal salvation.

8. They make progress in purity of conscience and consequently in all virtue through the monthly confessions and the care taken to see that they are decent in their speech and virtuous in their entire lives.

9. They draw much greater merit and fruit from their studies, since they make a practice of directing them all to the service of God from the time they begin studying, as they are taught to do.

For the people of the country or territory where these colleges are established, there are also the following advantages:

10. Financially, parents are relieved of the expense by having teachers to instruct their children in letters and virtue.

11. Aside from the schooling, they also have in the colleges persons who can preach sermons to the people and to those in monasteries and who can assist them through administration of the sacraments to quite good effect, as has been seen.

12. The people themselves and the members of their households are drawn to spiritual concerns by the example of their children, and are attracted to going more often to confession and living Christian lives.

13. The people of the country have in our men people to inspire and aid them in undertaking charitable works such as hospitals, houses for reformed women, and the like, for which charity also impels our men to have a concern.

14. From among those who are at present only students, various persons will in time emerge—some for preaching and the care of souls, others for the government of the land and the administration of justice, and others for other responsibilities. In short, since young people turn into adults, their good formation in life and learning will benefit many others, with the fruit expanding more widely every day.

I could elaborate further, but this will suffice to explain our thinking here about colleges of this kind.

May Christ, our eternal salvation, guide us all for his better service. Amen.

FIGURE 3   An anonymous eighteenth-century painting (conserved in
the sacristy of the college of Alcamo, Sicily) listing the network of Jesuit institutions in Sicily: the branches of the tree
bear thirty-eight fruits, such as colleges, seminaries, residences, and professed houses.

CHAPTER 5

Considerations Regarding the Multiplication of Colleges (1553)

Juan Alfonso de Polanco

Following advice given in the Spiritual Exercises, *Jesuits often produced lists of pros and cons before making decisions.[1] Here Polanco deliberates in this fashion on the question of increasing the number of Jesuit colleges at a time when the Society was under mounting pressure from cities and sovereigns to expand its educational work, especially in Italy. By the time of this letter, the Society had already accepted responsibility for colleges for external students at Messina (1548), Palermo (1549), Tivoli (1548/49), the Roman College (1551), Venice (1551), Ferrara (1551), Bologna (1551), the German College (1552), Florence (1552), Naples (1552), Perugia (1552), Padua (1552), Modena (1552), and Gubbio (1552). Several material reasons, particularly the limited number of suitable Jesuits, seemed to counsel restraint. Furthermore, the entire apostolic direction in education was still a quite recent decision; rapid expansion could be overwhelming. On the other hand, multiplying colleges was attractive because this kind of work seemed perfectly in line with the two primordial purposes of the Society as expressed in the* Formula of the Institute: *(1) defense and propagation of the faith and (2) the progress of souls in Christian life and doctrine. Polanco finally counseled prudence, requiring good income and other material conditions as prerequisites for considering these involvements. The way he structured his reflection is telling: he considered individuals, neighbors, and then the Society.*

Juan Alfonso de Polanco (born December 24, 1517, Burgos—entered the Society in 1541, Rome—died December 20, Rome, 1576). A prolific and influential secretary of the order for twenty-six years, Polanco helped Ignatius turn the Society into a teaching order, particularly through his substantial contributions to part 4 of the Constitutions, *on the colleges and on the spiritual and academic formation of Jesuits. To his effective organizational mind we might attribute some of the impetus that soon let the Society establish its worldwide network of colleges. Polanco is known also for the many letters he wrote for Ignatius "on commission" and for his extensive* Chronicon, *the first detailed chronicle of the early Society.[2]*

Source: *Monumenta paedagogica*, nova editio, 1:446–49 (original: Spanish)

---

1   See George Ganss, *The Spiritual Exercises of Saint Ignatius* (St. Louis: Institute of Jesuit Sources, 1992), 77–80 [no. 181].

2   The *Chronicon's* official title is *Vita Ignatii Loiolae et rerum Societatis Iesu historia* [The life of Ignatius Loyola and the history of the Society of Jesus], MHSI vols. 1, 3, 5, 7, 9, 11, ed. D. Fernández Zapico (Madrid, 1894–98). A selection of the *Chronicon* has been published

1—The Usefulness of Multiplying Our Colleges

Regarding the Individuals Themselves

(1) Both those who govern and those who obey practice and test themselves in public as well as at home.[3] (2) They are inspired to do more things, as they see that it falls to them to answer to expectations and to take care of spiritual needs; and with care and diligence and discreet charity, the teaching can be enhanced. (3) It does not hurt the young men's doctrine to practice teaching others and to deepen their understanding of literary culture, even if they are detained for a year or so longer in language-related matters before they begin theology.[4]

Regarding Our Neighbors

(1) Even those who are not very educated will always assist in spiritual needs, and perhaps they will do so more than those others in hearing confessions and in giving exhortations. (2) They could serve well enough in teaching Christian and Catholic doctrine to those who are very simple.[5] (3) In managing these schools it can only be helpful to take care to assist the children in their habits, all the more as these works expand. (4) They will always be adequate to teach children their letters, and the more this spreads, the better. (5) They always help through their example.

Regarding the Society

(1) It is an advantage to have somewhere to send those who are received in a house to carry out their work. (2) There is an advantage in being able to accept more people in the Society from among whom a choice will later be made of those who are more suitable. (3) There is an advantage in beginning many institutions where the service of God is carried on.

All things considered, three things seem good in Our Lord: (1) We should accept and provide what we can to those colleges that are endowed with a good

---

in English as *Year by Year with the Early Jesuits: Selections from the* Chronicon *of Juan de Polanco, S.J.*, trans. John Patrick Donnelly (St. Louis: Institute of Jesuit Sources, 2004).

3   "At home" means within the communal life of the religious residence.

4   There soon emerged in the Society a typical formational path for Jesuit scholastics: after the two-year novitiate, if not already well grounded in humanistic studies, they would spend two more years in humane letters and rhetoric and then three years in the arts course (philosophy), after which they were usually required to teach in a lower school in their province for three to five years before beginning theological studies. Sometimes they began theology while teaching humanistic studies.

5   Teaching doctrine stood at the core of the Jesuit identity since the very beginning, being one of the ministries expressly mentioned in the Society's most important founding document, the *Formula of the Institute*. It is not surprising, therefore, that Polanco lists this work among the first advantages of running colleges. The first Congregation of the Society of Jesus approved a decision obliging the professed to teach catechism occasionally. Ignatius had already set a period of forty continuous days of such teaching for Jesuits. See *Institutum*, 1:481.

income and placed in a good location.[6] (2) If they lack such an endowment, but they want to maintain some students and priests, we should not hastily accept such colleges until we have suitable individuals to send, always being careful not to deprive the most important places. (3) As humanistic literature is studied in the colleges, so in some colleges or in some one of them the arts and theology should be studied, so that there might arise fully trained workers who are more suitable to work in the Lord's vineyard.[7]

2—There Are These Reasons Why We Should Not Multiply Our Colleges Much until We Have More People to Supply

Regarding the Same Individuals

(1) Because it demands sending too soon those who are not sufficiently tested to help in such assignments. (2) Because, not being able to send to such assignments persons of authority and experience and knowledge of the matters of the Society, it would be necessary that those who go to their positions will not be helped so much in the Society's spirit and way of proceeding. (3) It greatly impedes the members of the Society in studies that are not suited to them for their benefit, and they will not become well and fully formed workers, or they will become so only later. (4) We are forced to commit youths who are neither learned nor experienced to the ministries of confessing, preaching, or directing others, which is something that they do with a danger that is proportional to their ministerial incompetence.

Regarding Our Neighbors

(1) There will not be enough done for their spiritual needs, since they [i.e., the ones assigned to these teaching positions] are not instruments that are as adequate as is necessary. (2) For the same reason, they will not be of very much help in teaching language and literature. (3) Those who hear them are deprived of the fruit they would have if those of the Society who preached were more resourceful.

Regarding the Society Itself

(1) Its reputation would suffer under its responsibilities and its sending inadequate people to new institutions; this suggests that more is lost than gained. (2) It would suffer much distraction and anxiety with so many changes that would be going on almost constantly. (3) For so many assignments, the Society would have to accept a less select group of people and it would have more and more subjects

---

6 Since Jesuit education was offered for free, colleges needed a guaranteed income to operate. Ignatius and his successors were always unwilling to open colleges without the provision of adequate yearly revenues.

7 In the documents of this Reader, "arts" typically refers not to the contemporary idea of "liberal arts" but to the course of philosophical studies that were usually undertaken in a university before going on to any of the professional schools in theology, law, or medicine.

that are not the way they ought to be. (4) Waiting a short while until some have finished their studies, our colleges could gradually multiply, with more foundation; and it would always be easy in the way that things have now begun in Italy, where it seems quite improper to take hold of what cannot be well grasped.

CHAPTER 6

The Aim and State of the Roman College (1553)

Ignatius of Loyola

The Roman College opened on February 22, 1551, in a house owned by the Aquilani family, thanks to an endowment from Francisco de Borja (1510–72), the fourth duke of Gandía. Despite its less than inspiring start, Ignatius maintained his high expectations. He wanted it to be a jewel shining brightly in the city of the Holy See, furnished with the best teachers that the Society could provide and offering a full-fledged curriculum, from grammar to theology. After a year of operation, the college moved to another house, near the Piazza del Gesù. There, the college succeeded so well and so quickly that Ignatius had to deal with ill-will coming from two quarters. Joachim Christiaens (1529–56), called "the Greek" because of his superior knowledge of the ancient languages, began his course only to find himself the victim of violence in his own classroom. The perpetrators were two private teachers from the neighborhood. One of these was later imprisoned on the order of Cardinal Juan Álvarez de Toledo (1488–1557), protector of the college and inquisitor of Rome since 1552. Then there was the response of the institution known as the Sapienza, the old Roman university founded in 1303. It began to suffer under competition from the Roman College when the latter began teaching arts and theology using an apparently superior pedagogic method. This background frames the letter written by Ignatius to Francisco de Borja's son, the fifth duke of Gandía. Here Ignatius showed both his pride in the success of his best educational institution and his chagrin at seeing it still so financially feeble despite requests made to people like Cardinal Alessandro Farnese (1520–89). Ignatius's last statement of loyalty to the house of Borja seems to be not least a plea to increase the endowment.

Ignatius of Loyola (born c.1491, Guipúzcoa, Spain—co-founder of the Society in 1540, Rome—died 1556, Rome). Chief founder of the Jesuit order, Ignatius was a great supporter and administrator of Jesuit studies from its earliest days after official papal approval. Though he did not at first intend the Society to be an organization that administered schools, he quickly made it into one when he saw its great apostolic results and promise. He readily took on as many colleges as feasible, showing a special enthusiasm for the Roman College. His own journey manifested a deep investment in studies in Barcelona, Alcalá, Salamanca, and Paris, and the Society itself was uniquely tied to the University of Paris, where all of the founders were students. Ignatius is often listed as one of the great figures in the history of education.

Source: *Monumenta paedagogica*, nova editio, 1:44–46 (original: Spanish)

Ignatius of Loyola to Carlos Borja, Duke of Gandía, and Diego Hurtado de Mendoza, Count of Melito[1]

Rome, November 6, 1553

[...] What moves me now to present to Your Lordship what I am going to report to you here, after having given it so much attention and after having so fully entrusted it to Our Lord, is nothing but his greater glory and praise. And if Your Lordship thinks the same, he will think that the author is the same as the author of all good. If not, he will ascribe my deception to the special attachment that I feel towards the service of Your Lordship, and I wish to owe much more to the one to whom we all owe so much in Our Lord.

I think that Your Lordship is already informed about the college that began to operate here in Rome thanks to Father Francisco de Borja's donation, which was intended to provide for both the college and church.[2] The reason for establishing this college was the importance for both the service of God and the common good of the Society, to the greater glory of God Our Lord, that colleges of the Society, as well as professed houses, would take shape here at the seat of the Apostolic See, under the eyes of the vicar of Christ and of all Christianity.[3]

And not only do we never have occasion to regret what was begun but every day we take more satisfaction, because we can see in an ever better way the importance of this work in the service of God. And so we have decided to develop it as much as we can, with the grace of Our Lord. And where there were twenty-four people in the college, who were studying Latin, Greek, and Hebrew, now there are about sixty people, and all the major subjects and higher sciences have begun, as Your Lordship will be able to read in a document which is attached here.[4] For this, we have drawn many good teachers and scholars of the Society who together are starting three courses of arts and every branch of theology and giving order

---

1 Carlos de Borja y Castro (1533–1606), fifth duke of Gandía and son of Francisco de Borja; and Diego Hurtado de Mendoza (1503?–75), ambassador of Charles V (1500–58) and viceroy of Aragon from 1553/54 to 1564.
2 Thanks to the financial support of Francisco de Borja, duke of Gandía up to that time, the Jesuits were able to open the Roman College (February 2, 1551). The sign hung on the main door has become a kind of icon for the early phase of Jesuit ministry of education: "School of Grammar, Humanities, and Christian Doctrine, Free."
3 The same argument can be found in a letter addressed by Polanco to all the superiors of the order on March 31, 1553, about the beginnings of the Roman College. *Monumenta paedagogica*, nova editio, 1:427.
4 The college opened under modest circumstances, but, just one year later (January 1, 1552), Ignatius could state that "the college is getting better and better. Good teachers give lessons on Latin, Greek, and Hebrew and I estimate that there are about 250 students attending" (*Monumenta ignatiana*, series prima, 4:59). One month later, Polanco wrote in a letter to Francis Xavier that the general attendance was increasing and the number of Jesuit students at the college was about twenty-two to twenty-four (ibid., 4:131). This letter testifies to the further rise in the general enrollment from twenty-four to sixty in just one year.

to the exercises that is the most valuable thing for making the students into real doctors.[5] The result is that no university of which we have knowledge here is able to produce students as learned in literature in so short a time as are ours and whatever others are studying here.[6]

Furthermore, beyond the many learned people this college will send forth, there will also be this advantage, that, in light of our testing of what works best here, the school will help to give shape to other colleges of ours. The same goes for the books and doctrine that should be studied in each course. Some very learned people have started to think about this issue,[7] and we hope that sound doctrine will take shape, in both pagan and in Christian authors, purged of additions that are not coherent with it,[8] that it might spread not only among our colleges but even among other studies outside of it, in humanistic studies as well as in the higher faculties.

Now these intentions of ours have been implemented and are truly working with hope in Christ Our Lord, whose honor and service in helping his beloved souls are all that we seek, that he might help us in this, and that concerning temporal goods as well he might move the heart of whoever might be served to help keep such a good work in operation. And it is true that someone wanted to buy the house which currently hosts the college and use some revenue in order to maintain it, being himself the founder and installing his coat of arms.[9] But this proposal seems definitely unacceptable to us: we are drawn more by our

---

5 The list of renowned professors who were brought to the Roman College is a long one. Francisco de Toledo (1532–96), Benet Perera (1535–1610), and Juan de Mariana (1536–1624) were among the earliest philosophers and theologians. Francisco Suárez (1548–1617), Robert Bellarmine (1542–1621), and Christopher Clavius (1537–1612) fostered the reputation of the college in the fourth quarter of the sixteenth century.

6 Two years later, Polanco could write that the Sapienza, the university of Rome, was generally thought to be giving "cold" and "almost useless" instruction in comparison with what was being offered at the Roman College (*Monumenta paedagogica*, nova editio, 1:458).

7 Ignatius refers to Jerónimo Nadal (1507–80) and Martín de Olave (1507/8–56), who laid out two plans for studies at the Roman College. See *Monumenta paedagogica*, nova editio, 1:133–85.

8 On the opportunity of censoring and emending the ancient texts in order to provide a safe education, see the above-mentioned letter from Ignatius to Andrea Lippomano (1549). The Jesuits used to adopt the metaphor of the "spoils of Egypt" to refer to the legitimacy of using pagan texts, though amended or expurgated (Padberg, *Constitutions*, 152). See Kristine Johnson and Paul Lynch, "*Ad perfectam eloquentiam*: The 'Spoils of Egypt' in Jesuit Renaissance Rhetoric," *Rhetoric Review* 31, no. 2 (2012): 99–116.

9 The financial status of the college was precarious, since Borja's endowment proved insufficient. Moreover, a part of the endowment had to be devoted to purchase a house where a church was to be built. On October 20, 1553, that is, only ten days before Ignatius wrote this letter, Polanco complained that "the endowment of the college is faith and hope, because a great part of the legacy has already been spent in purchasing a house for the church" (*Monumenta ignatiana*, series prima, 5:595).

devotion to Father Francisco and to your Lordship along with him. As the Society owes you so much, it would like to keep you as the patrons and founders of this work, which is and will be, with God's help, the most prestigious and distinguished one in the entire Society and the one that is most productive of the universal good […].

CHAPTER 7

The Origin of the Colleges (1556)

Pedro de Ribadeneyra

In 1555, Ignatius had two ideas in mind when he sent Pedro de Ribadeneyra to Flanders, which was at that time under the rule of Spain's Philip II (1527–98): solidifying the settlement of the Society of Jesus in that region and explaining the recently approved Constitutions to members of the Society there. As a Jesuit of noble ancestry, Ribadeneyra seemed to Ignatius the best intermediary between the Society and the Spanish crown. The order needed the king's favor to defend itself from the hostility of the local clergy, which typically saw the Jesuits as unwanted competition. Thanks to the help of the royal advisor Gómez III Suárez de Figueroa y Córdoba (1520?–71), the fifth count of Feria, Ribadeneyra was finally able to win the favor of Philip II, who later asked him to go to London and assist his wife, Queen Mary I of England (1516–58). In 1556, at Philip's accession, she had become queen consort of Habsburg Spain.

This letter was one of Ribadeneyra's first attempts to win the king's protection for the Society in Flanders. It presents a manifesto for the educative mission of the Jesuits, citing the order's most important documents to gain Philip II's support. In his persuasion of the so-called "most Catholic king," Ribadeneyra emphasizes the importance of educating youth as a way of countering the spread of heresy, one of Philip's chief worries about the Low Countries.

Pedro de Ribadeneyra (born November 1, 1526, Toledo, Spain—entered the Society on September 1, 1540, Rome—died September 22, 1611, Madrid). Ribadeneyra had taken up residence with the Jesuit community in Rome shortly before his fourteenth birthday. He spent time at Jesuit colleges in Paris, Louvain, Rome, and Padua. Showing special talent in the communicational arts, he taught rhetoric at the Jesuit college of Palermo (1550–52) and gave the inaugural speech at the German College in 1552. After many years spent mostly in administrative and delicate political missions, and after producing a valuable biography of Ignatius at the request of Superior General Francisco de Borja (1510–72), Ribadeneyra was sent back to Spain in 1574 by the following superior general Everard Mercurian (1514–80, in office 1573–80). He stayed there until his death, writing so prolifically and so well that he is to the present day known as one of the canonical writers of the "Golden Age" of Spanish literature, with contributions mostly in history, hagiography, and spirituality.

Source: *Monumenta paedagogica*, nova editio, 1:474–77 (original: Spanish)

Pedro de Ribadeneyra to King Philip II of Spain

Antwerp, February 14, 1556

[…] Our Father Master Ignatius has instructed me that after kissing Your Majesty's hands on his behalf and on that of our entire Society I should present to Your Majesty the desire that God Our Lord has given all of us, a desire now grown great, to use the trickle that he has kindly shared with us for his glory and for the good of souls in service of Your Majesty. Master Ignatius said that I should state plainly that our Society's Institute is such that those who live in it not only are concerned to profit spiritually themselves but also are interested in attending to their neighbors, each one of them, according to the talent that God has given them; and because this is so, the Society should try to gain their salvation, whether they be faithful or unfaithful or heretical. And since the light of wisdom is most necessary to instruct and teach the people, it has been a necessary matter for us to establish endowed colleges in the Society (because studies are encumbered when the necessities are lacking) in which those who enter our Institute without adequate education, after being trained in the matters of religious life, may be taught the sciences necessary for their final goal of helping souls.[1]

Since it seems very difficult for those grown old in sin to be renewed and to strip off their bad habits, put on new clothes, and give themselves to God; and since the good of Christianity and the entire world depends on the good education of the young who, being soft as wax in their childhood, more easily take on the shape of whatever impresses them;[2] and since we sorely lack enough virtuous and learned teachers to do this, people who unite example with doctrine, this same Society, with the zeal which Christ Our Redeemer has given to it, has reached down to take up this less honored but no less profitable task of educating children and young men. And so, among the other services that it performs, this is one, not the least of them:[3] to run schools and colleges in which to teach not only its own members but external students as well, for free and without any worldly reward, in addition to the virtues and what a good Christian needs, all the main sciences, from the rudiments and principles of grammar to the other,

---

1   This paragraph echoes the preamble of part 4 of the *Constitutions* of the Society of Jesus (Padberg, *Constitutions*, 130–32).

2   On the image of youth as a soft and blank slate, see the letter Polanco addressed to Laínez above (Chapter 2).

3   Pope Julius III (1487–1555, r.1550–55), in the bull giving a second and final confirmation of the Society (*Exposcit debitum*, 1550), approved the revised version of the *Formula Instituti*, which stated that the ministries of the Society were "to strive especially for the defense and propagation of the faith and for the progress of souls in Christian life and doctrine, by means of public preaching, lectures, and any other ministration whatsoever of the word of God." Among the *consueta ministeria* (ordinary ministries) of the Society, there were listed also teaching Christian doctrine to children and unlettered persons and works of charity. Padberg, *Constitutions*, 4.

deeper subjects, according to the different possibilities of the colleges that have been founded for this purpose in different parts of Spain, Portugal, Italy, and Germany.[4] This enterprise has been received very well, with great popular support and gratitude wherever schools and colleges have been founded, and it has won approval with great profit everywhere, as can be gathered from the success and spread and propagation that our Lord, in the few years since it began in this region, has given this work, like something coming from his own hand.[5]

Our Father Master Ignatius, seeing how universally successful this way of teaching was in all regions, and on one hand thinking over how profitable and necessary it would be for these states against the damages and ravages that heresies and monstrous new manners of sects and errors started bringing about in them, as Your Majesty knows all too well; and considering that heretical fathers must necessarily pass on to their children their own heresies and errors; and, on the other hand, marveling that Our Lord God has been so good as to call many individuals of virtue and learning from this nation for the establishment of our Society, and other young men of good talent and prospects, who with time would be able to be faithful instruments of his glory in these states; it seemed to him that he would not be fulfilling his duty to the health of souls and to the service of Your Majesty if he did not at least show the desire he has to serve Your Majesty and not offer all our least Society with its works to your perpetual service in all regions, and especially these as they are more in need of aid and rescue.[6]

What especially moved him to this was seeing how many important people, zealous for God's honor and Your Majesty's service, such as are the inquisitors and others who know well the evil that exists and the profit gained by some members of our Society through the grace of the Holy Spirit, are asking him to send over here people to help them to defend our holy Catholic faith by means of their example and doctrine, since it has been challenged in so many ways and places. And he was also moved by the knowledge that complaints have arisen because many promising capable young men and individuals that could be productive in this region have gone off to enter the order in Italy. This has been necessary

---

4   In Spain, the Jesuits were running colleges that had previously been opened to external students in Burgos (1550), Medina del Campo (1551), Córdoba (1553), and Plasencia (1554). A list of the colleges in the other countries can be found in László Lukács, "De origine collegiorum externorum deque controversiis circa eorum paupertatem obortis," *Archivum historicum Societatis Iesu* 29 (1960): 189–245, here 242–43.

5   See Luce Giard, "Les collèges jésuites des anciens Pays-Bas et l'élaboration de la *Ratio studiorum*," in *The Jesuits of the Low Countries: Identity and Impact (1540–1773)—Proceedings of the International Congress at the Faculty of Theology and Religious Studies, KU Leuven (3–5 December 2009)*, ed. Rob Faesen and Leo Kenis (Leuven: Peeters, 2012), 83–108.

6   The phrase used here, "our least Society" (nostra minima Societas) was frequently used to indicate the small size and poverty, and perhaps even more pointedly, the youth of the Society when compared with the older, larger orders in the church. The Latin phrase "minima natu" signifies "the youngest."

as there is no house here, nor a college, nor a location belonging to the Society where, being called by the Lord Our God, they could gather and take shelter.

And he has likewise seen that the bishop of Cambrai[7] wants neither to welcome into his diocese members of the Society, even though it has been confirmed and approved by recent popes,[8] nor to grant them faculties to preach and to perform the other offices to the profit of souls, claiming that our Society has not been approved by Your Majesty in these regions. And he realizes that some others might say the same. So the desire to remedy this has also moved our Father [Ignatius] to send me to Your Majesty to plead that he kindly take this least Society under his wings in these regions, just as he has already done in others, and grant us license to be able to run colleges. This is to say that if some city, or lord, or particular individual intends to perform a service to God Our Lord by leaving some house or college or revenue for some individuals from our Society to teach the young or study in order that they might later apply what they have learned to the good of souls and to the service of Your Majesty, they might be able to do it freely. This is not so that our members might come to a locale against the will of these people, but rather so that those making a request to have members of our Society can be granted this favor and assisted. […]

---

7   Robert de Croÿ (1500–66), archbishop of Cambrai from 1519 to 1556.
8   He refers to Paul III (r.1534–49) and Julius III (r.1550–55). The latter had died just a year before this letter was written.

Part 2:
Administration

CHAPTER 8

Constitutions of the College at Messina (1548)

Jerónimo Nadal

In 1548, Ignatius agreed to send ten Jesuits to Messina to open a college as the city had requested. This group included Jerónimo Nadal, who would be the rector and teach Hebrew, Scholastic theology, and cases of conscience; Benedetto Palmio (1532–98), Hannibal du Coudret (1525–99), and Giovanni Battista Passerini (dates uncertain) to teach grammar; Peter Canisius (1521–97) to teach rhetoric; and André des Freux (c.1515–56) to teach Greek. As soon as they settled in Messina, Nadal set out the rules, which follow in general outline the common practices of the most celebrated Parisian colleges.

Nadal divides the rules into two parts. The first concerns morals and spirituality, referencing the fundamental apostolic aims of the Society (the glory of God and the help of souls) and thus supporting this new ministry in education. Spirituality stood so much at the core of the Jesuit self-concept that Ignatius wanted the ten Jesuits in Messina to teach Christian doctrine in the church of San Nicolò every Friday and to preach frequently there despite their many obligations at the college. The second part of Nadal's rules focuses on studies. It surveys the entire curriculum of Jesuit education from basic grammar classes for children to Scholastic theology, counterpointed by the teaching of cases of conscience. The success of the college was great and immediate. Polanco enthusiastically reported in his Chronicon *that he could hardly believe that an institution could make so much improvement in its students' knowledge of the humanistic literary arts.*

Jerónimo Nadal (born August 1, 1507, Palma de Mallorca, Baleares, Spain—entered the Society November 29, 1545, Rome—died March 25, 1580, Rome). The first rector of the college of Messina (1548), Nadal was chosen by Ignatius as the one who could organize the Society according to the Constitutions. *Nadal's importance for Jesuit education cannot be overemphasized. He endeavored to provide useful and suitable rules for governing the colleges, traveled all over the provinces to survey the situation and provide educational directives, and wrote a number of letters to make Jesuit pedagogy as consistent as possible.*

Source: *Monumenta paedagogica*, nova editio, 1:17–28 (original: Latin)

[I. What Pertains to Religious Devotion and Good Morals]

[1] Everyone should attend Mass daily, and it should be celebrated before the first class.

FIGURE 4   A drawing by Filippo Juvarra (1701) of the front of the Jesuit college
at Messina.

[2] Christian doctrine should be taught Friday in every class according to
everyone's level of understanding.

[3] Everyone should go to confession each month, and if there are any who are
devout, they should receive Communion, but following their confessor's
advice.[1]

[4] On every Sunday and also on holy days they should hear a sermon.

[5] Each of the instructors should pray before the start of the class,[2] and they
should encourage everyone to pray together; in the classes for boys, they
should also have the boys answer aloud. They should do the same in the
evening when the students are dismissed.

[6] All students should be taught the general examen, and they should be
encouraged to make it every day. See that everyone knows Christian doctrine and the way to make a confession.

---

1   Although the idea of frequent Communion was not new, the other orders often criticized
the Jesuits for their promotion of the more frequent reception of this sacrament over the
customary practice of receiving it once or twice a year. This conflict probably suggested to
Nadal the consultation of the confessor in this matter. See Robert A. Maryks, *Saint Cicero
and the Jesuits: The Influence of the Liberal Arts on the Adoption of Moral Probabilism* (Aldershot: Ashgate, 2008), 19–26.

2   This translation generally uses "instructor" as the translation of *praeceptor*. The standing term
for "teacher" in the *Ratio studiorum* of 1599 is "professor." *Magister* can also mean "teacher."

[7] They should pray at least twice a day in silence or aloud, when they get up and when they go to bed.[3]

[8] No one should swear an oath of any kind. But if anyone uses the name of God and the saint in some objectionable way, some penance should be given.

[9] No one should utter obscenities.

[10] No one should play dice or any forbidden game, under some penalty.

[11] Everyone should keep in mind reverence for God and they should embrace this with all their heart. And they should believe and feel that worldly glory which is contrary to the law of God is a most certain and deadly plague to the whole world.

[12] They should firmly set the honor and glory of God as the goal not only of their studies but also of all their activities as well.

[13] They should always and urgently beg God to give them a good and holy mind, and no one should decide anything about his state [in life] without first praying very diligently with great devotion and with complete denial of his own will.

[14] Everyone should very diligently manage their time so that what ought to be of greatest value to everyone is not wasted in idleness.

[15] No student should come to class with a sword or dagger, and there should also be a penalty for doing this.

[16] All pre-adolescents should be subject to the switch; the adolescents should be verbally chastised in the strongest terms in front of the class, or expelled completely when they are found to be incorrigible.

[17] All the students should be examined and each assigned to his own class according to his ability.[4]

[18] Appoint someone to keep a complete register of all the students and make a note of those who are absent; the parents should be informed of their absence.

[19] Everyone should be speaking Latin at all times and there should be someone to make a note of those not speaking Latin.

[20] There should be a syndic in each class to find out what everyone is talking about and he should report on this to the instructor. This syndic should be secret and he should make his reports in secret.

---

3   The teaching and promoting of mental prayer was one of the Society's "special campaigns," as it derived from a method they had learned in making the Exercises. O'Malley, *First Jesuits*, 163.

4   This pedagogical principle matches the idea stated in the *Formula* about the appointment of each of the Jesuits, who were required to achieve their main goal (the glory of God) "according to the grace which the Holy Spirit has given to him and according to the particular grade of his own vocation." See Padberg, *Constitutions*, 4.

[II. What Pertains to Studies]

[1] Those studying Donatus should be given considerable pedagogical attention, and their characters should be formed to be holy and devout in the Lord.[5]

[2] The group should be split into two parts and a competition organized to see which part outdoes the other in memorizing the greatest number of verses: and this should happen such that each student has his own adversary to compete with. But instructors should watch for two things: first, that wherever possible equals are partnered; and second, that nothing really detrimental arises from such competition, such as hatred and mischief, or excessive eagerness to win or not give in (which has become obsessive in some students), or even the dispiriting of one person to match the insolence of the other, both of which extremes the teacher will use his own judgment to keep under control.

[3] Every Saturday, there should be no new lesson, but they should only recite whatever they commit to memory over that whole week, and at the same time, they will be stimulated by little challenges, as for example, if someone says, "Give the future tense of *fero*, give the perfect tense of *doceo*," and so forth.

[4] At the same time, they should be taught Christian doctrine and devotional prayers, and they should take examples from the authors they are reading to use as the basis for exercises of imitation in class.

[5] Those being taught the principles of grammar will learn by heart all the rules of the grammarians.

[6] They will note in their own exercise books everything they hear, and there they can easily add their own glosses. And after the grammar class, they will be examined individually by the instructor in the manner given in the rule. The same procedure will be followed in the exposition of authors, where individual sections will be analyzed according to the method of grammatical rules.

[7] They will have debates every evening, in addition to that day's classes, split into two sections and driven by an honorable desire to win.

[8] On alternate days, they will change [partners] according to their capacities.

[9] Every day, a theme will be composed, and they will recite and correct it according to the instructor's model.

[10] Every Saturday, nothing [new] will be taught in the morning; there will only be a review of all the lessons of the previous week. After lunch, one

---

5 Aelius Donatus (*fl.* mid-fourth century CE) wrote an elementary grammar (*Ars minor*) which was among the most popular textbooks for children's education from early Middle Ages onwards. The children's *cursus* (curriculum) usually began with learning numbers and counting; they then learned to use the abacus and learned the psalter by heart (without understanding it). Finally, they started to learn grammar with the so-called *Donatus minor*. Before reaching this grade, children were called *pueri a tabula usque ad Donatum*.

person will propose either a theme or some lesson or a rule to be defended, and all the others will debate this.[6]

[11] In that class, it shall be ensured that no vulgar expression is used, but that everything is Latin and pure; so that only pure and appropriate Latin speech should be fashioned and looked for in this class.

[12] In the second class, after any lesson is taught, a single person designated by the instructor should first review it. Then, the students themselves, divided up into two sections, should discuss it. Afterwards, the instructor will examine what relates to elegance of expression and offer other observations about the Latin language. Every day, they will compose a theme. Every day, they will vary it and debate it. Every evening, they will compose verses in friendly rivalry in the summer, but in the winter let them pay more attention to prose, but still according to the teachers' judgment.

[13] On Saturday morning, no lesson will be taught. There will only be a review of whatever was presented in the previous week. After lunch, one student will defend either some composition or reading selection or rule, and the others will discuss this.

[14] Everyone in the class should speak Latin, under the supervision of a fellow student.

[15] Also a student will be appointed to keep track of the absentees and give the full report to the instructor.

[16] The rhetorician will test his students first by having one repeat the lesson and then everyone discuss among themselves. Then by having them make daily variations upon a set theme. Also by having one give a declamation in any style, with the others declaiming against him. Someone should support something from the lesson in a dialectical manner, and others should challenge him. These two things will take place by turns on alternate Saturdays.

[17] The philosopher will always be most diligent; in any given lesson he will first tell one student to review the lesson in front of the others; then all should discuss it among themselves. Before the next lesson the instructor will always review the preceding one. But on every Saturday, a single lesson will be given in the morning; nevertheless the remaining time will be given to a review of the week. After lunch, a student will defend the positions and all the others will challenge it. On all Sundays and feast days, he will go through Aristotle's *Nicomachean Ethics*, and he will tell his students to review and discuss the preceding lesson before the new one.

[18] He will teach mathematics outside of the ordinary schedule at a time the rector judges most convenient. First he will teach several books of Euclid, until they have learned the proofs. Then he will teach the practical arithmetic of

---

6 *Disputare* can mean "to discuss." It does not always refer to a formal, structured disputation in the Scholastic mode.

Orontius and his *Sphere*, the *Astrolabe* of Stoeffler, and the *Speculations* of Peurbach.[7]

[19] The Greek scholar will give time before noon to his Greek students. He will teach partly grammar, and something from some author that everyone, even the untrained beginners, can understand; and partly, so that he may also be able to satisfy the more advanced students, he will go through some important author, reviewing as many exercises as time allows, and so forth, in the manner of grammarians and rhetoricians.

[20] The Hebrew scholar will give time after noon to his students. He will always teach some grammar and something from the sacred scriptures; and according to the schedule and ability of the students, he will prescribe exercises in the manner of grammarians.

[21] The Scholastic theologian will have one student review the lesson after he teaches it; then everyone will review this among themselves and repeat it in the presence of the teacher, so that if they have doubts about anything, dispute it, or do not know it, they can be taught by the instructor before he teaches. This will be taken care of as far as it can be. There will be a discussion on the lesson under consideration, and every Saturday after lunch one student will hold the positions and the others will challenge it. Before lunch, all the lessons of the entire week will be reviewed.

[22] On all feast days and Sundays, Paul's letters will be covered.

[23] If cases of conscience have to be explained, some lesson on Scholastic theology will be omitted, so that the cases of conscience may be fully covered in its place.

[24] During a week that has no feast day, there will be no class after lunch, but there will be a break in all studies. But this should take place in such a way that the young men enjoy some wholesome recreation.

[25] Also, every month an instructor will nominate one student to defend his positions in public at St. Mary's church or in our own, with the teacher presiding while the instructors stand by each of their students as they make their defenses.[8] The theses should be posted publicly at crossroads so that everyone may know about the event, and the place for the scholastic competition should be an accessible one.

---

7 Oronce Finé (1494–1555) was a French mathematician and cartographer who published his *De mundi sphaera* in 1542. Johannes Stoeffler (1452–1531) was an astronomer and professor at the University of Tübingen. He was also a maker of astronomical instruments and his *Elucidatio fabricae ususque astrolabii* was published in 1512. Georg von Peuerbach (1423–61) was an Austrian mathematician and astronomer who wrote his successful *Theoricæ novæ planetarum, id est septem errantium siderum nec non octavi seu firmamenti* in 1454.

8 Santa Maria Assunta, the cathedral of Messina, where Nadal would occasionally comment on Saint Paul's Letters. Juan Alfonso de Polanco, *Chronicon*, in *Monumenta paedagogica*, nova editio, 1:510. The Jesuit church was San Nicolò dei Gentiluomini.

[26] The division of the classes into two parts, even though helpful, will nevertheless be varied every Saturday, so that the same students are not always standing in the same places and enmities perhaps fostered. It will be done in such a way that the individuals will sometimes be adversaries and sometimes allies.

CHAPTER 9

Rules for the Rector of the Roman College (1551)

Juan Alfonso de Polanco

Opened in 1551 in a very humble fashion, the Roman College was destined to become the most renowned of Jesuit schools. Ignatius himself strove to make it the best educational institution possible so that it might shine at the heart of Latin Christianity in Rome under the pope's sight. He wanted it to offer a full curriculum, from grammar to theology, and to stand as the model for Jesuit colleges everywhere.

Here, Polanco provides the rector of the college with the most comprehensive set of rules that the Society had so far produced, largely following Nadal's rules for Messina (see Chapter 8) but introducing some features that would much later find a place in the definitive Ratio studiorum *of 1599. The structure significantly separates the rules for spiritual and moral education from those concerned with instructional practices. The presentation suggests a ranking of Jesuit educational goals, with character formation being its main pedagogical concern. But the body was not ignored: the order gave to the students' physical well-being an attention that was distinctive in its time.*

Juan Alfonso de Polanco (born December 24, 1517, Burgos—entered the Society 1541, Rome—died December 20, 1576, Rome). A prolific and influential secretary of the order for twenty-six years, Polanco helped Ignatius turn the Society into a teaching order, particularly through his substantial contributions to part 4 of the Constitutions, *which concerns the colleges and the spiritual and academic formation of students. His effective organizational mind inspired the march towards the creation of a worldwide network of colleges. Polanco is known also for the many letters he wrote for Ignatius "on commission" and for his extensive* Chronicon, *the first detailed chronicle of the early Society.*

Source: *Monumenta paedagogica*, nova editio, 1:64–92 (originals: Latin and Italian)

IHS

The rector of the college should apply very diligent care especially to four things: The first will be to exercise the youth in spirit, virtue, and piety. The second, to see that the time that should be spent on spiritually profitable studies is not frittered away uselessly. The third, to see that their physical health should be preserved for the worship of God. The fourth, to see that the college's goods are used frugally and as well as possible.

Part 1: Concerning Spiritual Progress

1. Everyone should endeavor to have the right intention, clearly not seeking an education for any end other than the praise and glory of God and the salvation of souls; and from this, they should each strive steadfastly and zealously to attain that hoped-for end of their work, always mindful of obedience. Finally, with abundant prayers they should beg God's help to make greater progress both in learning and in the spirit.

2. Every day, everyone should attend Mass (except for those who might be dispensed by the rector for some good excuse, such as sickness). They should know how to serve the celebrant and have the responses thoroughly memorized. They should attend Mass with devotion, not sitting on a bench or leaning against the wall, but kneeling or standing at the appropriate times.

3. Everyone should try to keep their minds pure. To attain this purity of mind, twice every day, they should examine and weigh their conscience. And in the day they should spend an hour reading from the office of the Blessed Virgin and praying other devotional prayers assigned to them by the rector (for it is part of his role to decide what is more beneficial for each person).

4. Every week (not more frequently or less without the agreement of the rector), everyone will confess his sins to the priest assigned to him and take the holy sacrament of the Eucharist at Mass as reverentially as he can. Everyone, that is, either together on the same day or separately on different days, however it can be managed, so that every day there are some communicants.

5. Be sure that the exercise of virtue does not grow cooler as the burning zeal to acquire learning increases, nor on the other hand should education suffer a loss either through overextended prayer or through extraordinary mortification or through an excessive debilitation of the body. Therefore, beyond the fasts sanctioned by the church, none should be undertaken without the knowledge of the rector. He should also make the decisions about the use of disciplines, hair shirts, vigils, and mortifications such as these.[1] What of public mortifications? These will be adopted for no reason at all without the advice of the superior (to whom it belongs to know the medicine that should be applied to each, on the basis of how each of his flock appears to him).

6. Students should attend the sermon every Sunday and on feast days, in the morning or at noon, and in the afternoon they should go to hear the lesson at the church, and also they should attentively listen to the lesson in Christian doctrine that should be held in the college. But they should also be carefully trained in preaching in different tones (especially in connection with those days).[2]

---

1 A discipline is a small whip, sometimes made of knotted cords, used to mortify the flesh lightly.

2 For the practice in tones (*toni*), see O'Malley, *First Jesuits*, 100.

7. Moreover, each one will strive to have his own inner modesty shine out, certainly in his facial expression, his speech, his posture, his walk, and in such external personal features, as an edifying example for his neighbor (beyond the support that these things provide to his own consciousness). To do this more effectively, someone should be assigned to report to the superior the observed shortcomings of those who fail in these respects unless perhaps that person himself has permission from the superior to give penances to such students.

8. To eliminate any occasion for offending God, no one should go out without the superior's permission (unless in some situation the opposite would seem better to that superior) and without a companion who has been assigned to him from the college. However the superior himself should be sure that during the Bacchanals (as they call them)[3] while maskers are wandering through the city, he gives no one permission to go out, unless an urgent matter comes up.

9. Neither outside nor inside the house (where excuse can find a place) will they speak with non-religious externs, nor will they bring such individuals into the house unless they have permission from the superior. And still they should have no conversation with these individuals other than that which bears on the spiritual life or academic progress. In fact, they will not be permitted to speak indifferently with just anyone at all in the house, but only with those that the superior designates for them. His position and his office alike impose on him the task of selecting for them the individuals who can not only not undo them but also edify and support such students.

10. They will write no letters or receive them unless the superior has first examined them. It will be left to his discretion whether it is helpful for the letters to be read or written by them or not.

11. Subjects will have no additional funds in the college. If some happen to bring them, they should deposit them for safekeeping with the superior or with another person who is to provide this service.

12. No one will take anything belonging to someone else for his own use or as a gift or favor, however small it is, from another person, whether from the house or from outside it, apart from the superior's knowledge. Far less will anyone presume to loan or borrow anything. He will leave all concern for this to the superior.

13. No one will dare to instruct another person beyond what formally falls to him to do on the basis of his office.

14. At lunch and dinner, before beginning the meal and after it has been eaten, thanks should be given with due reverence and devotion. During lunch or dinner, either some spiritual book should be read or there will be preaching so that along with the body the soul will be restored with its own food.

---

3   The most famous in Rome was the Carnival.

15. No one should take the liberty of intruding on another person's office. But if he notices that there is any deficiency, he should correct his brother fraternally or try to have him corrected or advised through another person whose suggestions might possibly be more effective.

16. Every corner of the house should be cleaned of dirt so well that it shines. In brief, any particular individual should have such a lively care for his own particular room, clothing, bed, books, and all such things that their external appeal and beauty exude the pleasing odor of the appeal and beauty that exists within him.

17. Everyone should comply with the rector of the college and with someone to whom the rector has given authority. But if among the other upright students a son of damnable disobedience [cf. Eph. 2:2, 5:6; Col. 3:6] is caught, he should be deprived of bodily food; a house dedicated to respectable obedience will not long allow such a person to go unpunished.

18. The rector will take care to apply the appropriate medicine to each one's spiritual infirmity; for example, by exercising someone inclined to pride in the lowliest offices of the house, and by not at all sparing those on whom penances have to be imposed, even in the least shortcomings, so that greater ones will be more easily avoided.

19. The older ones will lodge with the younger ones, either in the same room, if it accommodates several, or in a neighboring room, if each one has a private room. The doors of the room should be open to the superior, especially if two are lodging in the same room. Doors should be shut in such a way that they can be opened without difficulty.

20. In short, everyone should be linked to each other by the bond of charity, all quarreling excluded. But if perhaps someone notices that (God forbid!) the bond is being dissolved through fighting and mutual blame, or even through a secret hatred, he should report it to the superior, with no thought of putting this off. Anyone who suffers serious confusion or temptation should run to him in the same way.

Part 2: The Structure of the Studies

1. Each one will comply with rector's decision in regard to taking classes, the structure and manner of studying, and the time to be spent on this or that exercise. When asked, he will honestly let the rector know what and how much he knows so that he might get from the rector a class suitable for his learning. The rector himself will also be sure that in every subject solid doctrine and the better authors are being taught; but also that no students who are ignorant of grammar are graduated to the higher sciences.

2. The rector will arrange the lower and the upper classes in such an order and sequence that the more advanced lessons are taught to the more advanced

classes, the middle-range ones to the middle-range classes, and the easier ones to the lower classes according to their intellectual abilities. And he will see that these are taught at the determined times, not at other ones. Nevertheless, classes will be able to be moved up or back, in keeping with the opinion of the rector and seasonal changes in schedule.

3. Before Mass there will be a class for an hour or so; after Mass, one for two hours. But another hour will also have to be spent on raising discussions on the basis of the lessons that have been learned, certainly as far as the midday meal. After this, for half or quarter of an hour, if some book is not being taught, there will be a repetition and a conference on the lesson taught before the midday meal. The following two and a half hours will be given to composition and to previewing and explaining the lesson. When this is finished, there will be a lesson that should last two hours. After that is done, review or discussion will take another hour, and dinner will follow it. But three times a week there will a repetition or discussion of everything that has been taught. As has been said, however, the lesson can be moved back or up, according to the various changes of the times. It must also be said that immediately at the sound of the bell everyone should quickly go off to whatever exercise they are being summoned.

4. On feast days that occur during the week, there will be class at least for an hour in the morning and for a second one in the afternoon.

5. On feast days, each individual will be able to choose for himself some hour to be given to review the lessons so that they might be readier to give to the rector or to someone acting in his place an account of what was learned. Additionally, after lunch, at the designated hour, conclusions will be given out, taken from what was learned during the entire week, so that this way everything learned in the same week can be considered and discussed. Or someone should present his own compositions to be examined by the others and even corrected (if perhaps some mistakes turn up now and then in them). Themes can be proposed by the teachers of the school for them to compose on the spot, for those teachers to listen to and correct. Or one of the students appointed as censor should evaluate them, equally alert to catch mistakes. Occasionally the more advanced students will deliver speeches or declamations previously analyzed and memorized. Or if this exercise better appeals to the prefects, after a theme has been given, they will give a speech or a declamation on the spot.

6. During the week, they will each work hard at the practice of composition. The instructor, if it pleases him, can devote some part of the class to examining and correcting what they have written.

7. Everyone should speak Latin. And when someone makes mistakes, he should be corrected by the one who notices them.[4]

---

4   This paragraph is only in the Italian version.

8.   During the classes, everyone should be attentive and diligent, not look-
     ing around but keeping their eyes on the instructor and at the same time,
     sharply intent (like bees), gathering all the best substance, storing it away in
     their beehives of paper, especially what the instructor dictates. But if they
     have a question about something, they should remember to bring up the
     issue with more learned individuals for them to solve.

9.   But if, through lack of talent or memory or health or will, someone is caught
     getting nothing of value, the rector will inform the superior general of the
     Society, so that such a person might be expelled and make a place for some-
     one who can profit there. But if he was yet not to blame, he might be kept in
     the house to serve God in some other way.

Part 3: Preserving Bodily Health for the Service of God

1.   There should be a set schedule for going to bed, rising, eating, attending Mass
     and classes, studying, praying, and so forth. The schedule can be altered by
     the rector in accordance with seasonal changes, as has been mentioned.[5]

2.   Six hours should be allowed for nightly rest, or even seven, and everyone
     should get up together at the same time, awakened by someone assigned to
     this duty. They should sleep in their underclothes in their own bed, not in
     one that belongs to someone else. In the day, no one should sleep, at least not
     on some bed, unless bad bodily health makes that necessary; in that case, the
     rector and the physician should be advised.

3.   The amount of food should be moderated: it seems that every day a pound
     of meat (or even less) with the addition of a few other items should be
     enough. But there should not be another measure imposed for bread than
     that which the nature of each person demands, but it should be what is help-
     ful and healthful.

4.   The drink will be wine that has been sufficiently diluted. The amount
     offered each person should not exceed three measures at individual meals:
     the more sober the stomach, the more alert the intellect and the more reten-
     tive the memory.

5.   They will not review books at times that are not suitable (like right after
     lunch or dinner), but they will exercise by taking a walk either at home or
     (with the rector's permission) outside if the house lacks a garden fit for this.
     This should be done especially after dinner. Or it will be better for them to
     postpone their study time as they refresh themselves with good and modest
     conversation with their approved conversation partners.

6.   They should all individually have a regimen for maintaining their health.
     Therefore, if it should happen that if they lack something, then without any

---

5   See above, part 2, no. 2.

delay and dropping all interest in mortification, it should be made known to the superior, but still with a prefatory prayer so that they better decide in the forum of conscience whether that is good for them. But when they have made their proposal to the rector, they should set aside every concern and worry, leaving this matter to the rector's discretion.

7. There should also be someone to work as an infirmarian for preserving the current good health or restoring it for those who are failing. To him, or to the rector himself, each person will take care to make his illness known (if any has crept in), leaving aside, as I have said, every interest in mortification or delay. Also, each person will comply with him and with the physician, always mindful of patience, humility, obedience, and such virtues. Meanwhile, the infirmarian (as we might call him) should himself see that he offers nothing special to the sick person without telling the physician and the rector.

8. Bodily dress will preserve decency, honor, and modesty but especially the makings of health. To conclude in a word what has been, is being, or will be said should depend upon discretion, the shrewdest governess of all.

Part 4: Accounting and the Preservation of Supplies

1. There should exist in the house, even in the possession of secular procurators of the college, a single register containing the founding charter and the legal instruments of all the accounts or real properties of the college itself, so that there is clarity about the college's revenues and when they come due.

2. There should be in addition another register in which there are individual records of the money received from the ordinary as well as from the extraordinary accounts of the college. Moreover, it should be set forth in such a way that the temporal and external status of the college may be easily known.

3. All of the money received from anywhere for the use of the college, and the accounts that come due yearly, should be reported to the procurators. It will be their job, of course, to spend it for the uses and purposes of the college.

4. The financial officer should get directly from the procurators the money needed for expenditures. He should likewise record these, itemized in a notebook, ready to render an account every week to those procurators. Finally, in his financial accounting, he will endeavor to adhere to the format that they are to lay out to him.

5. If anything in the house happens to need repair, the gentlemen procurators should be advised so that it might be taken care of before things get worse.

6. Then we should have inventories of the supplies of the entire college, such as beds, books, clothes, and movable goods of that sort. One copy of this goes to the rector, a second to the procurators.

7. Finally, there should be care not only that the goods of the college are not wasted but also that they are better kept from being worn out. So rags and

linen cloths, underclothes, towels, and so on, both for this reason and for greater decency should be washed in the house and even repaired if possible.

8. There ought to be no less care to obtain provisions of wine, wood, and the like at a good time. In this matter, the procurators should be consulted.

9. Only the financial officer should involve himself in this and take on these worries connected with food, clothing, beds, and so forth. Still, he will take care of them in the house according to the rector's decision, and outside the house according to procurators' advice.

10. Clothing will be from cloth that is useful rather than fine and expensive. In its purchase, when a great expense has to be made, the rector will see that the procurators are informed.

11. There should be such a large supply of books that they suffice for all the subjects taken in the college. Moreover, there should be care that the books of some value do not get defaced with annotations or ink. In fact, better to have chapbooks put together for writing the notes that need to be taken.

12. For the preservation of those who are healthy and for the healing of those who are sick, it seems more convenient that the procurators make an agreement with a certain physician and pay him an annual sum for his efforts than that they pay him cash for each and every visit he makes.

13. Even though the college's doors should not be shut to benefactors, nothing will be accepted from the parents of the students attending the classes of the college, as if it were a compensation, or a reward, or a repayment for our efforts; we expect these only from God (in whose name this work is undertaken).

How the Rector Should Deal With Youth from Abroad Who Want to Attend the College's Classes

First of all, only those will be admitted who know how to read and how to write legibly.

1. Students from outside the college, no matter of what condition, whose heart aspires to acquire the ornament of learning and the virtues will be admitted. Nevertheless, if the parents are unwilling, then in no way will those individuals who are subject to them be admitted.

2. The rector will find out from everyone who is planning to continue on in the numerous classes ahead what their intention is, if they are ready to obey their teachers in matters concerning doctrine and moral integrity, preserving modesty and guarding their speech from foul words and wicked conversations, and, to put it all in a phrase, preserving all honor. And if they answer affirmatively, they can be registered in the catalog of accepted students; but if negatively, then not at all.

3. Moreover, he should see that they realize that it is the custom of everyone living in the college to confess at least once every month and to attend the solemn rites of the Mass every holy day and to attend also, on Sundays and feast days, the sermon and the explanation of Christian doctrine. They should be enticed to these with devout and gentle exhortations, if they are not given to doing these things on their own.

4. Very diligent care will be given to those who have been admitted so that each one of them progresses in learning and in spirit and so that they themselves and their parent realize that they are not going to be treated any differently than are the members of the house, certainly with all charity and concern.

5. Those who are uncooperative, refusing to follow advice and corrections should first be scolded; then finally, if they think nothing of what they have been told, the disciplinarian should carry out his duty, if they are able to take sharper correction (and that disciplinarian will not belong to the Society but work for a set stipend). But if the correction does no good, the parents will be informed, and they will be separated from the flock, like a bad sheep, so that the others are not infected.

CHAPTER 10

Report on the Boarders of the German College (1559)

Lorenzo Maggio

In 1552, one year after the foundation of the Roman College, the German College opened its doors. It was primarily a residence for Germans seeking the kind of education that could help to reverse the directions of the Protestant Reformation. The cardinals Marcello Cervini (1501–55)—who would soon be Pope Marcellus II (r.1555)—and Giovanni Morone (1509–80) had urged Ignatius to establish such an institution. Despite these affluent protectors, the German College encountered difficulties from the very beginning. Few Germans took up residence there, and their number even decreased over the first years, with one new student in 1555 and none in 1556 or 1557. Superior General Diego Laínez (1512–65) was forced to admit paying boarding students, and these soon became a large majority at the college. Most of them were children of the Italian nobility, who often seemed to the Jesuits to be less than admirable. The mixed student body presented a difficult pedagogical challenge. How to attend adequately both to the needs of a crowd of children and to those of the older German students? How to provide a moral formation for such diverse groups? Lorenzo Maggio (1531–1605) was rector of the German College for four years, from 1557 to 1561. In the middle of this period, he composed a report that showed a well-balanced judgment about the educational situation. This was the first in a series of evaluations sent to the Jesuit curia during his rectorship.

Lorenzo Maggio (born August 10, 1531, Brescia, Italy—entered the Society on March 7, 1555, Rome—died October 26, 1605, Rome). A young man of noble ancestry, Maggio was given the Exercises by Ignatius himself. Shortly after he had entered the Society, he was appointed rector of the German College, an office he held from 1557 to 1561 while attending classes of philosophy and theology at the Roman College. He was rector of the colleges of Naples (1561–62), and Vienna (1563–66, 1578–80) and held other important positions such as provincial of Austria (1566–78), visitor (1576) and provincial of Poland (1580–81), assistant of Italy (1581–94), superior of the Veneto province (1596–98), and finally visitor of France (1599–1604).

Source: *Monumenta paedagogica*, nova editio, 2:799–803 (original: Italian)

So that your Reverend Paternity might be better able to make whatever arrangements seem right to you in the Lord concerning the admission of pupils to the German College, we felt obliged to set forth some of the many difficulties occurring here, even though it is impossible adequately to explain how we experience them in practice.

1. Our young companions suffer from many disorders, scruples, indecent
    fantasies, anxieties, and distractions which limit their spiritual progress.
    And since a man is a man and the war is continuous, there is danger of
    some scandal.

2. The particular trial for our novice brothers who have been accepted for a
    period of probation at the college, the ones who want to enter religious life,
    [is that] they seem to stand among the children in confusion.[1] And since
    they are novices and not yet mortified, they often take offense and say some
    derisive words to the children, which are taken badly and attributed to the
    Society as a whole. And yet if we want to maintain this work, it is neces-
    sary that there be members of the Society present, considering that a person
    from outside cannot be trusted, as experience has taught us.

3. Many things get in the way of our young companions' studies, so much so
    that they do not have much quiet time to study beyond the time they spend
    in class, as some of them say; and the same goes for the Germans, who quite
    often complain about such conversations, even though they have more free
    time for studying.

4. Taking people in as we do lets in many who know very little and who do not
    possess the talent to be able to learn. And even though at the start the fathers
    say this does not matter, they still complain later when they see that their
    sons have learned little, because their main desire was that their sons learn
    letters more than virtue.

5. Typically, the fathers want to put into the colleges those with whom they
    cannot live at home, and to resolve their annoyance they send them off to
    the college, thinking that the Theatines have broad shoulders.[2] And if just
    one of them is enough to throw a community into confusion, what would
    so many of them do together?

6. Some people consider us to be entrepreneurs in this, and profit-seekers,
    especially when they see that the procurator is very diligent in asking for
    money.[3] But this is necessary because more often than not they forget to pay
    their debt; and very often the procurator has to wear out his shoes and drag
    himself all over town before he can get hold of the money. And when some

---

1   Despite optimistic expectations, enrollment at the German college faltered, even well below
    the originally poor number of twenty-four in 1552. To save the college, Laínez was forced to
    allow the admission of paying boarding students in 1558, most of whom were from noble
    Italian families and under fifteen years old.

2   The Congregation of Clerics Regular of the Divine Providence, also called the Theatines, was
    founded by Gaetano di Thiene (1480–1547), Gian Pietro Carafa (1476–1559, Pope Paul IV
    [r.1555–59]), and others in 1524. Carafa was the bishop of Chieti, whose ancient name was
    Theate. Because their founders and those of the Society of Jesus were active at the same time and
    in some of the same places, Jesuits were often mistaken for Theatines, especially in central Italy.

3   The treasurer.

of them do pay, they think that they have made a donation and that their fee is charity and alms.

7. Our young companions are typically hated by the youths because, as they keep a check on the boys' unrestrained impulses, controlling them more by feeling than by reason, the youths attribute to malice what is done out of charity. And this gives rise to many suspicions about our companions when the boys see that, in order to admonish and correct one of the more needy pupils, they pay more attention to him than to the others.

It seems that all of these annoyances might be compensated with great profit by either gaining many of these same youths for the Society, or by reforming their lives so that the good seed lasts a long time; but it seems hard for us to expect either outcome. Concerning entrance into the Society, experience teaches us the opposite, since up to now none or very few have been won over, and in fact, some of those who had initially wished to join grew cooler after entering the college. The reason for this could possibly be the estrangement from our young companions that they feel at the beginning, knowing them to be the eyes of the rector and the minister of justice.[4] Because these individuals are so displeasing to them, they cannot be much attracted by our way of life.

On the other hand, it is apparent that they do not gain much spiritual profit. As much as they abandon their earlier laziness, it is nevertheless obvious that they are doing this simply because they cannot act this way anymore, not because they do not really want to. This is clearly the case, seeing that when they leave school and join their fathers on major feast days, they do foolish things, as they themselves confess. And in the college itself there is no safety, neither at night nor in the day, not in private places nor in public ones, not in bed or out of bed, and not even in the church itself, at least from groping. It could be that the same conversations and everyday joint activities of the youths and the children (eating well, playing games, and sleeping) harm them and cause their will to fail more frequently, although less when they are at their work than outside it, for objects that are present engage them more than those that are not. It is quite true that there are some who are helped, but for the fruit to last in them, they would have to stay at the college for a long time. This does not happen for a number of reasons, especially because when their fathers see them inclining even a little bit towards devotion, they pull them out of school. And so when the fire is taken away, the water returns to its normal state.

Your Paternity will see better what is appropriate and order it in the Lord: either enlarging the college and getting a bigger house, or sending away those who are currently here, or taking more on and letting them use it all, or doing

---

4   The *corrector*, a disciplinarian that the *Constitutions* recommended be a non-Jesuit. "For those who are derelict [...] and for whom kind words and admonitions alone are not sufficient, there should be a corrector from outside the Society. He should keep in fear and should punish those who need chastisement and are fit for it." Padberg, *Constitutions*, 186.

whatever else you wish. Whatever you may command, we will be sure that it will be for the best. It only remains to be said that if we keep this company we must have trustworthy and patient people to direct them.

On the other hand, it cannot be denied that [1.] the students are generally helped in learning Christian doctrine; in living according to church traditions; in getting accustomed to prayers, Masses, preachings, confessions, and so forth; and in restraining wicked inclinations, at least (as noted) in their outward actions, dishonesties, and other vices—such as cursing, swearing, and playing forbidden games—both in will and in deed, because they have few opportunities for them.

2. The Society wins the hearts and minds of many students' fathers, especially those who wish to see their sons well brought up; and many people praise the work even though others do not feel the same.

3. Thanks to this opportunity, the Society can manage a greater number of our young companions in Rome without difficulty, testing some of those who wish to join the Society and exercising those who have already been admitted in the practice of supervision.

4. It is a great help for the German College, because, even if one were to gain no more than what is sufficient for sustaining both the youth and those who supervise them, at least he would save a part of the expenses for those who are needed to supervise the Germans, seeing that the same individuals supervise the Germans and the children.[5] Furthermore, when the money has been obtained for them on schedule, the provisions can be arranged in good time.

Beyond this, we will not forget to remind Your Paternity that, in order to carry on this work, if we wish to pursue it, three things are necessary beyond having trusty ministers and so forth. The first one is that for those pupils studying grammar one person is needed to exercise them in their lessons very diligently, because children who lack this continuous stimulus produce very meagre results, as experience up to now has shown us. They produce as much as is demanded from them. But this cannot be asked of our young companions who are currently in the college, for they are busy both with their studies and with their many household chores. This would allow us to maintain the respect we are earning. Otherwise, fathers will complain about the little progress that their sons have made.

Second, it is necessary to have a house very close to the college of the Society, because many difficulties and dangers arise in sending them to school if it is at a distance, requiring a greater number of our young companions to keep accompanying them.[6] In addition, they would be completely deprived of conversation

---

5 This was the case for Ortensio Androzzi (1528–89), who was appointed to a role supervising children at this time. See the following chapter.

6 Students of the German College attended classes at the Roman College, which was moved closer to the German one in 1560.

with our brothers, which is of such help to them, so much so that proximity makes the life of the German College.

Third, in undertaking this enterprise it is most advisable to establish some kind of order and to make a selection of pupils with regard not only to their knowledge but also to their age, nature, and aptitude; as perhaps has already been provided for in arrangements for the Germans. This is because some confusion follows if one admits all of them indifferently, and one does not gather the expected fruit. Others have occasion to suspect that this (namely indiscriminate admission) is done for the sake of financial gain. In addition, these individuals would be occupying places where others would be able to profit much more. This is as much as currently occurs to me to present to Your Paternity regarding this matter; I leave everything to your holy judgment.

CHAPTER 11

Comments on the Effectiveness of the German College (1561)

Ortensio Androzzi

When Lorenzo Maggio (1531–1605) was sent to Naples, Ortensio Androzzi (1528–89), who had been supervising children for two years at the German College, became acting rector there for a few months in 1561. His report on student behavior is so positive when compared to what his fellows were writing in the same years that it seems difficult to take it at face value. The reasons for his attitude are obscure; perhaps they have something to do with his expressed desire to be relieved of the rectorship. Androzzi shows himself to be particularly committed to the college's youngest students, to whom he displays a very gentle and loving attitude. His desire for reassignment was eventually fulfilled: on January 1, 1562, Giovanni Peruschi (1525–98) became rector of the German College, and he was to hold that position until the middle of 1563.

Dealing with the organizational needs of the German College, this letter introduces the reader to some roles which have escaped scholarly attention. Although the rector was the undisputed leader of the college (even while he could sometimes have a superintendent), the roles of the minister and his assistant (the sub-minister) were of crucial importance, for they were responsible for the material aspects of the college. In Androzzi's view, their service was essential to the entire project.

Ortensio Androzzi (born c.1528, Montecchio [now Treia in the province of Macerata, Italy]—entered the Society on March 8, 1556, in Loreto—died January 24, 1589, Rome). He was one of three brothers that joined the Society. Fulvio, the eldest, was born in 1524 and died in 1575 in Ferrara, where he had been rector for more than ten years. Curzio was the youngest (1536–84). Ortensio became a Jesuit in Rome, where he was based at the time when Polanco was writing to Fulvio. He was entrusted with the care of young students at the German College (1559–62) while he attended philosophical and theological studies. He was then sent to Florence, and finally to the college of Forlì, where he was appointed rector.

Source: *Monumenta paedagogica*, nova editio, 2:804–7 (original: Italian)

Rome, 1561

First, from early childhood the young boys become accustomed to observing everything they should do according to the Holy Mother Church, such as believing; acting in accordance with that belief; giving themselves to prayer; attending Mass every day (during which they behave as a Christian should, or at least display an outward appearance as such); and reciting the holy office, the rosary, or other prayers. And if someone has not attended Mass because of some impediment, he immediately hurries to the superior with the sense that he has missed a very great thing. They hear on feast days sermons and holy lessons, learning how to stand still and remain quiet in church. This is no small task, especially for such awful children.

They become accustomed to holy confessions, and little by little to Holy Communion. Some of them go to confession and receive Communion every Sunday, even though they previously did not go to confession or know how to make a confession.[1]

They learn to keep a sensitive conscience in such a way that they become scrupulous in every little thing they say in ordinary speech. Furthermore, they learn to fast during given periods, and there are some who ask to fast throughout all of Lent, doing so with great perseverance and happiness. This is very untypical of small children. They learn to observe feast days and have reverence for saints and sacred images, unlike the treacherous heretics of our times.[2] They do not feel embarrassed to do this even in public, going to the stations [of the cross] and participating in devotions in holy churches.

But what seems to me more miraculous is that they learn to stay so reserved and restrained, keeping their passions in check and staying at their table all day long, not leaving it without permission. And when they are rebuked for their faults, they listen to the reprimands and accept the punishments, even doing these things in public, even if it should require them to lower their stockings.[3] This seems to me quite an amazing thing.

They learn to respect their elders and their parents, who feel (as is generally known) much edified by and attached to our Society. They respect and listen not only to their superiors but also to the others who take care of them. And they are so obedient in many things that even if they are in the middle of playing a game (which children typically enjoy so much), when the signal is given to return to the classroom, they go immediately. Previously, they had perhaps not even heard a single word from their parents.

I do not know how I can explain this great fruit and service that is being performed for our Lord God to the great displeasure of the "old foe": after many

---

1   On frequent Communion and confession, see above, Nadal, "Constitutions of the College at Messina," n. 1.

2   *Dulia* (the veneration of saints) and *hyperdulia* (the veneration for the Blessed Virgin Mary) were considered by the Protestants to be a form of idolatry. For a similar reason, some of the Reformers, such as Karlstadt (Andreas Rudolf Bodenstein von Karlstadt, 1480–1541), Ulrich Zwingli (1484–1531), and John Calvin (1509–64), encouraged the removal of the sacred images. An outstanding work on this subject, focused specifically on England, is Eamon Duffy, *The Stripping of the Altars: Traditional Religion in England, 1400–1580* (New Haven: Yale University Press, 1992).

3   Use of the switch was sometimes permitted in the Jesuit colleges. See Nadal's "Constitutions of the College of Messina" (Chapter 8), rule 16.

of these poor boys, being so inclined to the cursed vice of the flesh, have come to feel regret, they themselves are astonished and amazed that they have so much restraint.[4] And some often say that, if they had not attended the German College, both they and their household would have been tainted with a bad reputation. Sometimes they come to such regret and sorrow for their past lives, that we ourselves are encouraged and strengthened as we admire them and realize our own negligence. Furthermore, not only do they not think about that vice now, they do not utter even the slightest word that might incline towards carnal thinking; or if they do speak, they do it so secretly that I believe the fear of discovery sooner restrains than incites the concupiscence of the flesh. Moreover, if one of them hears some conversation containing indecent words, he immediately comes to report it to the superior, such that even if one of them had a bad intention, he would be unable to fulfill it, not knowing whom he could fully trust.

Many of them are so used to lying when they join the college that they almost never, or rarely, tell the truth; but after having spent a few days in the college, if it happens that they do something wrong, they would rather be punished than tell a lie.

This is not to mention that they abandon many of their former vices and sins, such as blasphemies, curses, detractions, swearing, unlawful games, and bad company; they learn to remain silent, to behave modestly at home, to use good manners at the table, and to be patient; and they are finally freed from all of those horrible sins which one sees youth more inclined to today because of the bad examples given by their elders. By the grace of God, not only are such things not seen in this college: we also do not allow anyone who begins to wish to be a bad example to others to remain here.[5]

Later they learn to live in a regulated manner, and they acquire at a young age the proper way of studying so that when they grow up they can advance effortlessly in every subject. This can be seen more clearly in those who have left this college as incorrigible: after a short time, almost all of them have expressed either in writing or in speech a great remorse for not having stayed in this college (and they have also made a plea to return).

This is not to mention that our Society not only makes great friends through this enterprise but also that those who were, one might say, enemies and less than friendly eventually change their mind and become benevolent, as has happened

---

4   "Old foe" (*hostis antiquus*) is a traditional phrase for Satan or the devil. Cf. Apoc. 12:9: "And that great dragon was cast out, that old serpent, who is called the devil and Satan [Vulgate: *draco ille magnus serpens antiquus qui vocatur Diabolus et Satanas*], who seduceth the whole world; and he was cast unto the earth, and his angels were thrown down with him" (Douay-Rheims).

5   The order's *Constitutions* recommends dismissing someone only "when neither words not the corrector avail and some student is seen to be incorrigible and a scandal to others." Padberg, *Constitutions*, 186. The decision was up to the rector.

a number of days ago to some old men, who left this college so delighted and edified that they made the sign of the cross.

One obtains great profit with the parents and friends of these children, for when they go home and are asked about their lifestyle, hearing that they often go to confession and pray, it becomes necessary for these parents and friends to begin to inspire their children and give a good example, if they are true Christians. Moreover, it is clear that when they come to visit the students or speak with us, we have the opportunity to advise and exhort them towards Christian piety.

And what goes beyond everything just mentioned is that through this means many of the students renounce the world, and either enter into religious life then and there or, if their families prevent them from doing so, maintain the same good intention, which I believe they would have never had if they had not been here.

It remains to be said, my Reverend Father, that perceiving these and many other fruits (which I was unable to gather) that have been gathered or are still to be gathered in this little orchard of our Lord, it remains, I say, that you ensure it is well cared for. To this end (I want to write now what I have often wished to say out loud), you need above all to obtain a good rector for it, most importantly a man of seriousness who surely knows that our brothers who are here can provide for many and many things thanks to the extensive experience we have with these people.

Next, the college needs the following: a minister, or sub-minister, who will be diligent in the house; a master to teach the children of the fourth and fifth classes; a coadjutor skilled as an infirmarian; and someone to teach ancient Greek to the children; and, above all, a good rector, because, to be honest, I myself am worthless. It also seems to me (to speak freely) that if the boys do not stand in front of me, they will be able to feel secure in many matters that they are ashamed of if I associate with them and spend time among them. I am not saying this because I am more diligent than the others, but because this is the impression that the children and the adults have among themselves. And I do not want Your Reverence to think I am saying this because I want to get out of this labor, for in fact I will undertake it appropriately if obedience would employ me in this college. Nor should the superiors need to worry about this, since I am ready to do whatever I am ordered. With this diligence, I will know what to do and I will be able to do it, aided by God's favor. I know that all the readiness and efficiency I have belong to the holy Society of Jesus, from which and through which I have received them, however paltry they may be out of my own negligence.[6] However, I will spend all of what I am worth, even though I believe it is little or nothing. Now it remains to ask Your Reverence to pray much more fervently for this college and for me, so that it might enjoy very beautiful fruits (which the Lord God will make good and amplify) and offer them to him at the heavenly banquet.

---

6   The *Formula* requires a Jesuit who has been enlisted "through the inspiration of the Lord in this militia for Christ" to "be prompt in carrying out this obligation which is so great, being clad for battle day and night" (Padberg, *Constitutions*, 8).

CHAPTER 12

Report on the German College (1567)

Ludovico Gagliardi

When Ribadeneyra's supervision of the Roman College was extended to that of the German College (1567), he asked some of his companions for a report on it. Ludovico Gagliardi (1543–1608) was among them, since he was prefect of studies at the German College from 1565 until his assignment as rector at the Roman Seminary in 1567. The college's economic and organizational troubles had now subsided; there were more boarders, as the enrollments of Germans and of young Jesuits had improved considerably.

Gagliardi thought that the confusion that had resulted from mixing two totally different kinds of students was being remedied. Yet the approach of the rector (Giuseppe Cortesono [1537–71]) seemed to be falling short: it was overly focused on moral concerns to the detriment of academic ones. Gagliardi included in his report some telling details, as when he refers to the large staff that a college needs, or to the way some of the wealthy students went about shabbily dressed. Curiously, Gagliardi's main complaint was about the lack of clear rules and order—the very deficiency that Cortesono would lament when he drafted his constitutions for the German College (see the following chapter).

Ludovico Gagliardi (born c.1543, Padua—entered the Society September 29, 1559, Rome—died March, 9, 1608, Modena). Brother of Achille (1537–1607), the renowned spiritual writer and teacher at the Roman College, Ludovico was appointed prefect of studies at the German College in 1565. He held this position for two years, while he was entrusted with the same position at the Roman Seminary. Despite his youth, he was appointed rector of the seminary in 1570. At the beginning of 1572, he was sent to Padua and made rector of the Jesuits in Verona, where he had to face the crisis of the Venetian interdict (1606), a conflict between the Republic of Venice and the papal curia. After the Jesuits had been expelled from Venice, he found refuge in Modena, where he died.

Source: *Monumenta paedagogica*, nova editio, 2:855–57 (original: Italian)

Rome, 1567

Care of the German College covers all these individuals: (1) the fathers and our young companions whose number is approaching that of a large college; (2) boarding students; (3) Germans who wear a religious habit and live at no charge; (4) novices; (5) lay people who serve in the house, such as bakers, carpenters, tailors, painters, and the like, along with others who are on probation before becoming novices.[1]

Concerning those of the Society who are called fathers here, they—unlike those in the Roman College—do not even have quiet scheduled time to study in their rooms, but they have more unscheduled time, as well as many more exercises of disputations.[2] Concerning spirituality, they lack much spiritual guidance, because they are never given any penances, nor is there any reading of the rules, nor are there exhortations; nor do even the superiors spend very much time with them, partly because of their involvements, partly because the father rector does not seem committed to this, but only to the children.[3] Concerning attire, there does not seem to be any definite rule; this leads to occasional improprieties, such as wearing shabby clothes and the like. About boarding students, let us first talk about their studies. From rhetoric on down, I understand that they make much less progress than the seminarians.[4] I do not know the reason for this, but sometimes I have wondered if this task is so difficult because of the large number of students and if it would be expedient for the superior to know and arrange everything in detail. I believe there is a shortage of good *repetitores* who are both diligent and committed to this task.[5] The father rector does not seem committed at all. It is far easier to manage the studies from rhetoric on up. And this matter depends upon the *repetitores*, who are currently average. There is one thing I have not been able to fix: the students find their teachers' notes and then have them copied. I have seen this very thing occurring even among our young companions. In regard to students' habits, things are going well, and there is a very great vigilance that they do not go astray. And this particularly seems to be both the talent and commitment of the father rector. Regarding Christian doctrine, it seems to me that they do not learn things by heart at the college. This seems to me most important. I would judge it necessary not only that they learn by heart

---

1   Polanco's *Chronicon* reported that, by 1565, the German College had students from many European countries and that it even had two from lands under Ottoman rule. See the selection from Polanco's *Chronicon*, in *Monumenta paedagogica*, nova editio, 1:569. Between 1563 and 1573, the number of boarding students at the college was about two hundred, twenty of whom were German seminarians.

2   Ordination to priesthood was usually conferred on Jesuits in their third year of theological studies, prior to their full profession in the Society. See *Institutum* 1:54. An ordained Jesuit received the title of *pater* (father). Nonetheless, in 1568, Pius V (r.1566–72) forbade the ordination of non-professed religious (this had been the Jesuit practice). Gagliardi's remark apparently testifies to a Jesuit custom common until Pius V's prohibition. In 1573, Gregory XIII (r.1572–85) restored the Jesuit privilege to ordain to priesthood before full religious profession.

3   Giuseppe Cortesono was rector at that time. See the following chapter.

4   Gagliardi refers to the Roman Seminary, which was founded and assigned to the Jesuits in 1564. It began operations on February 22, 1565.

5   A *repetitor* is a review-tutor. See the introduction and Chapter 16n11.

but also that they do some exercises on the material. There is neither concern about nor regularity with respect to the display of good manners. Concerning the quality of the food service, there is little regularity in making the portions bigger or smaller according to the students' ages. The same goes for sanitation and occasionally varying the menu. Regarding students' health, no one takes care of it beyond the infirmarian, who is very often inexperienced. Concerning the Germans, in short there is not any order, because it is impossible to observe the many rules that were made at the beginning. And now we do not know how many have to be kept, and good things are sometimes done happenstance. Students need to be well instructed in Christian catechism above all, but that is not happening. Moreover, they need to learn Italian better. The same point about language applies to all the German boarding students. Father Ruiz has care of the novices, but he rarely comes here;[6] so Father Benedict does it instead.[7]

Those other house staff workers would need instruction in Christian doctrine and the like. That is not happening. The same goes for those who are on probation. There is almost no attention paid to visiting the rooms and keeping them clean, and generally the college is not very tidy.

In general, it seems to me that the college needs definite standing rules drawn up, as well as written ones about everyone's duties, because I believe that we have no specific rules—neither for the rector, nor for the minister, nor for the other positions.

It seems it would also be very useful to communicate by letter with students' parents, so they know the care being taken for their sons, for students only seldom know the good that is being done, and also so the students themselves would be more mindful of this. This way we might greatly raise awareness of this work's importance.

---

6 Alfonso Ruiz (1530–99) was also master of novices at the professed house of Rome.
7 Probably Benedetto Negri (1540–91), who was a student at the Roman College in 1567.

CHAPTER 13

Constitutions for the German College (1570)

Giuseppe Cortesono

As the fruit of the late reflections of Giuseppe Cortesono (c.1537–71), this document, dictated to a companion as he suffered his final health struggles in his native Forlì, was far more than a plan of studies. It was his comprehensive spiritual, apostolic, and pedagogical vision with special reference to the German College, which had a singular place among the institutions entrusted to the Society of Jesus. Contemplating the school's difficulties with financing, teaching, and governance, Cortesono concluded that it still needed much attention. He emphasized the critical importance of forming competent administrators: apostolic success was impossible without good leadership. Piety and learning could not suffice on their own. Only the right policies and directives would allow the German College to achieve its ends. Cortesono expressed his most significant insights in the rough-hewn prose of this document, one more often cited than fully studied. Its heft and scope make it one of the most important documents in the entire Monumenta paedagogica. To form students, Cortesono suggests, an educator needs to know their particular inclinations, backgrounds, and desires. Adapting pedagogy in light of these personal features should be attempted not only by every teacher but also by the college as a whole.

Giuseppe Cortesono (born c.1537, Forlì, Emilia–Romagna, Italy—entered the Society on February 1, 1559, Rome—died January 14, 1571, Forlì). After entering the order, he attended the logic classes of Francisco de Toledo (1532–96) at the Roman College, where he also served for a long while as a confessor. In 1564, he was appointed rector at the German College, a charge he held until 1569, when he was sent by Pope Pius V (r.1566–72) to Montecassino as confessor of Cardinal Innocenzo Ciocchi del Monte (c.1532–77). He spent his last two years of life in Forlì, where he turned to the task of providing the German College with effective constitutions.

Source: *Monumenta paedagogica*, nova editio, 2:864–933 (original: Italian)

Constitutions or Advice for the Use of the Administrators of the German College

Proem of the Constitutions of the German College

It has pleased God Our Lord to allow many disorders in the college, whether because administration is a matter of importance and not very well known by those who have been engaging in it, or because administration was altogether new to them. And so in the process of remedying these disorders and finding ways to prevent them, they learned how to run the college. Thus extensive experience

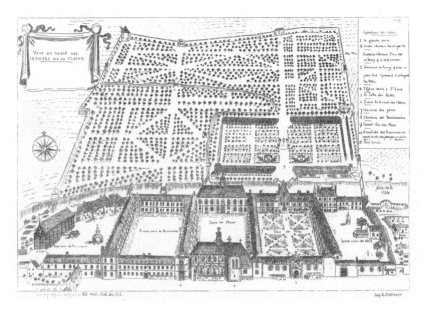

FIGURE 5   This bird's eye view of the College of La Flèche shows how well the architec-
ture of Jesuit school could be arranged. The quarters to the right of the central
chapel of Saint Louis belonged to the Jesuit residence. The central courtyard
was surrounded by the classrooms and the auditorium where the acts (or academic performances) took place; it was the yard where students had recess.
The quarters to the left of the chapel were the residences of the boarding students. Behind the college were the Jesuit community's garden and the vineyard, where students recreated on break days and during the summer.

Originally published in Camille de Rochemonteix, *Un collège de Jésuites aux
XVIIe et XVIIIe siècles: Le Collège Henri IV de la Flèche* (Le Mans: Leguicheux, 1889), 1:74.

has taught all that is suitable for this governance. And so that everyone does not
have to learn at his own expense and to the detriment of the college, the present
constitutions have been drawn up at the order of Father Superior General of
the Society.[1] These constitutions are based on experience as this task has been
entrusted to someone who has been directly involved in many aspects of this
undertaking. Beyond the fact that everything has been founded on very keen
reasoning that goes further than experience, these things have all been reviewed
(before and after their approval) by many judicious fathers expert in administration and finally by the assistants and by His Most Reverend Paternity.[2] These
constitutions were drawn up for this: to achieve clarity and to allow a prudent

---

1   According to Lukács, it is likely that Borja gave this order in 1567.
2   This does not seem to be true. Cortesono added this passage as if he were drafting the final ver-
     sion of the constitutions and therefore as if it had already passed the review mentioned here.

rector to choose (according to the times and situations) what seems more conducive to the college's purposes. But when it still seems good to him to try other
things that are similar to these with the consent of the superiors (and they ought
to give their consent whenever they find him to be a skillful administrator), if
these new things are tried and found successful, he should follow them; if they
do not succeed, he can fall back on these constitutions as a body of practices that
are already more tested and approved. This can be allowed with the intention
of perfecting and facilitating governance. It is also fine to change the manner of
governance according to the variations of times and people, all the more so when
the experience and judgment of administrators recommend it.

It only remains, then, to answer those who might possibly object that with
these constitutions we are exaggerating the importance of this work and making
it too grand a thing. The answer to this is first that insofar as the Society is a great
thing and has a great institute, it is not inappropriate for its works to be great.
Second, the works that are directed towards the honor and glory and greater service of God cannot ever be so great that they cannot become greater still. Third,
as the fruit is great, so the operation from which it arises ought to be the same.
The fruits are great—they are listed in the first chapter of the first book where
the college's institute is presented—and to harvest them, it is suitable that this
enterprise be great and maintained and governed as such.

When one is dealing with the salvation of souls and spreading God's worship and the Christian religion, there is no hard labor, no tribulation, no price so
great that it would not seem minuscule by comparison with its goal.

This is how to answer those to whom it seems that too many members are
committed to this work to the detriment of our Society and to the detriment
of its other ministries and works: First, the members who hold the authority
of the rector and the minister do not have to study and stand still. All the others can attend to study and at the right time they can be sent, some here and
some there, beyond the studies, to learn the way to govern and to deal with souls
and help them, since what is sought is the knowledge of how to carry out well
all the ministries that the Society performs for the neighbor. And the college
should become an excellent seminary for producing good rectors and ministers
and teachers through the *repetitores* that are maintained there. Thus nothing is
lost in any respect, and the college can maintain so many more in compensation
for its administrative obligations. In this way, it turns out to be an advantage for
them, because it has so many members. And if they say that the college ends up
impoverishing [the Society] by giving it its best, the response is that to be good
for the college one only needs knowledge and judgment, and those who lack
these two things will not be very good for the other ministries of the Society.
And so the college provides an opportunity to get to know the members and
their talents, and it refines them in what bears upon helping the neighbor. Lastly,
I say that when the college is well run, so many members and so many goods will

be gained, that you could say that on those assigned to administration we are making a profit.

To those who hold that with time this governance is drawing us into a great danger, the answer has been given above, and likewise in the first chapter, which could be inserted here.[3]

To those who say that the Society has to take care of running its own colleges, the answer is that if it is by a lack of subjects, the same college supports subjects through the costs of those who are entering the Society. If it is by a lack of administrators, I say that the German College helps because it produces administrators who learn to run not just this college, but many colleges of the Society; and from some leading ones there will, from now on, emerge those who are given to all of the colleges, even the smallest; all the others are readier to learn than to expend what has been learned.

To those who wish to know the standing this administration has in relation to others of the Society, I say first that since the Society is still in its early days, and since one can learn how to govern only by experience, it has not yet reached that perfection in governance which we are seeking for its institute. Some disorders and troubles have to come up first, and then things will go well when serious consideration is given to administration and the three things necessary for the preservation of the Society, that is, letters, spirit, and governance. I hold the last of these as more necessary than the others, because it is what draws forth fruit from them by disposing them towards their end. Without this one, the other two would be more harmful than useful. In raising people to the profession of four vows, as good as it is to see that they are individuals of spirit and letters, I judge it much more necessary that they be administrators because on them depends all the good governance of the Society. Good governance is that which will see that the *Constitutions* are fully observed. Without that good governance, it will be impossible to observe them. If they are observed but not in the right manner, there will be either little good result or damage and the rise of greater disorders. Someday, the Society will be on the right path when it finds the manner of the individual governances which properly belong to the office of the rector, who assigns individuals who are adequate for such an office, endowed with the talent for it and experience, and which sees that all things are uniform, because good governance is one, as everything has to be run on the same principles and rules. If this is lacking, I believe there would arise in the Society almost all the disorders that there are; or at least we would see the diminished progress that its subjects make in the spirit and in their abilities to help their neighbors to advance. This is the most important concern there is in the Society, but so far it has been neglected. If a little bit of order had not been established in the novitiates, things would already be going really poorly for the Society, and the spirit would soon

---

3   No additions were provided by Cortesono.

be fading away. But this remedy has kept it with us, yet not enough for what the Society intends because it is not looking for "someone who has made a start," but for perseverance.[4] The rectors are the ones who need to follow up the work begun in the novitiate, in order to lead the individuals towards greater perfection, or at least towards a balanced stability in keeping with the Society's Institute. We have to realize that the Lord has kindly granted the grace to discover how to run this college; he has given the grace of finding a way to run the German College in having us discover the way to govern the colleges of the Society, as that is far more difficult than this one.

Second, I say that agreeing to run many colleges is the Society's ruin. With time, the Society will be forced to leave them as a result of the troubles that will arise there. For example: (1) These colleges hinder the main aim of the Society, which is to produce sacramental workers and professed fathers, because in these colleges, the individuals, as far as school is concerned, cannot finish their studies in an organized way and then, because to maintain the colleges, there will have to be a concern to have a greater number of college personnel than professed and spiritual coadjutors. (2) It will be necessary to admit every kind of person in order to maintain the colleges, and this will be the ruination of the Society as it has been for other religious orders. (3) In order to maintain the colleges, we will need to tolerate everyone in the Society, even those who are undisciplined. (4) Finally, one day it will be an issue on account of the troubles that will arise; the ones that necessarily arise whenever the spirit is gone. And the multitude of colleges will give rise to a situation in which the spirit is lacking, and it will require the abandonment of the ministries of its Institute. Especially when the Society runs schools, it will be forced to "take in the chorus" for the management of the colleges. Once these have entered and taken their places as good members, everything will be done so as not to lose them.

In the third place, I say that colleges in accord with the *Constitutions* exist for two reasons: one is to produce instruments for the ministries and seminaries of the Society; a second is to educate the young in Christian devotion like tender plants; and to have the opportunity to do this, we involve ourselves in their humanistic education.[5]

Experience shows us that this last mentioned type is not successful, through the minimal fruit that the students ordinarily appear to produce in Christian life,

---

4 "Someone who has made a start" is expressed in this Italian text by a Latin phrase "qui inceperit."

5 Cf. Padberg, *Constitutions*, 130. In the preamble to part 4 of the *Constitutions*, the rationale given for the Society's investment in studies leans much more towards the first purpose stated by Cortesono here. But that preamble begins with a reference to the neighbor as well: "The end steadfastly pursued by the Society is to aid its own members and their neighbors in attaining the ultimate end for which they were created." Cortesono might have also referred to the *Formula of the Institute*. See the following note.

except for the boarding colleges when they are governed in the right way. And so, the colleges should be reduced to being only ones for the first purpose, while the second kind should be turned into boarding colleges in the manner that will be described, because there will be sufficiently more fruit and it will be achieved with less tribulation.

Fourth, I say that in every province it suffices to have one or two or three colleges of a hundred or two hundred individuals each, in a large city, where there are public schools, and together with them it should try to improve the populace. And where there are similar colleges there could also be boarding colleges such as will keep the following constitutions to serve the goal at which the [Society's] *Constitutions* aim, to instruct the youth in Christian life. Insofar as it sees that it is realizing very great results, it could also enjoy the advantage of having those whom it wishes to enter the Society study there, or a way to support them in this college to have them made members later. When they are later said to be formed subjects, they could be sent into the world.

Chapter 1—On the Institute of the German College

One of the great works currently in the hands of the Society is the German College. There, the Society perfectly carries out its Institute regarding its neighbor, that is, fostering his perfection through the frequent reception of sacraments and the hearing of the word of God, along with teaching him Christian life and doctrine together with other good literature.[6] After the religious orders, it is one of the great works that one can find in God's church. And insofar as the Council of Trent held that the reformation of the clergy depends mostly on the seminaries, one might expect that the reformation of every state and condition of Christianity depends on a college such as this, as a universal seminary for all the states belonging to the church.[7] And inasmuch as the heretics have caused such great ruin in the church through similar colleges, so we can hope that God intends to restore and expand it by means of these. And considering that the former, being the work of the devil, will soon founder, there is hope that the latter are going to be greatly increased through God's actions.

---

6   See the part of the *Formula of the Institute* that was incorporated into the Society's 1550 bull of confirmation issued by Julius III (r.1550–55): "He is a member of a Society founded chiefly for this purpose: to strive especially for the defense and propagation of the faith and for the progress of souls in Christian life and doctrine, by means of public preaching, lectures, and any other ministration whatsoever if the word of God, etc." (Padberg, *Constitutions*, 3–4). Note especially too the phrase "along with other good literature," which expands on the words of the *Formula*. Good literature (*bonae litterae*) was not seen as something separate from the religious sphere. Classical antiquity explicitly used "letters" to cultivate virtue; this connection was still strong in Cortesono's day and well beyond it.

7   See the Council of Trent, session 23 (July 15, 1563), canon 18.

From this work, all of the following goods and benefits will arise: (1) the young people's avoidance of many sins while they stay in such places; (2) the good discipline and inclination that they have the opportunity to adopt in the most dangerous period of their lives; (3) the opportunity they have to produce fruit in Christian life and literary compositions, and to learn early to use their time well and get used to living a life ordered in its actions; (4) the great service done to their parents, relieving them of the hard work of bringing up their children to produce such great fruit; (5) the hope that exists that each is such as to be able to help others, by becoming a prelate or a pastor or a person of significance in society, one who is a judge or the father of a family or one of the leading members of the republic or a religious or someone of another station; (6) the opportunity to bring together such a great variety of nationalities under the same discipline, most impressively the northern nations in the German College—it seems they are being given a convenient opportunity to bring it about that many return to the devotion of the Holy See, as they nourish their sons in the city of Rome in such a program of training.

The benefits the Society receives from it are the following: (1) the occasion to gratify its benefactors and friends by bringing up their sons, and (2) at the same time, to reconcile to itself some who currently hate or persecute it; (3) the good example it makes of itself to the world by taking care of such fruitful labor; (4) having against its detractors such a public witness in Rome of sustaining its many subjects who are studying; (5) the opportunity it has to exercise its charism in help of its neighbor as it learns how to administrate and to deal with neighbors to help them; (6) the gaining of many good subjects for the Society and keeping them until they are quite mature, that is, well advanced in both spirit and in letters, with proven perseverance and constancy; (7) everyone's benefit, satisfaction, and gratification in the raising of so many sons and giving them a good way to live; and as the Society cannot run colleges everywhere, this one, being universal, can benefit all the provinces and any particular city and large estate, so that with this college, its Institute comes to be known everywhere.

Those who maintain that the damage the Society suffers from running this college is greater than the advantages seem to me to be making a big mistake for these reasons: Assume that the Society is walking in the Spirit and in collaboration with God in works directed to his service (and to which this same God calls the Society) as it is in this, by being most pertinent to the Society's Institute, by there already being so many similar colleges in different countries and by appearing at first sight to be the Society's own particular work, without the like ever having been seen before, and not appearing to be, humanly speaking, capable of success if it were other than it is. And assume as well the good governance on which the benefit and advancement of every good congregation depends, and without which everything falls into disorder and ruin. Should the Society be lacking in spirit and good organization it will be forced to leave not only such a work but all the others that are in accord with its Institute and that are no less risky and dangerous than this one when they are not directed by the rule of the spirit and good governance. We note that no one in the German College up to now has lost the spirit or spiritual soundness, nor has there been any departure from the Society in these circumstances. Nor have any other troubles occurred, as has been seen in the case of other works of the Society. On the contrary, on the average, many people seem to be advancing and exercising themselves in many kinds of virtues. If someone without any spirit were to be sent there and not acquire it, this will stand out clearly.

As for the labor, it is quite true that just as the work is great and most productive, so there is need of great governance. Absent that, many troubles will arise there. In such a case, it will be better to abandon it than to continue on with it. We must either do it as it ought to be done or leave it. I do not judge it a good thing to create many colleges and to look after them as a duty, and this should happen only in a place where the Society has its own college with about a hundred brothers.[8]

In particular, the institute of the German College can be understood by its very name: "the German College under the care of the Society of Jesus." The very title lets you know the institute of the college, because "college" means nothing more than a gathering of students; "German" means it aims at helping others;[9] "under the care of the Society" means they are attending to the spirit and the main goal is the Christian life.

In order to lighten its load in the schools in a city where it has colleges, the Society could arrange that the community selects some fine young man of good talent and supports him in the German College until he becomes capable of being a teacher. Later, the community is repaid little by little for what it spent, since such a person would serve as a teacher there, while our companions attend to teaching Christian doctrine to the children and to the Society's exercises.

Our Father Ignatius, of holy memory, inspired by God, sought nothing other in creating the Society than to fill the world with Christian doctrine and spirit since these two things were in a very bad condition in his time. The Society has no better means to engage in these activities than the German College.

Staying in the colleges and going out to engage in the Society's exercises in service of the neighbor are two extremes. The German College is the means of going from one extreme to the other. And missions might be given those who are

---

8   In this document, "brothers" (*fratelli*) indicates *not* the "temporal coadjutors" (non-clerical Jesuits who assist in temporal rather than in explicitly spiritual matters), but rather members of the Society, particularly those in training, the "scholastics," who are still in their studies and assisting with the running of the school.

9   Cortesono plays with the word *Germanicum*, tracing the etymology back to the Latin meaning of *germanus*: brother (from the same parents). Therefore, the aim of this college should be to foster human brotherhood by helping the neighbor.

in the German College, because this way the talent that they have to deal with the neighbor comes to light.

Chapter 2—Admission Procedures for the College

In enrolling students, one should always keep in mind the proper end. Above all, as is true for every good action, the first and universal end of everything should be the glory of God; second, the common good in the Christian republic; third, the good and perfection of the same college. If during the admission process something arises that conflicts with the three ends mentioned above, there should be no acceptance of the applicant under any circumstances. Admitting someone solely for profit or for worldly esteem would be contrary to the first point. Admitting children or useless people or those who do not display much aptitude for letters and spirit is contrary to the second point. The third point is undermined if undisciplined pupils are admitted, ones who disturb and impede the good of the others. And I hold that one of the main causes of so many of the disorders that we find in governance is that the administrators do not take care to keep the proper end in mind when they make decisions. This is the reason why God allows many disorders to go on. But God has to give his particular care to one who in his actions continuously keeps in mind the right end. Admitting people because they enjoy human favors seems to be a kind of ambition. Admitting people because they are friends or relatives seems to be a kind of commerce, arranging such a work to fit a worldly service and convenience.

The more particular ends are the following: that the students can advance above all in Christian life; second, in studies; third, in good manners. Hence those who are admitted should be such that one can expect them to attain these three ends. And one should see that they achieve them as well as possible. Experience has shown us if some are helped only because they are popular or because they are sons or relatives of a certain friend, they most often tend to end up hurting themselves and the college and disappointing their parents and the Society; and also, the Society finds itself forced to take on certain features that do not comport well with the good of the whole work.

To reach the above-mentioned ends, the students need to be characterized by the following: (1) they should be between fourteen and twenty-five years of age; (2) they should be born from a legitimate marriage; (3) they should be well grounded in letters, at least in grammar; (4) they should be well behaved; (5) they should enter the college willingly with the aim of being helped and improving in letters, manners, and Christian life; (6) they should intend to continue on in the studies, including philosophy at least; (7) they should intend to observe the rules and allow themselves to be governed in everything superiors judge to be helpful for them and for the universal good of the college. Students who are twenty years old should not be admitted if they are not suitable for the course of philosophy. There should be good testimony about their manners; as soon as these get worse, the students should be dismissed.

One should admit those who are most suitable and alert, ones in whom the above-mentioned qualities are found more fully. There have to be some individuals who have responsibility for their worldly needs and who provide for them without their leaving the college for every little necessity; or there should be someone in the college who takes care of this.

Those who are in charge of the students have to be the ones who accept them so that they are well informed and know those for whom they are responsible. They could be the following ones, acting all together: the rector, the minister, the confessor, the prefect of studies. All of these four will talk with those who want to enter the college. They will be able to examine the students about the qualities mentioned above. But in particular, the confessor will determine the level of devotion. The prefect of studies will inquire into the level of learning; the others will inquire into students' attitudes towards the observance of the rules. Then all together they will decide for acceptance or rejection. And when they have made a decision to accept an individual for some good feature of his even though he lacks some of the above-mentioned characteristics, an appeal can be made to the father general for a dispensation, with reference to the qualities of the youth and the opinions of all four about accepting him. It should be done in a way that all of them are looking in the admissions process only for the good aspects and good qualities of those that they are to accept. They should be inclined to admit especially those who come to the college with the fixed aim of attending to the spirit, because these are at odds with none of the principal goals, and they are extremely useful for the universal good of the college, and we can usually hope to win them for the service of God. If such a person is lacking in some other respects, it should be easy to dispense him from them.

Those who have been admitted, after they and those placed in the college have been shown the rules, should be advised that if they fail to follow the customs of the college, they will be expelled. And the youth and the one who put him there should promise to be content with this insofar as it has been so ordered by the superiors of the college. Likewise, the youth should promise to follow the rules.

Chapter 3—Examination for Those Who Are to Be Admitted into the College

Questions for Learning His Spiritual State

This part particularly belongs to the confessor, who could ask (1) if the student has any regular devotions of his own, such as saying the office of the Virgin or any other prayer, fasting during certain days, and the like; (2) if he has ever made a general confession; if so, with whom and on what occasion; if not, whether he wishes to or not; if there is anything that is weighing on his conscience; (3)

how many times in a year he has been accustomed to go to confession and take Communion, and what is his opinion about the frequent reception of these sacraments; (4) if he has ever been acquainted with spiritual people, and if he has ever devoted himself for any time to the spirit; and if he has stopped doing it, on what occasion; (5) if he has ever felt the desire to dedicate himself to devotion, and how many times he has felt such a desire, and why did he not follow it from those moments; (6) what kinds of goods does he typically enjoy and, when he attended sermons, what tended to move him; and, if has he ever attended spiritual discussions, in which kinds of discussions does he feel most moved, that is, by the four last things, by the vanity and misery of this life, or by the benefits of God, and so forth;[10] (7) if he is under any vow; and how does he feel about progressing in spiritual matters; and if he knows their importance; and to which devotional subject he feels most inclined.

Questions to Determine the State of the Student's Education
(1) How many years has he been in school, and where did he stop? (2) Which authors did he read with understanding? How many of their books? (3) What was the quality of the teachers he had? Did they consider him a good student? (4) How good is his memory? How easy is it for him to understand what is taught? (5) Does he like studies? How has he gotten accustomed to studying previously, and what has been his manner of going about it? (6) How far does he think he has gotten in studies? To what kind of studies does he feel more inclined? What has his family decided about his studies? (7) Have him compose and parse and deliver some passage from the authors he has read.

Questions to Determine the State of the Student's Manners
(1) How did his relatives consider him, quiet or lively? (2) Was he obedient to his elders? And were they happy with him? (3) What kind of company did he keep? How did he behave with them? Did he ever run around with them and why? What kind of bad behavior did he find in them? What did he dislike the most? (4) Has he ever gone abroad? For how long and on what occasion? What were his business or leisure activities? (5) What kind of bad tendencies does he think he has? What kind of things does he feel is the hardest to overcome? (6) Did he ever have someone who taught him good or bad manners? What did he learn there? (7) Does he feel a strong desire to leave aside all his bad habits and learn good ones? Then, it might be read and set out clearly what good and bad manners are, giving him some advice about them, and the same for the other questions.

All of those who give the three above-mentioned examinations will take note of the responses so that the student's state can be known. Then they should report on it to father rector.

---

10 The four last things (*quattuor novissima*) are death, judgment, hell, and heaven. These themes appear in meditational traditions in the late Middle Ages.

These examinations can be given before admission, especially regarding those who are not already very well known. However, these examinations may be left for after admission, before their entrance, or until after they have entered the college. The proper examination for admission is the one with the seven conditions for finding if one is suitable for studying in the college.

Chapter 4—Advice to Give to Those Who Are Going to Be Examined

Concerning the spirit, they could be told what constitutes spirit, the benefit that comes by devoting oneself to the spirit, the things that are helpful for the spirit and the things that work against it. The same will happen with regard to behavior and keeping the rules. This might be done after the students have entered the college.

Commitment to the spirit is nothing other than doing what human beings were created to do, and what is proper to humanity and particularly to the Christian, and that for which God will ask everyone to account, according to the benefits and chances he has given him. He should have the opinion that God with his most holy providence has led him to the college for no other reason than to consider and attend to spiritual things in particular. And the spirit consists in properly knowing, revering, and loving God, by ordering oneself and all of one's actions towards him, and striving in all of one's actions to know him, revere him, and love him. This is done by observing his holy law. The benefits are boundless, but in particular they are the following: first, being freed from the tyranny of sin, the devil, and one's own passions; (2) the peace, freedom, and safety of one's own conscience; (3) receiving the friendship, grace, and goods of God, constantly growing in them; (4) coming closer to heaven every moment as one's own way gets easier; (5) walking in the light that dispels the darkness from itself, the chains, the dangers, and the miseries of the sin, being wary of them; (7) finally achieving blessedness.

The means are: (1) having a strong will and a great desire to attend to this spirit; (2) frequenting the most holy sacraments; (3) giving oneself to prayer; (4) often delighting in hearing the word of God and repeatedly engaging in spiritual conversations; (5) making sure always to busy oneself, but in things that are virtuous and wholesome, and persevering in good actions; (6) attending to the correction of one's own defects; (7) enjoying the company of spiritual persons.

The obstacles to the spirit are: (1) having a weak will for doing the good; (2) bad habits or bad inclinations; (3) putting little value on spiritual things and the means that are conducive to the spirit; (4) bad conversations and associations; (5) being too affectively attached to the things of this life, especially to conveniences and pleasures of the senses; (6) bad actions; (7) avoiding good company, and disdaining good conversations as one turns oneself into an enemy of virtue.

Studying is an action proper to humankind by which one fulfills the principal part of the soul, that is, the intellect, in the knowledge of things. Those who advance the furthest in this seem in a certain way to be superior in comparison with others. It is also one of the worthy occupations in which individuals can be occupied naturally. And it is an exercise and a labor which one has to begin in one's childhood in order to finish it at the end of one's life. Above all, it is important to have in studies the right end, which is the glory of God, the salvation of the soul, and being able to help the neighbor, that is, to study in order to know and honor God, to save one's own soul, and with these things to be of service to one's neighbor.

The benefits are: (1) occupying oneself, during such a dangerous time of life, in such honorable and useful activity; (2) fulfilling such a noble part of the soul as our intellect is, while getting rid of ignorance, which makes men so utterly vile; (3) making oneself fit to be able to help others and especially one's homeland, relatives, and friends; (4) by the honor given to scholars; (5) studies are usually a means for acquiring the goods of fortune and expanding one's wealth through these means; (6) the good satisfaction that is given through these studies to one's relatives and friends; (7) the satisfaction proper to a human being that derives from seeing that one has arrived at a good end in knowledge, with the good account that one can render of oneself, and with the ability to stand in the company of others who are known for wisdom.

The resources and helps are: (1) having a good intellectual talent, that is, good judgment and good memory; (2) devoting oneself totally to studies, discounting the labor; delighting in them, and abhorring everything that can hinder one in them; (3) having good teachers and good exercises, and always being busy about them in the time assigned to them; (4) having a way to study by progressing in them in an orderly way; (5) enjoying good associations with learned men, intending to get to know each one and having good emulation with one's peers; (6) detesting and loathing individuals who are trying to keep them back from their studies; (7) having a great desire to learn, submitting oneself to whoever wants or is able to learn those studies, taking some saint as an advocate for good academic progress, every day doing some good work for such an end, praying that God give him the grace of leading him towards his honor and glory, and towards the salvation of his own soul.

The obstacles are all the things that are opposite to the above-mentioned helps, and especially to letting one's soul indulge in pleasures and its own passions.

Good manners are the ornament of human actions, through which we make them pleasing and attractive to others. This ornament consists in doing one's own actions in due measure and order, paying attention to time, to place, and to the qualities of the persons, taking delight in always performing virtuous acts, avoiding the bad ones and those that could displease others, or rather that are strange. And this consists in the external actions of the body and in speaking; it includes the better part of good manners, that is, being humble, mature, and benevolent in one's actions.

The benefits are: (1) demonstrating oneself to be virtuous, the exterior very often being a sign of interior composure and order; (2) making oneself likable to everyone; (3) the praise that is raised about oneself; (4) the good example and the good report that one gives of oneself; (5) becoming worthy of imitation by others; (6) avoiding the many troubles that usually arise from bad manners; (7) gathering in the fruits of good associations; (8) the ease in acquiring every other virtue by means of these; it is like a foundation on which every other virtue can easily be built.

The helps and means for obtaining good manners are: (1) being provided with the natural disposition; (2) wishing to acquire and enjoy them; (3) knowing what good manners are, and striving hard to acquire them and to notice them in other people; (4) association with virtuous and well-mannered people; (5) knowing bad manners and watching out for them, and working hard to get rid of any bad manners that one has; (6) having someone like a teacher who gives notice when something is lacking in this respect; (7) watching over oneself and being mindful in all one's actions of what is being done and how and how one ought to do it; and above all being a friend of modesty.

The obstacles are everything that is the opposite of the items just mentioned, but they are especially these: being naturally animated, having little wit, being haughty, and easily giving in to bad inclinations and bad habits. The rule is nothing other than that of well-measured action organized to reach the intended goal.[11]

The following benefits stem from living according to this rule: (1) easily reaching the intended goal; (2) because it is typical of virtuous men, while living without this rule is typical of a man given to vice; (3) making actions virtuous even if they are not so in themselves, by the strength of obedience and the goal; (4) using one's time well; (5) learning and becoming used to living in an ordered way; (6) the merit which one earns before God; (7) making one's own way to the virtue easier through the good habit attained through the frequent actions performed.

The means are: (1) submitting oneself in every respect to obedience and to the rules; (2) enjoying them and often considering the end to which they are to be led, which ought to be desired above everything else; (3) not becoming attached to anything, except insofar as they help one to observe the rules; (4) always siding with those who see that the rules are observed rather than with

---

11 "Regula autem et mensura humanorum actuum est ratio, quae est primum principium actuum humanorum, ut ex praedictis patet, rationis enim est ordinare ad finem, qui est primum principium in agendis, secundum philosophum" [The rule and measure of human acts is reason, which is the first principle of human acts, as is apparent from what has been said, for it belongs to reason to order things to an end, which is the first principle in actions, according to the Philosopher]. Thomas Aquinas, *Summa theologiae*, I^a–II^{ae}, q. 90 a. 1 co. Editors' translation.

those who would like them put aside; (5) willingly working hard by following these rules, realizing that no good is gained without hard work and especially virtue, whose roots are bitter but whose fruits are most delectable; (6) pondering often the benefits that arise from observing the rules, as well as the damages that arise from not doing so; (7) enjoying the association of those who like to follow the rules, and keeping oneself away from those who do not trouble themselves to observe them; and maintaining the same spirit with which one entered the college, that is, diligently to observe all the rules, recalling the promises made about this.

The obstacles are the opposite of the things just mentioned, among which are also: (1) grumbling or listening willingly to grumblers; (2) being a friend of idleness and one's own will; (3) developing a habit in the opposite direction; (4) being an enemy of and avoiding those who report infractions of the rules, and being bothered by these kinds of reports, and agreeing with others to keep a distance from these people; (5) doing penance reluctantly; (6) being disinclined to and annoyed by them; (7) preferring to spend time with those prefects who overlook the observance of the rules rather than with those who more diligently observe them; and behaving differently when the prefect is present or absent because one needs the motivation.

Acceptance policies should favor those who are more promising and those judged likely to be more useful to the Christian Republic—like nobles, people of means, those who come from lands infested by heretics, those who intend to devote themselves to philosophy and theology. It is even necessary that they keep advancing in their studies to perfect themselves as much in them as in good manners and life to be able to help their neighbor all the more. Their relatives, uncles, or guardians should be informed: (1) about what necessities have to be provided for them; (2) about how the students are not to sleep outside the college, except for when they are ill; (3) that students should not visit their homes except on rare occasion; (4) that they can sometimes come to get information about their young man, so that when he needs it they can help to correct him; and that if he does not correct his faults he can be taken back; (5) that if they hear something about the child such as complaints or accusations, they might advise him and not believe him easily; (6) that they should be careful to keep him in fear, for external fear is usually very helpful; and that if they are outside of Rome, they should be advised of similar things by letter; (7) they should know with what kind of foreigners the student is allowed to talk; (8) they should know that the student is not to have any sort of work or responsibility; (9) they should be informed that students will be kept in the college for two months on probation; (10) information is gathered on the student's nature, behaviors, and manners, and about what needs attention; (11) they should be asked about their motivation for placing the student in the college and if the young man is coming willingly.

Chapter 5—On How to Deal With and Help Students Who Have Just Arrived at the College

Helping those who have just arrived is very necessary: (1) because in every matter it is important to start well; (2) because they are found more disposed to do everything and they tend to let themselves be governed easily; (3) because they tend to aim to do everything well, and for some time, they tend to put many things above them, keeping a spirit of great reverence; but later, when they begin to feel their oats, if their steps have not been well guided from the start, they suddenly begin to want everything their own way; they associate with those who are going astray; they begin to grumble; they shirk hard work, and little by little they detach themselves from every benefit; so it will be good to (1) give them some good advice, as we find in the fourth chapter of the first book; (2) give them healthy association with some fine young men; (3) arrange for some father to take special care of them, one with whom they feel at home and secure, revealing all their needs and discontents as they arise, and they can send these students to those who have charge of directing them in devotion, in the observance of the rules, in studies and in manners; (4) put them into a room of good young men and with a very discreet and experienced prefect, and it would seem better to have one or two rooms added on where all the new ones could lodge; (5) they should be given good treatment and they should be treated with all possible gentleness, endeavoring to make them grow fond of the college, its exercises, and to good people, and its administrators.

It is known that three sorts of people are accepted: those with a good nature ready for the good, who are easily directed to the good with the help of the examples of others; those whose natures are hard to turn to the good; and those who are inclined to evil. Once the last of these are known, they should not be accepted, if there is doubt about their success. And, if one decides to admit them on probation: (1) make an effort to learn the student's nature; (2) take away from him every opportunity for evil; (3) keep him humble and busy; (4) endeavor to help him through spiritual means in order that God might move him towards the good, means such as good conversations, especially about things that bring him to an awareness of himself, of sin and its fruits, and of virtue and its fruits; (5) have him make a general confession; give him the Spiritual Exercises of the first week, if he is up to that; (6) remove from him the opportunity to associate with people who fit with his own nature, that is, who tend to trouble him with their wicked talk and grumblings; (7) keep him in reverential fear, especially of dismissal every time he deviates from the right path; and try to make him a friend of hard work, and above all of perseverance, because everyone knows how to do some things after a bit of time.

Everyone should then attend to the direction of the students, according to his specific office: for example, the confessor should direct them in devotion, the prefect of studies in studies, the prefect of discipline in behavior, and the dormi-tory prefect in the observance of the rules, as will be said in the relevant passage about the office of each one.

If they are provided with a natural attitude for both good and evil, there needs to be very special care and very diligent observance of the rules just men-tioned, so that on account of the fault of one who has the oversight nobody is lost who with some diligence would have been won. All the hard work and trouble typically rests with these, as we will say in the next chapter.

In this, as in all other administrative matters, one would learn much by experience, trying many things and taking note of what is helpful for each one. Above all, care should be taken that the rules are being observed and that there is someone assigned to read and explain them, and that students are made to promise to observe them, having them say in what matter they think they will have the hardest time. Likewise, we should try to make sure they commit to memory some good advice given to them at the start to help them.

If they do not know how to say the office of the Virgin Mary, it should be taught to them. Similarly, they should be directed in prayer and examination of conscience according to their ability. And we should see that Christian doctrine is learned, so that they know it by heart in a short time.

It is very necessary that at the beginning they talk only with a very few assigned to them who could give them some help. And in some rules, in those important for removing the occasion of sin, it is better to be severe and strict than loose and easygoing. It is very important to know everyone's nature from the beginning and to treat each according to what helps him the best. What has to be done to know the natures and deal with them will be addressed in the following chapter. We should realize that for a month after entering they can be known only with difficulty because at the start everyone behaves well. But it is good to treat them tenderly to oblige them more, and it is good to remain atten-tive to their actions, giving them every chance to perform good actions.

If someone bad should come to the college, but with a powerful resolve to be corrected, just as with someone dangerous who had already begun to go astray, it is extremely important to help such as these from the start, because everybody tends to make great efforts at the beginning and have a great resolve to do well, but then he drifts easily, especially when he finds fellows to his lik-ing and similar to his nature. But it is very necessary to help these people from the very start, and it is almost necessary to provide such as these with a special place, before they associate with the others, because they would take liberties as soon as they are with others, and they always join up with those who cannot help them, so both of them fall. And of all of these things, the most important one is giving them good associations and getting them into devotions, assign-ing them to the care of one of our members and doing some other things as will be said in the next section.

It is particularly important to be familiar with the nature of northern people and to know how to deal with them.

The second book has to be divided into two chapters.

Chapter 1—How to Know and Deal With Diversity in the Natures of the Students

Knowing and dealing with everyone according to his own nature is very important for the good governance of the college. And although this is the charge for all of those who will be assigned to this governance, it still particularly belongs to the office of the rector, who has to have a special talent for knowing and directing everyone according to his nature, taking care to make himself *omnia omnibus* ["all things to all," 1 Cor. 9:22] as Paul says, that is, terrible with the terrible, humane with the humane, and so forth. And in this he has to apply special diligence and attention, endeavoring day by day to become ever more adroit and astute in this practice, because in this consists the entire importance of governance.

All natures fall into three categories, that is, the good, the bad, and the in-between, that is, those who readily do good or evil, namely those with bad inclinations who have not yet acquired bad habits and who can easily defeat their bad inclinations through some means.

The good qualities that good people tend to have are these: being well inclined, modest, well mannered, humble, reasonable, simple, respectable, shrewd, obedient, having few words and good conscience, reverent towards God, eager to do good. They love the virtues and associating with virtuous people and good conversations and are enemies of vice and bad associations and bad talk. They amend themselves when rebuked or corrected, and they do not involve themselves with evil, being eager to help others to do good things by setting an example and engaging with them in good conversation.

The bad qualities bad people tend to have are these: being wickedly inclined, having bad habits and manners, being immodest, proud, ambitious, suspicious, headstrong, not respectable, careless, comic, frivolous, unintelligent, fanciful, loquacious, quarrelsome, deceptive, self-centered, sensual, ill-disposed towards virtue and virtuous people and good conversations and hard work. They enjoy idleness, associating with bad people, and bad talk. They grumble easily. They want everything to their liking. They are ungrateful, impatient, disobedient, choleric, envious, lustful. Corrections make them worse, and they become more stubborn in their evil and more hostile to virtue and the means that lead towards it.

The qualities of those who stand in the middle tend to be some good aspects and some bad ones, that is, they have a little of each, but imperfectly, in such a way that there are principles for doing good and principles for doing evil; with the good they are good and with the bad they are bad.

The good ones are of three kinds: beginners, when they start to do good; progressing, when they go from good to better; and perfect, when they are well habituated and secure and can help the others.

Some are good by nature, others are so by good company, and others by God's activity, through which they have overcome the bad inclinations and the bad habits that they had.

The bad tend to be of three kinds: that is, the lustful, the proud and immodest, and the ones who are both, that is the lustful and proud.

Some of them are bad by nature; some become bad through a bad upbringing; some are good but become bad; some are proud; and some are hidden.

Some think that this work requires great labor, and no wonder, because it follows the command of God and nature that fine things are achieved with great effort. But the labor comes with the lack of good organization; yet when things are well ordered there will be superabundant results with very little toil.

Some suspect that disorders will eventually arise, but it seems to me that insofar as *bad things should not be done so that good things may arise* [cf. Rom. 3:8], so one should not abandon the present good because of the suspicion that an evil can possibly follow upon it, because only God knows what will happen. And as God is in his own works, while he keeps them under his protection, they cannot crumble; acting this way, he does not want to allow anyone to contradict him, because he certainly knows what is the best.[12] However, even with all that, in governance one should prudently prevent bad things and remedy them. Laws and decrees and statutes are made for this purpose, that is, to promote good order and to protect it from events that could occur in opposition to it. Therefore, the following constitutions are made to arrange everything so as to reach the intended goal easily and to preserve it from future disorders. And so this governance belongs properly to the Society and it depends on the Society not losing the spirit: such a loss would mean that this work and all the other administrations the Society has would fall into ruin; so the Society mainly has to see to it that the spirit more than anything else is preserved and increased. Nor should anyone think that the subjects lose their spirit in this governance. On the

---

12 According to Aquinas, substances can stand and act only by the power of God: "Sic ergo Deus est causa actionis cuiuslibet in quantum dat virtutem agendi, et in quantum conservat eam, et in quantum applicat actioni, et in quantum eius virtute omnis alia virtus agit. Et cum coniunxerimus his, quod Deus sit sua virtus, et quod sit intra rem quamlibet non sicut pars essentiae, sed sicut tenens rem in esse, sequetur quod ipse in quolibet operante immediate operetur, non exclusa operatione voluntatis et naturae" [Thus therefore God is the cause of any action insofar as he provides the power to act, and insofar as he preserves it, and insofar as it is by his power that every other power works. And when we add to this the fact that God is his own power, and that he is within any reality not as a part of its essence but as one supporting it in being, it follows that he himself is immediately at work in anything working, including the working of the will and of nature]. Thomas Aquinas, *De potentia*, q. 3 a. 7 co. Editors' translation.

contrary, it presents an opportunity to increase in spirit as this action is virtuous (1) since it is commanded by God and thus meritorious; (2) because God works along with his works and increases the spirit rather than takes it away; (3) because, since people know that the spirit is needed to run the college, they are inspired to acquire it in their own selves; (4) because an individual, especially one belonging to the Society, acquires the spirit and perfection when they gain it for others, as happens in this work.

Those who stand midway between good and bad are also of three kinds: that is, those who, though they have some bad inclinations, also have the counterweight of other good inclinations; others who, though good by nature, have been harmed by a bad upbringing; and others who despite their bad inclinations have not grown bad or gotten into the habit thanks to a good upbringing, or by respect and human fear, or because of their age and because they have not had the opportunity.

How to know someone's nature: First, notice in each individual the following things: (1) his nature, that is, what is his complexion; is he sanguine, choleric, or phlegmatic, or melancholic, or any particular combination of these? (2) His age, that is, if he is a child, a youth, or a mature man; (3) his station and condition, that is, whether he is of noble birth or common, lay or ecclesiastical, legitimate or natural; (4) his manners, that is, whether is he well behaved or not; (5) his inclination, whether it is good or bad; (6) his upbringing, that is, whether is he well or badly raised; (7) his dress, whether it is good or not; (8) what characteristics and special particularities does he have; (9) how does the above appear in his qualities of good and bad. Second, the individual's nature can be judged by his manner of speaking, by his external acts, and from what other people say about him; from the passions he reveals, especially in his face, from the company he keeps, from the goal at which he aims, and from the ease and difficulty with which he lets himself be managed, and by what does he rate things highly or give little attention to them. Third, tell the dormitory prefects to write down all the virtues and defects they notice in their students, and the rector should keep a list of everyone's characteristics in a book, and in addition, the good or bad progress each one makes, along with the means through which everyone gets more help. And by noticing this, he will get very well practiced in knowing the natures of individuals in a short time, and in knowing how to deal with them, because in this area one learns more through judgment and experience than with any other thing; and it is still necessary to apply oneself to this and enjoy it. When someone has a great dread of appearing before the superior, he is usually bad. Fourth, one should test the student through rebukes, penances, new room assignments, watching closely over him in the matter of observing the rules, giving him someone with whom he has to talk, giving him some particular advice, and the like. But in this it must be noted that the desire to know each one should not lead the students to get angry and feel slighted. This can happen with some who are partially known, both when there is good reason, and when they think that certain means are being used to correct or investigate them in order to find an opportunity to expel them. Fifth, one should inquire into different things relating to what one wants to know, especially what has just been mentioned. And one can gather the nature of the students by their responses to this examination.

The way to handle such a diversity of natures to the help and satisfaction of each one is very difficult and calls for special help from God. And it is good that one be a very careful and prudent person, provided with much charity and zeal for souls. (1) One needs to put oneself on the same level and make use of sweet or bitter measures as the occasion requires; (2) one should proceed deftly and not impatiently; (3) one should ask for the opinions of others, endeavoring to do everything in a reasonable and orderly way, as experience teaches; (4) one should aim always at the good of the others, and especially the common good; (5) one should avoid every kind of passion, especially [the desire] to do everything.

Chapter 2—On How They Should Deal With Foreigners

Is it essential for them to take care in talking with the foreigners (1) because this could occasion their being persuaded to do something to the detriment of those who have little interest in doing good; especially if they are persons who had previously misbehaved together; or at least, it could lead students to discover the discontent they might feel about their staying at the college; and so they can avoid being hindered or distracted from their studies with the visits.

One should give special attention to: (1) those who are new; (2) those who are dangerous; (3) the undisciplined ones; (4) those who have experienced some disappointment, until their feelings fade. One should also take care to keep anyone in the college from undertaking any kind of business. And if some necessity arises, it should be managed by someone from the college such as the procurator or those on his staff.

This order could be kept: (1) when a student enters the college, ask his relatives what person is the one with whom we can deal, and make sure they are instructed to come to take care of the necessities; this person should be trustworthy and reliable, and once the receptionist gets acquainted with him, one should inform the person about the times he can conveniently deal with the student without disturbing him. He should courteously try to learn what they talk about, especially when students are looking to get something. (2) When they are not commoners, or their relatives, or notables, the receptionist should not call the student to the door without first informing the superior. When not inclined to speak with the superior, the visitor can be informed about the superior's quality, and then he can be courteously informed about the order of the college and the intention behind it. If it becomes obvious that the person keeps insisting, the superior, in order to not send him away upset, could have the student called into his presence or into his room, and this way he would know the subject of the discussion.

When the students are at class and someone comes to talk with them, if he is neither a person of some standing nor a close relative who wants something necessary, do not allow him to talk with anyone, but the teachers should advise them to go to the students' college [residence] so that their studies are not interrupted. The young people should do the same, and when someone comes to talk with them, as soon as they are in the college, they should inform the superior.

When they go out in Rome, either they should not talk to him or they should be in the presence of the prefect or of someone who is accompanying them, if there is not a relative or ordinary person who has responsibility for this. And in this there has to be thought for the qualities of the young man, according to what has been stated above.

Chapter 3—The Order and Division of the College

Beyond everything else, order is necessary for governing: it is what makes it all the easier to escape confusion and also to avoid troubles.

Order consists in doing things at the right time and place both in the proper manner and with the subordination of one thing to another, such as getting up at right time, and then having conversation, and then doing what is to be done during the whole day until they go to sleep; and it is having things done in the right manner, for example, keeping silence during study time, and the like, at the right time. For this, everything is arranged so that disorder is avoided, as it is controlled throughout the rules; because working in an orderly way is the same as working according to the rules.

There should be order: (1) in time, that it is structured well; (2) in actions, that they are done in the proper manner and in the right circumstances to produce results; (3) in individuals, that is, in dealing with and instructing them according what is suitable for each one's level; (4) in removing opportunities for troubles; (5) in balancing one thing with another, so they last and so that they are less burdensome, as recreation in its time is more productive and more helpful; as is, after studies, ordering one's schedule to attend to the spirit.

The superior should see to the following: (1) being orderly in himself, careful to dispense things at the right time and to the convenience of others; seeing to it that what can be done one day is not postponed to another on account of not knowing how to use the time, as will be said in the passage about the office of the rector; (2) making sure everyone has a clear idea of what needs to be done, that is, the rules for everyone; and he should take care that everyone observes them; (3) making sure there is order in the college, both in the ordinary and extraordinary things, and seeing that everything is done properly. The same goes for the literary and devotional exercises. Regarding the things that are to be done which are not so ordinary, the superior should think them over in advance and at the proper time advise those involved so that they can stand at the ready to do as much as they have to do.

Among the goods of the college, the division of the students is what avoids many troubles and much confusion; it is most necessary for the universal good of the entire college and for smooth governance. (1) There should be a four-part division in recreation: the first section consists of the oldest, the second of the middle, and the third of the youngest; the fourth will depend on dividing whatever is the largest group into two parts. Without this division, it would be impossible to run the college. And even if there were few students, it would still be good to make such divisions. (2) There should be a division of rooms, according to which they will be divided everywhere they go, seeing that everyone goes or stays with those of his own room, without mixing in with others of other rooms.

Since this partition of rooms is a very important matter, the superior should be extremely careful in assigning the rooms in such a way that students are so distributed that they help one another, and no one does damage to someone else. In this, we need great experience and great speculative power and prudence on the part of the superior, because a great part of the good of the college depends on this. It is recommendable that he pay attention to the following: (1) He has to be careful to put together those who are similar in age, rank, and manners; (2) brothers and relatives should remain separate, unless there is a special consideration that makes it good to keep them together. Ordinarily, the dangerous or the badly behaved ones should be kept separated among themselves, unless it is not convenient to keep them all together since there are so many, so that they not do damage to others when they have been dispersed, as has been said above, and in separating these, they have to be kept among the trustworthy ones so that among many good ones you could put one of these others. If there are two, forbid association with the dangerous ones. The same goes for those who are beginning to decline, or who are not very trustworthy; and these, if they are dangerous because of their carnality, ought by all means to be set apart from each other. When there are other parts, they can be together, provided that there are many trustworthy students among them and association among the dangerous ones is prohibited, or someone watches over them whenever they are immodest, grumbling, annoying, disgruntled about staying in the college, inimical to hard work, and inclined to pleasure and idleness.

We have to be sure always to keep new students among good ones, as mentioned above. It is also useful to make changes frequently, at least when it is judged most advisable, such as during the resumption of studies, or at other times when many particular changes have to be made, or when there are many new arrivals, and it is suitable to make a universal change to accommodate them better.[13]

---

13 The resumption of studies is the commencement of the school year, that is, the return to school after summer vacation.

Sometimes particular changes are made in order to help someone by placing him among good fellows; or to test him by making him switch rooms; or to remedy some problem that has arisen or is about to happen; or for the good of a room, by removing individuals who are disturbing it; or to do a favor for someone who has insistently pressed to join that room, pledging to make some progress. But in this last case, one should be particularly careful about: (1) giving priority to the common good; (2) seeing if the request will really work to the good of the individual; (3) considering the aim of the request (why is he asking?); (4) even if it seems a good idea, granting it with some conditions, for the student's greater help.

Making students switch from one recreation group to another is also good, either for the good and advantage of that recreation group or for the other one, or for a separation from dangerous students, or for a particular help or probation for the one who has been changed.

To make the divisions and transfers well to the benefit of the college and the particular good of each one, it is necessary that there be many good individuals among whom some few bad ones are mixed, yet in such a way that these latter are kept in check so that they do not dare hurt the others. Otherwise it would be the ruin of the college because everything would fall into disorder, and the young instead of being helped would spoil one another. In such a case, it would be better not to keep such a responsibility.

Chapter 4—On Disorders and the Means for Remedying Them

What matters most for the administration is acting prudently to prevent and impede disorders from arising, or if they have occurred, using the proper remedies to put them in order.

Disorders tend to be (1) when there is no observance of the rules, and there is no discipline or fear; (2) when there arise many significant deficiencies; (3) when the spirit is not there, and the good students are pointed out and are loathed by those who look at them; (4) when students are not paying attention and there is no academic achievement; (5) when students are allowed to make friends in their way; (6) when they shy away from our companions and those who accuse them are persecuted; (7) when bad students get together and form cliques; (8) when students are immodest, disobedient, and refuse to do the penances given them; (9) when they grumble in the college over every little thing; and every little thing that happens in the college becomes known outside the college; (10) when students lead each other astray, or there are some from outside that try to lead them astray, or when they can easily go out and meet together, especially when they make plans about this in the college.

The principal cause of disorders comes about from the superior who does not understand governance, or who does not apply himself to it, or who is too benevolent or severe, or who does not know how to remedy matters in a timely way, or who is new and has not had the appropriate experience, or who does not have able assistants; (2) when the college is full of undisciplined students; (3) when people ignore shortcomings to show respect or exempt this or that student from punishment when they deserve it and it is appropriate for the common good; (4) when little infractions are not taken into account, and this leads to a feeling of freedom to commit serious infractions; (5) when one lets undisciplined students become arrogant, not restraining themselves as they should; (6) when one let disorders grow little by little, by not remedying them at the start; (7) not supervising students during vacation time or during special breaks, such as Carnival and Christmas time and the Feast of the King and in the summer trips to the vineyards;[14] (8) the hidden friendships that students establish with one another, especially when they are not trustworthy; (9) the summer, through the recreations they enjoy continuously all together; because in the recreation that each room enjoys during winter there are many disorders and usually at Eastertime the loose behaviors typically sown during the Carnival time begins to appear and they are fully enjoyed in the summer; (10) when students have someone other than the rector to appeal to; or when the rector is such as to make it appealing to diminish his authority; or when he, to escape hard work, leaves nearly everything to the minister to do.

The way to remedy these things in general are: (1) the wisdom, care and solicitude and proper manner of proceeding followed by the superior and the other administrators; and a delight in seeing things well ordered; (2) making sure that good orders are given there and that things are done in a timely fashion, and doing them in a such a way that they are followed; (3) being ready to forestall disorders at the start so they do not arise, and when they have arisen, fixing them before they get worse, by being careful not to use such remedies as to make the disorders increase, as happens for some who do things in haste without advice and without experience; (4) when the superior does not do things just out of his own thinking but gets the opinions of others experienced in such matters; (5) when one has the undisciplined students held in check, and when encouragement and honor are given to those who are virtuous; (6) when the superior notices some disorders, he should consider their causes and see that these are removed because otherwise no matter how good the remedies, they will spring up again; (7) the superior and other administrators should have the right intention in their actions, and take care to direct all their actions towards their true and legitimate end; (8) when some remedy succeeds in removing a particular

---

14 The *festa del re* was a goliardic feast day (January 14) celebrating the flight to Egypt; it occurred shortly after the feast of Epiphany (January 6). It was also known as *Feast of the Ass*, because, as with other "feasts of fools," it inverted the social hierarchy, giving the lowly ass the highest rank.

disorder, the superior should take note of it, and learn from it how to remedy other things; (9) when he encounters difficulties in remedying some things, he should make many attempts; and he should keep to the approach that seems most successful until the entire disorder is gone; (10) above all, he should turn to God for help, so that he might enlighten him about how much he should do, and having himself recommended to others' prayers, that the Lord might grant him his holy help in providing a good remedy for the disorders.

Remedies in particular are the good orders that are given, and everything contained in the following work in the particular chapters of each topic, since good governance is nothing other than governing things and directing them to their end without giving rise to disorders and remedying those disorders if they do arise. This is why these constitutions are being drawn up, the rules and the good orders which are proposed for everyone to follow.

When a particular order given has been restored and it needs to be observed, students can be reminded of it by giving a public penance to whoever has neglected it more than the others.

One of us should always be there to take responsibility for those who are staying in the house or for those who have returned from school.

Most importantly, one should keep an eye out for those who are going astray and who have some friendships with such students, and for those who do not easily allow anyone—especially the good ones—into their association and friendship.

Supervisors should be designated, especially in those places where disorders tend to arise, such as in the rooms, in the classrooms, during recreations, and the like; and reports should be made often.

Chapter 5—On the Offices of the Recreation Prefects and the Dormitory Prefects

Dormitory prefects are appointed (1) So that they might each help the college in their recreation time, seeing to it that the rules are kept and orders and advice given, keeping a copy of every instruction that they give.[15] (2) So that they might talk with the brothers about what might help their students, they should get information about their shortcomings to then update the superior. (3) So that in their presence, especially in recreation time or when they are all together, the students behave more respectfully. (4) They should take care that the brothers are uniform in governance and that they deal with the students in a helpful way; and they should make note of the brothers' shortcomings and advise the superior about them, see that the brothers observe the Society's rules as much as possible, and make progress in the spirit and walk forward in perfection. They should instruct the newly arrived brothers, and they should inform them of how

---

15 See *Monumenta paedagogica*, nova editio, 2:368–78.

much they have to do in the responsibility that will be imposed upon them. (6) On feast days and break days, and especially during solemn feast days like Epiphany and the days of Carnival, they should get particular reports from the prefects about how they behaved. (7) They should see that the brothers keep good watch over their own during the time they are in recreation or are all in the dining room, noting with whom they are engaging and associating; and no one should be able to leave that place without their permission or that of whoever is in that location. (8) They should take care that provisions are made for the brothers' recreation and for all their essentials. (9) They should take care to help some who give particular indications that they have need of it; and in general they should supervise their recreation, seeing that it is done with profit in the spirit, in studies, in manners, and in health; and they should take special care of the sick or convalescent ones in their recreation group. (10) They should be frequently with the rector, telling him how their recreation is going, at least twice a week; and as soon as something important happens, they should see that he hears about it right away.

Although it is good that the prefects be allowed to give some penances and spankings in order to maintain their authority, they should still give them as rarely as possible, preferably having the minister do this; because, although they should keep some authority, they still have to beware that they do not make themselves odious. On the contrary, they should behave with all mildness, especially with those who give some hope of being helped.

The dormitory prefects should know that in the German College they have to attend to helping themselves, chiefly in looking to make advances in their spirituality and in their studies and in observing their rules and those of their institute as well. Therefore, they should keep themselves from taking too much freedom or license, and above all from seeking the goodwill of the students and forming close friendships with them, making sure that their will to help others, as the proper Institute of the Society, does not stray from virtue and from the way of perfection; but they should seek with all their hearts to help others along with themselves, being obliged to it by Christian charity and by their own Institute.

The main help that the prefects will give to the students will be by their good example, showing themselves eager for perfection, exercising themselves in virtue, being frequently and devoutly at their prayers, diligent in their studies, and above all zealous for their good and their progress.

They should realize the opportunity that they have in the German College to attend to their own studies and at the same time learn how to deal with and help their neighbor to practice many virtues and to become such as is proper for the ministers of the Society. At least there is the opportunity to get to know their own shortcomings and their own weaknesses and how much progress they have made towards perfection.

They should deal with students in a pleasant manner in such a way that they can guide them sooner with reason and by showing them what sort of thing is for their good, than by using harshness and threats.

They should keep in mind the final goals of the college, which are the advancement in spirit, in studies, and in manners; and they should strive to guide the students towards these by the observance of the rules and the orders of the college.

They should be one with the other brothers, and strive to be uniform in governing the pupils, keeping away from the two extremes, that is, being too easygoing and granting the students too much freedom or being too strict and making them become exasperated over the slightest thing. The middle point is using the measure of discretion to hold them to an observance of the rules, in a manner that gives rise to fear and love at the same time.

Above all, they should address few words to students and avoid quarreling with them; but they should impose silence on them immediately. And if they insist, they should not answer them, but tell them that the rector will hear of this; and when it seems good on the occasion of some disobedience, they should send for the rector or minister. And they should find a good way of keeping them in fear.

They should try to get familiar with the natures of each student and deal with them accordingly; that is, the good ones with pleasantness, the in-between ones with a blend of pleasantness and intimidation, and the bad ones with intimidation alone, yet still with charity and patience.

They should not have the habit of rebuking students in the presence of others for every defect, or when they are angry, but at the proper time, such as during recreation, they should talk with them separately, recounting their defects to them and setting the final goal before them. And they should show them the way to benefit themselves, advising them in the end that if they see that the pupil is not benefiting, the prefects will be compelled to inform the superior so that the superior might take care of him.

When someone resists attempts to direct him, and particularly when there is a danger of others being harmed, the prefect should immediately discuss with the superior the way to help him: that is, the superior should get involved, first giving warnings and rebukes, and then penances and punishments. And if he judges that it is good to relocate him, he should be relocated.

The prefect should give the rector an account of his students at least once a week. If it is not possible to do that with him, then he should report to the recreation prefect; and if the recreation prefect does not provide a remedy for his students, the prefect should appeal to the rector.

The prefects should be informed about the associations of their students and should have someone to advise them about how the students are behaving in class. When the students go out of their dormitory all together, they should be provided with chaperones.

If anyone happens upon a good way to help his students, he should talk about it with the rector—for example, something like creating some kind of competition that of itself spurs students on to observe the rules.

During recreation, the prefect should strive to deal with them as well as he can, especially during winter evenings, with some pleasant and useful conversation.

He should stay with his students as much as he can, and keep them always in sight; he should take care that they not go wandering about the college, being sure not to do the same himself; and he should not easily allow them to leave their dormitory room during study time if they are not the trustworthy type or if it is certain that they would not have any need to do this.

When students go to another college, they should observe the same rules that the others do there, especially about entering the dormitory room of another person, about talking to those who should not be talking, and about repeatedly wasting time during study periods.

Chapter 6—On the Offices of the Receptionist, Infirmarians, and Chaperones

It is very necessary that the receptionist be diligent and alert, since the good of the college depends importantly upon him. And above all, he should be patient and devout, striving to edify all those who deal with him.

1. He should watch the hours, being careful to ring every hour on the hour, because it is basic to all the good order of the college.
2. He should leave the entrance as little as possible so as not to make anyone who rings the bell wait, and if he is too encumbered to summon someone, he should ask someone else to help him, at least during his busiest times.
3. When students are not in the house, he should take the things that have been brought to him, and he should try to return them without delay; while he is holding them, he should see that they are carefully kept so they are not lost.
4. He should notice those who are out of the college in the evening and inform the rector of this; and to those who are there without permission, he should not open the door without first telling the superior.
5. He should take notice of those who go out, seeing that it is with the superior's knowledge and that it is with the companion that usually accompanies them; and to those that return alone without the companion, he should not open the door without first informing the superior; and when those who accompany the individual return alone, he should send them to the superior, to account for why they are coming back alone.
6. He should take care of the things brought for the college, making sure they are delivered to the right person.
7. If someone carries something out of the college, he should try to know why it is that he is doing that and with what authority.

8. Above all, he should keep an eye on the staff when they leave the house, noticing if they are carrying anything out and if they have permission to do so.

9. He should not let anyone loiter at the door. He should see that the ones who are called down come right away; and he should try his best to hear what they are discussing; and when they are not ordinary and familiar persons, he should not call them without the superior's permission; and when something strikes him as wrong, he should tell the superior about it.

10. He should not call down to the entrance those who are dangerous, unless they have special permission, and he should especially keep an eye on them, noting with whom and about what they are speaking.

The infirmarian should be a person of great charity, patient and diligent in his duty.

1. He should be sure to attend the physician, carefully taking note of what he prescribes, and carrying out everything at the right time. And when he cannot carry out everything by himself, he should ask somebody else to help him, so that the sick do not suffer.

2. As soon as one feels ill, the infirmarian should inform the minister of health and take care of the person's daily life, putting him on a diet until the doctor visits him (should that be necessary); and when there is not the convenience of recovering outside the college, if he is lodged in a uncomfortable place, the infirmarian should see that he is put in a place which is comfortable for him and for those who have to interact with him.

3. He should see to it that the cook prepares food suitable for those who are sick and if necessary he should have something special for them, making sure that what is prepared for them is really tasty.

4. He should pay similar attention to the druggist, that he gives him good supplies. If they are running out, he should tell the superior.

5. When the sick get well, the infirmarian should see that they return to the responsibility of their prefects and that they pay both the doctor and the druggist.

6. He should see that they are not left alone, and if he himself cannot stay with them he should see that some other person is told to do this.

7. If someone is troublesome about letting himself be told what to do, the infirmarian should inform the superior of this.

8. If a dangerous or undisciplined student was removed from his dormitory room, the infirmarian should make sure that he goes back to it as soon as he begins to feel better.

Chaperones should be individuals that are spiritual and trustworthy and known well, and men of discretion, and every recreation group should include one of them.

1. He should avoid becoming too familiar with the young men, so that he can do his job more safely.
2. He can administer the students' money for that outing, spending it on their ordinary needs and keeping a good account of everything, not making extraordinary expenses without the permission of the superior.
3. He should pass through the dormitory rooms every day and, if someone needs something, he should take it to him in that very dormitory room.
4. He should learn everyone's houses, and when someone wants something from them, he should go there and carry a list of their needs; if there are things to talk over with the superior, he should do it.
5. When someone needs to go out, he should first inform the chaperone, who in turn will inform the superior, in order to get permission. If he has to go out with the student, the chaperone should not let him go where he does not have permission, being concerned to return soon to the college. Nor should he leave him anywhere if he does not have special permission to do that. And once back at the college, he should give the superior an account of what the other has done outside.
6. He should strive to keep good accounts of the money that he spends on the students; and he should give these accounts every time that they ask for it.

When he accompanies a couple of students, he should first see that they are all going by the same street, and he should have them take the one that is nearest when they stop in different places. And if it is too difficult to follow both at the same time, he should be careful to accompany one alone and go out with the other one another time.

Chapter 7—On the Causes for Expelling Students from the College and How to Do It

1. One should consider that tolerating undisciplined pupils in the college leads to all of the following troubles: (1) Their company spoils the other students, as the saying goes: *A single sick sheep ruins the whole flock.* (2) They hinder the peace and union of the college, which consists in spirit, in good orders, and in the union of hearts, because those students are enemies of devotion, cause every kind of disorder, and they are hostile to those who do not share their outlook and behavior. (3) They make work for the superiors who almost cannot do anything else because they need to hover continuously over them so that they do not ruin everything. (4) In addition to not reaching the final goal of the college in what is most important, they are in the college as a reluctant presence, and because they are not dealt with as they would like, they cultivate in their hearts a very strong hatred towards our members and towards virtue; and so when they leave, they remain inimical towards both virtue and us; and they tend to leave much worse than they

were when they entered there. (5) They give a bad name to the college, as it appears they have learned their bad manners there; and if the administrators do not do everything they can to expel them, I do not know how they can have a clear conscience after using some means of helping them.

2.   We have now to deal with those who need to be expelled and under what circumstances. Those who must be expelled are: (1) The ones who do not seem to be attaining the final goal of the college, such as those who are inept in their studies, so that they cannot occupy a place that others may have. (2) The ones such as the undisciplined ones, who are the sort that harms the others; these are the ones who are characterized by these two things: they are inclined towards what is bad, and they show little desire to be helped; you recognize them from the fact that (1) they are difficult to govern and satisfy, and (2) they grumble easily; (3) they dissatisfy our companions and the dormitory prefects; (4) they are enemies of devotion and of the good students; (5) they do not observe the rules, and they are hostile to those who want the rules to be followed; (6) they easily join the others who are behaving badly; (7) when they are keen on everything that concerns their own comfort, especially when they show themselves to be vain and sensual, and are eager to go out of the college often, and in the college itself they are aimless and idle. These and those like them should not in any way be tolerated in the college.

Also when there has occurred some public scandal, those who have caused it should be expelled; likewise those who are not willing to obey or do the penances imposed on them, and those who show that they are there against their will.

3.   This matter of expulsion could be handled this way: (1) When they enter the college, advise the students and those who are putting them there that just as they have the right to leave the college at any time after they have entered it, so every time that it is clear that they are not achieving in the college the result intended as a final goal, it will be in the school's power to dismiss them. And so they should promise to accept this in good faith, without showing any resistance; especially as every effort will be made to act honorably and to their satisfaction. (2) Advise them that they are admitted on probation for the first two months, so that they can be known; and in the event that they are found not suitable for the college, they will not be promoted. (3) They should be made aware, as experience has taught us, that those who are not suitable for the college not only are not suitable for it but they also soon become detrimental to themselves; and when someone is discovered to be this way, the sooner he is removed the better. (4) If someone is found to be unsuitable for the college, the rector with his consultors, who have the right of dismissal, will determine an appropriate course of action, and, concluding that the best course is expulsion, they should have

his relatives informed, explaining the reasons for it, as it is a matter of the order of the college, having regard for the common good, and as the administrators have made this judgment. And if this could be done without the young man knowing that he had been expelled, it would be better, excusing him as much as possible in their presence and advising them that it would be good that he take up another path, one for which he is better suited. And when it is not possible to dismiss him right away, a time should be picked, after one or two months, but so that this is done in a way in which the young man does not know that he has to leave, and he should be kept following the same routine. When it is realized that in some respect there would likely be harm to others and it would not be suitable to keep him, he must by all means be let go. But there should be an attempt to anticipate the time well in advance so that things do not come to such extremes that it would not be possible at least to inform his relatives, if they are outside Rome; or one should try to wait a little so that he can be set up in some other place or with some other party. (5) One should make the best effort possible to send him off with as much of a feeling of satisfaction as one can. The same should be done with all the others who will leave the college.

Accepting Students

Only the rector along with his consultors should admit students: (1) in order better to observe the rule already made about this point, because without it, he will be able to be corrected by the other superiors; (2) because as the one assigned to govern them, he also has to be fully aware of what kind of person he is taking in; (3) so that he can dismiss them without trouble, knowing the manner and the conditions on which he has accepted them; (4) to remove the complaints of those who say that some are not accepted except as a favor; (5) so that they are not accepted if they are not individuals who are suitable for such an institute; (6) so that those who are rejected are not so resentful as they would have been by a rejection from other superiors, who represent the Society more to the extent that they are greater; (7) so that other superiors do not have occasion to treat this as a temporal matter, doing a service for and gratifying this or that other prelate, while giving the rector all the charge of governing them even if the young men are ill-disciplined—just so that they might do a favor for someone; (8) so that they understand that this is a work of importance and that one must not be accepted without conforming to the orders and rules of the college; (9) to follow the usual approach that the superiors make the laws, but the execution of them is left to the other ministers because they, not being held to this, will easily go against them on every little occasion; and they have to be strict with those who break them; (10) because seeing clearly many disorders arise by failing in this respect, the superior has to consider that his authority is given only for edification, and woe to those who do the opposite.

Fourth Book

Chapter 1—How to Advance in the Spirit

The kind of spirit that one has to foster so that the students of the German College make progress consists in three things: (1) in devotion, which means *revering and loving God*; (2) in virtue, which consists in loving and taking the path of doing good deeds, and in hating and avoiding evil ones; (3) in defeating one's own passions and evil inclinations, restraining them through the rule of reason that comes from the Holy Spirit.

The means will be:

1. Walking with students on the path of prayer and examining their own conscience in such a way that they get the habit of doing it on their own; (2) each one's capacity, whether in mental or vocal prayer; and some assigned individuals should attend to giving them the way to do this.
2. Frequenting the sacraments, provided that it is in a proper way, that is, taking care that they understand (1) the importance of the sacraments; (2) the desired disposition before and after, in order to draw spiritual fruit from them; (3) the mounting results that come with frequenting the sacraments with the proper disposition.
3. Hearing the word of God, and knowing how to draw fruit from it; they can do this if they are disposed to do whatever they understand as their duty and what fits their status; second, when they go to hear the word of God with devotion and the desire to understand God's will and their own path towards salvation; then they will listen attentively to the word of God, taking care to stir their own feelings towards the good things that they are hearing; third, when, after hearing, they repeat it to themselves or with the others, noting chiefly what applies to them to put into practice, and that which has especially moved their feelings, keeping it in mind to remember it on occasion. They will be able to hear the sermons when they are given in our church, but in a way that does not bore them. It will be more helpful to give them some particular exhortations that can be given by some of our companions at the same college, treating of matters that particularly affect them; and they can be given at least every couple of weeks by the recreation prefects or those the superior tells to do so. This can be done on occasion publicly to everyone, by some leading father or by the superiors themselves.
4. Good associations with virtuous and devout people, along with good discussions; the dormitory prefects should give special attention to this, and they should take care to set up the discussions during recreation time, especially on winter nights, in such a way that students might draw fruit from them and be encouraged to make progress on the path of the spirit.

5. Making students understand the path of virtue and that they enjoy spending their time well and engaging frequently in virtuous actions. And above all, they should be mindful of obedience and they should be enemies of idleness, never fearing in anything the hard work involved in acquiring and making a habit of virtue.

6. Students should seek to be aware of their own defects, desiring their correction and employing the proper means to get rid of them.

7. Observing rules, since those rules have been made for obedience and are aimed at their final goal, leads to virtuous and praiseworthy works, and so they amplify grace and they promote progress on the path of the spirit.

8. Some emulation of virtue and some common exercises for those who wish to make a profession of it in a special way, namely the congregations, which help one to use well and fruitfully all the above-mentioned means.[16] I do not think it can be said how helpful and necessary these are if experience itself does not reveal that to us.

9. The superior should hold those who are virtuous in high esteem, showing them favor in every way possible and showing himself to be an arch-enemy of those who are bad.

10. Assigning someone to take special care of helping and setting on the spiritual path those who desire this; and they might be the same as those who take care of the congregations; the spiritual prefect next, and the confessor, together with the rector should make every effort that attention is given to the spirit, and they should work out what could be done to rouse the students to it, especially during solemnities that occur, by removing the obstacles that could arise, and by no means allowing into the college those who hinder good conversations in their example and company or who show themselves adverse to devotions and try to alienate others from them.

In particular, help could be given to some through the Spiritual Exercises, with general confessions and the like.

Above all, good administration and the good order of the college will be aided by a practical superior who is eager to achieve such order.

During solemn holy days, especially those of our Lord and the Virgin Mary, nice decorations could be prepared, prayers and poems recited, beautiful vespers sung, and some particular communions arranged. Arrange twice for a forty-hour devotion, or at least have one of twenty-four, during Christmas at the crib, and in Lent at the tomb, taking care to have these done as nicely and devoutly as possible.

There should be a particular attempt to seek to set the newly arrived students on the road towards devotion, because they are usually well disposed, the

---

16 Congregations are what are frequently known as sodalities.

larger part of them arriving with such a spirit; and they tend to be more compliant, readily accepting the first directive pressures applied to them.

It is good that the spiritual prefect understand how he has to treat and help the beginners, and how he should do this with those who are progressing, and how with those who are more advanced in their spirituality. With regard to allowing them the penances they ask for, one should rather be reluctant than easygoing; and, in allowing them to the students, the times should be kept in view, such as vigils of certain solemn holy days, and so should the circumstances, the persons, and the goal that they are able to expect from it.

Chapter 2—How to Have the Rules Observed

Three things are required for the proper observance of the rules: (1) the superior and the other administrators, who should be diligent and eager for the good of the college, which depends on the right observance of the rules; (2) the students' will, whether spontaneous, as with the good ones, or forced as with the bad; (3) the way of observing the rules: first gently, as befits the good students, and then there is the harsh approach, which is necessary for the bad ones.

As for the first, the superior, having the attitude and the makings sought for in a superior, has to be sure to have extensive practical knowledge of the rules, so that he immediately spots infractions, even minor ones that are committed against them. Also [he should know] the means he has to employ for their proper observance, along with a zeal and concern that surpasses the average.

As for the second, the will of students has to be moved, especially that of the good students: (1) to know that this is their duty; (2) to understand the fruits they can get from this; (3) and that they are pleasing those they are obliged to work hard to gratify, such as their parents and superiors who are working hard for their good; (4) and to know the goal to which they lead; (5) and to know the evils they are avoiding both in themselves and in others, as well as the goods attained that they acquire this way. The will of the bad ones has to be moved with the fear of not getting a penance, which consists in (1) losing the favor of those who are able to do good or bad things for them; (2) losing honor, becoming disreputable in the college and outside it; (3) being caught and punished.

As for the third, the means can be: (1) good directives for the college, for observing one rule often helps the good observance of another one; (2) that, after the superior, the other ministers and dormitory prefects are diligent and concerned to have the rules observed, by being present during their activities as much as possible.

(3) They should see that the other students know the rules by heart. But it will be good to have them read publicly every month, and every week the brothers should read in their rooms a section from them, clarifying them by noticing the good that arises from their observance and the evils that occur when they are

not observed. And they should inform the students generally about infractions, exhorting them to correction, demonstrating their intention to be virtuous. In particular, they should then advise each one of his shortcomings, pleading that he should be willing to correct them because otherwise they will be obliged to inform the superior and will do so shortly.

(4) The superior, once informed about some infractions of the rules, when they appear to involve the harm of others, either because those others will be exposed to bad example or scandalized, they should not fail first to expose them properly and second, to remove, in a suitable way, the bad effects that would arise from them. When it rebounds only to the harm of that particular person and he seems to be getting worse, one should proceed sensitively: after being warned in a kindly way by the dormitory prefect, he should then be warned by the superior as well, the second time harshly, and the third time with strong punishments and penances. When someone is going well enough and there is a single occurrence, when it is not clear or there are doubts about a change or a worsening, it is appropriate to look the other way about this matter, but noting his development and removing the opportunity so that he does not get upset and take a disliking to the college, the rules, and the superiors.

(5) Above all, one had better remove any opportunity for the dissolution and non-observance of the rules; and one should block every meeting and private association that they might be able to have among themselves, because ordinarily if they are not quite good, they tend to end up thinking very little of the rules in order to have more freedom to do what suits them.

(6) The superior should go to the dormitory rooms once a week or more, as is convenient, in order to take note of how the students are doing in observing the rules, and he should especially go into those rooms that demonstrate a greater need because of the type of individuals who are there, sometimes with warnings and admonitions, sometimes with rebukes and criticism, sometime with punishments and penances. Sometimes he should generally ask about how the rules are being observed; and then he should ask each individual in particular, in order that he might understand their behaviors. And if this can be done, he will be very thoroughly informed about everything. Other times he might leave it to the dormitory prefects to report on the disorders that arise in their own dormitory rooms.

(7) To interject a spirit of competition, prizes could be given to those who demonstrate greater observance, either privately in each dormitory room or publicly, as judged suitable, or at the time that the others are doing penance for their failures in observance.

(8) During superiors' visitations to the college, if someone is found deficient in following the rules, that person should never be left without punishment, rebuke, admonition, or at least the arrest of that behavior.

(9) Exhortations, public or private (that is, addressed to the recreation groups), should be made and used to persuade students to observe the rules.

In giving them the usual recreation periods at the proper times to reward and relieve their labor, one should see that as far as possible everything is done lightheartedly, everything depending on the superiors' affection, artfulness, prudence, and good manner of proceeding.

If the college were coming apart and needed to be pulled back together with a bit of force, one could resort to the following:

1. Being diligent about giving penances and punishments to those who fall short, especially those who have some standing with the others and are leaders among them; one should get progressively stricter with those who do not correct their ways.
2. Expelling students from the college, or imposing penances or restricting the students in such a way that they have to leave it.
3. Being strict about silence, greatly limiting speaking among them, and being diligent to see that this is observed.
4. Having some dormitory prefects who know how to be strict, and lodging them with the most terrible of the students, and being continually in supervision over them, appraising every little thing.
5. Summoning all of the students of a recreation group before the rector once or more a week, as if before a judge, examining and criticizing each one's defects, and rebuking these defects in the presence of the others. Even should this be routine, one could just give them warnings the first time, and exhort them to want to keep the rules; the second time, one could complain and tell them how they are falling short overall; the third time, one could get into the particulars, and give them the penances and punishments that they deserve, especially those who have been warned and have not corrected their ways.
6. The diligent observation of the catalog, and having it reviewed at the proper time by the person assigned for this.[17]

Yet one should hope that the college never has to come to such extremes that it should have need of such rigor, especially when it has been kept purged of undisciplined students. And one should hope that the superiors along with the other ministers will be doing their duty to maintain the college in its due observance of the rules, because these measures have a violent aspect, and they should not be continued for very long, but only until order is established and the students begin to live in discipline and reverence.

It should be noted that the catalog is a particular way to have the rules kept, and to know who is falling short in them; and it is an excellent way, but it does

---

17 This catalog was a kind of class register where notes were taken about students' behavior.

not fit everyone in the same manner: (1) With children, it can be used just as it is. (2) With undisciplined students, it can be done this way, so that the censors are some who are good and ordinary, sometimes one and sometimes the other; and the prefect himself should remain aware of what they are doing; and in his absence, a censor should be assigned; and at the end of the week, he should give prizes to one of the poorly disciplined students who has behaved best, giving him the hope that behaving well will get him a place among the good; he should give penances to those who fall short, according to his best judgment. (3) With the good ones, they should pick other censors by having an election by lot; the ones that they have should "pay" something like paper, images, pens. At the end of the week or the month, he should distribute them to those who have behaved the best. And above all, he will note carefully those who resist and are not being helped by the notations of the catalog and likewise of the censor. And when it occurs that some censor is unjust, one should make a pointed display of this as an example for the others.

Rules should be divided into four types, that is, into the rules for devotion, for obedience, for manners, and for studies. Here there have been listed the ways to have the rules observed insofar as they depend upon obedience, because the others have their own particular ways and their own particular circumstances.

Chapter 3—How to Advance in Modesty and Manners

Good manners consist of exterior actions exhibited in our associations through behaviors designed not to offend others, but rather to please and delight them. They are of three kinds. Some properly consist in modesty, which is behaving modestly and calmly. Others are properly political manners, like certain shows of external gallantry that courtiers tend to perform. Others are called Christian manners, like virtuous actions that consist in being patient, obedient, and the like; through these we rule our own passions. The first are necessary for the preservation of modesty, which has to be acquired among the youth, like a rein on their passions. The second are necessary as an enhancement of modesty. The last are necessary to acquire the habit of virtue. And these, together with the first, have to be acquired so the students progress in them, as the principal goal of the college. When the others can be learned, it would be good, but it does not matter too much, as they look more like the manners of courtiers than of religious, and they have to be learned at court and not among members of religious orders.

All manners consist either in the movements of the body or in conversation and the manner of speaking, or the manner of associating and dealing with different kinds of people, accommodating oneself to each, according to the relative stations between the parties, accommodating oneself to the place and the time involved, and in line with the custom of the country.

These three types of manners go by degrees, and they are acquired in succession. So one ought to see that first of all there is modesty in the college, which tends to be foreign to children and to some lively and restless natures. And it has to be acquired: (1) with the fear and the good discipline of the college, punishing those who fall short in modesty, being watchful during the time when they get together with the others, as in recreation, outings, classes, reviews, and the like; (2) with watchfulness of those who have them under their care, being sure that they are made to dress modestly.

Those who are already well grounded in modesty might be able to be taught good manners, according to what is necessary to each one's station. The manner is: (1) Note each one's bad manners and bring this to their attention; these tend to be found in some by nature, in others through bad upbringing, in others through carelessness. (2) Make a collection of some good manners and propose that they observe them. (3) Tell some who are better-mannered to teach the others or at least to make friendly comments when they fall short this way. (4) To be able to set up some competition among the students, by giving prizes to the best-mannered; and to give penances to those who fall short more than the rest, with a recounting of their bad manners. (5) The diligent and good care of the prefect of discipline, noticing carefully who falls short when he reviews the rooms; advising and teaching them and seeing that they know their deficiencies thoroughly, and seeing that some progress is made in this area in the college.

As for the third kind, it will be especially helpful for the acquisition of good manners (1) to attend to the spirit because there is nothing that governs our passions more, and better makes us virtuous than the spirit of God when he lives within us; (2) to rebuke and advise those who fall short and do things that are not seemly; (3) to give penances to those who go too far, such as those who fight with the others and act pridefully, and the like; (4) by having them understand the value and worth of virtue, and the damage and shame that vice carries with it; (5) to give help to particular individuals, and to stand above those who are known to be naturally inclined to some bad passions and vice, giving them remedies for this while watching over how they apply them.

Concerning manners we want at meals: the mistakes that are occurring could be noted, along with the proper behavior that should be followed, and this could be brought up with them in the dormitory rooms. These instructions are especially necessary for children.

Chapter 4—On How to Advance in Studies

Eight things contribute to academic progress:

1. Possessing real talent, which consists in good powers of comprehension, good reasoning, good judgment, and a good memory for retaining what is learned.

2. Being studious, which is usually a gift of nature, when the individual, on account of the pleasure he feels in studies and the eagerness he has to know, applies himself in such a way to his studies that he cannot be torn from them. Sometimes it happens with others, or in search of another goal, or through some fear or human respect, or the individual applies himself to studies, not knowing what else to do.
3. Good teachers, who should be (1) competent; (2) able to teach and explain themselves; (3) able to lead students in a way that goes forward, that is, in the exercises that he has them do.
4. Good exercises, that is, compositions, translations, reviews, tests and examinations, those exercises that train memory and debate.
5. Having the time for studying, that is, arranging one's time and setting aside other specific hours to work on the regular course of studies.
6. Studying in an orderly and methodical way, applied to studying what is useful and in line with the intention behind these requirements.
7. Emulation, that is, considering it a loss and a shame to see one's companions progressing in studies while one stays behind.
8. Incentives, that is, awards for the studious ones and penances and punishments for those who are negligent.

So there will be progress in studies when we take care to provide the eight things just mentioned. Those who are found to have little talent, those who are by nature negligent in studies, and those for whom no means of advancement are effective, should be dismissed from the college. If they remain there against the institute itself, we have to worry about the college: this removes a place from someone else, and often such individuals are the cause of disorders and limited progress among the others.

The means to be used on behalf of the college are:

1. Assigning each of the students to the proper class, so that he is able to progress.
2. Scheduling everyone's time so well that there is something to do in every hour, seeing that at a given time they are busy with what has been assigned them. And in addition to the dormitory prefects, there should be others assigned to oversee the students in everything that the prefects of studies and review will do.
3. Seeing that there are good review masters, who, beyond the reviews, might also be able to give private help and assistance in their studies. Concerning the reviews, they should follow an approach such that the student can profit in relation to what they have been told to do, taking care to follow the teachers. They should make sure that students are attentive and modest.
4. Seeing that students engage at the proper time in the usual disputations, readings, and speeches, according to their abilities. Those who complete the course should take part in some public acts; those who are competent should graduate.

5. Giving great care to their compositions (beyond their other usual exercises) in the humanistic classes, and having them frequently compose for the awards. And these compositions, both in poetry and in prose, should be posted publicly.

6. Making much of having them exercise their memory in everything; for the students of philosophy, by having them learn well the terms, definitions, divisions, conclusions, and various opinions of many on their faculty, arranging for them some public acts on these, with the award of prizes for those who perform the best; the others should be made to learn their readings, and they should be well quizzed on them; and in a few days, the same should be done with the winners.

7. Cultivating the academy and its rules, according to what has been instituted; they should see to it that the students go to it eagerly.

One should be particularly watchful that in the classes the students are attentive and modest, that they pay good attention to the teachers, with punishments for those who fall short.

At the recommencement of studies, one should make sure to give solid instructions, paying close attention to constituting classes according to everyone's level of ability. Yet changing classes calls for some careful considerations, especially when they are moving on to the next course, since not everyone is suitable: (1) the will of the student's relatives; (2) the young man's inclination; (3) his age; (4) avoiding harm done against the others; (5) the goal at which he is aiming with his studies; (6) how long he is thinking about staying in the college; (7) his benefit.

During vacations, one should know how to keep the students busy so they do not waste all that time; sometimes there should be some competitive exercises, as in the academy.

Be sure that those who attend rhetoric (or have in the past) get exercise in composing speeches, and they should recite them on solemn holy days or in a contest. The same goes for poetry.

Chapter 5—How to Keep the College Healthy

Concerning health, generally all these things need to be taken into account: (1) students should live in good rooms; (2) they should eat good food; (3) they should be kept out of the night air; (4) studies and other hard work should be tempered by their recreations; (5) in the exercises that they do, they should not be too forceful, and they should be kept from getting overheated or getting too chilly.

One should be particularly careful about the change of seasons, such as spring and fall; and care should be taken about the changing of clothes. In summer, when there is great heat, one should see that they are relieved of their usual hard academic work, taking them up in a more moderate way. Likewise, care should be taken in the changes in diet, as at the beginning and end of Lent. In the time of Lent, there should be great discretion in seeing which ones can do it and fast, and which are not able to do this, consulting the physician and being aware of each one's age, constitution, and disposition.

In particular, there should be special care for those who are characterized by a weak constitution, or who are naturally inclined to suffer some indisposition, even while one's attention should be given to not admitting into the college individuals sickly by nature.

One should be diligent and solicitous as soon as a student feels sick, have him well cared for and require the physician to be called in. The student should be provided with everything that is necessary, and he should inform his family as soon as possible. When the disease is serious or likely to last a long while, students should be sent back to their homes.

During dangerous seasons and whenever sickness tends to break out, special care should be taken.

During recovery, good care should likewise be maintained, not only with regard to food, but also with regard to exercise.

One should watch over those who might pretend to be ill in order to get out of classes, or to sleep a little more, healing them by means of *panatella* and *acquacotta*.[18]

In the same way, we should be watchful of the students' manners when they are sick and stay alone at home, so that nothing might happen that makes them lose what they have previously acquired. So one should watch over them.

When spring has arrived, about May, one should select those who need to be purged because of scabies or any other disease, or because this is their regular practice.

Chapter 6—How to Maintain Purity and Chastity in the College

Taking care of honor is very necessary, especially here in Italy, where such a misery reigns […], great disorder can arise in this area. So we have to be very watchful:

1. We need superiors to be very suspicious in this matter; and it is better for them to err in being too suspicious rather than in the opposite.
2. Special attention should be paid to those who seem inclined this way or who are in danger of it. In order to know individuals like this: (1) the information acquired at the beginning, when they enter the college, is useful; (2) by their actions and manner, which sometimes tend to be wanton and annoying, and they tend to wander around the college; (3) by the company they very soon tend to keep […]; (4) when they are too sensual and idle; (5) when they are enemies of the spirit and virtue.

---

18 Two dishes of the Italian traditional peasant cuisine that were commonly used for a sick person's diet.

When such a person appears, we should take care of the following: (1) keep him in great fear; usually this kind of individual is very shy; and when they lack this fear and have some anger, they usually tend to be incorrigible, and we should not put up with them in the college; (2) supervise their company, both in the college and outside it, and restrict it in the college so that they are able to talk and associate only with some select individuals who are safe; (3) be watchful of them when they have the opportunity to remain alone in the house; (4) they should only with difficulty get permission to go outside the college or to their houses, or to do other business in Rome; (5) point out to them all their least defects to divert them from getting into greater ones; and in particular they should be warned about every small action or sign that they address to others, and about getting too familiar with everyone, which they tend to do; and above all keep them from looking at and observing this or that person, seeing that they observe modesty more than the others; (6) see that they are set on the path of the spirit by showing them the miseries and losses that this miserable flesh produces, exhorting them to be quicker to subdue and punish it than to seek out ways to delight and take pleasure in it.

In general, it helps that (1) we remove every opportunity, seeing that they cannot get together with the others except in public places; (2) we are very watchful over their affections, seeing that they are impeded; (3) those who are dangerous in this way are kept in separate rooms and recreation groups; and we should watch that they do not leave college at the same time so that they can join up with each other; (4) there is good care in those times when they can fall into some dissolution, as during Christmas and Carnival, not ever mixing the dangerous ones with the others; but they should take care to stand near their prefects in such a time. Likewise, in the summer, and when in such a time they are accustomed to go for recreation at some vineyard, they should not unwind too much and this should happen with good order and under good supervision; (5) they should be kept busy, and we should take care that they do not go wandering about the college during the time for studies; (6) we should see that they are led on the path of the spirit; (7) when the least act of such behavior is noticed, they should be punished and dismissed from the college, especially when after some time and some attempts they do not correct their behavior or do not take the path of virtue.

One should never be trusting with these but keep them reticent, especially those who keep pressing to be together; and one needs to be astute to recognize the affections, the meaning of looks, associations, opinions, and acts.

Chapter 7—How to Keep the College Happy

On the basis of many good considerations, it is very necessary to make sure that the college is kept happy. Among other reasons, this is so that the students might be able to endure the hard work through the enjoyment they get from recreation. But knowing how to give recreations while avoiding damage and still profiting the young is very important, and the famous saying can be cited: "The one who has mixed the useful with the delightful has won every point."[19]

The way to keep the college happy:

1. The first is the manner of proceeding adopted by the superiors who act with loving kindness and in such a way that the students are well satisfied with it, especially the virtuous students, whom you can get to do everything through love.

2. When the college is doing well and no strictness and austerity are constraining it. And this can be done when the students are virtuous young men and the superiors are astute in their governance.

3. When the college is kept in good repute, both because it seems to improve day by day and to grow every day in greater esteem and because some worthy things are being done there.

4. When students have their needs and they are given their favors by their superiors, especially when they are just and honorable and they behave well towards them.

5. When students have some honorable recreations, which are of four kinds:

   1. Everyday recreations: which can be done this way to please them: (1) When they all assemble in the courtyard, we should see that each one is kept to his humor;[20] so that those who are of the same humor will be able to have good associations as similars with whom they can discuss virtuous matters; and three or four can be assigned or one whole dormitory room in the same association. To the others that are a little more restless in their minds, there can be granted certain kinds of honorable amusements, which do not involve much exercise; watching out for three things: quarreling; second, acting too immodestly and letting themselves go too much, or taking the game too seriously; because it is better that students such as these be allowed to enjoy their similar interests than that they be left in a melancholy state, disgruntled with the college, and it is better than letting them hurt one another in their associations as tends to happen since the dangerous and undisciplined ones tend to work all their mischief and intrigues during recreation time. (2) When they gather in their dormitory rooms during winter nights, each room separately: and the way to keep them there will be to discuss different things every evening, such as spiritual matters on Sunday and Saturday evenings, or recounting everything that occurs to them, or proposing something and having each one say what he thinks about

---

19 Horace, *Ars poetica*, l. 343.

20 "According to one's humor." Humor stands for "temperament." Cortesono adopts a Galenic point of view, according to which the individuals' characters correspond to their specific cognitive talents.

it or something that he has read or heard from the reading at table or the sermon. On Mondays, something from their studies, whether it be a story or fable, or a satire or something from doctrine; this way, the others in the group might be able to learn something. On Tuesdays, some should propose some problems or questions about a matter that has been taught, and the others should answer them. On Wednesdays, they should take up the rules, reciting them, clarifying them, and listing the ways that they are broken, or the ways in which they can be broken, and the usefulness that arises from observing them. On Thursdays, they should be at liberty for each one to talk about what he would most like to, or to play some amusing game of the sort that tends to be played on some proposed subject, with penalties for those who make mistakes, making them do some good thing. On Fridays, there should be discussion of virtue and some of their effects and properties, and of the evils that arise from the vices and the remedies to get free of them. All these materials will be treated according to their abilities; and the prefect will be able to have them proposed, with each one speaking his opinion, or one of the same young men whose turn it is.

2.   There are the regular recreations of the week: these should be devoted to getting exercise rather than to anything else. Therefore, they could go outside at the designated time to walk with all their roommates, and after a solid exercise, return to the college. When that same recreation is done in the college, they will be able to play ball and other games for exercise. When they want to go out to play somewhere, they should not do this without special permission. In such a case, more rooms could be sent with a person of standing going along in addition to the ordinary prefects of the dormitories, such as the recreation prefect. In the summer, when it happens that they go to some vineyard to eat, we should see that there is good order there. In this matter, when it is possible to have our own vineyard it would be much to the purpose and many other disadvantages would be avoided; there would be much recreation there. Concerning this, rules could be drawn up according to what experience teaches. One recreation group should go there at a time, so that it might have the convenience of playing different games.

3.   There are extraordinary recreations, such as the Feast of the King during Epiphany and the Carnival, comic stage productions, or public award ceremonies, large groups going together to the seven [stational] churches during vacation time, partly for devotion, partly for recreation, in the way that all of this will be described in detail.

One should see that in the college there is musical practice, both vocal and instrumental, in keeping with the students who enjoy it. Those who know some of the rudiments of music might make some progress in it by following those others, but a master should not be called in to teach them, except for the director of vocal music. This individual could be kept on staff in the college.

Concerning the above-mentioned feasts, there should be care taken to have something of what is great, pleasant, and virtuous; and we should be sure that the students do not let themselves go too much during the feast and take the opportunity for any mischief. This will be done through the good orders that will be given about this and through the prudence and diligence of the rector in such cases.

Chapter 8—How to Maintain the College and Bring It to Its Full Form

Many things are required to maintain such a work, because even if the things of this world are necessarily subject to change, administrations in particular tend to be more needy than otherwise, especially this one, by being subjected to so much turnover among students and administrators too; so there is a need to give good attention to its conservation: (1) The rector and the minister should stay steadily in office as long as possible, especially when they understand how to govern in this situation. (2) One should pay attention to the observance of the good old orders, not lightly changing them to try out other new ones at the opinion of this or that person—this is the downfall of governance. (3) Attention should be paid to accepting students who are in keeping with the institute of the college and to what is being sought there. (4) Those who do not achieve according to expectations and goals and who are not making progress in it, chiefly in Christian living, should not be kept in the college. (5) There should be no lack of ministers who are necessary and adequate and apt for the aim intended, especially the dormitory prefects. (6) The diligence and concern of these ministers.

As for the full realization of this college, first, concerning what is temporal: it should own a house and a vineyard for recreation.

As for the studies, the college should first foster the sciences, by making sure it is one of the main houses of wisdom and studies of Christendom in philosophy and theology, by having public acts performed, and by graduating in due time those who have merited it, taking care to have the degrees distinguished by some particular privileges from His Holiness.

As for the spirit, the college will reach its full form whenever the administrators consider it to be the principal institute, and so they will mainly attend to observing the means that lead to it, while keeping away from the things that impede it. And they will show themselves to be friends of the virtuous and enemies of the unhappy, not paying any attention in this to rank, nor to talent, friendship, or any other interest or human concern.

Since performing favors and acting for one's friends make it hard to maintain the rigor that one should have in admitting students, it is good to have a place set apart, such as for the Germans, and to assign someone as a temporal

minister for them, as we have done from the beginning. Or rather make him a
member of the boarders of the seminary who are maintained on seminary assistance; and when some good subject succeeds, he could be placed among these in
the German College.

To get around a disorder that spoils almost the entire effect (and it would
lead to many pursuing philosophy studies)—the disorder is this: that the students, in aiming to take a course in legal study—it happens that, going to Italian public schools, they lose all that they have gained in college; for this reason,
I would like to prescribe that those who have finished the philosophy course
in college and have made progress in virtue and are quite solid and firm in
it, I would order that they lodge together in an apartment of the college, and
there have a lecturer of the law come from outside for the first two years at
their expense. For the others that follow, send them to public study all together
with one of ours in their company, when it is not possible to have an adequate
reader come or stay in the college. In this, we should strictly allow no one else
than those mentioned above; here it would be at the discretion of the rector
and of the other appropriate administrators, in judging which could remain
and which could not, so that everyone would be in a position to achieve a
good outcome.

It is very important to take care at the beginning to determine those who are
not suitable for the college, and to put them rather in the separate place mentioned above; because in wanting to put up with the undisciplined with the idea
of helping them, they give rise to disorder and do harm to the others; and since
afterward they leave to their own and to their parents' dissatisfaction, and as
enemies of the college and the Society. The main remedy for this is to be careful
about accepting them and to be ready to dismiss them quickly.

Finally, to satisfy many nobles who gather there, there could be established
a separate table where they would have the same size of serving but of somewhat better quality; for example, the appetizers might be a bit elegant and they
might get more tender veal roasted when the others have it boiled; when it
comes roasted, in the later dish there should be the same consideration as with
the appetizer, but additionally they would contribute more to the expenses
than the others do. (2) Because it is good that they have some services done for
them and that they have their own servants, there is some difficulty, because it
would be good that the college maintain the servants and that they contribute
to the expenses, and that there be services in certain ordinary things, such as
in making up the bed and sweeping the room, in carrying water to the room,
breakfast, and so forth. If it can be brought about that every dormitory room
has its own servant it would be very good and some poor people could be
maintained in such a situation and given an education, and among the others
there would be some who might have a mind to enter the Society but not the
wherewithal for college.

To strengthen the college, it would be good to have such a system of governance approved by His Holiness.[21] And there should be a strong prohibition against those who might want to violate the given statutes and constitutions to favor their personal interests. Especially important in particular is the acceptance of capable individuals into the college and the dismissal of those who are found incapable; and in addition, granting some privileges to those who finish their studies to the satisfaction and edification of everyone.

Concerning those who wish to enter the Society, it is good for the conservation of the college to persuade no one but to let them be called by God. And those who are called should be tested first on their constancy: have them finish their studies and then with the consent of their family accept them. If the family members do not give their permission and the individuals are known to be good subjects who would be solid in their vocation, see that when they leave the college they state their intention to their families, since their permission is not being given, to join the Capuchins or the Carthusians, and then one day they should go off suddenly to other provinces to enter there. Those provinces should be given the work of seeing that they are admitted. This should be done so that rumor does not spread in that locality where the college is and where the person is known.

Concerning nobles: (1) If they have been badly brought up, in no way should they be accepted. (2) They should be treated politely in such a way that they still have a respectful fear, in an appropriate way. And this respectful fear is very important, the kind that they have of their parents on the outside. (3) We should be careful of their associations, to see that they are not with people who are not safe. And this should be arranged by them at the beginning. In this matter, do not trust anyone, because it is very easy for them to be spoiled, because if there is a desire to restrict them later, they show scorn, and because there is a crowd of individuals who want to take up their friendship. The sorry ones join together for this sooner than the others, to have that support and to have the nobles as companions in mischief when they make them fall.

Be as careful as possible to treat everyone in an ordinary manner so that some do not begin to have ill-will towards others.

At the end of the year, during vacations, on recommencement day, one should make a diligent investigation about those who have made progress neither in spirituality, nor in studies, nor in manners, and by no means should these individuals stay for another year; they should be given their dismissal.

If one has to keep some students alone, this should not happen if they are not very safe individuals, and they should be devout and studious, and well tested in college; and there should be someone who has charge of visiting them often; and those who are found to be rule-breakers should be put under the charge of the dormitory prefect.

---

21 New constitutions were approved by Pope Gregory XIII (r.1572–85) in the bull *Ex Collegio Germanico* (1584).

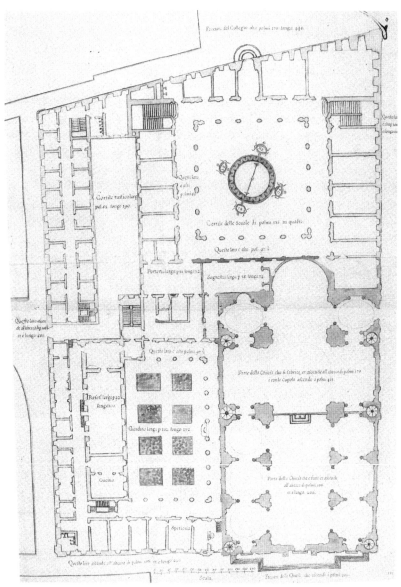

FIGURE 6   This plan of the Roman College shows the destinations of the
rooms and spaces within the building. Starting from the front (in
clockwise order): the school with the classrooms and the yard;
the church; a garden with the grocery, the kitchen, the refectory;
rooms and a kitchen garden.

Anonymous, *General Plan of the Collegio Romano,* Pen and ink and
wash, 65 × 90 cm., second half of the seventeenth century.

CHAPTER 14

Studies and Morals at the Roman College (1564)

Diego de Ledesma

Diego de Ledesma (c.1524–75), a man gifted with an organizational mind, was appointed prefect of studies at the Roman College in 1562. When Superior General Diego Laínez (1512–65) charged him with reforming the curriculum there, Ledesma organized a series of meetings with the professors; these discussions were recorded and officially transcribed. He also asked some of the most prominent instructors to submit their advice about the teaching of their own particular subjects. From this meticulous undertaking, we possess in the Monumenta paedagogica *several documents that offer a very faithful picture of what and, most interestingly, how the early Jesuits taught. In 1564–65, Ledesma summarized the results of his consultations in* De ratione et ordine studiorum Collegii Romani *(see Chapter 15).*

Using some progress reports, Ledesma prepared this review for Laínez in 1564, giving special attention to the issues of studies and morals in the college. He thought that too much professorial laxity had led to a loss of modesty, spirit, and humility, critically impeding the work. His evaluation almost surely refers to his conflict with Benet Perera (1535–1610), a professor of philosophy whose teaching seemed to him to deviate from orthodoxy and jeopardize the entire Society of Jesus. At issue were the boundaries of academic freedom and interactions among the college personnel.

Diego de Ledesma (born c.1524, Cuéllar in the province of Segovia, Spain— entered the Society on September 30, 1556, Leuven, the Spanish Netherlands—died November 18, 1575, Rome). Ledesma was a professor of theology in the Roman College and prefect of studies there from 1562. His work, De ratione et ordine studiorum Collegii Romani *[On the plan and order of studies at the Roman College] has been called "perhaps the most substantial contribution to the development of the Jesuit code of education."[1] In 1569, it was issued by Superior General Francisco de Borja (in office 1565–72). Known as the "Ratio Borgiana," it was the first universal plan of studies in the Society. It remained in effect until the 1591 Ratio was issued for trial use.*

Source: *Monumenta paedagogica*, nova editio, 2:481–90 (original: Latin)

Rome, 1564

Very Reverend Father in Christ,

I will report here what I feel about morals and literary studies at this Roman College of ours; but I will not speak of those things that please me, which are certainly numerous and substantial; I will only speak of some things through

---

1 Allan P. Farrell, *The Jesuit Code of Liberal Education: Development and Scope of the* Ratio studiorum (Milwaukee: Bruce Publishing Company, 1938), 169.

which some studies can, in my opinion, be furthered in some respect, and of some things through which some greater progress can be made in morals; and I will simply express them without attaching my reasons for what I have said.

In Morals

1. The mortification of the teachers [should be] greater, and [likewise] their subjection to superiors and rules.
2. [There should be] greater union, simplicity, sincerity, greater charity of the teachers among themselves, so that they may mutually feel positively and speak well of one another.
3. No privilege should be granted to the teachers [as a group] or to any one of them in food, drink, dress, room, work-duty, kitchen, refectory, exercise, service, attendance at sermons and exhortations, conversation, declamation practice, or penances; and therefore they should be set to work like the rest in all the household chores, even the dirtiest and the lowest; and all the rules should apply to them just as they do to the rest; and I think this is the most important point of all.
4. Treat the teachers in such a way as to let them know and be convinced that neither the college nor the Society depends upon them; and unless they conduct themselves as they should, they should realize and expect that they will be removed from their office and replaced by others, even if they are considered highly learned; God will not be lacking, and he is capable of raising up [what he wishes] from stones.[2]
5. No one, however learned, should become a teacher of any subject or class except one who has made much progress in the spirit, both in prayer and in mortification, one who can help others in word and example; otherwise in no way should he be permitted to teach; and the more learned he is, the less should this occur.
6. We should not make much over the learned; the good, even the unlearned, should in all things be preferred to the learned, even if he be the least coadjutor.[3]
7. The method of teaching should not be one adopted to please non-Jesuits with worldly style or speech, nor through self-promotion, nor in attracting students, etc.; but the approach to teaching should be simple, honorable,

---

2 "God is able from these stones to raise up children for Abraham" (Mt. 3:8–9).
3 The term "coadjutor" describes a grade or "stratum" in the Society's membership. A coadjutor commonly assisted the professed members. Although there were two kinds of coadjutors (spiritual and temporal), Ledesma seems to refer here to temporal ones, who were lay (i.e., non-clerical) religious called *fratres*, or brother coadjutors. They could not hold governance roles, but they could hold many positions that did not pertain to the priesthood, particularly those relating to domestic service. If they had the requisite talent, they could work in fine arts and teach in elementary schools.

true, and holy; and this applies as well to the manner of discussing and conversing with students.

8. In the college and among Jesuits, we should not even utter the name of nations, or their rivalry, either in the selection of teachers or in other matters, this certainly being the greatest seedbed of hatred and dissension; and what has already started should be smothered immediately.

9. The entire college ought to be granted more prayer and mortification, as seems best. Perhaps we need to work out ways to make more spiritual progress; for unless I am mistaken, we have lost some spirit over the last five years.[4] Perhaps it would help to create divisions of fifty, each with its own immediate superior; and then the rector would be in charge of everyone, so that at least the fifty would get to know one another, and so on.

10. Again, neither teachers, nor students, nor others should insert themselves into the academic ranks, outside of the prefect of studies and his advisors and the syndics appointed by the superiors; they should not criticize or praise, except in a very restrained way, the teachers, preachers, poems, orations, and so forth, especially by comparing one with another, or by expressing their preferences; and they should not be allowed to make judgments about the established arrangements, or state their opinions just as they wish; but they should keep to what has been prescribed for them, and each should carry out his own duty.

11. Again, when their prose compositions, poems, orations are corrected by the one who has that responsibility, each should be satisfied, even when they have been badly corrected; or if it seems good to him to do so, he should inform the superior; and perhaps we should compose a rule about this, one which would be read at table every month with the other rules.

12. Again, unless we effectively remedy the matters I have mentioned above, I fear that a longer-lasting evil will creep in day by day and become an incurable evil, especially in the mortification of the teachers, and so forth.

In Humanistic Studies, and First in What Is Common

1. A book should be written in which is contained, distinctly and in detail, the entire order of studies, both of this college and of others in which there are one, two, three, or more classes of grammar or of subjects; and this order by each of the classes and subjects individually; and by the individual duties of persons and the diversity of matters, acts, disputations and all other literary

---

4   The rector at the Roman College was Sebastiano Romei (in office, 1554–68). Ledesma was professor of theology from 1556 to 1562 and prefect of studies from 1562 until his death in 1575. His reference here to a decline in spiritual progress at the college "in the last five years" does not seem to refer to any particular situation, despite the coincidence with the beginning of Benet Perera's tenure as a professor of philosophy at the Roman College (1559).

exercises, distinctly and in detail;[5] and applying the judgment and opinion of superiors, that order should be established to be kept and never to be changed except by a general congregation, so that now at last there should be some definite rule for prefects of studies and teachers to follow.

2. It seems to me that Reverend Father Nadal should live in our college and he should be its prefect at least for a year; and the reason is both especially for the sake of morals, and for composing and solidly establishing the order of studies that I just mentioned, and on account of his extensive experience and knowledge of the many years of this college and its personnel, and so forth.[6]

3. Again, it would seem helpful for some individual to be prefect of studies, and he should have power to make use of counselors or to follow the order given. And he would also direct the studies of the German College and seminary, even if it is through those who are directly in place there. Perhaps the college's studies will do well to have three prefects: one up to rhetoric, inclusive; a second for the arts; and a third for theology.[7]

4. Perhaps the time for vacations and recreation ought to be changed and shortened, and the time for the other break days and the classes increased; for, apart from the humanities, the rest of the teachers of the other subjects, along with the rhetoricians, only teach for 130 days, more or less, so that they teach for hardly a third of the year; I once gave an account and reckoning of this number to Your Paternity.

5. It seems to be helpful that from each course of arts, students of theology be left at Rome, at least two or three of the leading ones who impressively exhibit a greater degree learning and talent, to finish the entire course of theology and afterwards perhaps even to be promoted in theology according to the *Constitutions*.[8]

6. It seems helpful that there be as great as possible a group of theologians and arts students at Rome, and likewise a group of rhetoricians; for then there will be greater results, and there will be a single excellent teacher for all of them, and we will in this way attain the fullness of disciplinary knowledge, and missions will go smoothly, and many teachers will be available for possible assignment at other colleges.

7. Perhaps at the start of the year there should be designated substitutes for each of the teachers in case they happen to fall sick or become exhausted; and this especially in the humanities.

---

5   By "acts," Ledesma means public academic performances, like defenses of theses.

6   According to the catalog of the Roman College from July 1564, Jerónimo Nadal (1507–80) was living there as the supervisor of the college (Archivum Romanum Societatis Iesu, *Rom.*, 78/b, fol. 28ᵛ).

7   This division reflects the classical stages of Jesuit education: "letters" or humanistic studies, philosophy, theology.

8   See Padberg, *Constitutions*, 183–85.

8. It would perhaps be helpful that the schedule be stable and fixed for the entire year; but I believe that this cannot be unless we change the clock, at least for our students, so that we might use, I say, the astrological clock, namely a clock of twelve hours, as in Spain, France, and Germany.[9]

9. Then non-Jesuit students would be able to be alerted by some rather large bell, placed in an elevated location, which would be struck every hour before the time for the lessons, as happens in Padua.[10] Then every hour, they would go to and from classes at the stroke of the clock.

In Grammar and Humanities

1. The *Rudiments* of Coudret should be better and more fittingly printed so that the boys might easily learn them.[11] And certain things, it seems, ought to be changed or added from the rudiments book of Coimbra.[12]

2. Perhaps we should be using another, more convenient book on syntax than the one we are using now.

3. The proper or optimal structuring of classes should be formally set, and a method of teaching and exercise-practice prescribed for each one, the books that they will teach, and so forth; and of course [this should all be put into] writing so that there is a definite way to follow.

4. On feast days, it would seem helpful for some literary exercises to be done, certainly in some classes if not in all of them, such as orations in poetry or prose, private declamations, rhetorical disputations, etc.; and [this should take place] especially in the rhetoric and humanities classes.

5. Public formal declamations should occur twice or three times a year, both in prose and in poetry, and also occasionally something in the same way in Greek, in poetry or in prose.

6. Public awards should be given out once a year.

7. Once a year, a single dialogue should be put on; but a comedy or tragedy in Latin only at the resumption of studies.

---

9   Astronomical clocks provided astronomical information in addition to the time. Ledesma's reference to the twelve hours suggests he was thinking about a mechanical clock based on a verge and foliot system, which was the most widespread form in Europe until the fourteenth century. One of the most famous of these clocks has been preserved in Prague.

10 The need for a bell was usually mentioned by Jesuits to those who had asked them to open a college.

11 Hannibal du Coudret (1525–99) was among the Jesuits that Ignatius sent to Messina to establish the college. His grammar lessons were collected in a booklet entitled *De primis Latinae grammatices rudimentis* [On the first rudiments of Latin grammar] and used as textbook at the Roman College.

12 The *Grammatices rudimenta* [Rudiments of grammar] was probably compiled by the humanist and famous Portuguese historian João de Barros (1496–1570), a professor at the College of Arts at Coimbra, about 1540.

In Philosophy and the Course of the Arts

1. They [i.e., the students] should follow some author, so out of the material that is available, let the best person be chosen for the individual books of Aristotle; for even if there are different things in individual books, it matters little or nothing, and this will be far more helpful than following no one.

2. But this method will be, in the first place, to describe the contents at length; then the teacher can add a few other points of his own or of others; and the teacher will treat the questions and matter in the order in which they are given there, not elsewhere; and he will not be quick to depart from the author's opinion, or from the common one; but some limited freedom of opinion should be allowed.

Method of Teaching

1. Again, this should be the method of teaching, and on it the entire usefulness especially depends, as it seems to me: they should teach in such a way that even average talents can learn a lesson by heart and repeat it from memory. Likewise, teaching should last three-quarters of an hour, more or less, and then for the following quarter the teacher should review the same lesson again, more concisely; later, he should put questions about that same lesson to one or more students that he selects. When this kind of review is done, groups of three or four students should review it among themselves, and if this is possible, in the teacher's presence, for at least some part of the time. Again, he should not overwhelm the students with a multitude of testimonies on Aristotle, I mean from those books that the students have not yet studied; for this is downright useless and more likely to confuse the students; but the teacher should emphasize the main elements in the foundational material, and the material that presents a particular challenge.

2. Again, he should not praise Averroes too much; no, in fact he should not even praise him at all, nor other non-Christian authors who comment on Aristotle; and he should not immoderately praise Greeks or Arabs;[13] but if anyone should be praised, it should be Saint Thomas or Albert the Great, or another Christian commentator.[14] He should not seem or appear inclined towards

---

13 This was one of Ledesma's main accusations against Benet Perera. See *Monumenta paedagogica*, nova series, 2:502 (doc. 73) and Christoph Sander, "The War of the Roses: The Debate between Diego de Ledesma and Benet Perera about the Philosophy Course at the Jesuit College in Rome," *Quaestio* 14 (2014): 31–50. Among the Greek commentators, Perera praised Alexander of Aphrodisias (*fl.* 200) and Simplicius (*c.*490–*c.*560), whose position on the human soul contradicted the standard understanding in Christianity.

14 The word here translated as "Christian" is *pius*, meaning loyal, devoted, and good among those who are in the circle of believers. Thus *impii authores* is translated here as "non-Christian authors," referring to those who do not have such a commitment and understanding as the *pii* do.

or devoted to the authors just mentioned: Averroes, or the Greeks, or other non-Christians, deprecating the Latin authors. He should not seem disinclined to the Latin authors, nor should he teach the arguments of the Latin authors against the Greeks, and the reverse; or at least this should happen only rarely. He should not alienate his students from the doctrine of the Latins, least of all from the doctrine of Saint Thomas; and he should not make serious criticisms against him, but he should depart from Saint Thomas's thought in a humble way if that ever has to be done, and this should be done with praise for him; the teacher should not seem to disagree with him frequently or to do so eagerly; but he should dispose the students well towards Saint Thomas and his doctrine.[15] He should not apply to himself or presume to adopt the name of Peripatetic, nor that of Peripatetic or Platonic doctrine; but he should merely say simply what he himself thinks. He should not be excessive in critiquing other authors, and especially not the one whose work he is teaching; nor should he do this arrogantly or with pride, and so forth; he should not be a lover of his own opinion, nor should he want to be considered an original thinker and one who has contempt for others; for the students take in such behavior; nor should he criticize any other teacher; nor should he show himself eager to disagree with him or to critique another's pronouncements.

3.   He should never criticize Scholastic theologians in general, but he should increase esteem for them and foster it among his students; and he should not assail any one of them, even on details; all the more should he be careful not to alienate his students from Scholastic theology or in any way criticize it.

4.   Again, when he is pleading for the faith and he falls into some question that bears on the faith, he should plead with all his strength and every effort, always following Christian interpretation, but not half-heartedly or with more energy for an opposing position.[16]

---

15 Albert the Great (before 1200–80) and Thomas Aquinas (1204–74) were two towering intellectuals of the thirteenth century, both Dominicans. The attitude towards Thomas evident here was similarly supported by the *Ratio studiorum* (*The Ratio Studiorum: The Official Plan for Jesuit Education*, trans. Claude Pavur [St. Louis: Institute of Jesuit Sources, 2005], nos. 15, 175).

16 Ledesma's words echoed the Council Lateran V (Session 8, December 19, 1513): "Each and every philosopher who teaches publicly in the universities or elsewhere, that when they explain or address to their audience the principles or conclusions of philosophers, where these are known to deviate from the true faith—as in the assertion of the soul's mortality or of there being only one soul or of the eternity of the world and other topics of this kind—they are obliged to devote their every effort to clarify for their listeners the truth of the Christian religion, to teach it by convincing arguments, so far as this is possible, and to apply themselves to the full extent of their energies to refuting and disposing of the philosophers' opposing arguments, since all the solutions are available." See Norman P. Tanner, S.J., ed., *Decrees of the Ecumenical Councils* (Washington, DC: Sheed & Ward and Georgetown University Press, 1990), 1:606.

5. Again, they will defend from what touches on the faith the opinions that I have listed in another paper separately; and they will attack positions contrary to these.[17]

The Rest of the Literary Exercises

1. The master's or licentiate examination should be a serious and determinative written one, given for the purpose of making it clear who ought to be promoted, how many should, and when; and an appropriate method should be devised so that this might occur without the rivalry of the rest who are not promoted, and so that only worthy ones are admitted [to the position of teacher].
2. Perhaps it would be helpful that there be distinct grades for the bachelor's, licentiate, and master's.
3. Perhaps it would be helpful that there be some special philosophical acts given during the year, either with those who are being promoted or with others.
4. Perhaps it would be helpful that at the end of the three-year course there be given a half-year following it, for holding the acts and for the preparation and the examination of those being promoted.
5. The full content of the arts course seems to require three and a half years to complete; and then a following half-year would be granted both for preparation for the examination and for putting on acts, as the *Constitutions* state; but I wonder if this can be done at this time and with the lack of personnel.[18]
6. Saturday disputations should last three hours, or two and a half; namely at the time of the classes.
7. Perhaps other private student disputations could be scheduled once a week, and they could be either on feast days when no sermon is given, or in the evening, or on Sundays, or on another day, and these disputations should last at least two hours.
8. It should be seen whether there should be a course on ethics and whether it should be given by the teacher himself or by someone else, and so forth.[19]

---

17 All of these counsels are repeated in (or drawn from) the "Report on the Consultation of Professors about Studies at the Roman College" (1564–65), which is published in *Monumenta paedagogica*, nova editio, 2:464–81.

18 The *Constitutions* explicitly show the same concern: "If because of insufficient personnel or for other reasons facilities for that arrangement are lacking, the best that will be possible should be done, with the approval of the general or at least of the provincial" (Padberg, *Constitutions*, 184).

19 Many Jesuits believed that most ethical questions should be left for the theological course.

In Theology

1. Only those who deserve to be doctors should become such, after many acts in the preceding years, and not before a five-year period at the minimum; indeed, if possible, they should be appointed according to the *Constitutions*, and not otherwise.[20]
2. It seems helpful to have other degrees before the doctorate, namely the bachelor's and the license, with certain acts preceding each.
3. If possible, it would make a great difference for complete coverage of the discipline, and for the frequency and attendance at the acts, and for greater help for the students, and for the learning of the instructors and for many other things, if there were here in Rome in this college ten doctors of theology who would engage in disputation in the acts, be present, support them, and also now and then act as examiners, and so forth.
4. These could all be busy, as in addition to two teachers of Scholastic and one of positive theology, one would teach cases of conscience, another controversies, another could be a preacher, another prefect of studies, one or others would write and take care of business and issues that come up, and so forth.
5. This should be the method of teaching theology: so that even average talents might be able to get the lesson by memory and repeat it by memory; at least in Scholastic theology this will be necessary; and they should exhort everyone to get it into their memory and review it as much as they can; for otherwise they can hardly make judgments, and they understand it badly, and they recall it worse. The result is that as class reviews get weaker, so do home reviews and the disputations as well.
6. He should not introduce new thinking, especially in an important matter, without the advice and permission of the superior; but he should almost always follow the common opinion, or that of Saint Thomas.
7. He should first say what Saint Thomas says, and just in the order in which he says it; he should explain the arguments, solutions, and the foundation for this concisely and elegantly; then, in a similar manner, some of Cajetan's most important comments, just about always following the same order; then he should add what seems to him to be good to include. For to teach his own treatises by their contents, in their own order and sequence of exposition is not especially helpful for the students; but they retain less in their memory, and they are not able to prepare themselves before the class; and they are more confused by the diversity of method and order and approach taken by Saint Thomas and by Cajetan.[21]

---

20 Padberg, *Constitutions*, 184.
21 The most renowned of Aquinas's commentators in the sixteenth century, Thomas de Vio Cajetan (also called Caietanus, Caetanus, Gaetanus, 1469–1534) was also cardinal and master of the Dominicans (1508–18).

8. Acts and public disputations involving those to be promoted should be held during the year, and in fact frequently.
9. Disputations on Saturday should last three hours, or two and a half hours, that is to say, during the entire time for classes.
10. Perhaps it would be helpful that there be, in addition to these, private disputations of students at least once a week for two hours, or in the evening on feast days that do not have a sermon, or on other days; for our students are really in need of greater [academic] exercise.

CHAPTER 15

On the Plan and Order of Studies at the Roman College (1564–65)

Diego de Ledesma

Ledesma's masterpiece was the plan of studies he composed for the Roman College. Although not mentioned in the Society's definitive academic charter (the Ratio atque institutio studiorum Societatis Iesu *of 1599), Ledesma's influence on that work was quite substantial. After collecting suggestions from the professors of the college where he was serving as prefect of studies, he laid out five books of instructions, the first of which dealt only with studies of language, literature, composition, and rhetoric (that is "letters," here called "humanistic studies"). In Lukács's edition, this document is one hundred pages long. We present here only the introductory letter in which Ledesma summarizes the goal and the method he had followed in constructing his plan for studies. It should be noted that the need to provide such a plan was Ledesma's main concern: he believed that only a reliable and fixed set of rules could offer the necessary guidance for every prefect of studies.*

A champion of uniformity of doctrine among Jesuit professors, especially in philosophy and theology, Ledesma also enthusiastically supported the idea of obliging teachers to adopt a single pedagogical method. Ledesma's pedagogy for the literary part of the course, despite its meticulousness, did not receive universal approval. Pedro Perpinyá (1530–66), a celebrated professor, would censure it as a clearly useless product of a thinker who had neither known nor taught humanistic studies.

Diego de Ledesma (born c.1524, Cuéllar in the province of Segovia, Spain— entered the Society on September 30, 1556, Leuven, the Spanish Netherlands—died November 18, 1575, Rome). Ledesma was a professor of theology in the Roman College and prefect of studies there from 1562. His work, De ratione et ordine studiorum Collegii Romani *[On the plan and order of studies at the Roman College] has been called "perhaps the most substantial contribution to the development of the Jesuit code of education."[1] In 1569, it was issued by Superior General Francisco de Borja (in office 1565–72). Known as the "Ratio Borgiana," it was the first universal plan of studies in the Society. It remained in effect until the 1591* Ratio *was issued for trial use.*

Source: *Monumenta paedagogica*, nova editio, 2:519–627 (original: Latin)

---

1   Allan P. Farrell, *The Jesuit Code of Liberal Education: Development and Scope of the* Ratio studiorum (Milwaukee: Bruce Publishing Company, 1938), 169.

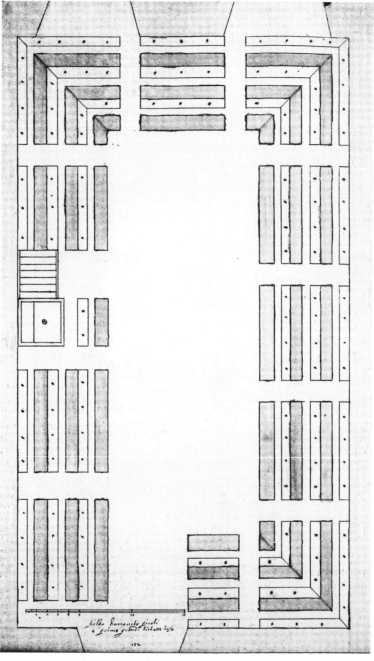

FIGURE 7   A scheme drawn by Henri Laloyau (*c.*1646–1723) for furnishing
a classroom in the Collegio Romano. This rational planning of a
Jesuit college shows the chair of the master at center-left and groups
of benches divided according to the students' skills and grades.

Very Reverend Father in Christ!

First:

In this office of mine to which I have been assigned some years now, I have been impelled for a long time by a desire to provide something that could contribute to the glory of Christ our redeemer and the service of the literary studies at this Roman College. And so, spurred on by my conscience, I thought it good to touch briefly here on what seemed best to me concerning this entire plan of studies and, as is proper and as the procedure of our Institute demands, to subject my reflections to the reckoning of my superiors for their judgment.[2]

Second:

1. Therefore I think it quite necessary to draw up some plan and order of studies for this Roman College of our Society (and indeed the best of all, if possible) and to establish by the order of superiors what has been drawn up so that it may not be changed except by the well-deliberated advice of the same; and this should be the case whether the judgment is that the present system should be maintained in all respects or whether it should be partially changed.

2. It is not enough to draw up the plan in general; rather, it is important to record the separate details about what each party needs to observe, item by item, through each of the subjects and classes.

3. We have to write not just what touches upon the plan of our studies but also what concerns the literary study and morals of non-Jesuit students.

4. Likewise, we should also prescribe for the individual teachers a manner of teaching and the form and manner of all other exercises, such as correcting themes, reciting, reviewing classes, testing on them, and so forth; for these things are very different according to the diversity of the classes themselves; otherwise, we will have as many methods as we have teachers; different ones will be used at different times, according to the teacher's judgment; and, as they say, "however many heads there are, that is the number of the opinions."[3]

5. Again, we ought to draw up for each of the classes which books should be read and which not; on what days there should be instruction; at what hour of the day and for how many hours; in what order; what should be done in the morning and what in the evening; on holidays, and Saturdays, and feast days, and in individual months, etc.[4]

---

2   As the prefect of studies, Ledesma was asked to write this report in 1562.

3   This proverb goes back at least as far as the *Phormio*, v.454, a comedy by the ancient Latin playwright Terence (Publius Terentius Afer, *c*.195/185–*c*.159 BCE).

4   The order's *Constitutions* themselves (at part 4, chapter 5, E [359]) suggest specificity in regard to course content: "Furthermore, it is good to determine in detail the books which should be lectured on and those which should not, both in the humanities and in the other faculties" (Padberg, *Constitutions*, 152).

6. Again, what should be done at the re-commencement of the school year; what in adjustments; what in vacation-time or holiday-time or in other times of the year, so that in everything a definite plan is evident.

7. Finally, it seems necessary to gather and to make a judgment about all the rules drawn up on this matter so far concerning the different offices and the persons necessary to staff them, such as the prefect of studies and the prefect of teachers, the beadles, the syndics, the examiners, the disciplinarian, and others; and it then seems necessary to write up the judgments and submit the final draft to be preserved so that in this way everything might be quite clear at last.

8. And indeed all that I have mentioned will have to be properly and systematically written, in a clear, distinct, and concise fashion, so that the points may be easier to understand and especially so that they may be adapted to actual practice.

Third:
The following considerations suggest that this should be done:

1. First, not just the apparently great necessity that we see, but the example of all other academic establishments that have their own fully drafted constitutions about all matters.

2. Again, some of the more famous colleges of our Society have drawn them up, or they have taken ones that have been written up and they are observing them.

3. Again, [this should be done] so that the prefect of studies might have something firmly established to follow, something that he has the power to put into practice through others; and from it he himself might be able to learn, especially when he is new, if it ever falls to him to make the decision [about some matter].

4. Again, [this should be done] so that the teacher may draw upon it when they are put in charge of classes or when they are hesitant about some matter; and the prefect might hand over to them, even in written form, their entire plan and order of studies so that it is not left to their judgment or so that there need not always be a new consultation or inquiry about what must be done.

5. Again, [this should be done] so that the syndics of the classes may also have something definite that they may be able and obliged to observe in the teachers and in those teachers' classes.

6. And finally, [this should be done] so that we might avoid a certain serious disadvantage that necessarily arises, namely keeping either the prefect of studies himself or the teachers or any other observer of the studies from wanting to introduce new practices or orders and methods that they think best, though it frequently turns out otherwise.

7. Or it happens that every day they fight and argue among themselves about those matters, while each one praises his own view but gives little approval to somebody else's method and plan, as experience has shown.

8. Again, it would be helpful for other colleges to have a best example which they might be able to imitate to the extent that it helps them.

9. Again, [this should be done] since teachers should go out from this Roman College as from the first source and origin, and since colonies should be derived from it and instructors sent to teach also in other colleges; and since we should nourish and raise those who may imitate and follow elsewhere the best that they have seen observed in this Roman college of ours.

10. Again, [this should be done] since, unless I am mistaken, in the *Constitutions* themselves, in part 4, it is asserted that some book ought to be composed by the Society for the governance of educational institutions and for the organization of all their offices and studies, a book that conveys one by one the things I have mentioned.[5]

11. Finally, since so many things that are both manifold and different in nature have to be done, and since they are neither common nor easy, nor a simple task for anyone even with an average education, in so full a plan of studies for the entire college, it seems necessary that there also be more completely drafted the complete order of everything, bit by bit through all the individual details; and if not everything belonging to it, certainly most of the elements and the main ones, and those things on which all the rest depend, the ones that follow from them and that can easily and reliably be gathered from them.

12. I have approached this task as well as I can given the poverty of my talent, relying on God's help, and using the advice of other experienced members of our Society and the entire present practice of our college, which I have written, and its rules and their observance. Even if these do not find much approval, at least may Christ our redeemer and our holy Society take up the attempt itself and the desire of our will. Amen.

An unworthy servant of Your Paternity in Christ.

Praise to God and to Our Lord Jesus Christ, and the most sanctified Virgin Mary his mother. Amen.

---

5   See Padberg, *Constitutions*, 180. The passage in the *Constitutions* points to what the Society finally achieved in the *Ratio studiorum* of 1599.

.

CHAPTER 16

Difficulties in the Governance of the Roman Seminary (1570)

Ludovico Gagliardi

In 1567, Gagliardi was appointed rector of the Roman Seminary, an institution prescribed by the Council of Trent only four years earlier. The choice to entrust it to the Society of Jesus troubled some Roman clergy who chafed at the idea of having their seminaries directed by a religious order as much as they disliked supporting those seminaries with their own parish revenues. Gagliardi ran the seminary with a seriousness and strictness that apparently went too far, as we can surmise from the complaints made by several Jesuits, one of whom even asked for his resignation. At the end of his appointment in 1570, Gagliardi wrote a report to Superior General Borja (in office 1565–72) in which he outlined the administrative difficulties he had encountered, providing his superior with an uncensored picture of the student population. The report reveals the real challenges experienced by every authority in the school: rector, prefect of studies, ministers, repetitores, *and even workers at the seminary were defied, mocked, provoked, resisted, or simply ignored by students who were constantly trying to take whatever advantage they could to get their own way. Gagliardi suggested two possible remedies: either resign from the task of running the seminary, as the students were irredeemable, or renounce the distinctive Jesuit pedagogical principles of (relative) mildness and exemplarity, as the seminarians' behavior required drastic measures.*

Ludovico Gagliardi (born c.1543, Padua—entered the Society on September 29, 1559, Rome—died March, 9, 1608, Modena). Brother of Achille (1537–1607), the renowned spiritual writer and teacher at the Roman College, Ludovico was appointed prefect of studies at the German College in 1565. He held this position for two years, while he was entrusted with the same position at the Roman Seminary. Despite his youth, he was appointed rector of the seminary in 1570. At the beginning of 1572, he was sent to Padua and made rector of the Jesuits in Verona, where he had to face the crisis of the Venetian interdict (1606), a conflict between the Republic of Venice and the papal curia. After the Jesuits had been expelled from Venice, he found refuge in Modena, where he died.

Source: *Monumenta paedagogica*, nova editio, 2:1011–25 (original: Italian)

1. The first thing is this: almost all of these youths are Roman, and one cannot find a more difficult people to govern than this, as they themselves confess. This is because they are by nature very proud, excessively inclined to all kinds of vice and very far from the fear of God. Also, they are a very cunning

people who lack any simplicity at all; meddlers who try to know everything, especially the defects of others, and they are quite bold, never surrendering except when they cannot do otherwise. In short, they are very dangerous when it comes to conversing with every other kind of people: they can lead them astray, however religious and upright they may seem.

2. Except for a very few, they are all common and of low birth, living in poverty.[1] And although they are treated well here—they are fed, dressed in a very honorable manner, and governed very graciously by religious people—such things all greatly increase their pride and all of the other undesirable qualities just mentioned. Above all, since they are of low birth, they have as one of their traits not making any effort that is not for their own gain.[2]

3. Being in their homeland and almost in their own houses makes them more troublesome, because our companions are usually from abroad, and so this makes the students more insolent towards us.

4. They stay at the seminary for a long time—seven or eight years—while our companions, on the contrary, change frequently. Not only do the students inclined towards evil grow older and become wicked teachers of others, and not only do all of them become more difficult as they age; but thanks to the long experience they have of everything in the seminary (that is, of all the occasions and times and means they can have, in addition to their experience with our way of proceeding), they also come to be very skilled in knowing our companions, and they lose all simplicity. Therefore, those inclined towards evil become old and very bad teachers of evil for others. And growing up, they become even more troublesome thanks to the long experience they have had of everything at the seminary, that is, of all the occasions and times and means that they are able to have; and in addition, they have long experience of our way of proceeding. So they become very acquainted with our companions and lose all simplicity. The result of this is that they are able to know one of us as soon as he arrives—how they might make him their friend and lead him wherever they want. And they succeed in doing so because our companions, however long they spend at the seminary, will remain novices with respect to

---

1   This was the intent of the Council of Trent, which decreed that "those admitted to the college should be at least twelve years old, of legitimate birth, who know how to read and write competently, and whose character and disposition offers hope that they will serve in church ministries throughout life. The council wishes the sons of poor people particularly to be chosen, but does not exclude those of the more wealthy provided that they pay for their own maintenance and show an ambition to serve God and the church." Council of Trent, Session 23 (July 15, 1563), chapter 18. See Tanner, *Decrees*, 2:750.

2   The pupils at the seminary were gathered from the Roman dioceses, which had to support it through a self-taxation of five percent. The same went for the suburbicarian dioceses and the neighboring abbeys, which were unable to run a program of clerical formation on their own. The budget plan, drawn up by a special commission of cardinals in 1564, aroused turmoil as well as a general hostility towards the Society of Jesus.

the students in all that pertains to its administration. And yet, many times our dormitory prefects are sooner controlled than in control of the youths,[3] and they just do not realize it or they only do so much later, especially since other nationalities are far simpler than the Romans.

From the same source, there arises the situation that, since the same students stay at the seminary for such a long time, they become ever more united with one another and stronger, and they set themselves to the task of maintaining their liberty and license as best they can, and of resisting all those means that our companions employ to help them. On the contrary, since our companions change so many times, they turn out to be rather weaker and also less united, because they, according to their different natures, hold different opinions about what should be done, while the seminary students, who are always united, get what they want from everybody, that is, to live more freely. And if they realize that one of our companions is well disposed towards them, they tempt him by murmuring criticisms directed at the superiors and the rules; and it sometimes happens that they win him over to their side, to the great detriment of good order. Moreover, with all of our changing assignments, some of our companions who have many imperfections arrive. Everyone has some imperfections, and one can sometimes fall into some grave weakness, and they know all about such things, even the most private things, and they remember it for a long while, reproaching us for it whenever they like, to the great detriment of the Society's reputation. This would not happen if the same ones did not stay so long at the seminary. Furthermore, since these same ones stay so long at the seminary, they are able to attend all of the classes and make great advances in their studies, so that, as a result, many of them are quite skilled in all types of writing and every day they will be all the more skilled. On the contrary, our companions stay there only a short time, and every day new students arrive who are less learned than they are. This lowers the authority of our companions a great deal, because students think highly of their own knowledge, and they do not want to submit; and especially when they have gone into theology a bit, the seminarians want to teach everybody, and they quite often defend their shortcomings with a doctrinal point.[4] Then their solidarity with each other

---

3   The center of daily life at the Roman Seminary was mostly the dormitories (*camerate*) where students were kept separated in groups of tens or dozens. At full capacity, one could count up to fifteen dormitories, each supervised by a dormitory prefect. Dormitories were the place where students slept, washed and bathed, studied, played, had breakfast, and prayed. Even during recreation time dormitory-groups were kept separated.

4   The Council of Trent established the following curriculum for the seminarians: "So that they may be more appropriately grounded in ecclesiastical studies, they should always have the tonsure and wear clerical dress from the outset; they should study grammar, singing, keeping church accounts and other useful skills; and they should be versed in holy

increases because they know that when they leave the seminary they have to remain close to each other, that is, in the same region, and they will not have to return to faraway places like those of the German College; so instead they strive much more to keep a friendship with each other than they do with us, whom they know do not have to stay here. The seminarians are therefore very careful to avoid upsetting one another. From such a great union as this, which originates from interacting for such a long time (as we said above), it turns out that it is impossible to find any one among them who would report even the slightest fault of a schoolmate, even if he had seen it with his own eyes; much less if the fault is serious. And so the superior has no trustworthy people to rely on; this makes governance very difficult, if not impossible. And I believe this is the main cause of all the troubles that are happening without notice or that are reported in the seminary.

5.   The Society's work in the seminary is rather in the nature of service, since we do not have the authority to admit and expel seminarians, as in the German College, and we are at work in someone else's house, since we have been commanded to do this. If we turn to another issue, that is, utility, the seminarians are expecting neither benefices nor positions from us because we do not have any; not even temporal loss produces a reverential fear for us, so that, since these people seek only their own profit, they do not care about how they behave with us, but rather they strive to gratify only those people thanks to whom they were given their places in the seminary. They do not care about our companions at all. And although they could be worried about the fact that their advantage or disadvantage depends upon the good or bad report we give to the Honorable Monsignor Vicar,[5] we have had no demonstration of this in the past. Moreover, since this thing is covered and surrounded by suspicions, only hatred arises, not any feeling of fear or reverence, such that they claim to have received from us nothing but strict rules, reprimands, suspicions, penances, and punishments. And if they are dismissed from the seminary, they will ascribe it to our hatred and malice; but if they receive any benefice or other help, they will not ascribe it to us, but to the one who gave it to them. There are only two things that they cannot deny to have received continuously from us, which are also more important than everything else: the first is education in and support of good morals and fear of God; the second is their education in letters. Concerning the first, whereas youths are generally barely capable of it, these are not capable at all, and they are so envious of those who are free and out of the reach of our discipline

scripture, church writers, homilies of the saints, and the practice of rites and ceremonies and of administering the sacraments, particularly all that seems appropriate to hearing confessions." Session 23 (July 15, 1563), canon 18. See Tanner, *Decrees*, 2:751.

5   Giacomo Savelli (*c*.1523–87), who was appointed cardinal vicar of Rome in 1560 and hosted many of the meetings of the commission for the foundation of the Roman Seminary.

that they consider being under our authority a great misfortune. Furthermore, they let themselves become so blind that they resent even those things which we do in order to help them. The second thing, concerning an education in letters, they admit to receiving from us and they hold it in higher regard than all the other students, and in fact they are truly grateful to their teachers; but this would be helpful only if those who have authority over them at the seminary were the same as those who teach them.[6] But since they are different, this situation ends up undermining authority, because teachers and prefects of the college have very different ways of dealing with them from our companions who are at the seminary, because they proceed very gently, not knowing students' tricks or defects other than those that pertain to studies; they have a very positive opinion of everyone, and they treat everyone with respect. And by the same token, the seminarians exercise great gentleness and courtesy towards their teachers. So it comes about very often that the worst ones are better esteemed by the teachers, because they are the shrewdest and they know how to come across as friendly. But they hate the dormitory prefects and the superiors, who know them and are constrained by circumstances and by their position to take a different approach. And the more the seminarians experience the different approach of the teachers, the more they hate the prefects and the superiors. Moreover, since they know that advancement to the higher classes and other things pertaining to studies for which they have great esteem depends on the teachers and the prefects of the studies of the Roman College, they come to scorn in all respects those who have authority over them at the seminary. For these two reasons, it sometimes happens that the same one of us who was hated while he had been prefect of the room or had held some charge in running the seminary was then loved by the same seminarians when he had a class. Finally, it remains to be said that this entire benefit of getting educated in letters for free is something attached to having a place at the seminary, and yet even if they receive the benefit directly from the Society, they are only grateful to the ones who had gotten a place for them at the seminary, rather than to us.

6. The other thing that hinders our Society's administration is that the seminarians have never had the desire to be governed by the Society, nor has such a desire moved those who have found a place here for them at the seminary; their desire is only for the comfort and convenience of having a place for free as long as they are being fed and are getting an education. They happen to be under our authority by chance, beyond every wish and intention of their

---

6   Since the students of the seminary attended classes at the Roman College, they held in esteem those Jesuits who taught them while they remained hostile to those Jesuits who supervised them at the seminary.

own. In fact, they even think it a misfortune to have to be at discretion of the Theatines (as they call us), and they make do with the fact that they cannot avoid it. So they pass almost all of their time at the seminary reluctantly and by necessity.[7] And since they do not want to leave so as not to lose the benefit they draw from it, they all spend their time reproaching and criticizing all the decisions and arrangements, grumbling among themselves and making every effort to avoid observing the rules. It seems to them that the more one cheats one of us in supervision and in the house rules, the more of a gentleman he is, making something like an offering to God, since they tend to believe that all the rules or commands issued are our own inventions, not the seminary's institute. And, to sum up, they stay at the seminary (in their own judgment) as if they were in a jail, dealing with us as prisoners behave with executioners, sometimes even making use of these words with one another.

7. The last difficulty is not exclusive to the Society but would be shared with whoever would be in charge of this Roman seminary because it pertains to the very nature of the seminary. But it becomes greater for us than for others for the above-mentioned reasons. The issue is this: almost no one who attends the seminary has the honest intention that they should have to serve in the ministries of the church. If they intend to be priests, it is with designs to gain fine benefices without trouble, or with high rank. And all of them have relatives or protectors outside who provide for them during their stay at the seminary. The large majority therefore does not depend upon the Honorable Monsignor Vicar's will to complete the course in the seminary, but rather upon their other friends, relatives, or patrons through whom they received their place at the seminary. Thus many of them have very little concern about being expelled, provided that they should not pay their expenses. They therefore do not trouble themselves to behave well, but they live however they like at the seminary, enjoying this present good that has been granted them and waiting for a comfortable and honorable life on the outside, having a good time on the church revenues, without any care for souls. Rather, they hold openly among themselves that being a parish priest or running parishes is a disgrace and reason for laughter and joking, which are both entirely contrary to the intent of the council.

All of the above-mentioned reasons make it very difficult for the Society to run this seminary, and though they are plain enough in themselves, the members of the Society will understand them better if we compare them to the running of the German College. To those who have no experience of either, that institution is considered quite similar to this one and practically the same, even with all that is very different.

---

7   On this mistake, see above, Chapter 10n2.

So I claim that you can conclude from this that running the German College is far easier than running the seminary: (1) Most of the students are from states other than Rome: many are Lombards, naturally humbler, more inclined to the fear of God and other virtues, not cunning or pushy; rather, they are simple, docile, and respectful.[8] (2) They are of high and noble birth, which fosters all of their good inclinations and ensures that if they are treated decently in room and board and regulations, they do not behave insolently on that account, since such things are all appropriate for their status, and they have been raised this way from their childhood. Above all, since they are noble, they are motivated by the good of virtue rather than by self-interest. (3) They are almost all away from their homelands and many are very far from them: this makes them much more humble and ready to trust and to allow themselves to be guided. (4) Most of them spend little time at the German College, but there is a continual coming and going of new people every year. As a result, these students do not become as well acquainted with the system as ours do; nor do they band together with each other, especially because they will each have to return to their homes and will not deal with one another anymore; nor do they see such frequent changes among our companions. In addition, they do not make so much progress in their studies and therefore hold our companions in higher regard, realizing that they themselves are less educated. (5) Our work at the German College is not servile, because we are absolute patrons there: we admit or expel whomever we like, something that gives us great authority. (6) What motivates the youths and their parents to come to the German College is not some particular interest, but only the high opinion they have of us, and their trust, by which they of their own accord decide to place themselves under our discipline, and even if they are there unwillingly they fear yet more a bad report coming from our fathers if they do not behave well, on account of the esteem they know their parents and relatives have for the judgment of our companions. (7) They all behave with good conscience, because they live by their own means and they do not commit themselves to some mischief that could cheat them of what they had paid for. Therefore, concerning the essentials of the Society's governance, the German College is a paradise compared with the seminary.[9]

There are two things I have always judged to be true and indisputable about this great difference in the way the Society is in these two places: one is that the Society needs to be more careful in sending its subjects and pastoral staff to the seminary than it is with regard to the German College, not so much looking to

---

8 According to the medieval university tradition, students coming from central-northern Italy were called "Lombards." Some of the students at the German College were from the most distinguished families there, such as the Dorias of Genoa, or the Bentivoglios and Buocompagnis of Bologna. Juan Alfonso de Polanco, *Chronicon*, 1:569.

9 Apparently, Gagliardi modified his more nuanced estimation of the students of German College after his experience at the seminary.

merit in this as considering that the greater the risk and the need the smaller the results that accrue.[10] The second thing is that our companions' way of proceeding at the seminary should be far different from the one that is implemented at the German College. This means that here (at the seminary) we should have less conversation, less familiarity, less coddling; we should not trust them so much nor believe them, being much more careful and cautious in actions and words, not giving in easily to their requests; and, finally, we should not go about so simply and informally as we do at the German College, because this way does not work with those who are so worldly-wise and masters of the art of tricking their superiors. No, I would even claim that what suits them best would be a supervision entirely full of authority and power. And yet, I conclude that such is not the governance of the Society, which ought not to abandon its own Institute of gentleness and kindness in order to adapt itself to a particular place. But, since getting this weight off our chest is out of our hands, we should make a careful choice among different people and accommodate our Institute as far as it can bear, as happens in all the Society's undertakings. Because there is one way of proceeding with students, another with soldiers; one with nobles, another with country-folk; one with our brothers, another with lay people; one in the pulpit, another in schools, and another in the confessional. And finally, this prudence in considering places, times, and persons is necessary in every ministry of the Society. Therefore, I infer that one way fits the seminarians, and another those in the German College. I have wanted to say this in more detail because, of the two things I proposed above, that is, the greater need of the seminary and another way of proceeding, it seems that the first is starting to be understood and admitted by everyone, and the second is not believed by many.

They think that we cannot possibly fail to produce good results at the seminary by adopting a happy, gentle, edifying way of proceeding, eager to be of assistance. I say that gentleness does not have to be set aside, but rather that a particular caution and prudence are necessary there, along with a charitable zeal, but one based on experience. And to whoever thinks it can work with some other way will realize it is impossible as soon as he has this experience. And since the ability to remedy disorders very much depends on the detailed knowledge of what is happening, I will strive to describe succinctly the way of proceeding with these seminarians, on the assumption that it is not possible to express it through words nor for someone without direct experience to understand it fully.

Let us start with obedience. They hate observing the statutes and rules of the seminary and the orders given by the superior. They consider submitting oneself to these things as the characteristic of an unworthy man, claiming that

---

10 The word for pastoral staff here is *operarii*. An *operarius* was an ordained individual who performed typical pastoral priestly services (saying Mass, hearing confessions, preaching, and so forth).

slaves themselves are not so constrained. And so they do not give it any weight at all. And they do whatever they can do secretly against the rules, keeping secrets among themselves and considering a traitor and enemy of their common freedom anyone who reports infractions of the rules to the superior, calling him a snitch, and other unusual words to unnerve him. And so, through the many things done secretly against the rules, their souls take on an inner disposition to disregard them. This is the origin of many evils, as anyone can see. Thus keeping money privately, loaning or giving to one another what they like, sending out and receiving letters in secret without showing them; talking to foreigners and borrowing writings from or loaning writings to them or other materials, taking household objects or making them their own; and finally, doing whatever they can without permission and against the rules or against the expressed wish of the superior—all of these are very common practices among them. And whoever does not do one of these things because he has qualms about not having permission or about breaking the rules is considered silly and useless and he is mocked so much by others that he finally decides to act as everyone else is acting. Furthermore, those who are most talented and are very well spoken murmur constantly against the rules and orders given, exaggerating their rigidity and providing apparent arguments against them.[11] This alone is enough to remove everyone's misgivings about breaking the rules or failing to observe them and it alienates everybody. As a result, everyone in the presence of his companions openly does whatever he likes, provided that none of us is present, because he can be sure that none of his peers will report anything. So now it is really impossible to find anyone among them who would report anything to the superior, even if it is regarded a matter of great importance.

More importantly, they have an amazing ability to sway the dormitory prefects, our brothers, and to induce them to have the same attitude by showing themselves so obedient to them and falsely affectionate so that the prefects acquiesce to this: not especially caring about keeping the rules. And it sometimes happens that the students find some easy-going person who, with good intentions, allows himself to be talked into not reporting infractions of the rules to the superior. They get such a person to veer so far from his office and duty that things turn out terribly. And they really love, respect, and very much esteem such prefects as these (if only any of them are found). And it is no wonder that some of us drift in this direction, because the students are so resourceful, shrewd and clever, and they are so talented in making their explanations that they would deceive anybody. If the prefect does not allow himself to be swayed but stands firmly in his integrity and is one with the superior, and if he does not allow things to be done without permission or against the rules, they immediately become his enemies, they do not obey him, they answer him arrogantly, they joke about him,

---

11 Rigidity was a complaint that some Jesuits expressed about Gagliardi's rectorship.

laugh behind his back, and persecute him so oddly that sometimes a prefect who does not give in to their cajoling or fair words right away is forced by such persecutions to do so in order to avoid having a continuous purgatory. If he just stands firm despite all that and aims at doing his job, then they all gang up against him and set about doing the worst things they know—not wanting to obey him, not paying attention to his corrections, and pulling every kind of prank they can—while making sure he cannot prove these things even though he has often witnessed them clearly—for once the students are called by the superior, they claim to have done these things without any bad intent, and they say that the prefect is a suspicious man and makes rash judgments. They also tell some past story against the prefect. From it, they deduce that it was then when the prefect began to hate them and that for this reason he takes badly everything they do in all honesty. So the superior cannot easily persuade them, and the prefect has an unbearable cross, nor can he make any headway with them on account of this. Finding the middle ground between these two poles (that is, of going along too much on one side or on the other standing separate from them) is supremely difficult for a dormitory prefect because if he tries to go along to some extent with them while keeping himself on the superior's side, he cannot last very long: for they are very free at home and in public and the prefect is forced to report their behavior to the superior. And as soon as they suspect this, however trivial it may be, they drop all friendship and they begin to undermine in the group his trustworthiness, attributing all his lovingness to pretense and regarding him as an enemy in disguise. So, given their wicked disposition, I believe for sure that every great saint would find it supremely difficult to remain in good favor with them. This is why it is not so easy to find a suitable prefect for the seminary, since it is a matter of very great prudence and virtue to know how to get along with students while maintaining the spirit of obedience.

   The same difficulty is shared as well by the *repetitores* and all of our brothers and fathers both in doing their jobs and in maintaining relationships with the students, because if our companions do not establish a bond with the students as they are,[12] the students take an immediate disliking to them. The superior has to face this difficulty more than any other, because he is praised by the students as their friend if he displays friendliness and does not command any sort of observation of the rules; but as soon as he shows that he wants modesty, obedience, and the house rules observed, under threat of punishment no matter how trivial, they immediately drop all friendship. And they say to somebody who has been punished: "Look how that superior, your friend, treats you, because he is a friend

---

12 The *repetitores* were usually Jesuits who were in charge of making students review and repeat their lessons. The *repetitores* themselves were usually students at a more advanced level of the curriculum who also attended the seminarians' classes in order to train them later. They had the profile of tutors rather than teachers. See Luca Testa, *Fondazione e primo sviluppo del Seminario Romano* (Rome: Gregorian University Press, 2002), 98–100.

of yours." And as a group they begin to be averse to everything that comes from the superior, even his very friendliness, since they hold as false the good words he uses with them. If he issues any rebukes, reprimands, or punishments, they complain and whisper against him as a cruel man lacking understanding. In fact, those students who wish to help each other have the same difficulty, because they are persecuted by all of the others with insults, mockery, pranks, and in other ways difficult to explain, so much so that they are forced to join the others, nor can anyone be found whose spirit will hold up against so many persecutions. In this way, many good students have been spoiled, because as soon as the others see one wanting to pull back a little and to dedicate himself to devotion, they start to suspect he will denounce the others, and so they call him a snitch, a Theatine, and a hypocrite in such a way as to arouse disgust and make him lose any desire of behaving, something that cannot be explained, so that they compel just about everyone to follow in their path, or drive him to desperation.

When their shortcomings in violating the rules come to the superior's notice, at the moment they are called in, they know very well how to excuse their conduct and subtly defend themselves so that, even if the matter is as clear as day, they can make anyone believe that it is not true, especially because one cannot find any witnesses among them who would be willing to tell what he has seen. And with their most appealing way of presenting themselves they suggest that the fault is either of the dormitory prefect, who provided them with the opportunity, or of the *repetitor*, or the teacher, or the superior; and if the superior did not keep his wits about him, they would persuade him in every detail.

Eventually, if the matter is evident and cannot be excused, in such a case, if the superior does not make some response, they immediately become utterly free in that matter, as if there had not been any rule about it, raising in their defense that the superior had once known about it and said nothing, and that this is a sign that the measure is no longer being observed. If the superior calls them in and admonishes them without a punishment, they immediately come back to their rooms and find the one suspected of having accused them—whether that is the prefect or someone else—and they say: "You tried to punish us, but you could not: our good intent is apparent." And they say this very seriously, not laughingly or in a playful manner, but out of a sense of duty and with an indication of their will to remember it and avenge themselves. If the superior gives a punishment, right away whispers immediately begin to circulate, and the claim that the student did not deserve it or that he has been wronged by the superior. And they begin to hate the prefect or whoever they think has informed the superior. They start to do the worst things they can with pranks, taking everything the wrong way, and they keep the smallest punishment in mind forever. They take revenge for this in every possible way on the prefect, the superior, and everybody; so in certain subtle ways they signal that their spirit is bad and eager for a vendetta, like stopping their speaking with the prefect and privately begging others not to speak with him, giving him the worst helpings at the table, stealing the written plans for their lessons, making him walk further than he can when they go out, and other things like these. And if one of them behaves in sincerity, taking the punishment without plotting anything, the others immediately prod him by saying: "What? Are you still talking to *him* (that is, with the dormitory prefect or the superior)? If I were you, I would remember this my whole life, and I would not ever talk to him anymore, nor would I ask him for any kind of license, even if I believed I were dying." And they would say other things like this. It very commonly happens that they take a superior's punishment as an offense and wish to take revenge when they get the chance. Some of them have even been found to have hidden knives and clubs for such a purpose. So in conclusion, neither ignoring them nor correcting them nor punishing them helps.

On the other hand, if one of the superiors shows them a bit of affection, speaking lovingly to them or showing them his good favor, they immediately become highly insolent towards the other fathers or brothers of a lower level than the one who has spoken to them. For instance, if the latter is the minister, they become insolent and disobedient towards the prefect; in the case of the rector, with the minister; in case of the primary administrator, with the rector and all the others. And whatever little support they receive from someone, they use it in order to disobey everyone else. And experience shows that the good ones are better preserved if the superiors do not talk to them very much or praise them aloud, but instead treat them with a certain seriousness, preferring to communicate through others, and when the occasion arises, answering kindly with only a few words.

Speaking generally, the students take offense at every command given and they let it be known that they do not want to obey. So if it is ordered that nobody do something without permission, first, if it does not very clearly apply to everyone, they justify themselves saying that they did not know it; then, if there is careful concern in expressing the command, they grumble that new rules and statutes are being made on unreasonable grounds; and lastly, if it is possible, everyone secretly does what they have been forbidden to do without permission. If someone cannot do it secretly, he prefers to suffer rather than to humiliate himself by asking for permission, and he uses this prohibition as an excuse to disobey some other rule. And if he must eventually do that thing, he does it without permission even openly, justifying himself by stating that asking for permission is not necessary when there is a need, and seeking somehow to incur the kind of punishment that they can call unjust. And they employ similar twisted ways of shaking off the yoke of obedience and living free.

They are also headstrong and very obstinate in their opinions, trying to persuade and convince each other in such a way that it becomes impossible for them to understand any other reason, and they stand firmly in their opinion, aiming at their own interests and at none other, such as whether to change classes or remain in the same one, and in other such matters. When they come to ask the superior for some favor or some permission that he does not think appropriate, they never cease to be worried, they always receive his reasoning and good words quietly, but they will always remain discontented until their wishes are achieved, nor will they let themselves be swayed by any decency, respect for the common good, prayers, or any other such reasonable things.

All of them have the habit of reporting immediately to everyone everything that the superior or someone else in the Society has told them privately, complaining and adding lies to their report, and they very often spread some completely false gossip either against the superior or in regard to any other matter that can incite everyone to do all kinds of mischief, as has been seen in the case of the notes.

Telling lies and tricking the superior are very common among them; for example, asking for permission to go to one place and going to another, falsely purporting to want to be corrected while conspiring otherwise, and innumerable other things in this vein, so that in all matters these students are as cunning and deceitful as can be said.

Fierce hatred and divisions often spring up among them for every tiny injury; they do not talk to one another for long periods of time; they ask all their friends not to talk to those whom they hate. They dishonor one another with terrible things, very often falsely. And sometimes, if they secretly learn something bad about someone, they report it to their peers out of hatred, but no one tells the superior, because even those who hate each other will work together against the superior.

On the other hand, friendships (or rather dishonorable affections and persuasions aimed at leading this or that one astray) are so common among them that it makes one cry, especially because only a very few remain unpolluted by this plague. And they commonly talk to each other about things like this when they have the chance. Some of them boast about this or that awful thing. They all do this making sure that the superior does not know anything about it. On the contrary, among themselves they talk freely about it. And this is very common when it comes to various misdeeds, that is, to have it widely known among themselves while keeping it hidden from the superior.

Concerning spiritual help, students do not show any sign of devotion, nor familiarity with prayer; and during the time for prayer they will often mostly lean in such a way that they seem to be stretched out in bed, either sleeping or, if they can, secretly reading some textbooks or other kinds of material. They rarely receive the sacraments. Concerning confession, they report to one another what the confessor tells them and complain about the penances he gives, and they do not feel ashamed of sometimes telling both the grave things they have committed and the penances that were given to them as consequence. Other students avoid going to confession to the common confessor and they go to confess elsewhere when they can. They rarely go to Communion, and so they do not pray either before or afterwards nor do they show any sign of thoughtful recollection. They listen very reluctantly to the word of God, and as soon as one of us talks to one of them separately in order to give him counsel, they all surround him and ask what he has been told. If he responds to them, they begin to joke and give reasons in order to persuade him of the contrary. But if he refuses to tell them right away, they look at him with suspicion and begin to claim that he wants to become a Theatine, and to annoy him greatly, so that they effectively cut off every possible way of being helped. They do not know anything about our Society, because they do not want to listen to anything about it; nor are they edified by things like that. On the contrary, they scrupulously criticize every one of our actions, seeking only matter for scandal and grumbling, neglecting all that which might be able to edify them. If one of our members sets about conversing with them, nothing comes of it, for either he has to bend himself entirely to their freedom in everything, which is not appropriate, or they cannot tolerate him once they find out that he actually wishes to help them. Once, it even happened that after one of our companions went with them for a walk during the school break, they each left him, one by one, until he was completely alone. On occasions, they started speaking with him to let him know that it was better if he kept away from them or they got together and agreed to begin to make jokes about him. In short, the students' behavior makes many of us feel that the best course of action is not to spend time with them at all.

Furthermore, they are supremely impudent, especially during their school breaks and on the streets out of the house, and in churches they are irreverent at the altars. They do not want to kneel down during Mass when they are out of the seminary, and they give other signs of very bad example. Moreover, concerning eating, they are very greedy, and they secretly get food to eat, and they are never satisfied with what is provided at the table, doubling their portions when they can or stealing things from the refectory to take to their rooms. If they can, they also steal books and other things whether they belong to the seminary or someone else, and they snatch those items for themselves, removing the owner's identification, and applying their own.

They have a very bad custom of attributing very bad nicknames to all of our companions and also to some of their own. They use these names while talking to each other and joking about this or that person. Similarly, they use other words or proverbs which they use to talk among themselves about what they want without being understood by our companions. In this way, they quite often make jokes about other people who are present but cannot understand the joke. This makes them lose all respect and reverence, for they will even put among these the superiors.

The most dangerous thing of all is that they know how to simulate modesty, obedience, and all of the other virtues at the proper time and place, so that they often succeed in tricking those who do not know them. It even sometimes happens that the worst ones among them are regarded as the best.

Moreover, they quickly teach and inform the newly arriving students about how they should behave in front of the superiors, persuading them above all that informing the superiors about anything is a great disgrace. And besides that, if the new student is simple and pure, there will always be someone there to tempt him and teach him about the vices and every other kind of sad behavior.

This is as much as occurs to me to say about their way of proceeding. It will not seem unbelievable to the one who ponders the reasons that I have provided regarding the difficulties in this place. I even hold it to be a very great miracle that, given the conditions of these youths and the other factors mentioned above, no great public scandal has yet occurred, and I attribute this to the grace that God Our Lord bestows on our Society. Let us always give thanks to his Divine Majesty for this.

Part 3:
Formation

CHAPTER 17

Best Practices in Humanistic Studies (1564)

Benet Perera

*After being asked by Diego de Ledesma, prefect of studies at the Roman College, to pro-
vide suggestions for reforming the teaching of philosophy, Benet Perera also found time
to compose this pedagogical treatise encompassing a wide range of issues pertaining to
humanistic studies (from grammar up to the beginning of the philosophical course).
Perera even showed an interest in education as a psychosomatic process, taking an
approach almost unknown in schools at that time. But we also sense a more traditional
classical humanistic background in his calls for moderation, for balance between intellectual and physical activities and rest, and for imitation based on ancient exemplars
as the most worthy models. Although the treatise offers advice to students on how to
improve their studies, it is especially addressed to teachers, providing them with suggestions on how to organize the material, how to present it, and even how to behave
when explicating an author. Perera's vision notably stresses the effectiveness that is
required of a fully diligent Jesuit teacher. Unlike his document on the philosophical
course (see Chapter 29), this work gives no hints of polemicizing against Ledesma, who
was in fact at odds with him over his pedagogic methods. Perera can be credited with
writing one of the few consistent and systematic educational philosophies that is still
implicit in some current Jesuit practices.*

*Benet Perera (born 1535, Ruzafa, Valencia, Spain—entered the Society in March,
1551, Valencia—died March 6, 1610, Rome). An acclaimed philosopher and theologian of the Society of Jesus, Perera spent all his Jesuit life teaching at the Roman College, where he began to give classes of physics in 1559. Despite a controversy with Diego
de Ledesma, rector at that time, and Achille Gagliardi (1539–1607), who accused him
of supporting Averroism, he was never removed from his office. He published an outstanding tract on natural philosophy (*De communibus omnium rerum naturalium
principiis et affectionibus *[On the first principles and conditions common to all natural things], 1567) and enjoyed renown in his theological career.*

Source: *Monumenta paedagogica*, nova editio, 2:670–85 (original: Latin)

Chapter 1—The Goal of Studies and Obstacles to Them

The immediate goal of studies is knowledge of the truth. That knowledge is the
perfection of the human mind; everyone naturally seeks after it.[1] But the final

---

1   This is a very common quotation from Aristotle, *Metaph.*, A 980a: "All men naturally desire
    knowledge." Perera's argumentation follows Aristotle's bipartition of immediate and final
    goals: the former could not stand without the latter.

goal of all our actions and thoughts and therefore of our studies as well, is God.[2] If there is anything we seek that does not refer to him, it is necessarily vain, empty, and devoid of all good result. Therefore, everyone should approach the acquisition of learning with the intent that he will not promote what is false or desert what is true, drawn by malice or influence or stubbornness, or by any other spiritual disturbance. For unless this fog of disturbances is driven off from one's heart, the individual will never be able to discern the truth nor gaze upon it simply and clearly. We must keep to Aristotle's maxim in every plan of studies: Socrates is a friend, Plato is a friend, but truth is even more a friend.[3] For the sake of truth, one ought not only dissent from others but also (if the truth demands it) change and repeal his own opinions and decisions. All vices but especially the pleasures of the body should be avoided by one who is eager to attain wisdom. For pleasure dulls mental acuity, forces the mind to earthly matters, and holds it bound there as if with a kind of chain; and however small it may be, it slows down the mind's progress like a kind of impedance.

Chapter 2—The Teacher and Classmates

There are three types of human beings, as Hesiod claims: one consists of those who are capable of acquiring knowledge on their own; a second, those who need teaching and instruction; and a third, those who are incapable of learning.[4] The last group should be kept entirely away from a literary education. He thinks that individuals belonging to the first category are both the happiest and by far the rarest of all. Thus, this discussion will be about those who are average: the first concern to have about them is that they get an excellent instructor. Above all, this teacher should possess four traits in order to assist his pupils in their studies: a precise knowledge of the material to be communicated; the experience, exercise, and skill of teaching; order, clarity, and fluency in setting out the content; finally, a great zeal and assiduous diligence. And in my opinion, this last element should be ranked among the most important. For I would prefer that a teacher have less learning than diligence. I would prefer some lack of precise knowledge to a

---

2   See Padberg, *Constitutions*, 179. The *Ratio studiorum* of 1599 would state the final goal of the arts and natural sciences this way: "Since the arts and natural sciences dispose the intellectual talents for theology and assist them in arriving at perfect knowledge and its use, and since *even by themselves* they help these talents towards the same final goal." See Claude Pavur, ed. and trans., *The Ratio studiorum: The Official Plan for Jesuit Education* (St. Louis: Institute of Jesuit Sources, 2005), 99.
3   Cf. Aristotle, *Nicomachean Ethics*, 1096a15.
4   "That man is altogether best who considers all things himself and marks what will be better afterwards and at the end; and he, again, is good who listens to a good adviser; but whoever neither thinks for himself nor keeps in mind what another tells him, he is an unprofitable man." See Hesiod, *Works and Days*, 295f., in *The Homeric Hymns and Homerica*, trans. Hugh G. Evelyn-White (Cambridge, MA: Harvard University Press, 1914).

lack of interest and care in moving his students forward in their education. My judgment is that anyone who thinks more about his pay or standing than about helping his students while he is carrying out the duties of a teacher should be dropped. Therefore the teacher should be the sort of person whom the student trusts because of his learning and ability to exercise, understands because of his skillful fluency in teaching, loves for his enthusiasm and diligence, respects for the integrity of his life, and, when the occasion arises, feels he can approach freely for advice because of his humanity and personal warmth.

A second concern must be the careful selection of companions and, as it were, fellow-soldiers for his studies. They ought to have the same level of interest and the same intention, and they ought to be eager to learn, not lazy, graced with good character so that they can be assisted in their studies and morally corrupted in no way. But enough about matters that call for external observation; now let us speak about the internal prerequisites for learning. These are nature, exercise, reading, and imitation.

Chapter 3—The Nature of the Body

We are each composed of intellect and body, and so we must therefore take account of each of these in our studies. To speak about the body first, since it is the instrument that the intellect needs in order to understand, we need to attend carefully to its health and strength. These are maintained and increased by a measured diet, sleep, and exercise. The quality and quantity of food needs consideration. For fasting and the deficiency of what is necessary as well as over-eating and an excessive supply of food severely diminish the mind's operations. The amount of food consumed should be as much as is necessary to satisfy the need and a moderate natural delight. But it does not help to eat refined foods and delicacies often. They soften the intellect and once they have taken hold of it with such delights and charms, they make it lax and slow to deal with the abstractions involved in studies. And so food and drink should be of the kind that better promotes bodily health rather than appetite and pleasure. Although sleep needs to be of varying lengths according to different temperaments and physical con-stitutions, the ancients nevertheless took seven hours as an amount that is proper and close to what is required. We should attend to this not less than diet since the mind uses the faculties of perception as a help and support for understanding, and in sleep these faculties are renewed, refreshed, and made more active and alert to serve the mind.

Bodily exercise is necessary, not to mention helpful, under three headings: First, so that the mind wearied by studying might be renewed. For what lacks occasional rest does not last. In the way that a bow violently stretched breaks, so the mind that gets no break from its effort necessarily weakens and in a fashion breaks as well. Next, bodily exercise contributes to digestion and to the proper fulfillment of the other vital functions. If anything goes wrong there, it is incredible how much harm eventually is done to the whole life of an individual. Finally, exercise helps keep away illnesses and harmful humors, which, as they appear frequently and in diverse forms among those who devote their time to scholarship, undermine the body's health and stability unless careful attention is used to repel them.

The following bodily exercises are prescribed and especially praised by the ancients: taking pleasant walks that do not cause a sweat; pitch and catch; the practice of running, jumping, and so on, provided it is moderated, for we must always follow that maxim that is so very famous, "Nothing in excess." Just so, health is badly affected by mental concentration that lasts a long time at a certain level of intensity. This is why, at least in my opinion, no one will do more than three hours of study without a break. I must also mention here what I have learned from a prudent and learned man. He used to say that an individual that has already made some progress in studies should never either undertake academic work while his body is tired and unwilling or strain in such work to the point of bodily and mental exhaustion. Just as it is considered wrong and destructive to begin a meal when the stomach has no desire for food and recoils from it, and to fill it up to the point of disgust, so in studies, what I have mentioned should be criticized and avoided. Finally, care of the body should be managed in such a way that it always obeys and serves the mind, but never so that the body fights against or overcomes it. But that is enough on the body. Next let us briefly cover what pertains to the intellect.

Chapter 4—The Intellect

For learning, the intellect of a person needs the assistance of inborn talent, judgment, and memory. In the talent, we have regard for acumen, speed, and nimbleness. In the judgment, we praise clarity, sharpness, and the ability to weigh, discriminate, and arrange matters. And in memory, we approve the power to understand many things easily and to retain them for a long while. The acumen of one's talent can achieve a great deal in the subject of logic and in all discussions of texts. Sharpness of judgment is especially essential in all areas of philosophy and in all the more important disciplines. But the study of law above all calls for an excellence of memory; the individual who has not applied at least an average memory for learning it thoroughly will not make very much progress at all. Among these three faculties, even though an excellent memory is something to be admired, people think a superior talent is the gift one is most fortunate to have—it is an almost godlike thing. Still, I give the first place to judgment, the second to talent, and the last to memory, for the supreme merit of wisdom resides especially in judgment. And in addition, we look for talent or memory among young children, but among mature men and those who are already a little older [than children], we especially look to their judgment. Finally, even though talent may be the thing that a person is most fortunate to have, since it brings up and pours forth on its own many things, nevertheless, unless this abundance is polished by the file of judgment, it necessarily remains crude and imperfect. Thus judgment puts, as it were, the finishing touches on and brings to perfection the works of the other intellectual faculties.

Chapter 5—Exercise

Even though what I have called faculties may rightly be called gifts of nature because those deprived of them can get them by no art or industry, nevertheless these abilities can still be enlarged, polished, and brought to a finished state through art, diligence, and exercise.

But the exercise of a learner's talent will take the form of striving with great zeal and mental intensity to discover something independently and always to see something new in the particulars of what he has learned by reading or by listening to his teacher. He will accomplish this without much trouble if he looks and considers the first principles and, as it were, the foundations, that a writer or teacher will have set down in any particular matter that is to be treated. Attention should be given, though, not only to whether those points that he knows from others can be deduced from the same principles but also to other ones, by which the proposed matter might be broadened and enlarged. He should also see whether other principles, other reasons, other frameworks can be applied to treating, corroborating, and elaborating upon the same subject. For example: if his teacher or a writer demonstrates anything by a material cause, he should see whether he himself can explain the same thing using a formal or final cause also, or through the effects and outcomes of an event, by connections, similarities, oppositions. Finally, like a good and diligent heir who increases the patrimony left to him in an inheritance, he himself should also be eager to amplify through new discoveries what he has received from others.

The exercise of the memory consists in three things: First, if he learns something by heart every day, however trivial. In this way, he will acquire in a short time a great ability to learn by heart what he chooses to. Next, he must notice and consider things more than once. For what the senses register tends to implant itself more deeply in the memory. Finally, method, or the arrangement of what we want to remember, helps memory substantially. When we have distinguished every element and set it in its own place, the very sequence of the material and their connection do not allow the memory to waver, but what precedes reminds us of what follows by their very connection.

What the rhetoricians have handed down about the art of memory, like the arrangement of images in a certain order, seems to me more troublesome and harder than it is helpful; remembering them demands another memory far more extensive and immediately available.[5]

Lastly, the exercise of judgment consists in diligently and attentively reading and listening to what we wish to judge, often considering and weighing it, and not being rash and reckless in making our judgments. Better to be charged at the start with slowness and delay in judging rather than to be accused of superficiality and recklessness. For that slowness leads to a certain weightiness, sharpness, solidity, and a kind of fullness of judgment. And since judgment holds the place of highest merit, and its fruit is most abundant, special interest and care ought to be given to cultivating and exercising it.

Following upon our treatment of nature, both bodily and intellectual and of the memory, talent, and judgment as well, we should next go on to the best way to read authors, first what ought to be read and then how to read it so that from the content we might take some fruit.

Chapter 6—Reading: What Should Be Read

First, then, I suggest that those studying some subject under a teacher be advised to invest special interest, effort, and time in perceiving well, reviewing repeatedly, and considering diligently and attentively what they hear and learn from the teacher. The ones who, neglecting the teacher's lessons, devote their time to reading many different books neither know what they are being taught and what they ought to learn by heart, nor do they take from the things they are reading so enthusiastically anything other than an understanding of many matters that is crude, confused, jumbled, empty, and likely never to be of any use to anyone.

So when they have done full justice to their own public lessons, they will be able to devote the remaining time to reading those commentaries that pertain to the same subject, and they will not shy away from what those works are teaching them. But be careful not to read either many or different or less than excellent ones, for too much reading undoes youthful intellectual talent and extinguishes it. Variety distracts the mind and stops any matter from ever being precisely and completely understood. It is a commonplace in the schoolrooms: perception focused on many things is less with respect to each individual one. Just as too great a variety of foods, even though it delights the palate, still does very great harm to the stomach and one's health, so a variety of reading matter, even though it tends to delight beginning learners who burn with the longing to know new things, is nevertheless terribly harmful to studies, and it hinders students from attaining a full and finished understanding of the subjects. Finally, to accustom students to teachings that are not the best and most important, and to

---

5   For this approach to developing memory, see Frances A. Yates, *The Art of Memory* (Chicago: University of Chicago Press, 1966). For a famous Jesuit application of this art, see Jonathan D. Spence, *The Memory Palace of Matteo Ricci* (New York: Viking Penguin, 1984).

set the mind at the start to matters that are trivial, empty, and devoid of true and solid wisdom is, at least in my opinion, the disaster, the ruin, and the destruction of all academic pursuits. This evil that is already spread far and wide through all subject areas is one I wish we were as able to remove altogether, or certainly to engage and heal it somehow, as we are to grieve over it in these times of ours.

So read those authors who in each subject area are considered distinguished for their authority and antiquity and excellent for their wisdom and scholarship and foremost in their fields. The students should be assisted not only by the learning of such authorities but they should also be able to adorn and fortify their own compositions by the authority and witness of those authorities when the situation allows it. And so the old writers should especially be read; in them there shines out the knowledge of many different subjects and a certain serious, solid, distinguished learning. Reading them produces the advantage that the mind not only becomes richer and more polished by a breadth of understanding of matters but is also rendered weightier, more mature, and keener in comprehension.

I have neither unqualified admiration for nor blanket condemnation of more recent writers. Just as I am aware that certain ones are especially observant of old learning and wisdom and very enthusiastic imitators of the ancient writers, so I also know that there are many who manifest only a degenerate form of the ancient pristine wisdom and learning so that their writings, when they are compared with the lasting testimonies of the ancients, are childish, cheap, and utterly devoid of all true learning and wisdom. With such writers, if you take away some passages excerpted from the ancients but still badly crammed into their compositions, the rest is completely filled with sophistries, sharp childish chatter, and to put it in a word, nonsense. I will attach at the end of this treatise a catalog of those authors who have written learnedly and brilliantly about all areas of philosophy (for I do not think I need to speak about other areas at the moment, although this list can be accommodated to include all of them).[6]

On the basis of what I have said, I think it is sufficiently clear what ought to be read. Now I must speak briefly about how we ought to read authors so that reading them is not entirely unproductive.

Chapter 7—How We Ought to Read

There are two types of writers: one consists of those who explain the opinions of others with their own notes or commentaries; the other consists of those who are not bound to anyone's interpretation and offer in their writing their own opinions, not someone else's.

In order to carry out the task of interpreting correctly, of course the former ought to first be knowledgeable about and skilled in the language used by the

---

6   According to Lukács, this catalog is missing.

author who is being interpreted. Ignorance of it has very frequently led interpreters (who are in other respects learned men) into many awful errors. Convincing proof of this can be found in the thousand silly questions and countless fictitious creations thought up by Latin philosophers in expounding Aristotle because of their ignorance of the Greek language. Next, it is appropriate that they are thoroughly knowledgeable about and well practiced in reading other writings by the same author so that they might explain the work that they are trying to interpret more accurately and reliably either by explicating or comparing on the basis of other passages how something similar or different or opposite has been stated by the author.

Lastly, it is proper that they are not ignorant of those who either earlier or later wrote on the same subject. This way they might point out anything that the author has added to his predecessors or anything that was added later by his successors; and also they might either reconcile or refute those who seem to have felt differently, if in fact these had great reputation and authority and this can be done without inconvenience. And this is the task of a good interpreter, first, to indicate the intention and, as it were, the aim of an author and to place in a way before one's eyes that to which everything that the author says should be referred. The next task is to organize the entire treatise under its main headings and to explain the connections among them and their sequence and the method and arrangement of the entire teaching. This very same thing should be furnished for the explanation of each of the sections (unless this might perhaps be omitted for what is clear and unproblematic). Then ambiguities that exist in simple or compound words should be explained. It should be made clear whether arguments are necessary or probable. Their sources should be noted. If the same thing is said by the author elsewhere, whether it is clearly similar or contradictory, it should be pointed out. Nor should one fail to take note of anything taught by the same author that seems worthy of being taken out or put in. But if the author is at variance with other celebrated statements of a writer, it should be stated whether the difference is merely verbal or rather substantial, and there should be a weighing of which idea is nearer the truth.

One should also disclose whether the matter treated by an author can be transposed and suitably shaped to fill out, build up, confirm and refute other issues. So someone eager to learn should diligently ponder these things in his commentaries. If he discovers that most of the things that have been mentioned here are lacking, I would urge that he not at all waste good time in reading them; but if he sees what we have said to be present, he should expend ample and eager study, effort, and time there. But enough about the first kind of writers. Now let us come to the second one.

Among those who write precisely and extensively about any particular matter, whether that content pertains to moral or natural or divine philosophy, these things or something like them (at least in my judgment) can be observed.

First the entire treatise should be skimmed casually. Then one ought to examine diligently and search out the goal towards which most of it is directed. Then, the treatise should be handily broken down into several major sections. Finally, each individual part should be given a careful, separate evaluation. In this matter, four things must be considered: one is invention, the second arrangement, the third is delivery, the fourth, some external factors involved in every composition.[7]

In invention, one should look upon the principles and foundations on which the entire argument rests, how sure and solid they are. The explanations and arguments should be weighed, whether they are merely probable or necessary; from which sources they have been drawn, whether they properly belong to that subject or are adopted from different sciences; whether the opinions of those who differ on the same matter have been ignored by the author or passed over or neglected because forgotten, or intentionally suppressed, or well refuted; whether in the invention there is anything that is unnecessary that can conveniently be trimmed off; whether other reasons can be adduced in treating the same issue, either stronger or certainly just as probable; whether in defining and demonstrating matters the author has kept the precepts for defining and proving an argument. Has he made use of a type of proof appropriate for the material that he is treating? Mathematical sciences require one kind of proof; moral explanations and elaborations demand another; and theories and arguments involving nature demand yet another.

Has an author in such a composition followed and imitated some earlier writer? What has he borrowed from him, what added or changed? Was he better or worse in his treatment of the same matter? Has he said anything new and unknown to others or even something paradoxical? Is the treatment philosophical or oratorical or poetical? Is it schematic, having only the bones and sinews of the arguments but lacking the flesh, blood, and color—that is, has it been embellished with different explanations of many matters, illustrated with fine and suitable examples, metaphors, comparisons, stories, and other material of that kind? And so, considering these factors or others like them, one will be able to make a judgment about a writer's invention.

There follows arrangement or method, which is twofold, one pertaining to teaching, and another to prudence. But some of these are oratorical, some poetic, some historical. So let him see which the author employed and how well. One method of teaching belongs to arrangement, another to division or definition, another to resolution; indeed, if we believe Galen, we see this in all

---

7   In rhetoric, "invention" is a term that means "thinking out true or probable things (*excogitatio rerum verarum aut veri similium*) that strengthen a case." See Cicero, *De inventione*, 1.7.9.

well-organized subject areas.[8] Therefore he ought to consider the following: whether he has begun from those things that are more known and shared, more sure and obvious to us, from causes and essential principles, from matters that are more simple or more completely developed; whether he has put at the beginning the things that he intended to treat; whether he makes use of metabasis, that is, of transition (the device by which we are told when some part of what has been proposed at the beginning has come to an end, and what has already been said, and what has to be said next, both assisting the memory of the foregoing and stimulating the expectation of the following, as the sequence and connection of the two is clarified).

Then he should consider whether the author has kept to the plan of the treatise at least in the overall structure, yet not at all in the explication of the individual sections. Some make this criticism of Aristotle and Avicenna.

He should also consider whether all the rules of division have been followed in the sections; and finally, whether in the sectioning there is an excessive division into small parts, or whether, when the matter calls for it, the author has not neglected the method or certainly not ignored it. For this is both a praiseworthy thing and sometimes quite a help for concealing one's art and also for avoiding tediousness.

In the third place, there should be a consideration of the delivery: whether it is philosophical or oratorical or poetical or historical; what style he has used, low, middle, or sublime; and how adapted to the matter that is being treated. He should consider tropes and figures of speech, whether they are excessive in this material or too sparing. With regard to simple words, he should consider whether they are barbarous, obsolete, strange, proper, or metaphorical, homonymous, synonymous, or univocal (which are commonly called analogous, but by Aristotle "one to one"); whether the words are humbler or grander than the matter demands. In the matter of compound words, that is, in speeches, it should be determined whether the speech is obscure, ambiguous, confused, rough, unrhythmical, smooth, or choppy; and if joined in the manner of dialogue, whether the speech is attached and attributed fittingly to each character; and even though it is not embellished by a writer of philosophy, and a verbal elegance is not required, whether he should have been yet expected to speak refined Latin, or even required to speak properly, distinctly, and plainly.

He should notice whether the author has gone on longer than he should, or not long enough. Finally, he should observe the pointed maxims and reasonings of the author, his striking oratorical embellishments, his wise utterances, his witticisms, and his jokes.

---

8   See Galen (129—c.200), *Ars medica* [The medical art], proemium and *De placitis Hippocratis et Platonis* [On the doctrines of Hippocrates and Plato], 9.5.9–14. For an exhaustive reconstruction of Galen's thought on this issue, see Michael Chase, "*Quod est primum in compositione, est ultimum in resolutione*: Notes on Analysis and Synthesis in Late Antiquity," *Annuario filosófico* 48, no. 1 (2015): 103–39.

In disputing, he will be able to make use of the author's pointed statements; in speaking, his oratorical flourishes; in managing and administering both private and public affairs, his wit; and in casual and social conversation, his jokes. He should see what measure the author keeps in praising things or persons, in castigating them, building them up, diminishing them, putting an end to them, or ignoring them in his digressions.

He should consider the parts of the oration: the opening, the setting forth of the matter, the narratives, the confirmations, the refutations, the conclusions, and the like. These should be considered in the composition itself. Outside of it, however, some circumstances that pertain to good form should be taken into account; for example, whether the composition fits the rank of the author or the place in which it was done, or the time or the personage to whom it was sent, and other things of this type if they occur. Now from what was proposed at the start, it remains for me to speak about imitation.

Chapter 8—Imitation

Imitation has a double meaning: the first and supreme one, on which those who are aiming for something great should especially spend their efforts, when we have the idea of that matter we want to express and achieve, that is, the intellectual comprehension of the perfect and finished form in itself, towards which we are eager to guide and shape our very selves. For example, the one who desires to become as great a philosopher as he can be, should set before his eyes the idea of a perfect philosopher, thinking of the way a perfect philosopher should be, from whom nothing can be taken away or added. Gazing on that form, he should be eager and strive to express that in his very self, and shape his very self according to the imitation of that idea. This aspect of imitating, as I have said, is the highest because in the idea of each thing there shines forth in an amazing way every perfection that can exist in that thing, without any error or fault being there. This kind of imitation was highly celebrated by the ancients, and even exalted by Plato and recommended by him in many passages.

A second manner of imitation arises when in a single discipline we propose to ourselves some author who has excelled in it as a model to follow as a leader. For even though making use of the form of a thing taken in itself is more nearly perfect than making use of a form that is situated in others, for the idea (as Plato has it) is always finer than the image which is shaped according to its likeness; and the author Aristotle has it that what is such on its own is more noble and pre-eminent than that which is such by participation—nevertheless, since the form of a thing situated in others is clearer to us and easier to imitate, and in addition since we are both moved and taught how we ought to behave by imitating, most people abandon the former meaning of imitating and embrace

202 JESUIT PEDAGOGY, 1540–1616

this latter one. They need to be careful that they only propose as models for themselves one who has excelled beyond all others in that discipline, and who by imitation has come closer than they have to that idea we have just mentioned and more fully expressed it in his very self. Next they should be sure they are not so bound and indentured to a single author that if some vice is found in him (and what mortal indeed is altogether without this?) they would wish to defend, approve, and imitate it, even as they critique, downplay, and despise anything better and finer that they might find in other authors.

But if they have no confidence that they can surpass or equal those whom they are imitating, they still should not lose heart and drop their zeal and effort of imitation. For in the imitation of great things, even to stand in the second or third places is a magnificent and glorious thing. But although more could be said about the process of imitating than I have briefly presented in this essay, what I have given here should suffice.

[…] And even if what we had resolved to say about the method of studying has all been explained and finished (unless I am mistaken), still, nevertheless, before I put the last touches on this composition, I have judged it worthwhile to add some commonplaces here. If anyone has them at the ready, he will be able to speak and to write about any proposed subject promptly and extensively.

[1.] Therefore, when some subject has been proposed for a speech, let him first think over the names and terms attached to that matter, those by which it is addressed in all or the leading languages, in which there resides some meaning that can be used to test, embellish, amplify, diminish, or treat it somehow.

2. He should search for the actions or the results of that matter.

3. The accidents both proper and common.

4. The conjoined, or what is termed the "adjacent," such as place, time, and the like.

5. The causes of things, such as material, formal, efficient, and final.

6. The genus and the particular, and from this, the combined definition and description of the thing.

7. Similarities and comparisons, that is, greater, lesser, and equal.

8. The contraries, both those that are properly called contraries and the contradictories, privatives, and relatives. To this add the oppositional or disparate.

9. Whatever has been said and written about the same matter finely and brilliantly in the writings of authors, such as proverbs, maxims, and oracles both divine and human.

Finally, if anything has ever been valiantly done for its sake by an individual so that honors or rewards have been presented either for that thing or for those who are zealous for it; if any have ever undergone great dangers and sought death for the sake of its defense and preservation.

These items do not all have to be investigated or expounded; nor should they be with every subject. Rather take account of the particular content, persons, place, time, and other circumstances.

A clear and ready knowledge of these categories certainly helps the memory to discover what you should say. The mind running through these categories either in all or in some respects will discover many things that can be transferred and accommodated to the matter proposed for treatment. Then it is a considerable help in the arrangement of what has been discovered, for they can be handled in approximately the same order in which such categories have been handed down to us.

Finally, it makes a great contribution to forming a judgment about the writings of others, in which there is an extensive treatment of any particular manner. It should be considered which of the things we have mentioned an author has explained concerning this matter, and which he has left out. And this way, we can pluck the greatest fruit from the reading of authors, if keeping such categories in mind we recall them and those things that seem to pertain to each one of them.

[1.] But to clarify and facilitate the use of these categories, let us take a single example for illustration. For example, one must talk about the human person. First we should ponder the names for this. In Latin, the word is *homo*, or from *humo* (from the ground), which illustrates his low state; or from *humanitas*, which encourages him to cultivate humanity and maintain it with other human beings. In Greek, *anthropos*, as if "looking upwards."

2. The actions that are proper to a human being are the functions of the mind, will, and memory, which are numerous and amazing: to understand, to combine single elements and to divide them, to reason, to remember the past, to understand the present, to look forward to the future, to know not only individual realities but universal ones, not only material ones but those that are without material aspect, not only things that are created and finite but even infinite God. The works of a human being are all the arts and sciences and all things that arise from creative activity.

3. The accidents proper to his body, namely upright stature, the knowledge and power of his intellect.

4. The place of a human being during his time here is all the land and sea; after death, it is heaven for the good, hell for the bad. His time, if you look at the beginning, is finite, but if at the end, infinite and perpetual.

5. The human being's material cause is a body of amazing dexterity and art fashioned by nature both from so many different parts and from parts having such diverse functions. His formal cause participates in reason and is like God, and his efficient cause is immortal God, by whom our mind is created from nothing. God himself is his end.

6. The genus of the human being is animal insofar as he is similar to the beasts and less than angels, even while endowed with divine reason.

7. The human being is like a small universe, greater than whatever is under the moon, less than the angels.[9] If you consider nature, he is altogether like every other man. Therefore nothing is more linked with man than ignorance and vice, and nothing is able truly to harm him while he is reluctant and unwilling. Still there is practically nothing that cannot impede and harm his body in some fashion, and nothing that does not typically do so.

So, many things both human and divine have been spoken about man, such as that famous saying, "Know yourself." That man is a microcosm and a sort of "hay" of this world, that is to say, a shadow.[10] That he is the "entire tree," all things, either because by his sense and intellect he understands all things that are or because in him exist the perfections of almost everything.[11]

Finally, many individuals, on account of their excellence and a certain divine quality of their virtue and achievement, have on occasion earned not merely human but even divine honors and have been listed by the ancients among the gods.

This is the gist of what I have to say here about the method of studying. If I have perhaps left anything out, it will either not be of great importance and it will not pertain to the general method of studying that I have decided to pass on here, or it will certainly be easily understood on the basis of what I have stated here.

---

9   The image of man as a microcosm was a classic commonplace and one of the pillars of Renaissance humanism. See the *Oratio de dignitate hominis* [Oration on the dignity (or "rank") of man] of Pico della Mirandola (1463–94).

10 Hay or grass is a biblical image of humanity: "For all flesh is as grass (*faenum*); and all the glory thereof as the flower of grass. The grass is withered, and the flower thereof is fallen away" (1 Pt. 1:24). Also Is. 40:6: "The voice of one, saying: Cry. And I said: What shall I cry? All flesh is grass (*omnis caro faenum*), and all the glory thereof as the flower of the field."

11 The "Porphyrian tree" was a standard feature of medieval logic books, as in the *Summulae logicales* [Little summaries of logic] of Peter of Spain (*fl.* thirteenth century). The tree illustrated the entire "scale of being."

CHAPTER 18

Spiritual and Academic Progress (1564)

Giuseppe Cortesono

In his report on the German College (1567), Ludovico Gagliardi (1543–1608) criticized Giuseppe Cortesono (1537–71), the rector, for not carrying out his administrative duties rigorously enough. Three years earlier, at the time when Cortesono composed this document, he had already spent two years as a confessor charged with the care of young souls and was not yet rector, so it is understandable why Cortesono focused here on the general formation of young men rather than on curricular or didactic issues: he explicitly promoted the improvement of spirit and morals as the main goal of the Jesuit college, even at the expense of learning. These two aspects of education, spirit and letters, had always been linked in Jesuit practice, but Cortesono's most pressing concern was fostering unity—among professors, between professors and prefects, and between staff and students. This was critically necessary for an institution facing its early organizational troubles: rumors were spreading quickly through suspicion and gullibility, confessors were being ignored, students were being restrained by fear and sometimes punished without any proof. Cortesono's solution was the opposite of Gagliardi's: for Cortesono, gentleness and moderation should always be the hallmark of Jesuit pedagogy, since no other means, whipping or spying, denouncing and sentencing without a fair trial, could promote the students' spiritual well-being.

Giuseppe Cortesono (born c.1537, Forlì, Emilia–Romagna, Italy—entered the Society on February 1, 1559, Rome—died January 14, 1571, Forlì). After entering the order, he attended the logic classes of Francisco de Toledo (1532–96) at the Roman College, where he also served for a long while as a confessor. In 1564, he was nominated rector at the German College, a charge he held until 1569, when he was sent by Pope Pius V (r.1566–72) to Monte Cassino as confessor of Cardinal Innocenzo Ciocchi del Monte (c.1532–77). He spent his last two years of life in Forlì, working and dictating instructions providing the German College with effective constitutions.

Source: *Monumenta paedagogica*, nova editio, 2:632–35 (original: Italian)

Rome, 1564

1. The foundation for all the good administration of these schools seems to me to consist in our being persuaded that the goal we are aiming for is to help the students spiritually and morally more than educationally; and therefore we should all be united and in agreement on this point.

2. Our way of proceeding with students must be such that they understand and see through their experience that we are seeking nothing else from them except to direct them, help them, and raise them up.

3. I have always held discipline and punishment to be necessary for children, but only so far as they are necessary for correction, and no more.

4. Using the whip as soon as a student commits a sin makes them lose the good idea that we want to help and direct them. On the contrary, they get the idea that we are only looking to catch them in the wrong in order to punish them. So complaints oftentimes arise: "The teacher harasses me." "The prefect is picking on me." And this is not what the children alone say, but their parents complain of it too, ones who sometimes come to us with the intention to teach us the way to govern children with gentleness and mildness, as I have heard from the parents themselves.

5. I do not think that there is any better way to make use of the corrector than what our Father Ignatius describes, that is, first to use gentle words, exhortations, and threats of punishments; and when this is not enough for their correction, then one should make use of the corrector to punish them. And if even this is not enough to correct the student, he could be expelled from our schools, if he represents a scandalous example to the others.[1]

6. Even if we proceed this way with a gentle spirit, we should not be concerned on this account that the bad students will not be punished, because a bad student will either change his ways by means of the gentle words and good advice or not. If he changes, we will have already achieved our aim; if not, there will be other chances to punish him.

7. When the teacher or prefect can remedy the situation on their own, I think they should do so, particularly if the issue is private and carries disgrace, because doing the opposite would, it seems to me, be against charity, justice, and the goal for which we are aiming.

8. Nonetheless, the teacher should not feel offended or take it badly if the prefect or others were to apply a remedy to some problem in his school without informing him of it; and the same goes for the prefect, if he has not become aware of some problems, provided a remedy has been applied; in fact, he should be thankful.

9. When a teacher or prefect learns of some sin of a student, it seems to me that they ought to consult with the confessor before anyone else, and then take what they judge to be the best way to correct and help the pupil, even though sometimes it might require that we remain a little bit in the background. We need to be very careful about this, since often we fail to employ the proper means to help pupils, saying that otherwise we would lose our authority over them.

10. If a teacher or prefect should receive some complaint from one student against some boy, it does not seem to me that he should immediately proceed to punishment, and not even to a special inquiry, if the accuser does

---

1   See Padberg, *Constitutions*, 186–87.

not name other witnesses; and if he does name them, only those who have been named should be questioned. And this should be done very skillfully, because otherwise it seems to me that he would do wrong and an injustice to the accused.

11. I do not very much like the practice that tends to be used, namely that when the teacher or prefect has some evidence or slight suspicion, even one raised by someone else, they usually call the child in and tell him: "You have done this and that." Very often the charges are not well founded, and beyond the confrontation and the injustice that is done to the boy, the teachers themselves lose much authority and esteem. And even if the teachers later rightly catch the boys and accuse them, they would nevertheless hold the teachers' previous imprudence against them, and finding themselves on high ground they say: "What Your Reverence is telling me now is just like before." And they complain about this to their parents, as I know has happened, since a boy's father told it to me.

12. If someone should commit some error that has scandalized everyone, then he will certainly have to be punished, without any recourse; but if the scandal is not a pressing matter, I would not consider it improper if in such a case the confessor judged in the Lord that remitting the punishment on the strength of his own intercession had a greater chance of helping the pupil, the boy should be excused. In these cases, the prefect and the teachers should trust in the prudence of the confessor, who will always keep the common good in view.

13. Concerning matters of honor, one should be aware that once the pupil loses his sense of shame, it becomes almost impossible to help him. And it can often happen that, once a pupil had previously been solicited by no more than one or two individuals (because the others held him to be honorable and virtuous and did not dare to solicit him), once many questions are raised about him and inquiries are made, he will begin to be solicited by as many as have become aware of his fault, or at least suspect it. This happens because the mere suspicion that the teacher and prefect show with so many inquiries regarding the pupil's goodness is enough for other students to take it as the ultimate truth.

14. One should not rely too much on pupils' accusations, especially when they have not been interviewed, because everyone knows that they begin to lie as soon as they have barely learned to speak, and they take delight in seeing their fellow being punished.

15. Let me repeat that the unity of understanding and agreement among teachers, prefect, and confessor is extremely important for governing these schools, and each of them should highly value being helped by the others. And I believe it to be a very vain, even pernicious thing when one of them thinks that he will lose his reputation if someone else with a better

opportunity has resolved a problem for which he himself should have provided a remedy. For in this way it seems we are not looking to help the students but rather to enhance our own reputations for diligence in performing our assignment.

16. During the two years I have now spent in this office, I have never heard about any rumors or problems in the schools that are worthy of mention, except for the past year, when the teachers did not want to have anything to do with the confessor anymore;[2] and this year, three months ago, when neither the teachers nor the prefect conferred with the confessor about current affairs. I do not mean that this lack of communication was the cause of the problems, but that there were no similar problems except when this communication was lacking.

The confessor should not discuss with the prefect what he does with the teachers in order to help students, such as removing them from some practices, changing their place, and so on. Nor should the prefect confer with the teachers, because trouble would follow. But teachers should do what is proposed to them, if it seems to them right in the Lord, and if it does not, they should tell the confessor that it cannot be done.

---

2   Cortesono had been a confessor at the German College from 1562 to 1564.

CHAPTER 19

Refined Education (1565)

Pedro Juan Perpinyá

Already considered a great orator when he arrived at the Roman College in 1561,
Pedro Juan Perpinyá (1530–66) began teaching rhetoric there with notable success.
He had just come from Coimbra's renowned Colégio das Artes, founded in 1542 by
João III, king of Portugal (1502–57, r.1521–57) and soon entrusted to the Society.
This document reveals Perpinyá's great esteem for the pedagogy of his former college
in comparison with what he regarded as the low level of humanistic literary instruc-
tion in Rome. Given Ignatius's great ambitions for the Roman College, this judg-
ment may surprise us, but we must realize how high an institutional standard was
being used: the Coimbran institution was established as Portugal's worthiest possible
response to France's Collège Royal (founded in 1530 by King Francis I [1494–1547,
r.1515–47]).

When Prefect of Studies Diego Ledesma (1519–75) asked Perpinyá for sugges-
tions on the curriculum, he responded with this trenchant evaluation of the human-
istic pedagogy there, a sharp rejection of the status quo: textbooks, teachers, and
manners were inadequate. The insults Perpinyá directed at the author who had
dared to provide rules for teaching grammar and syntax—who was nothing but an
amateur of humanistic literature—were an especially bitter pill for Ledesma, as the
author in question was none other than Ledesma himself, whose name Perpinyá
had perhaps furiously written down on the paper and later rather prudently erased.
The mastery of humane letters appears here as the core of a refined education, which
encompasses both the learning of higher disciplines—a badly written philosophy is a
bad philosophy—and the formation of one's character.

Pedro Juan Perpinyá (born 1530, Elche, Valencia, Spain—entered the Society on
September 30, 1551, Coimbra—died October 28, 1566, Paris). Perpinyá's reputation
as a great preacher in Portugal began very early. He taught humanistic studies at the
Jesuit college of Lisbon (1553), gave the inauguration speech at Évora, and held the
chair of rhetoric in Coimbra from 1555 to 1561. In 1555, he delivered the funeral
oration for Prince Louis of Portugal (1506–55), brother of the king. He was called to
Rome, where he taught at the Roman College (1561–65). There, he was able to make
contact with such famous humanists as Paolo Manuzio (1512–74), and he tried to
reform the curriculum on humanistic foundations. In 1565, he was sent to the college
of Lyon, and finally to Paris, where he died before his thirty-seventh birthday.

Source: *Monumenta paedagogica*, nova editio, 2:658–65 (original: Latin)

Those Who Want a Refined Education to Flourish Should Take Care That These Things Are Done as Diligently as Possible

1. A Latin grammar should be composed by some man well skilled in this art and experienced in teaching boys, someone such as I have described in the second chapter of "On the Method of Teaching Boys Greek and Latin."[1] The grammar being used at the Roman College is quite unsuitable.[2] The Coimbra grammar is less bad, but you could not call it good.[3] Of all who are now in the Society, the Portuguese Manuel Álvares will most easily compose such a grammar and he will do it best.[4]

2. Following the opinion of the best instructors, a definite order should be established for the individual classes by a truly learned person who has had a long and extensive experience of teaching boys. This has been fully achieved at Coimbra through extensive deliberation and considerable experience. How much trouble the neglect of this arrangement has brought the Roman College is evident from the plain reality there and from the complaints made by many. I think it best if someone transferred both the number of classes and the entire structure of the college at Coimbra to the Roman College, with a few changes if anything does not seem to fit with Italian customs. What someone has written up on syntax and on the arrangement of classes seems to me completely without merit.[5] Nor is that surprising, since the author has neither this kind of disciplinary knowledge nor experience in teaching.

[3] Someone should be put in charge of the gymnasium to function as a supervisor and overseer [*episkopos*] so that no detail of the system is neglected. He should be a man of competence, energetic and learned, and a leader with considerable influence in the public sphere. He should be free from all other work and he should devote himself solely to seeing that the individual classes are well arranged and managed. And first of all, he alone should have the power to admit those who wish to contribute to our efforts, and he himself should gauge their disciplinary knowledge or their ability and assign them to whatever class will be appropriate. Likewise, at set times he should transfer boys to other classes according to each one's ability; and neither

---

1 See Chapter 24 in the present volume.
2 Perpinyá refers to *De primis Latinae grammatices rudimentis* [On the first rudiments of Latin grammar], composed by the Jesuit Hannibal du Coudret (1525–99). The book on syntax by the Renaissance humanist Guarino da Verona (1370–1460) was also used.
3 The *Grammatices rudimenta* of João de Barros (1496–1570).
4 Manuel Álvares (1526–82) published a manual of grammar which soon became successful in Jesuit colleges. The *De institutione grammatica libri tres* [Three books on the teaching of grammar] (Lisbon: Barrerius, 1572) was mentioned in the *Ratio studiorum* (in the versions of both 1586 and 1599) as the standard grammar used in the Society's studies.
5 Ledesma's name had been written here, but it was later replaced by the word "someone." See *Monumenta paedagogica*, nova editio, 2:659n8.

in this matter nor in any one of those that pertain to the arrangement of classes should anything be allowed to the rector of the college (either the pontifical or the German one) and to the prefects, whose concern should be kept within the community walls.[6] Likewise, whatever has to be performed publicly, whether they are dialogues or comedies or tragedies or orations, he should review carefully to keep anything from being done in the vernacular. He himself should make decisions about the Latin material as seems good to him. But he should see to it that public performances are very infrequent, and that nothing goes out from us that is not entirely polished and brought to its final form. The deliveries of speeches can be frequent, in the manner and style of the college at Coimbra. He should make rounds of the gymnasium frequently when an assembly is being held, and, if it is necessary, he should keep the young ones at their duties by the gravity of his presence and by his temperately administered correction. He should make frequent class-visitations, and afterwards in private he should remind the teachers of his own responsibility. In sum, he should be something like the mind of the entire school, and he should have the supreme power to structure the studies. Here there is a superintendent wonderfully trained and educated at Coimbra, but no one [trained there] has been at Rome up till now, or [such persons] have been distracted by other matters or not trained in this kind of thing, with the exception of Father Olave.[7] And so we see classes so troubled that it seems that they can hardly be motivated even with great effort.

4. Teachers should be selected according to their suitableness for teaching boys. What I mean by suitable is that they are so talented that they themselves can profit greatly by teaching others; and they should be so masterful with the material that they can very readily exercise their students in whatever they are teaching; and they should be so expert that there is nothing new for them in their job; and so industrious and diligent that they teach even difficult subjects easily and refuse no chore. If anyone is not so well practiced, he (provided the rest of these features are present) will acquire great facility, given the attention of the prefect and a short period of steady application. At Rome, many of the Latin teachers fall short in many respects, and in particular, the ones who are in charge of the lower ranks are profoundly averse [to teaching] and good for nothing.[8] That is why we have heard many complaining with good reason that

6 The pontifical college was the Roman Seminary.
7 Martín Olave (1507/8–56): See José Malaxechevarría, *El doctor Martín de Olabe* (Rome: Pontificia Università Gregoriana, 1940).
8 We know that, in 1554, there were five teachers of grammar (*Monumenta Ignatiana*, series prima, 7:258), but Villoslada, who listed all of the early professors at the Roman College, did not mention them. Ricardo García Villoslada, *Storia del Collegio Romano dal suo inizio (1551) alla soppressione della Compagnia di Gesù (1773)* (Rome: Pontificia Università Gregoriana, 1954), 322–36. A class of grammar was added in 1568.

with us "those who could not sing to the lyre, sing to the flute."[9] Those who think that in the lowest classes any ignorant person whosoever can manage the role of a teacher are mistaken, because it is more acceptable to fall below the average among the highest ranks than among those where the boys first have to be initiated into the practice of Latin. "The jug long keeps the smell of what first wet it fresh," as a most insightful poet says.[10]

5.   In what bears on this type of learning, the prevailing counsel and authority should be that of those who are leaders in practice and disciplinary knowledge, not of all those whosoever as boys [merely] got through the rules of grammar in their primary education; and the entire system should be managed according to the thinking of the former, not on the basis of the opinions and errors of the inexperienced. Nor in our planning should we consult those who seem eager to talk about everything at the prompting of someone asking their opinions, but we should look to those who truly and without ornament can and wish to explain what they themselves feel. For it is better to be instructed privately by members of the household on something that you may correct, than to be blamed publicly and criticized by outsiders on things that you don't want [to correct]. It is hard to say how many blunders there have been and are every day among us at Rome through the neglect of this one principle. The reckoning of sharp and substantial voices shows how we have lost it all for no other reason than this, and I do wonder if we will ever get it back.

6.   No author should be taught, neither orator, historian, nor poet, unless approved by his long-standing celebrity and by his style of writing. Thus I would not want recent writers being taught, however excellent they may be. I think a certain person named Verino and Cato should be rejected.[11] I think that we need to rid ourselves entirely of those copybooks that are so slender and so poor in words, and the sample-books for composing letters. Source material should be gathered from the reading of all the best authors. That other method helps little or not at all, and it does a good bit of damage since it removes all judgment and choice. For this reason, we see that it is approved by no one who is average in composition; it belongs to those whom no wise person ever wanted to be like. I approve the booklets of Father Cipriano on rhetoric since they have nothing but what is taken from the ancients.[12]

---

9   A Greek proverb indicating levels of musical talent. Cicero (106–43 BCE) cites this idea in *Pro Murena*, 29.
10 Horace (65–8 BCE), *Epistulae*, I.2.69.
11 Miguel Verino of Majorca (1469?–87?), author of *De puerorum moribus disticha moralia* [Moral distichs on good morals for children] (Lyons: [no publisher], 1540). Cato here refers to a long-used medieval text for children, The *Distichs of Cato*, attributed to Dionysius Cato, an author otherwise unknown, perhaps writing in the third or fourth century CE.
12 Cipriano Soares (1524–93), *De arte rhetorica libri tres ex Aristotele, Cicerone et Quintiliano* [Three books on rhetoric based on Aristotle, Cicero, and Quintilian] (Coimbra: Barrerium, 1562).

7. The more difficult passages for philology concerning money, weights and measures, notations of numbering and other passages in the writings should also be clearly explained. Nothing demands this support more than the art of speaking well. It is unbelievable into how much ignorance and ineptness we have fallen.

8. All the teaching of the greatest arts should be treated in pure and blameless speech, and in it each one should strive on his own to convey an elegance and quality of expression that matches the grandeur of the contents. For as things are explained now, a constant habit of speaking badly and ineptly deforms the speech of those who are learning; such a great distaste for pure speech is produced as to remove all hope that they can possibly be called back to a better manner of speaking. But that situation discourages both teachers and students and causes them to despair. After the teachers have lost every hope of a more refined education, when they realize that every attempt of theirs and all their considerable effort will be futile, with what attitude would they carry their daytime and nighttime burdens? But would the students not abandon all concern for and interest in Latin and Greek, if they thought that it made no difference how you speak in a gathering of wise men? What now could be thought more revolting than that such great matters are being buried in the filth of defiled speech, and the light of knowledge darkened by verbal murkiness? And if it is not supposed to serve elegance, certainly much less should it serve the monsters and deformities of words, but rather flee them, and take that [pure speech] as a fellow and companion to shed light on matters divine and human, not that these may serve it, but on the contrary, so that it may render service to them. If truth by its attractive and beautiful appearance alone awakens an amazing love of itself in the minds of people, how much more intensely would it inflame everyone's wills if the adornment of words like pearls and the glow of speech were to be joined to that brilliant shape? If ever it was necessary that these things be joined together, it seems to me to be especially necessary now. If it is right for any rank of men to strive in this direction, we ought to be doing this already ahead of the rest; if any from our community [should be doing this], those (beyond the rest who are living in this residence of the Roman College) [should be doing this], when they profess that they are going to be assisting Germany and France in oratory.

But we should not listen to those who say that it is impossible to explain elegantly what is involved in obscure technicalities. Perhaps we should listen to them if they were to say that they *themselves* are not capable of treating these matters elegantly. For indeed even if wisdom possesses no particular speech of its own, certainly what is expressed so poorly by those ignorant of Latin and Greek can be explained more suitably by men both learned and accomplished. I do not deny that certain words are proper to each art; but

I want them taken from the most reputable and ancient authors, not from mobs of amateurs. Nor do I strip from prudent individuals the power to attach new names to new realities, but I think that the extravagant license of certain people should be limited, so that no new word is made except by necessity and good reason. But necessity should not be judged on the basis of an individual's lack of knowledge, but on that of the reality itself. The measure of things is not whatever happens to occur to an extremely immature person, but what the leaders and the authors of Greek and Latin speech have taught. I approve neither the position of those who in their eagerness to seem elegant corrupt Aristotle's ideas; nor the position of those who in an excessive concern for the words show contempt for the meaning of the actual content. I say we have to strive to express the fullness of the greatest realities with proper, clean, and serious speech. But this belongs to orators, not philosophers or theologians. I do not want philosophers and theologians to speak "oratorically" but correctly;[13] that is not the proper possession of orators more than any free citizen. But those who are not trying to speak in Latin are very obscure; those who do this correctly do not speak obscurely except to those who have barely attained the rudiments of Latin as children. There is in Portugal some concern for this situation, as the writings of Pedro da Fonseca show.[14] There is almost none of this concern at Rome, where it

---

13 "Correctly," that is, "in Latin." *Latine* here has the meaning of "in clear Latin that is most appropriate for the content and the idea being expressed."

14 Pedro da Fonseca (1528–99), a Jesuit philosopher and theologian who became known as "the Portuguese Aristotle." In the "Address to the Reader" of his *Commentaries on Metaphysics*, Fonseca shows his concern about the relationship between philosophy and speech: "[...] illud primum efficere conati sumus, ut contextum Aristotelicum et sincere ad veritatem, et commode ad usum verteremus. Namque interpretationes ad verbum, quae circumferuntur, dum fidem servare volunt, non intelliguntur plurimis in locis; et, cum Graece Latinis verbis loquantur, nonnunquam aliam sententiam pro alia subijciunt. In iis autem, quae magis sunt tractabiles, et si maior intelligentia, minor tamen fides cernitur; in iis praesertim, quarum auctores plus studij in poliendo sermone (quod Philosophus non valde curat) quam in vero sensu eruendo, & reddendo ponunt." (We have above all attempted to translate the Aristotelian text both faithfully and usefully. For the verbatim translations now circulating, while they wish to be faithful, are not comprehensible in various passages; and when they speak Greek with Latin words, sometimes they say things that are quite different from the original. In the translations that are more useful, though they are more comprehensible, you find less fidelity, especially when their authors have put more effort into polishing their speech [which did not really concern the Philosopher very much] than in searching out and rendering the real meaning.) These words are taken from the *Commentariorum Petri Fonsecae theologi Societatis Iesu, in libros Metaphysicorum Aristotelis, Stagiritae, tomus primus* [Commentary of Pedro da Fonseca, theologian of the Society of Jesus, on the books of the *Metaphysics* of Aristotle the Stagirite, volume one] (Leuven: Porta, 1585). In "De cultura ingeniorum" [The cultivation of talents] of Antonio Possevino (1533–1611), part of the introduction to Possevino's *Bibliotheca selecta de ratione studiorum in historia, in disciplinis, in salute omnium procuranda* [Encyclopedia of the plan of studies in history, in the disciplines, and in procuring everyone's salvation]

ought to be at its strongest. In order for the concern to be everywhere just as great as is appropriate, it has been put in the power of those who are in charge of the colleges. For if they should show in words and deeds that they place a high value on the elegant expression of doctrine; if they bestow some favor on those who are enthusiastic about that elegance, and if they do not allow them to be ridiculed and insultingly called asses by others who are incapable of achieving the same thing, a kind of unimaginable concern to beautify wisdom will inflame everyone's heart.

9. Young men selected from the entire group, who possess robust native intelligence and whose age supports their efforts and who are inclined to this type of learning, when they have done all the rest of their studies—these men should be taught rhetoric for three years, or no less than two, and they should practice in such a way that they attain high proficiency in every type of composition. Then they should attend to philosophy and take theology classes for several years before they are put in charge of the upper classes. Unless this is instituted quickly, I am afraid that in a very short time we will have no one who is able to teach. For up to now, students quite uneducated in practically everything have been sent to the rhetors, and even before the end of the year, they (except for very few) were told to confess publicly what they did not know.

(Rome: Typographia Apostolica Vaticana, Domenico Basa, 1593), Fonseca was listed among the great philosophers who could write in a very stylish manner. One of Fonseca's students, Luis de Molina (1535–1600), became famous for refining his teacher's ideas reconciling God's grace and humanity's free will.

CHAPTER 20

Promotion of Humanistic Studies (*c.*1584–90)

Fulvio Cardulo

Two documents contributing to the debate over the Ratio studiorum *carry Cardulo's plea for the proper recognition of rhetoric among the disciplines. In the sixteenth century, the ranking of the arts and sciences had palpable symbolic reverberations in daily life, as for example in the seating arrangements for faculty at public events. In a parallel way, Jesuit education was structured along the lines of grades and classes: these had their own spaces, schedules, and identification badges (like colors or patron saints). Cardulo's complaints about rhetorical education found support in parental dissatisfaction with the literary course of studies. He therefore pressed for a substantial change in the symbolic representation of rhetoric in the eyes of both students and teachers. Cardulo thought this change particularly necessary because the families' main concern was having their young men trained in "letters" (language and communication arts, but also classical culture), since these were essential for employments carrying higher prestige. These expectations were quite different from those of the Jesuit scholastics, who were looking especially to philosophy and theology to go as far as they could academically. The tension between these two orientations eventually made it clear that serving a mixed population required adjustments in the plan of studies.*

Fulvio Cardulo (born 1529, Narni [Terni, Italy]—entered the Society in August 1546, Rome—died May 15, 1591, Rome). One of the first Jesuits sent by Ignatius to the University of Padua to complete their studies, Cardulo attended the classes given by the renowned humanist Lazzaro Bonamico (1479–1552). He taught humanities in Venice and Bologna, and thanks to his reputation of being extremely learned in classical studies, he was appointed to teach rhetoric at the Roman College in 1552, where he spent the rest of his life. Polanco entrusted him with the corrections of his own Latin translation of the Constitutions, *and Jerónimo Nadal asked him to provide Latin translations of the reports from the Indies. A great orator, he was often invited to preach at the Sistine Chapel during the pontificates of Paul IV (r.1555–59), Pius IV (r.1559–65), and Pius V (r.1566–72).*

Source: *Monumenta paedagogica*, nova editio, 7:128–30 (original: Italian)

I

Among all the means that our Society uses to attain its goal, which is to help souls, there is one that experience and reason show us to be especially effective: teaching, beside other disciplines and sciences, humanistic letters. We greatly need to support and maintain this enterprise, undertaken to the honor of God and the universal help of the Christian commonwealth, in quite a different way than we find in our schools today. There we see such slender results that the Society suffers great dishonor and blame, along with a bad reputation. And this general reputation, as we can all see, has arisen from the judgment and testimony of princes, prelates, and people of discrimination and learning who both love the Society and grieve that we are not doing our duty. We seem to be tricking people with promises to give the young a good education in letters and then failing to fulfill that obligation when we assign teachers who are inadequate and inept.[1] This troubles our conscience. The result is considerable harm, and we are kept from being able to help students in Christian devotion (our main aim). We lose our credibility and authority, as is evident.

To remedy such a serious shortcoming and to fulfill our duty, we should state first that in this area the intent of the Society should not be the teaching of grammar and Latin in any way we like. Rather, we ought to strive for a nobler goal, that is, forming good citizens who can contribute to society, and instructing so many of the youth and nobility in a way that with time they may show what they can do in pulpits, senates, secretariats, and ambassadorships—these students that our companions subject to school-discipline throughout the world. So the prudence and eloquence that we should be teaching in our schools will serve the Christian commonwealth and produce good preachers, senators, secretaries, nuncios, ambassadors, and others who serve the common good.

To do that, we need both a method of teaching and men. This is what the method would involve:

1. Collecting from good authors various contents and commonplaces that serve the above-mentioned Christian moral and political goal.

2. Beginning to teach and exercise students in this way and to this end, in due measure, from the lowest classes of grammar, where nothing but Cicero and such are read.

3. Methodically and diligently practicing, in the upper classes of humanities and rhetoric, oratory, declamation, history, and poetry.

4. Keeping them more years in such exercises, since one cannot acquire eloquence without great labor, diligence, and a long period of time. All these are very necessary for such exercises. When the students of the lowest classes have been instructed and exercised in the stated method in the direction of the intended goal, and when they have reached the highest class of rhetoric, they should stay there for three years and follow a kind of course of rhetoric. They should practice verse and prose of every kind, ordering all the literary exercises to the office of a good preacher, senator, ambassador, secretary, and

---

1   This was not an uncommon criticism addressed to the Jesuits, as one can see also in letter from Annibale Firmani (1530?–95) to Francisco de Borja (February 17, 1565), requesting better-trained teachers. *Monumenta paedagogica*, nova editio, 3:373–75.

so on, making use of commonplaces, subjects, maxims, and different collections, as stated.

And since such an important undertaking requires enough suitable individuals to support and maintain it, it will not be very hard to find them in the Society. And if they are not there, we should form them; and to form them, some who are talented and disposed to this profession and these exercises can be selected. Our Lord by his grace has given talent to many, as one can see, and the inclination and application rests with the superior, at whose judgment and will the subjects act. They typically apply themselves to what they see is pleasing to superiors. And so for a while now those who are in charge have turned all their interest towards theological and philosophical studies, discounting the study of fine literature and actually snatching away literary schoolmasters and professors through their deeds more than through their statements. In the hearts of many who had the greatest talent for these studies, an aversion to them is raised, along with an attraction to the higher sciences, so that the scholars might then be esteemed and follow careers and acquire ranks that are denied the humanists. Hence, our Society's youth shy away from both the teaching and the learning of humanistic letters, under the influence of this way of proceeding and the inequality of status (as it appears to them and as they say). Therefore, many people who are definitely suitable and talented for this way of life devote themselves to other, more highly esteemed exercises for which they have neither the talent nor the touch; and they therefore work hard at it, happier to be well thought of than to be producing fruit for their neighbor and attaining merit before God.

Those who knew our Father Ignatius can testify very well how much this saint esteemed these studies, and with what high a standard he wanted our brothers to follow in them. His successors should maintain this opinion, and, thinking over this subject in the Lord, I hope in our Lord's goodness that they will find abundant consolation there as they see humanistic studies flourish in the Society, with the fruit that the blessed Lord seeks.

To have a number of good teachers of rhetoric, two things are necessary: the first is good natural talent, the second, practice over a number of years. For practice, one must persevere in the class-work. For natural talent, superiors need to be careful not to assign those who only have four sentences and a little poetry at the ready; the professors should be individuals of good judgment and knowledge, and they should also possess the talent to profess them. And so that such people devote themselves to rhetoric, one needs to remove the obstacles that pull them away from it. Of these there are two: hard work and the typical neglect of these letters.

Two things make for hard work: one concerns dealing with students, and the second involves lowering oneself to give and read compositions, keep discipline, and stay two hours without a break in class. This does not seem to me at all degrading. On the contrary, it seems to me necessary that the teacher be very diligent in keeping his students of rhetoric busy, making them compose, repeat, and recite their own compositions, and so forth. This hard work could be alleviated in the following way: first, by letting the teacher take one year to be able to prepare lessons and topics and to become familiar with the authors. During this year, the teacher could be put in charge of the academy. And thus every three years the teacher should have a year of rest and again be the moderator of the academy or have some task in the seminary.

Second, the hard work could be alleviated by proposing that there be no lessons during vacation times, and, if there are no philosophy classes, even in September. Experience teaches us that during these days students make little progress because the external students either do not come or do not compose, or, if you want to force them, you need to lower yourself to indignities that are unworthy of a person who has those qualities we want in a teacher of rhetoric. During this time, some students are thinking about taking up another state or manner of life, or of going back to their homeland, or going to the country for vacation, or of studying something else. As a result, coming to school is merely *pro forma* for the external students. It is even worse for our young companions, because some are in retreat, and some are at Frascati, and so the school stays empty and the teacher disgusted.[2]

The other point concerning hard work for the rhetoric teachers is the matter of constant compositions, either to satisfy the external students or to satisfy the school's demands. This could be alleviated by the strength of our companions' correction skills if they are quite content to avoid criticizing little faults in work that is generally good enough. This is a very important point, because when some students realize that work does not please their teachers, or that they are being criticized, they lose heart, and they turn their efforts to less challenging projects that win more approval. So in this, it is up to the superiors to lighten things for their subjects in holy simplicity, speaking well of them right away or being silent about what might be criticized, because criticism, beyond the other stated effects, causes additional harm. What is also helpful in removing this problem are the remedies that serve to take away any devaluing, because lowering something's value in general leads to the lowering the value of its particulars.

The neglect of rhetoric arises first from the fact that superiors show few signs that they esteem these studies; and second from the great desire everyone has to study or teach philosophy. Therefore, rhetoric is often discredited, for both our younger companions and for the external students, with the talk that rhetoric does not have anything but words, or that it is unproductive and useless,

2 The Jesuits had a villa residence in Frascati (in the Castelli Romani area close to Rome) affiliated with the Roman College. It was used especially during summer vacations.

and so on. And this goes so far that sometimes the teachers who must teach the classes influence the students of humanities (directly and indirectly) cheat them of their humanistic studies so that they go on to logic without wasting a year of both money and time, as they say, in rhetoric.

The remedy for this would be for superiors to demonstrate an equal regard for teachers of rhetoric and logic. This could be done, first, by assigning individuals to teach rhetoric who are also suitable for other positions. Second, by repositioning rhetoric among the higher classes and granting it all the privileges logic has, namely: (1) The same vacations. (2) Rhetoric should have no supervisor other than the highest prefect of studies. (3) They should go to the vineyard with the metaphysicians.[3] (4) They should be provided with a person to take care of their rooms. (5) They should not be obliged to attend the ordinary meetings of the teachers of grammar, except for a particular reason. (6) At the disputations, they should sit in the higher section of seats, if they wish to go there. (7) When they deliver a formal oration, they should be recognized in the refectory just as the teachers of philosophy and theology are.

In addition to this, it will help if teachers of philosophy and theology show their esteem for the teachers of rhetoric, especially by inviting their students (seriously and not as a joke) to go to hear orations when they are delivered in the hall. The practices diverting students from rhetoric to logic should be abolished in every respect.

That the teacher of rhetoric deserves as much attention as the teacher of logic is proven by the following reasons: first, because his profession does not require less talent and fewer abilities (as for example, judgment, taste, and memory), but rather more of them. Second, because it requires at least the same amount of hard work. Third, because this profession is no less necessary than that for the common good and the reputation of the Society. Fourth, because very few are endowed with outstanding abilities in this field, so that those found to have them should be kept satisfied as much as possible. Fifth, because the world holds this profession in such great esteem, and if we do not match their opinion with some of our own demonstrations at home, they feel disappointed and suspicions can begin to arise. Sixth, although it might well happen that sometimes a very young teacher teaches a class in rhetoric, the teachers of rhetoric are usually older religious and they have been working hard in the lower classes for many years; this is not usually the case with teachers of logic.

---

3 Students would often stroll in the vineyard to get some rest during recreation. By rule, students usually recreated by class, so they might not share the same place at the same time. Cardulo's argument is that the dignity of rhetoric teachers should be recognized publicly: they should be allowed to share recreation time with the highest-level class, namely that of metaphysics.

CHAPTER 21

Specificity in Doctrinal Content (*c.*1574)

Diego de Ledesma

Ledesma's concern about the uniformity of doctrine among the Jesuits continued to his last days. Differences of a more than personal nature lay behind his opposition to Benet Perera, who was freely praising "impious commentators" at the Roman College to the detriment of the safe doctrine of Latin Scholastics. Nor was he motivated by a merely political concern to keep the Society out of trouble, as one might discern in Superior General Acquaviva's own commitment to constrain Jesuit academic freedom. It was mainly a problem of vision. Ledesma believed—and he was not the only one—that the Society should strive to be recognized as a solid army of philosophers who, as Saint Paul says, all speak alike (1 Cor. 1:10). He wrote a commentary on Borja's list of doctrines prohibited in a Jesuit college, providing references to support their elimination. He also outlined two documents in which he intended to provide a summary of the doctrines that should be taught.

Despite Borja's seemingly positive attitude towards his efforts, Ledesma failed to win his battle. In fact his adversary won a promotion rather than a rebuke: he became a theologian at the Roman College. In 1576, Perera dared to write an introduction to his philosophical masterpiece (De principiis [On first principles]), still acknowledging the "impious" Averroes (Ibn Rushd, 1126–98) and Alexander of Aphrodisias (fl. 200 CE) as the best commentators on Aristotle. This work received an imparimatur *from his superiors. Borja's list was never applied, and even the idea of the* Delectus opinionum *[Selection of opinions], which Ledesma himself had instigated with his lists of approved doctrines, was abandoned by the Society. This document is Ledesma's last stand, a letter written in 1574 to the new superior general Everard Mercurian (1514–80, in office 1573–80). The general was not disposed to support its vision, and Jesuit philosophers still had some time to cultivate a wider range of opinions.*

Diego de Ledesma (born c.1524, Cuéllar in the province of Segovia, Spain—entered the Society on September 30, 1556, Leuven, the Spanish Netherlands—died November 18, 1575, Rome). Ledesma was a professor of theology in the Roman College and prefect of studies there from 1562. His work, De ratione et ordine studiorum Collegii Romani *[On the plan and order of studies at the Roman College] has been called "perhaps the most substantial contribution to the development of the Jesuit code of education."[1] In 1569, it was issued by Superior General Francisco de Borja (1510–72, in office 1565–72). Known as the "Ratio Borgiana," it was the first*

---

1   Allan P. Farrell, *The Jesuit Code of Liberal Education: Development and Scope of the* Ratio studiorum (Milwaukee: Bruce Publishing Company, 1938), 169.

universal plan of studies in the Society. It remained in effect until the 1591 Ratio
was issued for trial use.

Source: *Monumenta paedagogica*, nova editio, 4:196–204 (original: Latin)

To Father Everard Mercurian, Superior General of the Society of Jesus

Rome, 1574

Very Reverend Father in Christ,
May the Lord Jesus kindly keep the learning in his Society always true, good, and
sound, just as we hope it will be. Amen.

The following three points concerning the opinions prohibited in the Society are now being called into question—not without considerable danger, in my
opinion: First, whether any specific opinions should be prescribed for teachers
in the Society to follow or avoid, or whether a general prohibition of harmful
doctrine is sufficient. Second, granting that some particular opinions are to be
prescribed, whether those that have been laid down should be retained or not.
And third, whether it should be in the manner in which they have been posited.
So I will take these points in this order and say what I think best.

I.   [I think] not only that should there be a general prohibition that no one should
      teach against the faith or teach things that are out of harmony with the faith, and
      so forth, but also that some particular opinions should be prohibited, and those
      that seem advantageous and necessary for sound doctrine should be prescribed.

1.   These opinions, either those that are erroneous or those that are out of har-
      mony with the faith, have given rise to so many turmoils, scandals, divisions,
      arguments, and dangers in our college over the last ten or so years, that it
      was all but impossible even to mute them.[2] And we only hope that they will
      not sprout up again in a worse form than before. This is why it is clearly
      necessary that some of these opinions be prohibited not only generally but
      even particularly, and why it is also necessary that we should prescribe those
      opinions that can suffice to maintain the true, sound, and secure teaching of
      the Society. Reason on its own seems enough to support this; indeed, so does
      experience, which, as they say, is worth a thousand witnesses.[3]

---

2   Ledesma is referring to an acrimonious battle he had been fighting against Benet Perera,
    professor of philosophy at the Roman College. Ledesma had accused him of extravagantly
    praising the "impious" Averroes and of teaching doctrines contrary to the Fifth Lateran
    Council (1512–17), which imposed on Christian scholars the task of defending the unity of
    faith and reason. See Christoph Sander, "The War of the Roses. The Debate between Diego
    de Ledesma and Benet Perera about the Philosophy Course at the Jesuit College in Rome,"
    Quaestio 14 (2014): 31–50; see also Paul Richard Blum, "Benedictus Pererius: Renaissance
    Culture at the Origins of Jesuit Science," *Science & Education* 15, no. 2 (2006): 279–304.
3   This proverbial saying is a variation on the form cited by Quintilian (Marcus Fabius Quin-
    tilianus [*c*.35–*c*.100]) in his *Institutio oratoria* [The education of the orator], V.11.41),

2. I also tend to think that it would be too cold and ineffective a remedy simply to prohibit these ideas generally (for example, "No one should teach against the faith or what is less favorable to the faith, or against what is commonly held, etc.");[4] for this can easily be side-stepped and they can say on particular points that what they are asserting is more compatible with the faith and favors the faith more or is more commonly held. This would give rise to daily arguments, disagreements, etc., of the teachers themselves or others with the prefect or with the rector over particular issues; and this is just what we see from our experience.

3. Likewise, if a general prohibition is issued, it should therefore be observed in detail in particular cases; otherwise it would be vain and useless. Therefore, it helps to have particular prescriptions so that it is clear and known what the general one includes.

4. Likewise, the unity of doctrine in the Society can be maintained with difficulty or not at all except on the condition that some points, at least the chief ones, are set forth in particular, the ones on which the rest depend; and certainly this will greatly help to maintain that unity of doctrine.

5. Likewise, it is hard or even impossible to maintain the security of doctrine in the Society in any other way; and especially in philosophical matters in which today one can find such great and destructive license in certain provinces and universities to the extent that we have seen. But a good, solid, and secure doctrine, one that is both stable and wholesome, is in the greatest interest of our Society. Further confirmation comes from the fact that apparently the main reason why the attempt is being made to have no particular propositions or opinions set forth is, I say, on account of the school of thought: some do not want to join in the common teaching of Saint Thomas's doctrine, or not even that of the Scholastic theologians; but they either want to teach just as they wish or they want to follow Averroes or other Greeks or Arabs (who are in reality not spiritually wholesome) and other modern philosophers who are very much the same.[5]

"Conscientia mille testes." *Conscientia,* later "conscience," originally referred to "shared awareness" or "shared knowledge *(scientia)*" so that its connection with "experience" *(experientia)* is a close one.

4   In 1564, Ledesma himself had put forward two very detailed lists of theses that Jesuit philosophers should be obliged to defend and a listing of the dangerous and erroneous doctrines Perera had taught at the Roman College. These lists were transcribed in *Monumenta paedagogica,* nova editio, 2:496–504.

5   Ledesma is clearly referring to Perera here. See Cristiano Casalini, "Pererio 'cattivo maestro': Su un *cold case* nella storia della pedagogia gesuitica," *Quaderni di Noctua* 2 (2014): 59–110. A short list of "modern" philosophers recommended by Perera can be found in Chapter 29 of this volume.

6.   In many different Jesuit colleges where the rectors, or even provincials or prefects of studies are not so learned that they can make judgments on their own about all these matters, they would not be able to stand up against those troubles. But this way they will be greatly assisted, and they will have fixed points to follow, so that they cannot easily be deceived by themselves or by others.

7.   In addition, the teachers themselves will have a light to follow, a way to go, and a recognition of the rocks they need to avoid. And alien and inquisitive intellects, if there should be any (and they are never lacking, so corrupt is this nature of ours)—these will be kept to their charge and within bounds, so that they do not get carried away.

8.   Likewise, especially in matters that somehow concern the faith positively or negatively, doctrinal freedom would be a supreme disaster, not only in the Society but also in God's church. Certainly, seeking after freedom in doctrine and permission for it at one's own level (if any seek it) is like the request and permission for freedom of religion and faith that the heretics of our age are pursuing with such great effort today, even if it is, as I have said, at a lower level; and as that liberty is most pernicious and not to be granted, so neither is this one. The argument is strengthened by the fact that otherwise sects would easily be introduced into our Society, both novel ones and the old ones of philosophers and others; people would be following different schools; and all kinds of strange teachings would be imported into the Society. But this is clearly against what the rules and the *Constitutions* state, that diversity of doctrine should not be allowed either in oral or in written form.[6]

9.   Finally, the Lateran Council under Leo X, session 8, teaches some particular things, and in other matters it instructs teachers to try to defend them as well as they can with arguments and in resolving opposing arguments, etc.[7] Therefore it helps, and it is in accord with the council, that the teachers should be provided with those particular points concerning which they especially ought to perform this task.

---

6   "As far as possible, we should all think alike and speak alike, in conformity with the Apostle's teaching; and differing doctrines ought not to be permitted, either orally in sermons or public lectures, or in books" (Padberg, *Constitutions*, 120–21).

7   On this point, the bull (session 8—December 19, 1513) states: "We strictly enjoin on each and every philosopher who teaches publicly in the universities or elsewhere that when they explain or address to their audience the principles or conclusions of philosophers, where these are known to deviate from the true faith—as in the assertion of the soul's mortality or of there being only one soul or of the eternity of the world and other topics of this kind—they are obliged to devote their every effort to clarify for their listeners the truth of the Christian religion, to teach it by convincing arguments, insofar as this is possible, and to apply themselves to the full extent of their energies to refuting and disposing of the philosophers' opposing arguments, since all the solutions are available." See Norman P. Tanner, *Decrees*, 1:606.

10. Again, the decree of the third congregation, stated in canon 46 on the basis of three congregations, says that "our teachers who are expounding Aristotle should use great discretion in reading those interpreters who have written in a spiritually harmful way against Christian dogmas, and [our teachers should endeavor] especially to assail whatever opposes the Christian truth; and they should teach philosophy in such a way that they make it assist and serve authentic Scholastic theology."[8] Therefore it helps and it is especially fitting to designate these issues where impious interpreters have made the worst mistakes, and where they twist the meaning of Aristotle in a spiritually unwholesome direction, and where it ought to be serving Scholastic theology.

Finally, this plague has invaded not only our college, but, as I hear, also some other provinces and colleges of our Society or it has certainly begun to invade them, and I wish it were not so, and that it had not already driven its roots deeper in some other places and even here has not been entirely uprooted.[9] Therefore, it seems best that, far from removing this remedy, we should all the more rigorously make it the rule and put it all the more effectively into practice. This is as much as I have to say about the first point. Let us now speak about the second one.

II. [I think] that these opinions which have been prohibited or established as the rule by Reverend Father General Borja, and which the general congregation has set forth for the teachers, and which have been circulated through the other provinces of the Society should be retained and proposed in the normal way to the teachers.[10]

---

8   The canon is actually number 47 (though in the manuscript the number is d.72). See *For Matters of Greater Moment: The First Thirty Jesuit General Congregations—A Brief History and a Translation of the Decrees*, ed. John W. Padberg, Martin D. O'Keefe, and John L. McCarthy (St. Louis: Institute of Jesuit Sources, 1994), 149. The Society's Third General Congregation (April–June 1573), summoned after Borja's death, elected Everard Mercurian as the new superior general.

9   Ledesma is referring to the German province, where Peter Canisius (1521–97) had complained about some former students of the Roman College who were spreading Averroistic theories there in the name of Benet Perera. In 1568, the provincial congregation of Upper Germany declared: "We greatly desire that a severe law be promulgated throughout the whole Society, so that the opinion of either Averroes or any other philosopher that contradicts the Christian faith or the common doctrine of the schools in any respect may not be defended or confirmed." *Monumenta paedagogica*, nova editio, 3:40–41. On the spreading of the Perera affair in the German provinces, see Marcus Hellyer, *Catholic Physics: Jesuit Natural Philosophy in Early Modern Germany* (Notre Dame: University of Notre Dame Press, 2005), 30–32.

10 In 1565, Francisco de Borja, third superior general of the Society of Jesus, issued a circular containing a list of philosophical axioms to be imposed and taught as true "according to Aristotle, true philosophy, and natural reason." Borja's list was first reproduced in Le P. Camille de Rochemonteix, *Un collège de jésuites aux XVIIe and XVIIe siècles: Le Collège Henri IV de la Flèche* (Le Mans: Leguicheux, 1889), 5–8. This list was eliminated during the editing process of the *Ratio studiorum*.

[1.] First, almost all the reasons just mentioned, if anyone examines them somewhat carefully, confirm this point. For they are those opinions that for about
a decade gave rise in our college to those feverish turmoils that I mentioned
above: disagreements, scandals, divisions, etc. The fire they stirred up was so
great and of such a kind that the fathers could hardly put it out. Nor were the
turmoils confined to this college but they spread even beyond it, and somewhat beyond the Society to its own great peril. So unless we want this fire to
be re-kindled, it is necessary to keep everything that had been established.
Indeed, after these decisions had been made, peace ensued in our college
(praise be to Christ) and we stopped being tossed about.[11]

2.   These very points that were laid down, if anyone considers them, can contribute greatly to preserving the unity and security of doctrine; to introducing
and promoting the best kind of doctrine; to putting a check on a pernicious
doctrinal freedom; to restraining talents that are too self-indulgent or, to
put it bluntly, reckless, keeping them within the bounds of sound doctrine;
to providing great assistance to rectors and prefects of studies in this very
effort; and to clarifying matters for the teachers; and to establishing the
goal of wholesome devotion [*pietas*] and the true philosophy at which they
should be taking aim.

3.   If anyone considers the individual propositions that have been laid down, he
will find that all of them are of the faith or more consonant with the faith,
or certainly that they more strongly favor the faith when one or two points
have been removed; but there is still an accepted philosophical axiom; and
against such axioms it would not be permissible to teach even when not
under any restrictions. But the contrary ones are either plainly wrong and
adverse to the faith or they favor wholesome devotion less, and they can
promote waywardness or certainly lead someone in that direction.

4.   These very same propositions, insofar as they touch on character, are a very
great help; for they are thoroughly religious and, as experience shows, they
preserve devotion and simplicity and intellectual honesty, and they render
the mind tranquil and humble before God, and obedient to him, and they
rouse hope in God and confidence and love and gratitude. But (as we unfortunately have more than adequately discovered also by experience, and we
say this with considerable heartache) contrary doctrine and contrary opinions dry up one's devotion, and they offer a good number of temptations
against faith and religion, and they often make the mind doubtful and hesitant and wavering, and so forth.

---

11 Ledesma provides a version of the story which is not entirely true. There had not been
such great turmoil as he attempts to depict during the Perera affair. Ludovico Gagliardi
(*c.*1543–1608), who fought harshly against Perera, had to move to a new location, whereas
Perera was simply "promoted" to teach theology at the same college, a position he held for
the rest of his life with a very positive reputation as a theologian.

5. These very things are consonant with Scholastic theology and the teaching of Saint Thomas, which the [Jesuit] *Constitutions* praise so greatly and want to be taught and commonly followed. But it is not the *Constitutions* alone that approve Scholastic doctrine and that of Saint Thomas; the church itself does.[12] It is almost under the very rule of the teaching of Saint Thomas and the Scholastic doctors, and it often follows them in its decrees and in other matters.

6. These established teachings are in large part those that are expressly stated in the Lateran Council under Leo X, session 8, such as what concerns the immortality of the soul, and that it is not a single entity in all human beings, and that in itself it is essentially the form of the body, and that it is multiplied and to be multiplied according to the diversity of bodies into which it is poured.[13] And the rest of the issues are included under the general statement of that council: "We enjoin upon all and upon every individual teaching publicly that when they have taught or expounded to their students the philosophers' principles and conclusions in which they are known to veer from orthodox belief, such as the teaching about the mortality of the soul, or its unity, or the eternity of the world, or other such things, they should be required to make the truth of Christianity clear and to teach it as persuasively as possible; and to eliminate or resolve as powerfully as they can and with all their attention the arguments of such philosophers since there are solutions for all of them." This is what the council said. Therefore it helps that these points be kept and observed; indeed, this is consonant with the council, that teachers both know what those points are and how they ought to handle them; and all the more so as the council enjoins that this statute and mandate be published as binding under holy obedience every year at the start of studies in universities and where *studia generalia* are operating.[14]

7. Moreover, if you consider the matter correctly, these are some of the chief headings which are the sources, as it were, from which almost everything else in philosophy that pertains to spiritual devotion depends and is derived, as if

---

12 Pius V (r.1566–72) declared Thomas Aquinas a doctor of the church with the bull *Mirabilis Deus* in 1567, only seven years before Ledesma's document.

13 The bull aimed to counter the doctrines of Pietro Pomponazzi (1462–1525), which were being spread in Padua, and contained the ideas of Alexander of Aphrodisias (*fl.* 200) concerning the unicity of the intellect and the mortality of the human soul. Pomponazzi justified his doctrine by distinguishing between truths of philosophy and truths of faith.

14 In this case, Ledesma is adopting a juridical distinction among European universities that can be traced back to Gregory IX (r.1227–41), who in 1229 authorized masters of the University of Toulouse to teach in any other *studium* without examination. Although there is no official definition for *studium generalis*, this kind of institution started to be known as a university: it taught the higher faculties (theology, law, medicine) and was provided with a similar papal dispensation.

from first principles in a way, so that they have been selected and annotated by that great council for that purpose, and that is why these propositions also can especially preserve the unity and security of doctrine that I have mentioned.

8.   For many years now, these points have been analyzed and discussed and finally, by the judgment and agreement of the fathers and many other learned men, they have been chosen and approved as true and safe propositions that we ought to hold; and Francisco de Borja, who was the reverend father general at that time, instructed us to observe them; and at the General Congregation of the fathers and in the presence of the same reverend father general they were proposed and promulgated to the whole body of teachers who had been summoned to the Congregation, and they were also communicated to all the other provinces so as to be observed in this same way; and that has been the practice thus far in our college up to the present moment, when there is a truly dangerous threat that they might be ripped away again.

Here is additional confirmation: as Emperor Marcian rightly said in the Council of Chalcedon, actio 3, a person does damage to the Holy Synod if he endeavors to bring something back into doubt again or argue over it once it has been defined there.[15] But if some mistake has been made in local or provincial councils it has to be corrected by a greater universal council not by some person or persons at a lower level. Therefore, if anyone opposes some proposition, the proper procedure is for him to express it in written or oral form to our reverend father general, and then of course the reverend father general will pass it on for discussion to those to whom it seems good to entrust the matter. And clearly, since they have been circulated to all the provinces and a matter which pertains to the faith concerns all of them, before there is a contrary decision, if anything needed changing, it would be proper to write also to the other provinces so that they might reply by saying what they felt about these matters; and so, after the matter has been thoughtfully considered for a good while, reverend father general with his assistants should decide, or certainly some general congregation should make a full decision about these matters if the determination of the reverend father general did not seem sufficient, so that every weed might finally be plucked up [cf. Mt. 13:24–30].

9.   Likewise, since every change of law in itself is odious, the law should not be changed unless there is clear and certainly not a trivial but rather a great usefulness in doing something different, as Aristotle says.[16] But plainly this

---

15 Marcian (Flavius Marcianus Augustus, 392–457, r.450–57) was the Byzantine emperor who convoked the Council of Chalcedon (451), famous for the definitive Christological declaration of two natures in one person.

16 Aristotle, *Politics*, 2.8.1269.a 12–20: "[T]he law has no power to compel obedience beside the force of custom, and custom only grows up in long lapse of time, so that lightly to change from

is so far from being the case that nothing would be less called for [than to make this change].

10. If these definite propositions were not retained or if they were no longer set forth for the teachers, we would already seem to be approving them or at least to be willing to allow them; and thus whoever wanted to follow a less wholesome teaching or opinion would think it permissible for him to do so. Likewise, we would seem to be condemning those old fathers of either error or ignorance for having made those decrees, or we would seem to be condemning those who made those decrees of imprudence.

11. But in fact, if there are any who follow a less wholesome doctrine or would want to follow it, they would by that very fact be saying and boasting that reverend father general and the fathers now share their own opinion; or at least that they tend towards their way of thinking and for that very reason have changed some of the propositions or commanded that they not be retained; and they would spread about such rumors to defend their own faulty cause. And the reputation of the fathers could be partially damaged by the statements of such people—God forbid!

12. Likewise, they themselves would think that permission had now been granted to them; and so they would with all proud self-satisfaction dare to proclaim contrary teachings boldly and repeatedly; and those who are perhaps lying low now would stand up and be counted. In fact, even now some do not bother to conceal themselves; no, latching onto some strange sort of hope, they openly break out in words and deeds. If this matter is not addressed as soon as possible, we will really have something to be afraid about. But now let us speak of the third point, namely about the manner in which these things have been posited.

III. Whether opinions ought to be posited as they have been, namely affirmatively, or whether the same opinions ought to be posited negatively.

We reply that it is not enough that these propositions merely be set forth in negative form and changed from the affirmative, as they now are, into negative ones. Such a change would never be sufficiently protective, and the propositions could easily be circumvented, as for example if someone makes this sort of proposition: "No one should teach that there are three souls in the human being according to philosophy or Aristotle" and someone were to say, "I do not teach that there are three souls, but only two, namely an intellective and a sensitive one in the human being, or a sensitive and a vegetative one in an [irrational] animal"; or if he were to say "I do not teach that there are several rational souls in the human being," as this is another way that these teachers typically circumvent and interpret canon 8

---

the existing laws to other new laws is to weaken the power of the law." *Aristotle in Twenty-Three Volumes*, vol. 21, trans. H. Rackham (Cambridge, MA: Harvard University Press, 1944).

of the synod (actio 10, can. 11).[17] So also, if there is such a prohibition: "No one should teach according to philosophy or Aristotle, that God does not have providence," someone will say, "I do not teach that God does not have providence, but that he does have providence, but only over the heavens or universal causes, or that he has providence only over natural things or necessary ones," and so on.[18] This is why putting prohibitions into negative form this way would never be enough. As those formulations were established for this very reason, and with foresight, we rightly should have the more wholesome opinion taught in affirmative form so that no one is able to veer off towards anything less spiritually wholesome or in fact wayward out of ignorance or disciplinary knowledge, or from their own will, or from error, deception, or craftiness.

So as not to say more in this matter that is of such great importance and as obvious as it is wholesome, I think that what I have said shows not only that the established statements should be retained and proposed to the teachers but that these very same propositions should also be confirmed and that, if any changes ought to be made in any statements that do not concern the faith, these others should be amplified rather than diminished in any way, so as to be a better and more effective remedy in the future.

Judgment of a second: (name).

In all respects this statement seems [approvable], the way it has been written above.

Praise to God and to Our Lord Jesus Christ and to the most holy Virgin Mary his Mother. Amen.

---

17 Beneath Ledesma's reference to a general plurality of teachers who seem to use this kind of argumentation, one might see a specific charge against Perera. In his above-mentioned lists of propositions, Ledesma twice cites the example of the number of souls in man. He states that Jesuit philosophers should defend the following axiom: "Quod non sint plures animae in homines, sed una solum rationalis, scilicet anima" [There are not many souls in human beings, but only one, namely the rational soul]. See *Monumenta paedagogica*, nova editio, 2:497, 501. Ledesma reports that Perera has taught the opposite statement: "Quod sint in homine tres animae totales: vegetativa, sensitiva et rationalis" [There are three souls in human beings: the vegetative, the sensitive, and the rational]. See *Monumenta paedagogica*, nova editio, 2:501.

18 In his list, Ledesma stated the axiom concerning God's providence as follows: "Quod Deus habeat providentiam istorum inferiorum, etiam rerum singularium ac rerum humanarum" [God has providence over those lower things, even of particular events and human affairs]. See *Monumenta paedagogica*, nova editio, 2:496.

CHAPTER 22

Uniformity of Doctrine (1613)

Claudio Acquaviva

Shortly before the end of his very long generalate (1581–1615), Claudio Acquaviva drew up this testament on Jesuit education. One of the hallmarks of his tenure had been the Ratio studiorum *(1599), a project that had been in the making at least implicitly from the opening of the school in Messina (1548). Though a master administrator ready for every internal and external challenge to his policies, Acquaviva nevertheless failed to attain one of his main goals: a catalog of safe doctrines that Jesuits should be obliged to teach. The reasons were both external (the inquisitors disproved of such a list) and internal (there was strong Jesuit resistance to restrictions on professors' freedom of interpretation). Acquaviva therefore sketched this brief account of his long effort to achieve uniformity in the teaching of doctrine, instructing all administrators of Jesuit colleges to observe the rules of the* Ratio studiorum *and to oversee the opinions being taught. Astute about possible circumventions of the directive to adhere to Thomistic doctrine, Acquaviva forbade any argumentation, even of a probabilistic type, that tended to undermine the Angelic Doctor's authority.*

Claudio Acquaviva (born September 14, 1543, Atri [Teramo, Italy]—entered the Society on July 24, 1567, Rome—died January 31, 1615, Rome). The fifth superior general of the Society of Jesus, Acquaviva used the longest tenure ever in that position (1581–1615) to organize and centralize the Society, most notably with the plan of studies known as the Ratio studiorum *(1599). Acquaviva took a continuing special interest in this project. He oversaw the drafting committee's two major preliminary documents in 1586 and 1591, both of which rested upon extensive consultation with teachers and administrators. The final version marked the culmination of over half a century of the Society's experiences, reflections, and attempts at codification. With adaptability explicitly encoded in its directives, it stood for centuries as the defining and premier document of the* studia Societatis Iesu *(the studies of the Society of Jesus), covering not only the schools but also the entire academic formation of all Jesuit scholastics.*

Source: *Monumenta paedagogica*, nova editio, 7:660–64 (original: Latin)

Father Claudio Acquaviva to All Provincial Superiors: Decree on the Solidity and the Uniformity of Doctrine

Rome, December 14, 1613

A long time ago, in reference to the considerations I wrote out on May 24, 1611, I expressed the opinion that we ought to exercise a very special kind of care for the solidity and uniformity of doctrine.[1] These aspects are so necessary and of such importance for the obedient service of the holy church and for the preservation of the Society that for that reason we see them greatly commended by Our Blessed Father Ignatius in the third and fourth parts of the *Constitutions*. So it came about that we entrusted to all the European provincials the task of gathering a certain number of leading theologians to weigh what could be done in this direction and then send us their judgments. This they have accomplished. When I received them, I saw quite clearly, and much to my great delight, that everyone was aiming at the same place, and everyone searching after just the same thing. For although different things were mixed together in proposing the means, over which several provinces were at odds, still, in most matters, either many or even all agreed. But some of the measures called for a longer delay; others were difficult to put into practice; others caused more commotion than they provided help; finally, others were too harsh and highly unusual in the Society, for example, by imposing on teachers and revisors under obedience or by binding them under oath to adhere to this or that opinion or to oppose it.

[1] Therefore, after the entire matter had been commended to the Lord God with many Masses and prayers for that intention, when it had then been fully considered and finally taken under review with the father assistants, we finally settled on this one thing: all problems would be more than adequately foreseen, as far as circumstances allowed, if we carefully keep to our *Ratio studiorum*.

This has made me want to impress more strongly upon the provincials that they should scrupulously follow their rules which are clearly and fully detailed in that book for our studies, including the rules of their office (chapter 6) concerning literary studies;[2] then I would impress upon the rectors that they should take care to observe their own rules; I would do likewise with the prefects of studies and the teachers of the upper faculties, but especially with those who teach Scholastic theology. If everyone strives earnestly to accomplish this, everything will go smoothly and as we wish, with the help of Christ.

---

1   *Monumenta paedagogica*, nova editio, 7:657–59. Acquaviva refers to the commission he summoned in 1583 in order to draft the *Ratio studiorum*. His intent was that commissioners work both on a plan for studies and on a summary of approved doctrines (the *Delectus opinionum*).

2   Pavur, *Ratio*, 7–30, nos. 7–74.

[2] And as far as the solidity of doctrine goes, if we follow Saint Thomas alone, as is prescribed in can. 9 of the Fifth General Congregation, we will protect ourselves on this side, and likewise we will not stray far from uniformity.[3] For both aspects of doctrine, namely solidity and uniformity, were the objects of the General Congregation's attention in decrees 55 (41) and 77 (56), the source of that canon. And plainly nothing will lead someone to say that the mind of Saint Thomas is not always clearly in view, since all doubt is in fact removed by that decree.

For if it appears that some doctrine conflicts with Saint Thomas, there is now absolutely no need to examine whether that doctrine is solid or not, because we should not be following it at all. But if there is certainty that it is in agreement with the holy doctor, then both those aspects of doctrine that we seek will be equally sure. On the other hand, however, where it would be in doubt, and many important and long-established Thomists interpret it in various ways, it will be permissible to defend along with them the opinion that is thought more probable and that is akin to the mind of Saint Thomas. But at this point care must be taken, and certainly very seriously, that no one under the influence of a peculiar doctrine tries to persuade others that it is like that of the holy doctor, twisting a certain few expressions scattered here and there in the works of the doctor, pasting them together in support of his own special meaning, so to peddle his own opinion as if it were that of Saint Thomas. Instead, sound doctrine and the proper sense must be drawn out from passages where St. Thomas formally presents an argument, not from passages where, while discussing something else, he briefly touches on a topic in passing.

[3] These arrangements obviate the need to compose a catalog of the opinions we ought to embrace or reject as probable or not. For if we follow a single author, all that work has already been eliminated. Nor does this bind talents but it only puts them within certain bounds. Indeed, they can confirm the teaching of their author with reasons, dilate upon it and add illustrations. And so a truly wide field is afforded them, one in which the teacher's energetic activity can range widely even in following the tracks of an approved author. For indeed, although something is subordinate, an example does not everywhere answer to the matter now being taken up. And yet the abundance and variety of the holy doctors who published so many commentaries on the sacred scriptures as if they were so many treasures of precious materials and still did not turn even slightly from the right road seems to express appropriately enough what I mean.

[4] But some have thought that that variety of opinions which is found in many writers of the Society can injure the uniformity of doctrine, if anyone should believe that he can freely on his own follow any one of ours, since their books

---

3   See *Acta Congregationis Generalis V: De studiis*, in *Monumenta paedagogica*, nova editio, 7:351.

have already been published with the permission and approval of the superiors. But I have plainly declared that teachers or writers so following others are not permitted to depart from Saint Thomas on that account. If some opinion has been allowed in print because it is very probable and defended by learned authors (doubtful opinions have already been treated above), it will certainly be defended from the charge of novelty, recklessness, and error; but it is not on that account assured that others ought to follow it, especially if it is known to stand in conflict with Saint Thomas.

[5] And so it will be worthwhile, at the start of the every school year, to read out in the presence of the teachers the letter I composed for this purpose on the solidity and uniformity of doctrine. It will also be beneficial if the superiors of seminaries where philosophy and theology are being taught have at that very time an exhortation to promote the decree on Saint Thomas's doctrine diligently, and likewise the practice of the ordinances, either the ones that I have issued or that have been written out in the book of the *Ratio studiorum*, so that nothing is omitted through carelessness.

Provincials should above all remember the principle given in their ninth rule in the book on studies that only those positively disposed towards Saint Thomas and profoundly disinclined to novelties either in theology or in philosophy should be promoted to teaching chairs. Unless they are of such a mind, or if they are following opinions that are sketchy and not solid, those who are already engaged in teaching should be removed without question from their teaching positions and assigned to other ministries of the Society.

[6] Whoever might teach opinions contrary to those of Saint Thomas, or come up with new ones on his own in philosophical matters, or introduce them from obscure authors, should be told to retract them as soon as possible, and there should be no waiting until the end of the year or the academic program. For not only does the trouble ripen over the course of the delay or even increase, but the students themselves, who have heard nothing contrary clearly set forth during the whole year, are being confirmed in that novelty. And the prefects have no legitimate excuse for ignorance, since it is incumbent upon them in the very exercise of their office to know about it. And this they can do in many different ways: first, if they attend the instructors' classes from time to time, according to rule 17 of their office;[4] second, if they regularly attend the review-sessions and the disputations, both public and in-house; third, if they put questions to the students and sometimes look over the notes that those students had taken down. If they apply diligence to this matter they certainly will not be able to keep from finding out the ones who are going astray.

---

4   "The prefect of studies should make class visitation now and then, at least once a month. Sometimes he should also read the notes taken down by the students." Pavur, *Ratio*, 43, no. 115.

But then, a censure will have to be worked up, with accompanying penances and public or private reproaches, but still with serious admonitions, even obliging a retraction, so they may realize that we are taking this seriously, not perfunctorily, and that the Society and its superiors are quite earnestly promoting this undertaking insofar as it is incredibly important for the goal of the Society and for the good of the church and the obedient service of God. This is why prefects ought to be drawing the reins in rather than letting them out.

But if anything doubtful arises, or if a teacher wants to defend his own opinion stubbornly, then, for things to move forward more smoothly and with greater authority, the prefect and the rector will meet together about this matter and turn it over for a more probing examination by other Jesuit teachers. After this, they will enjoin the teacher to assent and to let himself be guided, because we are involved in education to please the divine Majesty, and if we offer that Majesty anything besides an obedient will, it can in no way be accepted.

In the same way, we must take care that colleagues do not criticize or assail one another. But if somewhere they find themselves in disagreement—as must happen only in a very few matters if we are following a single author—then it should be done respectfully, and they should remember to engage each other with all due moderation. When the provincial makes his visitation, he should look into these matters with interest, and he should apply a suitable and effective remedy, removing from the classroom (as mentioned) those who have not at all complied with the expressed will of the general congregation and my way of thinking—in fact, with the thinking of our Blessed Father Ignatius himself, who so enthusiastically recommended this solidity and uniformity of doctrine.

But in addition, the provincial should diligently see to this and make it happen: the opinions that are taught in philosophy should be of service to theology, and our philosophers should follow Aristotle alone, wherever his doctrine does not conflict at all with Catholic truth.

[7] But in matters that have not been fully treated by Saint Thomas, where for that reason his opinion cannot be known, it will be right first to observe whatever can be drawn forth from his principles and whatever is least inconsistent with the rest of his doctrine. For even though he has not discoursed about that issue himself, if it still opposes his principles and does not cohere with his doctrine it should never be taught. No one will be free to invent or to teach some new doctrine on his own, even if it falls short of incurring censure, unless serious and approved authors exist who support it. And we do not believe it is right to be guided on a little-used path by one's own understanding, which has very often given occasion for wandering off and falling headlong.

[8] We ought to choose prefects of studies who are especially positive about the doctrine of this Holy Doctor; for many reasons it is not helpful that they be teachers at the same time.

[9] If any Jesuit adds anything without permission after the correction of books according to the censures of the revisors, he should be severely punished. For that is to impose upon the Society in a matter of great importance.

[10] Finally, this noteworthy item remains: indeed, it is deplorable the way that talents are confused and the solidity of doctrine weakened by the fact that some teachers occasionally are so problematic that they assert just any opinion as probable.[5] Of course, it then happens that the scholastics never have any certainty on which they might take a stand. And so teachers are to make a very circumspect selection of the more solid opinions that they are intending to assert.

[11] But since only one of the special chapters on doctrine touches on grace, which is the one subject, more than any other, where I wish to encourage uniformity among Jesuits, I have written a decree which your reverence will find attached to this letter. I mandate that it be communicated to every schoolmaster and to every teacher of theology, and that it be observed everywhere with equal diligence.

And these are the things that, as it is very important to me to follow them accurately, so I would especially wish that they have been commended to your Reverence. Lastly, I commend myself to the prayers and the holy sacrifices of everyone. The grace of Our Lord Jesus Christ be with all of you. Amen.

---

5   On the Jesuit engagement with probabilism, see Robert Aleksander Maryks, *Saint Cicero and the Jesuits: The Influence of the Liberal Arts on the Adoption of Moral Probabilism* (Aldershot: Ashgate, 2008).

Part 4:
Teaching Practices

CHAPTER 23

Teaching Composition (1554)

Ignatius of Loyola

Towards the start of 1554, Pierre Le Gillon (c.1520–c.1565), a French Jesuit teaching in Padua, corrected and sent Ignatius a sample composition to elicit his advice on such assignments. Ignatius's brief response, written only about two and a half years before his death and twenty years after his own college days, reveals several things: his serious commitment to the educational work, particularly in humanistic studies; his readiness to engage the collaboration of others in formulating an approach; his interest in developing students' own inventive powers by not restricting the work to dictation alone; and his take on the Erasmian approach to correcting themes. The ever-pragmatic Ignatius suggests that this method is not feasible with the greater numbers of students that were found in Jesuit classrooms. Cicero, a favorite author in the Renaissance, is recommended here as the model for Jesuit eloquence. This preference was later confirmed in the Ratio studiorum, *which would influence the Society's humanistic studies for centuries.*

Ignatius of Loyola (born c.1491, Guipúzcoa, Spain—co-founder of the Society in 1540, Rome—died 1556, Rome). Chief founder of the Jesuit order, Ignatius was a great supporter and administrator of "Jesuit studies" and the educational apostolate from its earliest days after official papal approval. Though he did not at first intend the Society to be a teaching order formally involved in opening and running schools, he quickly made it into one when he saw its great apostolic results and promise. He readily took on as many colleges as feasible, showing a special enthusiasm for the Roman College. His own journey manifested a deep investment in studies in Barcelona, Alcalá, Salamanca, and Paris, and the Society itself was uniquely tied to the University of Paris, where all of the founders were students. Ignatius is often listed as one of the great figures in the history of education.

Source: *Monumenta paedagogica*, nova editio, 1:451–52 (original: Italian)

Rome, March 17, 1554

Pax Christi [Peace of Christ]!

My dearest brother in Jesus Christ, Master Pierre, I have given some very capable individuals the task of figuring out the way to correct themes and compositions. They include Father Master Pedro [de] Ribadeneyra, Master Rafael [Riera], and Master Eleuthère Dupont.[1] They finally settled on this: several times, or at least

---

1 Notice Ignatius's care to use the academic title "master" when addressing Pierre Le Gillon and when naming these individuals. For Pedro de Ribadeneyra (1526–1611), see Chapter 7. Rafael Riera (born in Vich [Catalonia] *c.*1526—entered the Society on September 25,

once a week, take care that your students practice composition on their own, without your dictating anything, so that they improve in invention and find the encouragement to undertake greater things. You could allow them to take some sentences from Cicero and other authors that they choose, because, by overlooking some things at the very beginning, you will encourage them and they will adopt good usage in speaking and writing as they imitate good authors. On the other days, you could dictate other letters, as you usually do; and above all take care that they imitate Cicero and the other authors you are teaching them in class, because this constitutes the fruit of their studies.

As for correction, they think it enough to correct six or eight compositions each day, provided that the other students remain attentive and patient. And in correcting, each day take a different one and at the end give your Latin to all of them, so that your students benefit in the correction of their own work. And it will not be useless to take a letter of Cicero and dictate it to them occasionally in the vernacular, and then show it to them in Latin. And it will be good to have a bit of composition every day.

Although the meticulous method you propose in your letter for correcting compositions sounds good if it could be done, it does not seem possible with large numbers. It is true that Erasmus proposes this method, which someone who has one or two pupils could more easily follow than could someone who has as many as we have in our classes.[2] So this method should be praised. And let it be followed when it can be. It is true that the theme being sent from here had quite a few mistakes, and so we send it back to you thoroughly corrected.

Nothing else occurs to me except to commend ourselves to your prayers.

1547—died January 1, 1583). He founded a college in Palermo and wrote a history of the 1575 jubilee in Rome and some treatises on the sanctuary of Loreto, such as *De miraculis B. Virginis Lauretanae* [On the miracles of the Blessed Virgin of Loreto]. Eleuthère Dupont (Eleutherius Pontanus, born 1527—entered the Society on April 6, 1550—died January 31, 1611) was born in Lille (France) and taught rhetoric in Padua (1553). He was later appointed rector at the college in Tournay and died in Brussels.

2 Erasmus, *Ratio studii ac legendi interpretandique auctores* [A method for studying and for reading and understanding authors] (Paris: J. Granion, 1511).

CHAPTER 24

How to Teach Children Latin and Greek (1565)

Pedro Juan Perpinyá

A member of a noble family of Genoa, Francesco Adorno (1532–86) was a Jesuit who attended the college in Coimbra and was later appointed rector at the college in Padua (1559). From there, he played an important role in providing essential sources to the Coimbran philosophers compiling the Cursus Conimbricensis (Coimbran commentaries) *a very important set of Jesuit commentaries on Aristotle. Adorno always maintained close connections with his companions in Coimbra. When he moved to Milan in 1564 to be rector of its newly established Jesuit college, he asked Pedro Perpinyá, one of best teachers of rhetoric in Coimbra, to draft a treatise on the literary education of children. Stefano Sauli (dates uncertain), a learned Genoese patrician whose family had helped establish a Jesuit college there, had already asked Adorno for such a pedagogical work. Perpinyá responded with the following essay. It is a distinctive kind of Jesuit educational text: it was not addressed to any superior, nor did it deal with college life but with the education of young nobility, in the manner of many treatises written by scholars employed as tutors of noble pupils. Despite its special character, it follows typical Jesuit pedagogy, for Perpinyá did not deviate from his basic beliefs about the teaching of grammar and rhetoric.*

Pedro Juan Perpinyá (born 1530, Elche, Valencia, Spain—entered the Society on September 30, 1551, Coimbra—died October 28, 1566, Paris). Perpinyá's reputation as a great preacher in Portugal began very early. He taught humanistic studies at the Jesuit college of Lisbon (1553), gave the inauguration speech at Évora, and held the chair of rhetoric in Coimbra from 1555 to 1561. In 1555, he delivered the funeral oration for Prince Louis of Portugal (1506–55), brother of the king. He was called to Rome, where he taught at the Roman College (1561–65). There he was able to make contact with such famous humanists as Paolo Manuzio (1512–74), and he tried to reform the curriculum on humanistic foundations. In 1565, he was sent to the college of Lyon, and finally to Paris, where he died.

Source: *Monumenta paedagogica*, nova editio, 2:644–57 (original: Latin)

To a Nobleman Concerning How to Teach Children Latin and Greek

Chapter 1—The Teacher

Before all other considerations, we have to choose a teacher who manifests personal integrity, passionate interest, keen intellectual talent, and refined powers of expression; one who has not wasted all his time on trivialities or on the idle speculations of grammarians as is the custom of public school teachers but rather has at the ready a few precepts that have been taken from all the best authors; a person who is thoroughly acquainted with the finest writers of each genre and well practiced both in speaking and in writing. We have to watch out for two things especially: he should not be plainly inept in Greek, nor should he, out of a conceited exaggeration of his wisdom, think that he has to teach grammar as if it is some special one of the greatest arts.

Chapter 2—The Grammar Book

Then we either have to pick with great care the handbook for language-learning from the many that are available or, if none is found that is suitable, compose it. It should not overwhelm students with its length or its abundance of rules; nor should it drive them to despair with its obscurity; nor should it slow them down with contents concerning matters remote from everyday experience; nor should it accustom them to using a corrupted type of language with its rules or examples. And at the beginning it should have the forms for nouns and verbs apart from any rules, and to these a few irregular verbs should be added, namely the ones that occur frequently, like *volo, nolo, malo, fero, sum, fio,* and any others that there may be. Only the indication of the first person of each tense should be written in the vernacular as properly and neatly as possible. They should get the first elements of inflecting forms and the rudiments of grammar, as it were, those which, starting from the letters and the syllables, give an understanding of the parts of speech that seem likely to be easy for the boys to understand and useful as well.

Afterwards they should put a certain small number of rules, the ones especially common, about the connection of words (called "syntax"), for instance concerning the subject and the verb, the substantive noun and the adjective, the relative and the antecedent; which cases all verbs require before, which after; with which cases *sum* agrees, and anything else like this. The types of nouns should follow, and the rules for declining them. I include among those words the ones that are called preterites and supines. But we should not heap up everything that can be found anywhere, without making a selection. We have to omit what occurs either rarely or never in speech. Nothing common to all the inflections should be left out. What is proper to each form and has no great variety should be explained in a few words. Those things that are quite various should be put into one comprehensive category and kept for reference and practice. Then the nouns and verbs, both those that are defective and those that are irregular in some respect, should be carefully listed and described in groups, but there should be nothing that the authority of good writers does not confirm; and what seems to be most commonly used should be separated from the rest, so that the boys might more easily memorize them.

Immediately after this, there should be an explanation of how to connect words and arrange speech, that is, what we call "syntax." In this also, there is a need for the highest level of good sense. For not everything that Ennius, Accius, or even Plautus at some point said should be cited in this handbook, but it should teach only what rather frequently occurs in the works of the best authors.[1] Nevertheless, among these, we should take note of the conventions of the poets and the historians so that the boys may take care to avoid them in ordinary conversation. The expressions that radically differ from vernacular speech-habits and are rare should be presented separately. But the rules themselves should be written down, first generally according to the parts of speech, then particularly, according to their meaning, since the boys must understand the use of words before they can see to what rank they belong.

The last part should be that which introduces the way to compose verse and explains the system of acute and heavy tones. Here certain common reminders about long and short syllables should be set forth. Lengthening of nouns and verbs can be skipped; or if explaining them is desired, set aside those that have such manifold variety in the third declension. Concerning the first and middle syllables, the entire passage regarding the reading of the poets and regarding usage should be eliminated. Of the last syllables, since their treatment is brief, there should be careful instruction. Then a few things should be added from the ancients about the heavy and the acute tones. Finally, the most frequent kinds of verses should be taught in such a way that there is a constant demonstration of what makes for elegance in each style. And in treating all these matters an effort should be made to ensure that nothing is taught or said that is not correct Latin.

The inflections, the rudiments, and the syntax can be taken from no better place than from Linacre.[2] On the heavy and acute tones, one must gather passages from the prose of Cicero, Aulus Gellius, and Quintilian.[3] I have said nothing about orthography for the reason that I know that this is more of a matter of observation and long practice rather than of rules. Nevertheless, since certain common precepts for writing can be given directly, if desired, they can be excerpted partly from Quintilian and partly from others at the very end.

Chapter 3—Teaching Grammar

Whether the grammar book is chosen or composed, it should be used especially with a concern that the boys write their letters with some refinement. When they have made enough progress in this skill that there is some hope that they are

---

1 Ennius (Quintus Ennius, *c*.239–*c*.169 BCE), Accius (Lucius Accius, 170–*c*.86 BCE), and Plautus (Titus Maccius Plautus, *c*.254–184 BCE) were very early Latin authors.
2 Thomas Linacre (*c*.1460–1524), *De emendata structura Latini sermonis libri sex* [Six books on polished expression in Latin] (Paris: Robertus Stephanus [Robert Estienne (1503–59)], 1527).
3 Marcus Tullius Cicero (106–43 BCE), Aulus Gellius (*c*.125–*c*.180), and Quintilian (Marcus Fabius Quintilianus *c*.35–*c*.100) were considered scholarly and educational authorities.

going to improve day by day through their daily writing practice, they should memorize all inflectional forms along with the most common irregular ones and they should very diligently practice the different types of nouns and verbs they are given to inflect. Writing down first on paper whatever they are going to recite from memory every day greatly supports the strength of the memory, and the practice of writing, and the recognition of how words change in spelling according to their cases. But for speed in giving the various forms, sometimes they should inflect nouns and verbs in reverse order; sometimes they should be asked to produce promptly whatever case the teacher has randomly proposed; sometimes they should inflect many different declensional forms joined together, such as *consilium forte et prudens* [a brave and prudent plan];[4] sometimes they should take a sentence down through all the tenses, numbers, persons, and moods, such as *Ego lego Ciceronem, Ego legebam Ciceronem*, etc. [I am reading Cicero, I was reading Cicero, and so on.] But care must be taken that all these things are pure and adapted to common speech.

From here, go on to the rudiments, without ever stopping the inflection-exercises. Along with the rudiments, teach in the vernacular some author who is both polished and straightforward. They should also be made to write and to compose something every day, despite their lack of skill at this point. When they have gone on from those elements to the genders and declensions, pay attention that every day they both learn something about the rules and hear something about a good writer. What they have heard they should present from memory; they should practice the declensions and conjugations; they should be frequently quizzed on the rudiments, genders, and declensions; and they should write something in Latin.

When they have a good grasp of these grammatical elements, they should be moved on to syntax, the teaching of which should keep the same order as in the earlier studies, employing sometimes inflection-practice and sometimes quizzes on the rudiments, genders, and declensions, so that the boys do not start losing what they have learned. Present a more important prose author and some very easy poet, and start a practice of writing somewhat longer exercises. After they have understood the pattern of linking words and have begun to write more and with fewer mistakes, begin the last part of the grammar, which pertains to composing verses. Meanwhile, practice on the earlier parts should not be dropped, especially that part pertaining to syntax. A more significant and likewise more difficult poet should be taught, and when they have made a little progress in this author, it is very helpful for them to practice composing verses on alternate days. Then if the teacher likes, at times certain selected passages on orthography and

---

4   The Latin word translated as "declensional forms" is *nomina*, which later came to mean "nouns." However, adjectives and nouns were long considered the same part of speech, following the same sets of declensional endings.

at other times passages on the finer and rarer points of syntax can be taught from the sixth book of Linacre; then the standard best authors, orators, historians, and poets of each genre should be presented.

Chapter 4—Greek

Since not only the understanding of the finer arts but also fullness of expression has flowed from the Greeks to the Romans, we must join Greek with Latin, as Cicero prescribed for his son.[5] And yet I should hardly agree with Quintilian, who wants Greek grammar to precede Latin.[6] This was helpful at that time to those people for whom Latin was a native tongue; now we must confess that this does not make things easier. And so I think that Greek must not be started before all of Latin grammar is grasped and the exercise of writing in Latin solidly strengthened by systematic practice. Concerning the rest, the same things I said about the art of Latin can and ought to be transferred to Greek.

Chapter 5—Rhetoric

At the same time, the boys should be taught the rules for speaking well, so that they even speak oratorically, that is more impressively. Therefore, as soon as they have learned Latin grammar thoroughly, they should hear every day at different times something from Cicero's speeches, something from a premier Latin poet, a bit of Greek, and some rhetoric. And certainly in rhetoric, the most preferred method and approach is that the entire art first be laid out concisely in an order that is as transparent as possible, with very clear words, putting aside tedious disputes about doubtful matters, and by teaching principles rather than by disputing questions. Then the most ancient and important writers on the subject should be taught at length and broadly, and all the finer points of the discipline should now be divulged as if they are mysteries being revealed to initiates. But at the same time, the boys should use frequent exercises to fashion all their speech after the customary style of Cicero and Demosthenes.[7]

Chapter 6—Authors

New and recent writers should be rejected altogether. Only the ancients, and not even all of these, but only the very best of them should be presented to the boys. Although there are also those who are outstanding in their elegance, we must be discriminating, and all indecency of words and content should be removed. So I do not think Terence should be presented to the boys, although he is an excellent

---

5   *De officiis*, I.1.
6   *Institutio oratoria*, I.4.
7   Demosthenes (384–322 BCE) was the preeminent Greek orator.

teacher of Latinity.[8] This is not so surprising to anyone who has ever read Fabius.[9] In fact, he wanted his contemporaries to be forbidden to read any comedy at all. Cicero, at least in my opinion, is useful for all ages and seasons: even his letters can be accommodated to boys' abilities. Those who have made some progress will find very great value in the more serious and harder letters and some of the books on morals, such as *On duties*, *On friendship*, *On old age*, and *Paradoxes*; and the *Tusculan Disputations* and the other dialogues on philosophy nourish the mind of any educated person. We have no Latin speeches by anyone else; and if we had them, I would still think that these should be put ahead of all those from other authors. From the historians, I think Caesar is first because of the neatness of his expression. From this area, Livy and Sallust should be added, quite different from one another and from Caesar, but each pre-eminent in his different style.

Among the poets, the first place seems due to Ovid on account of his fluency of expression. To avoid all indecency, books can be selected from his *Sorrows* and the *Letters from Pontus*, and many passages of the *Metamorphoses* and fragments of the *Fasti*.[10] I would put Virgil next, third Horace, leaving aside all the poems that have some trace of impurity. There can be added some selected poems of Catullus, Tibullus, Propertius, and Martial that are completely free of anything offensive to common decency.

In Greek, I recommend starting with Isocrates or Xenophon; their speech is pure and clear. Demosthenes, foremost of the orators, will follow. Homer is the most brilliant of the Greek poets and the first in every compositional merit. Others will follow him, in the same way that I explained about the choice of Latin authors. In history, the notable figures are Herodotus, Thucydides, Pausanias, or if you want a shorter account and one that is not so continuous but in a way segmented and pleasing in its variety, Aelian, *Historical Miscellany*.[11]

Even though there are many compendia of rhetorical precepts, I approve of none of them except that which Cipriano Soares, a man from our Society, published not long ago at Coimbra and which I have had re-published now

---

8   Terence (Publius Terentius Afer, *c*.195/185–*c*.159? BCE) was a Latin dramatist much admired in the Renaissance for his pure colloquial speech.
9   Fabius is another name for Quintilian.
10 Ovid (Publius Ovidius Naso (43 BCE–17/18 CE) was well known since antiquity for his love poetry and mythological works. There follows a list of other major poets of Latin antiquity: Virgil (Publius Vergilius Maro, 70–19 BCE), Horace (Quintus Horatius Flaccus, 65–8 BCE), Catullus (Gaius Valerius Catullus (*c*.84–54 BCE), Tibullus (Albius Tibullus, *c*.55–19 BCE), Propertius (Sextus Propertius, *c*.50/40–*c*.15 BCE), and Martial (Marcus Valerius Martialis, *c*.38/41–*c*.102/4).
11 The Greek writers mentioned are Isocrates (436–338 BCE), Xenophon (*c*.430 – 354 BCE), Demosthenes (384–322 BCE), Homer (*fl.* eight century BCE), Herodotus (484–425 BCE), Thucydides (*c*.460–*c*.400), Pausanias (*c*.110–*c*.180), Aelian (Claudius Aelianus, *c*.175–*c*.235).

at Venice with [Michele] Tramezzino;[12] it is a thoughtfully gathered collection taken almost verbatim from the three most highly praised authors, Aristotle, Cicero, and Quintilian.[13] I consider the rhetorical handbooks of these three the ones that are the most highly finished. But not all of Quintilian's books should be expounded indiscriminately. While books 3, 4, 6, 8, and 9 are quite profitable, the rest are more fruitful for scholars than for inexperienced teenagers. Not even all of Cicero is equally valuable. The entire plan for speaking well is contained in the book *The Divisions of Rhetoric*, and likewise in the second and third book of *On the Orator*. *The Orator*, while it seeks after the most finished form of eloquence itself, almost bypasses the precepts, and it explains in a straightforward fashion hardly any part except delivery. Only *Topics* covers the categories for invention. *Brutus* is very useful, certainly, but it says nothing about style, except perhaps fleetingly. I do not consider someone remiss about looking after the boys' interests if he were to teach *Topics* after *The Divisions of Rhetoric* and finally two books of Quintilian, the eighth and ninth, in which what Cicero overly abridged in *The Divisions of Rhetoric* is given rich and expansive treatment. The three books of Aristotle's *Rhetoric*, commonly ascribed to Theodectes in error, are certainly insightful and rich in content and refined, but they can be more of a help to scholars than to boys.[14]

Chapter 7—The Manner of Presentation and Reception

The manner of presenting and following what is presented in class is one and the same in Latin and Greek. The rules of grammar have to be explained in simple, clear speech, without inquiries into trivia, and with frequent repetitions of the same contents. This should happen abundantly from examples, by which the boys are taught how the rules are applied in practice. I would prefer that the teacher be occupied in this than in heaping up all kinds of useful and useless items from hither and yon with great effort. At first, the authors' writings should be explained simply and only in the vernacular, so that the teachers' concern might be more focused on the words than on the content; and in individual classes, some outstanding features of style should be noted and the boys taught to make use of them with examples that have been appropriately constructed. Later, a Latin explanation should accompany the vernacular one; and a moderate care should be applied to illustrating the contents: so individual sentences should be explained with single

---

12 The first edition of Soares's work was *De arte rhetorica libri tres ex Aristotele, Cicerone & Quintiliano praecipue deprompti* [Three books on rhetoric especially based on Aristotle, Cicero, and Quintilian] (Coimbra: João de Barreira, 1562). The Venetian publisher Michele Tramezzino printed it for the first time in 1565.

13 Aristotle (384–322 BCE).

14 Theodectes (*c.*380–*c.*340 BCE) was a Greek playwright who had studied in the school of the rhetorician Isocrates (436–338 BCE).

sentences and words with other words meaning the same thing, suitable to the
matter at hand; and poetic styles of speaking should constantly be pointed out
in poetry, historical ones in history, and oratorical ones in oratory, with what is
common being pointed out in all of these genres; and the distinguishing feature of
each type should be understood so that they do not use poetic styles in speeches
or in histories or vice versa. Whatever seems necessary to grasp the content should
be recounted, whether it concerns history and antiquity or the fables of the poets.
Any noteworthy artistic devices should not be ignored. As long as the boys are busy
learning the grammatical rules by heart, the teacher should continue pointing out
the usage of those rules in the authors. Certainly I would prefer that at the start the
teacher should be tedious in impressing valuable contents rather than dismissively
disdainful in skipping over them.

After the students' talents have "grown up" in age, learning, and experience,
vernacular explanations should be put aside and the Latin ones should be more
fully elaborated both in the content and in the words used concerning grammar
and expression itself, except in the case of anything very abstruse, which should
receive no comment. Poetic and oratorical devices should be clarified as diligently
as possible. In all the divisions of teaching, we ought to use elegant, polished, and
precise speech. Sometimes we should also employ a certain greater display and a
more striking embellishment of both words and contents to provoke the students'
minds more vigorously to engage in their studies. At all times, the teacher should
strive for explanations of authors (whether lengthy or brief) in matters of both
style and content that fairly well match the boys' talents, so that however much
their understanding increases, so also does the method of interpretation.

The boys should very diligently write down at home whatever must be presented, putting it into notebooks in elegant handwriting with careful attention to
the spelling and leaving wide spaces between the lines and for the margins. The
teacher should often review these notebooks to spur the boys either by fear or by
shame to a greater interest and to more care in their writing.

In class, they should listen very attentively to the instructor as he speaks and
they should take down the very short summaries of books that he dictates, leaving as much space before each individual book for that item as seems sufficient.
Then they should interpose between the lines themselves the interpretive para-
phrases, each in its own place, and they should write down in the margins the more
important figures of speech illustrated with examples by the teacher, and likewise
the somewhat longer explanations of the contents or the difficult words.[15] But this
practice should be followed only for so long as a few things, or not too many, are
still being presented about each individual author. Later it will be sufficient that the
especially important or obscure things be indicated in the notebooks.

---

15 Figures of speech (*formae loquendi*) include, for example, simile, metaphor, hyperbole, per-
    sonification, and synecdoche.

Chapter 8—Exercise

Exercise is extremely important in this subject, just as it is in others, and it takes many different forms. The first is that of inflecting forms, about which I spoke in the method of teaching grammar. The second specifically concerns memory. All grammatical rules are to be grasped and known by heart (leaving aside the exceptions I mentioned above). Likewise the authors (one in prose, one in poetry), provided their exposition is not too advanced. Also the figures of speech and the more exact interpretations of contents and words. Not all the words of the rhetoric textbook ought to be memorized, but the maxims should, so that the boys are able to present the individual rules, if not word for word, then certainly with only minimal differences.

The third exercise consists of question and answer. An industrious teacher should have a fixed and definite time for quizzing the boys on the rules and the authors. And in grammar sometimes the rules themselves should be asked for, such as what gender are nouns in *–is*; sometimes many different things should be asked about, and there should be an attempt to see whether they can apply their reckoning from the rules, for example, about the gender of *corbis*; sometimes short vernacular statements should be proposed for them to translate into Latin on the spot. In this practice, we should avoid the foolishness of typical schoolteachers when they utter certain unusual sayings dredged up from God knows what dark places, good for nothing but producing laughter; they perversely teach their students to speak perversely contrived Latin; it is better that those statements be fashioned according to the rules of grammar that have been explained earlier or that are being explained at that moment, and that they adopt the vocabulary that the boys have seen in the authors. In dealing with the authors, first we ought to ask for an opinion that at the start they express only in the vernacular, later also in Latin, and finally only in Latin, fully and elegantly. Then if there is anything notable in words or in content, they should be told to say it from memory, whether in the same words or with some variations. And while they are beginners, they should be exercised in those figures of speech which they have written down in the margins of their notebooks. Later, when they have become experienced users and practitioners of the language, they should turn all their attention and study sometimes to reciting the contents more fully and impressively, sometimes to telling in varied and appealing ways the histories and stories that have been touched upon. In rhetoric, they should sometimes have to use examples to illustrate individual rules, in words of their own choosing, and sometimes they should have to show the rhetorical principles at work in examples taken from the writings of the authors and trace each one back to its own place. What remains is shared by both the rhetorical writers and the other authors.

The fourth exercise is that of speaking, which I do not deny has great utility, but only on these conditions: that the boys work at their studies so that they always speak well and in a polished way; that they are corrected by the teacher as soon as they make any mistake; and that the special vocabulary of each genre (especially for common content) is supplied by the teacher bit by bit to those who do not know it. Otherwise, without care about or interest in their constantly speaking incorrect Latin, they will necessarily start speaking it incorrectly and in a corrupted form.

The fifth exercise is writing, all the more useful to the extent that verbal address can be polished more by writing than by speaking. Therefore, every day one hour should be given to writing. But they should write in the presence of the teacher, and what they have written they should present to him before they leave school so that no deception is possible and so that each person's talent and diligence may be observed. At some time, exercise in writing verse will be added to the writing of prose. The best arrangement is to have each done at the same hour on alternate days. But the type of writing-exercise should not always be the same. When they are just starting out as students, the teacher should dictate sometimes nouns and adjectives, sometimes nouns and verbs, sometimes antecedents and relatives out of agreement so that they themselves may easily connect them; a little later, vernacular statements as short as possible which they will put into Latin. They will easily be able to do this even without skill if the statements are so connected with those that have been explained in some writer that the boys can use the same expressions with minimal modification. But when they have touched on syntax, it will be good to dictate longer communications that are both illustrative of the rules which they have heard concerning the connection of words and also very near the ideas of the author who is being presented; this way, the boys may become accustomed both to observing the rules of grammar and to using good and respectable words. When they are more practiced in writing and their speech seems sufficiently free of errors, propose in Latin only a very brief idea taken right from ordinary life so that it is better known and easier material, and with equal brevity note the passages that can be used to expand upon it at length. Using oratorical words and expressions, they should sometimes present stories from the poets and descriptions and even entire speeches with fictional characters inserted. On occasion, they themselves should fill out speeches for which historians have written out only the main points, taking on the character of those by whom the speeches were said to have been given. Cicero thinks that reworking in different words whole and direct speeches such as are often found in the works of these same historians is more of a hindrance than a help. This does not seem to hold when dealing with the poets since the poetic style of expression is far different from the oratorical one.

Lastly, when they have already grasped the skill of speaking, they should compose separate sections of speeches according to the purpose of each section: introductions, narratives, demonstrations and conclusions, and they should get practice in treating oratorical arguments, comparisons, examples, descriptions, fictional characterizations, amplifications, and other important stylistic devices.

Next, move on to speeches of praise and blame; from these to deliberations; from here, if there is an inclination to touch upon this part too, they should be taken over to judicial cases; and they should get so accustomed to writing and speaking that they are always inwardly looking to Cicero and trying to attain by imitation some similarity to him. But these longer and more difficult works should not be composed in class but brought in from home, worked out in the evening and well polished; the poets and historians will supply the matter to fill them out. The teacher should correct their compositions this way: at the start, he should only criticize verbal mistakes, then not so much those mistakes (of which there should be none), but rather if there is anything that is an old usage, or poetic or out of place or even at odds with the composition, or awkwardly put or too unrhythmical, or anything of this kind. This is what I have to say about prose.

The first exercise of poetry should be to put back together the words of a poet the boys do not yet know, after the teacher has taken them apart. The next is to compose a true poem on a given theme, using half-lines of verse or even full lines, which should not be too difficult. The last is to take an idea briefly stated by the teacher and expand it into many verses. In making corrections, these things should be noted: first, mistakes in verse and speech, if there are any; then, if anything has not been said poetically enough or said too boldly; if there is anything foreign to poetic practice; and other things like this. And in both types of correction, namely of prose and of verse, it is often more helpful to ignore some mistakes than to bring them all to light by criticizing them; and if there is anything good, it is better to spur the boys' spirits than to deter them by blaming them too sharply and to extinguish all their eager enthusiasm if anything is bad. When the harshness of criticism is tempered by the gentleness of praise it easily corrects the writing mistakes, nourishes the boys' hope, and strongly kindles their interest. Although the teacher should know the talent of those he is teaching so that he may shape his instruction to each one's nature, he should hold in check those who are too freely exuberant in their expressions, he should spur on those who are hesitant and almost shy, he should restrain those who pour themselves out using a rich supply of rhetorical resources to take extravagant risks, and he should add sap and strength to the dry and arid by his art of cultivation. Much profit also comes from having each person deliver before the class his own speeches and poems after these have been carefully corrected by the teacher.

The sixth and final type of exercise is the exposition of the authors. When they have amassed a good bit of scholarship and have achieved some facility in speaking well, it will be helpful to have the rest listen while one person presents with care and precision some passage of a good orator or historian or poet. But they ought to come to this exercise as prepared as possible, taking time not just for thinking it out but also for writing it up, so that they may learn to do this splendidly. And the more the content proceeds from their personal understanding, the more their confidence and spirit will grow.

Chapter 9—On Spurring the Boys' Interest

As I have mentioned above, nowhere is it more necessary to know the nature of each person than here. There are some who are motivated by fear, some who are motivated especially by an easy-going nature and friendliness. As some fear ought to be attached to friendly kindness so that laxity does not undo the boys' spirit, just so some of that good-heartedness should be attached to fear, so that the boys' industry is not broken by despair. But actually a person's interest can be neither enduring nor productive if, like a worthless servant, he is not motivated by anything except whipping and blows. There is far greater promise in those who are motivated enough on their own and who are afraid to offend the teacher's gentleness and who are drawn by modest and decent praise. So for these, even if there ought to be some prospect of fear if they ever abandon their duty, there should still rather be the prospect of rewards if they recite anything from memory best of all, if they inflect some word better than the others, if they surpass the rest in writing or in repeating the content of the lesson or in the care and fluency and completeness of the presentation. The rewards can be: a more honored place to sit, fuller praise spoken by the teacher, booklets decorated with gold, and many other things of the same type.

CHAPTER 25

Reflections on Literary Studies (1593)

Iacobus Pontanus (Jakob Spanmüller)

In 1591, a version of the Ratio studiorum *was distributed for trial use for three years in all Jesuit provinces. It modified the previous version of 1586 that had been sent out merely for advisory purposes. The new version provoked some criticism and it enjoyed only limited application, especially in the German provinces. In 1591, Paul Hoffaeus (1530–1608), the provincial superior of Upper Germany, reported to Acquaviva that the reception of the* Ratio *was "not excellent" and urged him to have the superiors of the German provinces see more diligently to its applica-tion. The Austrian provincial likewise appealed to Acquaviva to stop criticisms of the new plan.[1]In response, Acquaviva shrewdly engaged some scholars to support what had been written pertaining to their own areas of expertise. One was Iaco-bus Pontanus, who Acquaviva hoped would be the champion of humanistic studies. Pontanus readily accomplished his task, drafting several documents supporting the* Ratio, *answering any possible criticisms, and offering advice on how best to teach such courses. He also wrote an interesting document about the relation of rhetoric to dialectic that evidences a Jesuit debate about the boundary-line between human-ities and philosophy. Pontanus argues in favor of the* Ratio, *distinguishing rhet-oric sharply from dialectic on the grounds that they demand quite different aims and talents. Thus he agrees with Pedro Juan Perpinyá (1530–66) and supports the approach being followed at the Jesuit college in Munich.*

Iacobus Pontanus (Jakob Spanmüller) (born 1542, Most [Bohemia]—entered the Society May 17, 1564, Prague—died December 3, 1589, Augsburg). He was himself a great product of Jesuit education. He attended the Jesuit college of Prague and soon started to teach elsewhere while he was completing his stud-ies. In 1581, he began to teach rhetoric and humanities in Augsburg, where he was also appointed rector of the college. His teaching of Latin and Greek was so broadly praised that Superior General Acquaviva approved and promoted his method. Among his writings, the Progymnasmata latinitatis *(4 vols., 1588–94)—aimed at correcting and replacing Erasmus's method—was widespread among the colleges of Europe, even beyond those run by the Society. In 1582, he established an academy in Augsburg for the teaching of philology.*

Source: *Monumenta paedagogica*, nova editio, 7:88–104 (original: Latin)

---

1 See *Monumenta paedagogica*, 7:27*.

I

Proposals for Literary Studies in the Society according to the *Ratio studiorum*

1. It is undeniable that the *Ratio studiorum* has made more thorough and zealous provision for these literary studies than some and perhaps many individuals can digest. There are two reasons for this reaction: First, because, having a very superficial knowledge of humanistic studies, they do not very well see how valuable they are, either in themselves or when linked with our spirit. Second, because they appear convinced that these studies are taken up by the Society merely incidentally, but the higher ones are taken up for their intrinsic worth, as if all of ours, provided that they have the talent to do it, ought to become philosophers and theologians and train others in those areas.[2] The *Ratio studiorum* corrects both errors, for in it the Society reveals clearly and eloquently that it has a profoundly earnest desire for certain career-teachers, not just a few of them, individuals endowed with remarkable talent, to spend all their lives in these lower literary studies. And so it seriously enjoins provincials to make every effort to get such individuals, as many as they can.[3] It calls it a praiseworthy goal to dedicate oneself to these studies in perpetuity. It exempts absolutely no one from the three-year period of teaching these studies, no matter what work the individual may be finally destined to undertake.[4] Away with those two erroneous ideas, then, and let it be resolved that these literary studies, if we make good progress in them and realize how to use them well and in a way that promotes well-being, are extremely useful for arousing the knowledge and love of God without any theology (for I would not say without philosophy), and for the sake of this very goal the Society engages in them on the basis of their own intrinsic merits.

2. The *Ratio studiorum* has two parts. The first part is in a way the mother, source, root, foundation, and essence of the second one. It prepares the higher ones for educating our own, so that they turn out to be good teachers of others. The second part teaches how we should share our learning with others. Now there is the deepest silence concerning so many rules for provincials, rectors, and prefects. The rules for teachers are pushed, and among these teachers there arise complaints, dispensations, omissions of many of the rules, despair, nit-picking, and finally vast unhappiness. Rightly so, but through no fault of the

---

2   The distinction is given in well-known philosophical terms: *per accidens* (incidentally) and *per se* (intrinsically).

3   The *Ratio studiorum* of 1591 deals with this issue in the rules for the provincial superior (esp. rules 62–65): "Omni ope contendat, ut quotcunque potest, perpetuos habeat magistros" [He should make every effort to see that he has as many career teachers as possible]. See *Monumenta paedagogica*, 5:238.

4   See rule 66 in ibid., 5:239.

Ratio. It has not ordered us to follow the rules in this manner and to follow itself in the way we have up to now. It has not ordered us to fight without pay and weaponry, to build without brick and mortar, to pick grapes from thorns and figs from thistles, to hold onto lesser things and neglect the more important ones (especially when without them the lesser ones can in no manner be preserved); it has not ordered us to fashion a new world outside but to change nothing at home. The brothers are not allowed to study as much as they need to. Many teachers lack intellectual talent; they misuse their time; they shirk exercises; they study just as much and in just the way that they wish; they are not willing to go on teaching. But even if anyone really and truly wants to make progress and teach for a longer while, he is snatched away; every year, new teachers are sent down. After theology, no one comes back to us. After ordination to the priesthood, a person preaches, hears confessions; and if he does come back, he does not want to teach grammar, simply because he still does not know it well; he insists on teaching humanities and rhetoric. All these things are quite inconsistent both with the *Ratio studiorum* and common sense. There can be no other result than the daily deterioration of our classes and our literary studies, not to mention of the entire Society, while we feign ignorance and give no answer to the complaints except to say "We are not able, we do not have the resources," at the same time making no effort to become able and to get the resources; in fact we are doing the opposite so as to avoid being able and getting the resources.

3.   In our school here (and perhaps elsewhere as well), the execution of the *Ratio* is so truncated and imperfect, with so many of even the more important points being ignored, that we should not even call it that. Setting aside the rules of the higher faculties and the other instructors, the rhetorician has forty rules and the humanities teacher the same number. If you ask how many they keep, you will hardly discover four. Nor can they be keeping many more if we include what both instructors and students are missing, namely the rules about which they still do not know a thing.

4.   Seven years are required to connect the two curricula, [but] the brothers do not put up with two years of taking classes in rhetoric. In a single year, not considering what little progress they have made outside of these classes; although they have learned nothing in Greek earlier (so that many do not even know the alphabet); although they do not know how to compose verses; given that they have not looked at any book for the two years of the novitiate; and given that some of them are fairly dull and hardly suitable for literary studies—they nevertheless must attend three different classes every day, they must review, discuss, compose (and in a four-fold manner at that: in Greek and in Latin, and in prose and poetry in each language). Whoever thinks this can happen in a single year is showing his own utter lack of experience and judgment.

5. Unless we change our ways and, applying force, break through all the dif-
    ficulties that certain individuals are setting up against us, our good odor
    will perish. It is as obvious as can be that our greatest recommendation to
    every kind of person is our teaching the young religious devotion and virtue
    along with letters, returning to every parent children twice as dear. Certainly
    the colleges are not sought out by princes and civic concerns on account of
    philosophy and theology. All the rest of our services will be unappealing if
    this is lost. But the difference between practicing something badly and omit-
    ting it altogether is a small one. We, however, study badly, teach badly, and
    blindly lead the blind.

6. In this affair it is no small evil that superiors do not take more care when it
    comes to these studies. What do you expect? They have been educated the
    same way their brothers were; they drank like the proverbial dogs from the
    Nile.[5] They swallowed their Greek on the run; they hardly tasted a sip of
    Latin; many of them have never taught these languages. And nevertheless
    these are the ones to whom we give the decision-power regarding studies;
    they customarily decide what should be taught, how it should be taught,
    who the teachers should be, what their talents are, how great their progress
    is. Many things are entrusted to the prefects who themselves prove to be
    rather too uneducated to be able to be in charge of all the classes and to
    direct and correct the teachers. So when the superiors themselves are not
    educated in these subjects, the prefects in no way excel; the brothers are
    plucked out of studies prematurely; the ones who finish the courses are not
    sent to teach, or those who are sickly and untalented are; the better ones are
    always kept back, while the teachers themselves are not one step ahead of
    their students but two or three steps behind; what hope, pray tell, is there
    that we are going to make progress with non-Jesuits? Physician, heal thyself!

7. If the superiors should say that they are not able to follow their own rules
    because they are hindered by serious matters while their rules depend not at
    all on our rules, why would they call for our help? Surely our [rules] depend
    on those in the way an effect depends upon a necessary cause.

8. Ultimately, all those who assail the *Ratio studiorum* ought to know that if
    they take away from the brothers the two years of study (and also three for
    the more talented and promising ones) and also the three years from the
    teachers, and so even more importantly the career-teaching of this literary
    study, they have both murdered humanistic study among the non-Jesuit stu-
    dents for no good purposes and annihilated this most excellent work of the
    Society, so very pleasing to God and to humanity. The teachers are those
    who bear the burden of the day and its heat [Mt. 20:12], who have left their

---

5   The old fable presents the idea of dogs drinking very quickly at the Nile so that the croco-
    diles cannot attack them.

fathers and mothers [Mt. 10:37]; they have to somehow come to be; such great labors and worries do not trouble anyone, even the master of a large household, as much as they do the faithful teacher of a single class.

9. So please let those individuals who have not thought deeply enough about this matter stop complaining that there will be too few workers for too long if the brothers teach for two years, and instructors for three (except for the career teachers, whose virtue and charity can never be sufficiently praised); and they should not treat us so unfairly, wanting to take four out of five years away from us when they do not want even half of their seven years to be taken from them. This clearly betrays that they regard humanistic literary study as worthless. And how, pray tell, are we not workers of the Society if teaching is a work of the Society? It is embarrassing to prove that the sun is shining at noon.

10. I will put very briefly before your eyes, chiefly from the rules of the provincial, just a few things that are to be provided especially and above all; without them all our work will be empty, not to mention senseless.

1. The brothers should be left in rhetoric classes for two years; those who show great promise should be left for three. And this is all the more important to do if no one is being sent to the course in humanities. The years spent at other institutions outside the Society should not be counted, but we should look carefully into what each has learned and how much he ought to learn according to the Society's practice.

2. We have to acquire career teachers; and they ought to be requested, not plucked away; those who stop might also study some theology when they are not able to teach any more. For the study of theology, if it interrupts their teaching career, will create serious disadvantages.

3. After the course of study, everyone should teach not less than three years; whoever does not find a position should return to take classes in rhetoric.

4. Groups of two or three who are well educated in the humane letters and higher studies should always be sent back down to help us maintain a model for good teachers and to support the province's academic programs.

5. Whoever is in charge of classes should have studied philosophy.

6. Everybody should speak Latin, even superiors.

7. The theologians should teach grammar, since our school is one of humility, not ambition.

8. Neither an adviser nor a superior should show that he is so delighted and so extol the talent of any brother and his efforts in the coursework that the person begins to make plans to profess those things and begins to despise grammar and humanistic literary studies. People like this should be humbled.

9. The good morale of the teachers should be maintained and we should think that in that morale resides the entire surety of our running the school well.

10. All those who use ignorance as an excuse and refuse to teach humane letters should take lessons openly or in private.

11. Superiors should see to the dissolution of the opinion born of ignorance that those speaking Latin well and fluently are not intellectually gifted; also, the theologians along with the philosophers should speak in good Latin and hate barbarism.[6]

12. The teachers of humane letters should not be burdened more than other teachers with house services; in rooms, in clothing, and so forth, they should have no less consideration than the others, especially insofar as they are engaged in a less appealing and more bothersome work than the others are.

13. The rector should attend the declamations with the older fathers and encourage his community to participate in the exercises.

These are the more important rules we should follow without neglecting the rest of them. Indeed, I see legislated extensively in this book of the *Ratio* whatever I myself could have hoped for concerning the proper management of our humanistic programs for our men (and this has always been a concern of high priority for me).

II

The Importance of Not Mixing Rhetoric with Dialectic

1. As far as I know, in the Society, where the philosophy course is not being taught, this does not occur, or it just happens in one or two places. I will take up the case of Munich later.[7]

2. It is a shame to do what you perceptively criticize in others. And yet whenever one of us devotes himself to two or three subjects at the same time, we have made the decision to act imprudently and impractically. Even our Blessed Father Ignatius used to blame himself for having done this very thing. But dialectic should no more be studied with rhetoric than some part of mathematics or theology should be. No, in fact, those subjects would be more easily combined with it.

3. Either we will have to add a fifth hour, or we will have to teach Greek more seldom, or we will have to correct compositions more infrequently (as they necessarily ought to be corrected every day for an hour; and if possible, each

---

6 Pontanus refers here to a commonplace according to which those who are talented in eloquence are not suitable for philosophy and vice versa. This commonplace had found a scientific justification in a work by Juan Huarte de San Juan (1529–88), *Examen de ingenios para las sciencias* [The examination of talents for the professions] (Baeza: Juan Montoya, 1575), where the Spanish physician tried to demonstrate the Galenic reasons for the difference between temperaments and talents.

7 The Jesuit college of Munich (then called Old Academy or Wilhelminum) was established in 1583 on request of Duke Wilhelm V of Bavaria (1548–1626).

person's own compositions should be corrected, both in prose and in verse, to the extent that it is badly composed). First, that idea about the hours is not customary in the Society; for everywhere the rhetoricians have only four hours, and the Roman schools will never require more. Moreover, in this approach, the time at home is diminished, time that would have to be given to the compositions and reviews. Second, as for Greek, they have made very little progress at this point and bring with them almost nothing of the basics because in our schools it is taught very negligently and our teachers shy away from it; and now they will make even less progress—that is, none. But against ignorance we must push on, not give up. The Roman *Ratio* has a long and full chapter giving many reasons why Greek should be diligently taught; one of these reasons is this, that since the Society generally gets its members from our own schools, if they have been badly trained in Greek, the Society will not have Greek scholars; and so it will not be able to help the Catholic Church in that area of study, though it should certainly be able to do so. I am very eager to see this problem solved. And there is now a third consideration: composition is the one matter before which the rest shrink to nothing: this is what the public wants most of all, valuing our students most highly for that reason.

4. Rhetorical reviews, compositions, memorization, and the reading of Latin books are now being given much less care and time, since dialectical subtleties and obscurities occupy our intellectual talents considerably, especially those that are not so great. The more capable ones will always be given to dialectic, and its study will be preferred more insofar as the students will enjoy that in which the teacher, if there are two, helps them most markedly. But this happens to the ruin of rhetoric; for dialectic is not introduced into rhetoric for the purpose of it taking the leading students.

5. On account of these and other reasons, I think even Munich's rhetoric ought to be removed, and it has been put aside by Reverend Father [Georg] Bader.[8] I do not think that great results can be garnered from the linkage that is made there. If there is progress in dialectic, I dare say that there is less than this in rhetoric. Who is able to serve two masters? But those at Munich bring up an argument that can also be made in my own college as well. Many become priests who cannot go off to study the course for a three-year period. But more than a thousand times I have heard our fathers lament the ignorance of parish priests not in dialectic but in grammar. And I know that there are those who have been made priests who after taking the entire [theological] course knew neither the course nor grammar. They would have a more persuasive argument if they were promoting the reading of cases or sacred scripture, for which dialectic is not so necessary; even country dwellers can be educated apart from syllogisms. Sufficient is that dialectic that is part of

8   Father Georg Bader (1540–1612) was the Austrian provincial superior (1585–89).

the study of rhetoric; for many things dialectical are necessarily mixed in with rhetoric's rules on account of their close relationship. Any argument against this? Look how many individuals have become and are becoming priests on the basis of humanistic letters and rhetoric. Do they not carry out their professional obligations without first studying dialectic? No, some of these do better than those who have taken courses on marvelous subjects.

6. Brothers are sent here to study, and the one to whom they are being recommended knows how much they have completed in grammar and each language and poetry. Will they study or not study that dialectic? If they study it, they will be drinking hot and cold at the same time; we will be building and tearing down at the same moment; we will be burdening weak shoulders with an unbearable burden. Then they will study it again at Ingolstadt. If they have passed it at Augsburg, they will be more learned than the students at Ingolstadt who do not cover Fonseca in two or three entire months; they themselves will take classes for six months or a whole year and they will perhaps have more exercises.[9] If they have not passed it, they will not pass even in a third and fourth year, especially in such great haste. I leave aside the fact that all their studies will fail, and they will limp as much in them as they will in public on account of dialectic. Will they not take classes? What a trial! They will think themselves hated, and so forth. Actually, the more I think about it, the more monstrous a thing it seems to me. The matter deserves approval, but approval ought to be sought in another way, and we should rather agree to do what is useful for the students and what we might be able to approve for men of good sense who have had experience of both types of material.

III

The Society's Studies and Humanistic Classes

Five reasons why the Society rightly values these studies greatly and ought to so value them.

1. Because this is the portal through which we enter into the biggest cities. By way of these studies, we acquire the friendship of great princes. They strongly commend us to every social level, high and low, since indeed, everyone deeply hopes to see his own children well furnished with education and virtue. Without this work, the rest of what we do will hold little appeal for the public. Take away our classes and who will look directly at us afterwards?

---

9   The Jesuit college of Ingolstadt (in the duchy and electorate of Bavaria) was founded in 1556, the same year of the foundation of the German province of the Society of Jesus. Pedro Fonseca (1528–99), author of the *Institutionum dialecticarum libri octo*, first published in 1564 in Lisbon by Juan Flavio. This book was recommended in the *Ratio studiorum* and soon adopted by the majority of the Jesuit colleges.

2. Even if they do not rival the others in rank, they nevertheless are preeminent in richness and impact. For those pertain to few; these to many; you will always find among educated people that hardly a thirtieth has touched upon the more profound writing since such works are generally considered to belong to the domain of churchmen and religious. Our humanistic education wanders broadly through the human race; it cultivates its seedbed throughout towns and cities; and it makes a sowing whose expansive crops we have seen and do see.

3. These studies are supremely moral, whether you read history or poetry or oratory, Greek or Latin; on almost every page we have an opportunity to exhort to virtue or to discourage from vice; this does not happen in physics, metaphysics, dialectic, nor everywhere in theology. However, even though we want both, we prefer to produce good rather than learned people. In one address of yours and a conversation, you will sometimes bring it about that no longer does the usurer want to lend, nor does the libertine want to have his way, and just so with other reprehensible behavior; but the good instructor accepting a boy not yet allured by any vices, with continual exhortations and a kind of fatherly care, like a judge, will fashion him at a profound level and shape his life into a Christian one, so that he will not so much have to become good after starting out with a deformed character as he will not know how to turn out bad after starting with a good one; certainly he would be deeply repelled by such a thing. In this matter, just as in the teaching of literature, the second teacher follows the first, the third the second, the fourth the third, and so forth.

4. Our literature takes reserve, modesty, and caution from the spirit. From the literature in turn, the spirit takes likeability, good sense, and effectiveness. Since these three things are great and necessary for engaging honorably with people, they seem more likely to be derived from humanistic study than from the other subjects. For those are more rigorous, these milder and far more fit for regular companionship, from which they also draw their name.

5. The rest of the studies are chilly without the humanistic one; in a certain way they are mute and dead. These humanistic ones are their life, spirit, movement, blood, and bone. Without them, their splendor and worthiness lose all their luster.

IV

Eight Impediments to Humanistic Studies among Jesuits and Our Students

1. The first root of so great an evil comes from the lack of good sense on the part of superiors who in the enrollment of young people into the Society

consider—quite rightly—a calm disposition, devotion, and virtue; but they
do not attend much to intellectual talent and a disposition to learn. But
these are even more important for them to consider. The young people can
acquire the first set of characteristics with us if they lack them; nobody can
give intellectual talent. Since coadjutors are not being designated and on
account of the numbers all of them cannot be made ministers and procurators, they are being put in charge of classes while they themselves are
unpolished and inexperienced; they are teaching others, and what is more
insufferable, they move from one school to another. Since therefore the
Society without literary studies seems not so much maimed as non-existent,
it seems we should reject even young men who are good but dull and intellectually weak so that then there would be no need to answer the complaints:
"What can we do? What will we do? Be patient—he is a good brother; he can
be a minister," and so forth. And what a strange thing it is that so important
an office, right next to the rectorship, after all, seems to be considered the
office of the dull and dimwitted.

2.   After their introductory time is over, the brothers are left only a single year
     of humanistic studies, and some not even a year. The reason proposed is that
     they have studied two years outside the Society. They suggest therefore that
     they have made progress in such a period of time. The reality itself, however,
     shows that things are otherwise: in Greek, they have laid no foundations,
     they compose verses badly, they write badly. It is not years of classes that we
     need but learning. If someone has not gotten it, let him get it in the Society,
     even if he has studied rhetoric for ten years. And so we have to consider not
     how long anyone has studied but how far he has gotten, and neither rectors
     nor provincials should be the judge of this, but the teachers to whom they
     are entrusted.

3.   Each thing ought to be learned in its own class. Now when all the brothers,
     even those who perhaps had only studied syntax outside our schools and
     those who had hardly entered into the humanistic literary class, are automati-
     cally being sent after the novitiate to rhetoric, who does not see that this causes
     confusion, inequality, struggle, and unhappiness? This one needs tutoring on
     Cleynaerts;[10] another, on prosody; another one still needs to avoid solecisms.
     Fine and proficient in rhetoric indeed! But they say that the brothers would
     be downcast if they should be sent to the humanistic literary class. This is
     the great trouble that superiors are now bringing about, doing what pleases
     brothers of a proud and petty spirit, no, even those who are high-minded.

---

10 Nicolaes Cleynaerts (1493–1542), also called *Clenardus*, was a philologist and a renowned
    author of grammar manuals such as *Institutiones Graecae* (1530), *Meditationes graecanae*
    (1531), the *Institutiones grammaticae Latinae* (1538), and *Tabula in grammaticen Hae-
    bream* (1529).

Who lays foundations along with the walls? Who sows before the ploughing? But of course we, with all our good sense, mix Cleynaerts with Demosthenes, prosody and grammar with Virgil and Cicero, and when we join such disconnected things, we weary the mind, we trouble and afflict the instructors. Here we build, there we tear down, we get nowhere. In order to avoid something displeasing to a little brother, we have to become absurd and ridiculous. But from the beginning it was not thus [Mt. 19:8].

4. From badly and incompletely trained brothers arise inept instructors. From this same source come superiors who are uneducated and truly ignorant of cultural matters, so much so that there are not a few of them who cannot write a grammatical letter; and these come in a similar way from another source, namely not allowing many to teach for at least a three-year period after the course in philosophy and forcing them even at the peril of their own health to cover another course of studies without interruption. Indeed, these two reasons are why we have all those in the Society (and there is unfortunately a vast number of them) who have no more than rudimentary literary skills and little experience. In this province, and I believe it is the same in others, no rector (except perhaps one or two) has set foot in one of the lower classes to teach, and still school-related problems and literary educational matters are put before them. They are the ones who especially have to decide, correct, and change things. If superiors had taken more of the literary course, we would not be struggling so much to follow the plan of studies.

5. There follows another considerable difficulty, the inordinate freedom of instructors in private studies, and their very frequent transfer. Each one is allowed to read what he wants, to study as much as he wants, and in fact even when he wants. It is enough if he just teaches. The rector and the prefect are not very inquisitive about how he teaches; they do not correct the wayward. Nobody is pressed to compose; most write very rarely and very badly. We live in such great tranquility and have every year new teachers who are always boys so that our schools are becoming all the more contemptible. Before they have begun to teach, they have to stop. What authority do such teachers have? What good are they? Why are we not ashamed of our own stupidity? A city does not want to change a bodyguard or an executioner every year, and we think that in the pursuit of wisdom that kind of instability is going to be helpful, whether you consider the teachers themselves or the students? Fine if they would complete a three-year period; the best thing, though, would be if certain selected people spent their lives in this service and still became priests at the proper time, as the rule says, so that they would not be inferior to others and yet leave theology to others. If theology is introduced, then there is no hope for our having career teachers. They will come back, if they do come back, at a more advanced age, not capable of enduring the work we do, indeed, worn out by their other labors,

and because of their knowledge of more refined and greater matters they will be self-important, they will disdain the teaching of grammar, and they will be thinking about the theological course of study. In addition, they will partly be teaching, partly preaching, partly hearing confessions, and sometimes they will be engaged in missions, and it will be necessary to provide substitutes who will upset the students and bring other disadvantages into the school. Should the eye hear and the ear look and the hand walk? Being many we are one body; not all the members have the same function [1 Cor. 12]. There will be strong opposition to this rule about career teachers with the priesthood but without theology and as a result without the other activities of priests; and for that reason it will have to be very sharply countered. For there is nothing better in the whole book, nor anything more useful for protecting and extending the reputation of the Society.

6. We perceive an amazing contempt for these studies, arising from the perverse opinion that they are neither so useful nor so necessary as those higher studies; but for those studies themselves to be of any profit, they need other things, such as languages, knowledge of antiquity, a range of learning, and also the skill of speaking—all of which come from nowhere other than from our workshops. With this impediment, I join the honor that is always considered great enough for them, but that is slender or non-existent for us. And yet, "honor nourishes the arts, and whatever individuals find worthy of blame lies ever uncultivated."[11] The one who hears confessions during the week and sometimes on Saturday, who preaches every eighth day, who teaches philosophy—that person is called and considered a worker. But the one who by the sweat of his brow [Gen. 3:19] teaches five hours every day and prepares at home three or four lessons a day with concern and great effort, that person is not a worker. If teaching is a work of the Society, how are those teaching not workers? Indeed, they are most splendid workers. Truly such people do not know of what spirit they are [Luke 9:55], and while they have knowledge of profound matters, they are making the most embarrassing mistakes in extremely obvious ones.

7. Most of the superiors are cheap and tight; they do not want to buy good books. But still they avidly buy theological books and certain others that are not very necessary for their own colleges; and they do not shudder at the price. They are also too limp and soft, they pretend not to notice, they do not want to impinge on anyone, and in their excessive caution they lose esteem themselves; not wanting to offend certain unrestrained individuals, they offend those who have a better understanding and those who love the Institute [of the Society]. What a fool is that doctor who applies ointment when the wound calls for the scalpel. But now such is

---

11 Cicero, *Tusculan Disputations*, I.2.4.

the condition of literary study in the Society that we must no longer keep looking the other way, pretending ignorance, and waiting; better to rave devotedly than to flatter fecklessly.

8. I do not cease to wonder why penances are given out daily in matters of a most trivial and sometimes ridiculous nature, but in academics, a matter of the greatest importance, they are never given either to instructors or to students. Does it therefore pertain more to the glory of God and the salvation of souls that one has not made his bed at the right time, or that one has broken an old jar while using it to wash, or that one has petted a cat, and so forth, than that one teaches well and diligently learns, reviews, composes, and so on? Do we not stand in very great need of these things? In the dining hall, our superiors hardly suffer reviews, lessons, and recitations—no doubt so that their ears may not be healed completely.[12] About other matters they exhort us well and devoutly; but about the passion to study for God's sake, they never do. That is why, I believe, none of the brothers has the slightest scruple about neglecting study, nor is he admonished by confessors about this matter. It is also to be attributed to a faulty leniency that very often our superiors have in oral and in written form received ways and means to support our studies, and they have demonstrated their approval, but they have done not a thing about it afterwards.

V

What Response Might Possibly Be Made to the Great Volume of Objections and Complaints Raised against the *Ratio studiorum*

I. It is impossible, and even were it possible, it would not be a necessary effort to answer the objections, doubts, complaints of each college in each and every province regarding all the classes.

1. [One might respond] that the Society is sending this second educational charter, fashioned on the basis of critiques of the first one; treating us very graciously and prudently indeed, it has offered this one for us to judge in all freedom. Very learned men, chosen for this task, have carefully considered the critiques, forging and composing anew a single body of text. But if this one does not prove to be fit (and it will not be fit if so many doubts and complaints prove to be substantial and valid for a great part of the project; for I would not want to deny that some few of these criticisms do hold up) even a third would be drawn up, and it will possibly happen that finally a

---

12 Is. 6:10: "Make the heart of this people calloused; make their ears dull and close their eyes. Otherwise they might see with their eyes, Hear with their ears, Understand with their hearts, And return and be healed."

fourth would be called for. But everyone realizes that this would be an impropriety unworthy of us, just as everyone realizes that citizens ought to accommodate themselves to the laws and not the laws to the citizens.

2. Since there have arisen so many doubts in opposition to the thinking of the Society, and since there are so many people criticizing, so many despairing, then one of these follows, if the things they are saying are true: either the Society is treating us in a truly clumsy and harsh manner and does not yet know itself adequately; or we are really uneducated, inexperienced, and sluggish, which I would prefer to affirm.

3. If it makes many changes and concessions in response to the complaints, the Society will lose not just a little of its authority among its sons. For since we should be firmly of the persuasion that the Society is being governed by God, this should all the more especially be the case in a matter of such great importance which contains something like half of our Institute and which is in a way the second portion of our essence, something into which so much work has gone for so many years with such great diligence, and for which both divine and human assistance have been sought. But if much weight is given to those complaints, then the Society will appear to have acted inadvisably in many matters, and to be incapable of instructing its sons, who are more learned than their mother, and it will seem that God has not been with us, but that the entire business was a kind of collection of so-so discussions and random opinions, not lawful and holy commands. So what will happen when lesser things are being decided?

4. [One might respond] that almost all the judgments proceed from a kind of great lack of good sense and an incredible blindness. First, because all those scribblers imagine the *Ratio studiorum* is nothing other than academic regulations. Superiors allow them this opinion, and they say nothing whatever about what is taught by so many rules and how everything depends on them as effects from causes. They are surprised at how elaborately humanistic studies are treated; everything for them resides in theology and so forth. Then there is the fact that all of them make judgments about this charter on the basis of the present thoroughly confused and vexatious state of affairs. And those things that cannot be done now, as things stand, they boldly declare simply cannot be done and ought not to have been prescribed. The students, they say, are not willing to do this and that, claiming that it has not been done up to now. The students of humanities are told to ask each other about the precepts for elegy, epigrams, and so forth, to interpret hieroglyphics, Pythagoras's symbols, and so forth, when the professors themselves do not know these things. What then? So because the instructor is not learned, is the law not good? The

watchmen are for the most part drunk, so there should have been no instructions about guarding the city? The instructors should learn what they do not know and cause the children to want what they do not want; and to know that they should get used to being required to do not what is done but what is not done. In addition, they should know that the *Ratio* proposes a certain optimal state, and it gives its laws for that. But if we are not now prepared for them, we should make ourselves so, and we should strip off the old man [Eph. 4:22] with his ignorance. We need to become altogether different people and, digging up the old foundations, we need to lay new ones. Otherwise we will never raise up this building as we have been told to do.

II. Those objections were written up not by veteran teachers or experienced prefects but by instructors of individual classes at the behest of prefects. Those instructors, however, are almost all new; most of them began to teach after only a year, and some of them after only six months, with no experience up till then, with almost no understanding about academic matters, almost children themselves according to their age. O the shame of it! And such people are making judgments about the laws of the whole Society?

III. There is no reason why anyone should object to the idea that the students of the heretics are making better progress than ours despite the fact that their regulations are not as refined and fully developed as ours. This can be answered: if they are producing learned individuals with laws that are less carefully worked out, we with our more carefully framed regulations will be able to make ours yet more learned and even supremely learned—unless we are perhaps being commanded to do what is impossible rather than fully developed, which is false. Their regulations agree in many points with ours; in certain respects theirs are more scrupulous than ours, gathered from Seneca, Pliny, Quintilian, and so on. Read Sturm, Celio Secondo, Erasmus, Brun, Camerarius, and so on.[13] Our regulations do not speak about correcting themes and assigning them so clearly and abundantly. Ours do not detail so completely the office of the teacher. Ours do not name the helpful authors in each individual genre, and they are quite sketchy in prescribing books.

13 Protestant learned men: Johannes Sturm (1507–89) set up the Strasbourg Protestant Gymnasium in 1537; Celio Secondo Curione (1503–69) was an Italian humanist who became a radical reformer; Otto Brunfels (1488–1534) was a renowned botanist. Joachim Camerarius (probably "the Elder," 1500–74) wrote copiously, mostly on Greek literature and culture. Following a current view that made Erasmus a precursor of Martin Luther, Pontanus includes him here. See Paul Grendler, "The Attitudes of the Jesuits towards Erasmus," in *Collaboration, Conflict, and Continuity in the Reformation: Essays in Honour of James M. Estes on His Eightieth Birthday*, ed. Konrad Eisenbichler (Toronto: Centre for Reformation and Renaissance Studies, 2014), 363–85.

They have career teachers and men; we have temporary ones and boys. They are most diligent for the sake of money, we most negligent for the sake of God. They keep theirs longer at the humanistic studies; we rush too much for the sake of the theological course of studies. These, and other points that I am leaving out, can be put against those who say that the method of the heretics is less finished than ours. In certain respects this is true, in others not. And so we may learn from them.

IV. Something in certain rules can be forgiven ours so that the teachers are not overburdened. But it seems good that we keep all the prescriptions in the first part for provincials, rectors, and prefects, and especially those that pertain to the studies of the brothers.

V. Some make the objection that certain contradictions occur, and certain things are repeated in different classes. This is a strong argument. In so great a range of considerations, "the scribe has wandered off." Finally, many things are cited in those pages that are not worth reading since they are the doubts and laments of unpracticed and untrained individuals that prefects ought to have confronted, and the entire heap of them can be overturned with one great solution, namely that we should be eager to make ourselves learned first, then others; this is what superiors are wisely instructed in the first part of the *Ratio*.

Corollaries

1. In the items that I call the more important parts of the law, that is, the rules for the superiors, some sixty apply to the provincial, about thirty concern our classes. In each of the rules so much is important, so prudently and learnedly are all things prescribed, so necessary are the individual items, that even if we lacked the second part, which covers the rules for the classes, I would think that we would have a *Ratio* that was good enough if its rules were kept; otherwise all our effort is empty and ridiculous.

2. In this general congregation, where all the provincials and many rectors will be in attendance, a decision will have to be made about what should be kept permanently; and we will not have to wait until the *Ratio* receives more testing.[14] It has been sufficiently tested, and we have learned by experience that there are superiors who are not very enthusiastic about doing what they have been told; it seems that reverend father general has to use his power in dealing with these.[15]

3. We should not be too concerned about the multitude of those voicing opposition, and we have to maintain that a few people with eyes can discern more than a thousand people who are either blind or vision-impaired. In the

---

14 The Fifth General Congregation of the Society of Jesus (1593–94), the first to be summoned without the aim of electing a new superior general.

15 Claudio Acquaviva (1543–1615; in office 1581–1615).

Catholic Church, in civil matters, many have permission to express their opinions (as also happens among us). Deciding belongs to a very few.

4. In the fifth impediment, I made mention of the extraordinary carelessness of teachers in [their] private studies, which they arrange in such a way that good time is badly managed. All too many have no idea of how to study, and as perpetual students they never arrive at knowledge [cf. 2 Tim 3:7]. Therefore I think a guide should be written to teach them how to study so that they may in a short time and by a direct route arrive where they vainly aspire to go by way of so many detours over so many years.

VI

A Very Brief Method for Making Progress and for Teaching, Intended for the Humanities Instructors

When they are put in charge of classes, instructors should think that it is the highest will of superiors that they themselves not only form the young people well but also (something that is also a prerequisite for that task) that they make progress in their spare time in all sorts of humanistic studies, in Latin, in poetry, in Greek, in the knowledge of antiquity, and that they in this way emerge as fit for higher classes also. Two things are especially relevant here, reading and composing; unless we engage in these diligently and attentively, all our work will be pointless and we will waste our time miserably.

Reading and Composing

1. The teachers should therefore not deceive themselves into thinking that the library is theirs and that they can read good material on impulse. Better to read deeply rather than to read many. I say: you should read a few but read them often, Cicero especially; not so as to read his entire works, and then a second and third time—that is senseless and almost useless. What we take in we should also organize. Writing is organization, and for it those readers leave no place. They should believe, however, that they will never achieve a reputation and will be most justly scorned if they do not frequently produce compositions. Their writings will be worthless if they are not learned, serious, attractive, and rich.

2. We have to unlearn our barbarism. That is why indices and collections of low words and the detritus of Latinity should not be scorned. Then you should make use of some leaders and translators who teach us the use and the meanings of Ciceronian words and expressions, lest seeing we do not see and hearing we understand nothing [Luke 8:10]. For this, Adriano Castellesi and Anton van Schoor will serve especially well.[16]

---

16 Pontanus refers to a renowned manual of Latin written by Adriano Castellesi da Corneto (*c.*1460–*c.*1521), *De sermone Latino and modis Latine loquendi* (Basel: Froben, 1513) and

3.   It will help to have something like a reference notebook in which you may jot down things that you especially like and think will be useful, noting pages or chapters of books if they contain witty responses or clever stories or ancient rites or somewhat rare patterns of expression or other things of this kind; provided that later you do not spend time in changing such notebooks, organizing them, and writing them out.

4.   The goal and aim of writing is the ability to set forth our feelings easily, cleanly, neatly, and fully. This does not happen for those who write a little piece of prose once or twice in an entire year or for those who write often but with too little variety, especially when they realize their own inadequacies as they write. Likewise, it is a great help to enter a club, where members can compete and correct each other, both in poetry and in prose composition.

How to Teach

1.   They will be very diligent about preparing the presentation, not so as to knot themselves up by consulting all the commentaries and scholiasts they have available, but rather to be content with one or two of the better ones and to take from there whatever they think necessary. They should not search through books by the Nizolio's and Calepino's and the other lexicons unless compelled by necessity, and they should not read more than the passage requires.[17]

2.   They should set forth the argument of the next reading fully and clearly, and they should refresh the students' memories of the preceding material with a brief review.

3.   In explaining they will follow the order of the syntax. For example:
Arma virumque cano, Troiae qui primus ab oris
Italiam fato profugus Laviniaque venit
Littora […][18]
Cano arma virumque [I sing arms and the man], *qui ab oris Troiae primus venit Italiam Laviniaque littora* [who from the shores of Troy first came to Italy and the Lavinian beaches] *profugus fato* [an exile by fate]. Often there will not be any need for any other explanation.

4.   While teaching they will accommodate their delivery to the reading of the words and passages of the authors, to the passages themselves, to the matters under discussion, and to the characters. This wonderfully strengthens both the clarity of the material and the pleasure of those listening. For example: That line from the *Aeneid*, book 1: "You want me to give up on what I have

---

the works of Anton van Schoor (1525–52) who wrote several Ciceronian *thesaura*, that is, collections of Cicero's words and sentences.

17 Celebrated authors of dictionaries: Mario Nizolio (1498–1566) and Ambrogio Calepino (1435–1511).

18 The example is a classical reference for Renaissance schooling, the beginning of Virgil's *Aeneid*.

started, a conquered woman? Not have the ability to turn the king of the Teucri from Italy?" I would read angrily and like a person full of indignation. That line from book 3, "O happy maid of Priam, happy alone before the others," and so forth, I would read with sighs. The same approach will hold in letters, in speeches, in history, and in everything.

5. Outside rhetoric, nothing should be dictated in any class except for the themes of compositions.

6. In correcting the compositions, they should keep the rules set forth in the annotations of volume 1 of the *Dialogues* of a certain person.[19]

VII

A Brief Directive for Instructors, Especially of Humanities and Syntax

1. They should read commentaries diligently, but only a few of them. If there is one and that one happens to be the best, it should be enough; do not take up another. But they should provide what the boys can grasp and what the passage demands.

2. In explaining, they should keep the order of the syntax. They should adjust their voice in sound and intonation or control the contents and the words of the authors and the persons speaking. They should also have discussions with the authors and sometimes speak in the character of the authors.

3. A little more material should be expounded than that which should be committed to memory; this is so that a larger store of words and expressions is available for speaking and writing, which is the reason that the authors are being expounded. In Virgil, I would think that it is possible that twenty-four lines can be expounded in the time period, and fifteen or twelve can be committed to memory. In Ovid, around twenty can be expounded, ten learned by heart. A similar number will be the norm maintained with the letters of Cicero and in the *De officiis*, or *Tusculans*, or a little more, considering of course the passage's level of difficulty.

4. They will not use Nizolio or Calepino, or the *Thesaurus*, unless necessity forces them, and only to the degree it forces them.[20]

5. The themes of compositions should be varied, frequent, brief, both in poetry and in prose.

6. They should be assigned to do Virgil, Ovid, Cicero, and the *Dialogues*.[21]

---

19 Pontanus himself. The work is *Progymnasmata Latinitatis sive dialogi*, vol. 1, *De rebus literariis* (Ingolstadt: Sartorius, 1588); vol. 2, *De morum perfectione* (Ingolstadt: Sartorius, 1591); vol. 3, *De variis rerum generibus* (Ingolstadt: Sartorius, 1592).

20 The thesaurus was possibly the work of Robert Estienne (1503–59), *Dictionarium seu thesaurus linguae Latinae* (Paris: Robert Estienne, 1531).

21 See footnote 19 for the work mentioned here and in the following note.

7. In the correction of the compositions, they should follow the rules laid down by Pontanus in his annotations on dialogue 27 in volume 1.

8. Beyond the explanations, they should not speak in German unless it is necessary, and then only briefly. In speaking Latin, they should also try to employ the expressions and words that they are interpreting [in the texts]. They should certainly not learn any other words and they should unlearn any words of their own.

9. It is not necessary for each student to recite the lesson in its entirety. The second and third students can finish it off. Sometimes they will correct each other's letters, and the one who has been too careless in correcting mistakes will pay the same penalty as the one who made them.

10. As instructors would think nothing of all the industry and progress of the student if the student did not compose and they would rank the student higher if he composed better; so they should consider it certain that they will be imperfect and lame teachers, despite all their diligence in teaching, if they themselves did not compose, so that in this area also they might be of some help to their students. Certainly no one will make someone a writer nor will he be a good judge of composition if he writes nothing himself. For this reason, I urge that teachers not let three days go by without putting effort into writing four or five verses. And they should rest entirely assured that they will the better trained and the more fit for teaching the more they have taken a liking to the use of their pen.

VIII

Certain Obstacles to Progress in Humanistic Studies

It has been noted that our very dear brothers pursuing their humanistic studies are making less progress than they should be, given the excellent intellectual gifts that many of them possess, or given the passion for this literary study that burns in many of them, or even given the time that they spend on it. Those who seek the reasons for this situation find many answers, but I think the problems can easily be solved and I think they should be.

Among these, not the smallest is the fact that when our brothers are sent to these studies, we do not have a sufficient knowledge of each person's talents, progress, and disposition of mind to this or that type of study, and since we do not know in what subjects each person desires and is able to make the greatest progress, there is no doubt at all (and I will give the reasons later) that those who will make the greatest progress in the literature of the humanities are also more engaged in such studies. In the same way, we should endeavor to see to it that among the students of the humanities those who seem to have more capacity for poetry (for example) than for eloquence should be more intensely and frequently trained in poetry, and vice versa for those gifted in eloquence. Nevertheless, since there is an affinity between these pursuits, students should be given more training in all respects, especially in those that are necessary.

Still, there is no approval at all for that approach that has them on their first entry into these studies driven to read van Schoor and Cardinale and Greek grammar, so that generally they are forced to use up a large part of the year, and the best part of it, namely the first months when their hearts are eager, without any more liberal and pleasant exercise.[22] But this is not to say that therefore the foundations (so to speak) should be neglected, but that we should not stick with them too long nor to them alone, but that it seems we should always be building something on top of them. If there is anyone who is clearly ignorant of Greek grammar, no one doubts that there has to be a diligent effort to learn it thoroughly. Likewise for the one who does not know prosody. But perhaps some instructor might say, "There is no one just beginning these studies who knows the elementary material, and so they have to work on it for a long time." I know some teachers make this objection. But often it is false and harmful. Even if they do not know these things perfectly, many of them still know enough to make progress on their own if they are encouraged. If they are forced to apply themselves to points they are already sick of, they even forget things they already knew. And there are plenty of examples. This is the reason why it is necessary that instructors have good expectations of their students and show it. And even if they are deceived about one or the other person, it would be better that they be deceived in thinking that the students know more than they know of the fundamentals, than in thinking that they know too little or nothing at all. They have been neglected to the extent that they were falsely thought to know nothing. But however much they know should be put into practice immediately and they should not just learn the rules but the use of those rules should be shown immediately in writing, composing, just as it happens in Latin so also in Greek and poetry, starting from expressions, maxims, letters, and so forth.

Next, we can hardly approve the fact that those who should be practicing the art of eloquence are being excessively constrained to reading dialogues; even though they can learn a great abundance of expressions from these, they still do not represent a sure and uniform style. And so I think that this reading is helpful but that it ought to be available to those who have at least an ordinary command of Latin.

Perhaps many were hindered because for an entire year or the better part of it they were only told to write letters and they began to write speeches either never or very late, when of course they had gotten thoroughly bored with grammatical studies on account of the schoolboy exercising. Moreover, if they learn to write speeches, they will also be able to write letters, not the reverse. Intellectual talents dry up too much if they write nothing but letters. And still Cicero

---

22 Adriano Castellesi da Corneto, the above-mentioned author of a *De sermone Latino*, who was created a cardinal by Alexander VI (r.1492–1503) in 1503.

recommends that their speech be rich and abundant; so there is something to be trimmed, as with productive vines. Letters ought not to be rejected but mixed in; and greater variety should be provided in the exercises so that there is something to tickle their talents and not merely what offends their tastes. Indeed, they ought to be spurred even to undertake greater things on their own. It will nevertheless always remain proper, if need be, to call back to the foundations those who are attempting things greater than they can manage.

Nevertheless, to promote these studies we clearly will need more exercises and compositions than we have had up to this point, not the elementary kinds, but those that are more humanistic; we should not so much eliminate as focus the more important efforts of our Jesuit brothers. For example, there might be someone attracted to eloquence and devoted to poetry who would like to write [poetic] dialogue even though he does not yet write poetry of the highest order. There are some instructors who would think this a grave failing, and they would reprimand such students and deter them. But I am not sure that they would be very prudent in doing that. Why should such a student not be instructed how a dialogue should be fashioned rather than turned away in this manner from all desire to write poetry? Something has to be allowed to students even though they are attempting things greater than they can manage, because this very attempt is quite praiseworthy and often more useful than those little exercises. The students should have some freedom and not be stopped from taking pleasure in these studies in which they are engaging out of obedience. This especially should not be forbidden to the older or more advanced students.

In this matter it will also help if the instructor gives some assistance and prodding (as it were) in the sort of writing in which the student seems likely to make progress. For example, for a student who likes poetry, some poets would be better, even modern ones. Or for someone who likes Greek, some Greek books and authors the reading of whom would seem to be a sort of privilege for those who are making progress.

We should truly hope to put aside that useless method of dictating long commentaries in rhetoric; for the students are kept back during that time from exercises that are far more helpful, and they become accustomed to grammatical fine points that they in fact merely track down in those dictations; they plunder only old and variant readings of Turnèbe, Vittori, and so forth, in which there is hardly anything that boys can use but rather only fights over particles and comparisons of passages and different authors that the young men do not understand; and meanwhile the necessary exercises are being neglected, the hands are being wearied, and paper is being wasted.[23] And does any student later reread these writings of his or think them useful in his life?

---

23 Adrien Turnèbe (1512–65) had been professor of Greek at the Royal College in France for many years. He provided many translations of ancient Greek poems and writings in Latin

In improving the speeches or poems of our students and in correcting their errors, we take account only of the style, but there is no concern for invention and arrangement.[24] We do not correct the things that infringe upon decorum, nor do we give advice on topics for amplification, on the clarifying features that might be employed or on those that have been badly employed, about the power of the arguments or the order in which they stand to each other; and finally, we neglect entirely the issues that concern the very content of the speech. If there should be no solecisms and barbarisms, then the speech is considered good, whatever can be said about the matter. This results in the talents of ours in composition typically creeping along the ground and writing wretchedly, for they will never learn these things elsewhere if they do not learn them in rhetoric, unless they do so either with great effort or through the special virtue of intellectual ability.

If all these points are observed, namely that everyone's talents are well known by the instructors, and the instructors adapt themselves more to each one of them and do not lead them all to speeches in the same way or by the same exercises; if they do not wear down the talents of the students in grammar, prosody, and dialogues either too rigorously or for too long; if they have better expectations of their students and put some trust in them; if they teach them usage along with the rules; if they promote progress in many ways, there is every hope that more will make greater progress. And to put it in a nutshell: the most important element lacking to our students so far has been frequent exercises and ones that are useful and stimulating and adapted to the intellectual talents of ours.

IX

Advice on Reprinting Greek Authors for Use in Humanistic and Rhetorical Classes

1. Our province in these two schools struggles every year from the scarcity of Greek books, either because it does not find the ones it wants and ought to want, or because it does not find enough copies even for one class of one college. The reason for this is that we have almost always gotten them from the heretics of Strasbourg and Basel, and to these we have provided up till now large profits. And still they have often abandoned us and are doing so. They also have forced us ever to sing the same tune, since they have printed nothing more than Demosthenes and Isocrates. Hence our catalogs very often lie, promising books that are not expounded when the time arrives.

---

and French. Piero Vettori (1499–1585) was an Italian philologist and professor of Greek and Latin at the University of Florence, who published his *Variarum lectionum* (more than thirty-eight books) between 1553 and 1582.

24 Or "content and structure." *Inventio* refers to the thinking out of the contents of the argument to be presented about the subject (*materia*); *dispositio* refers to the arranging and proportioning of what has been "discovered" in the *inventio*. See Chapter 17n6.

2. To stoke up an interest in the Greek language among our students and, hope-fully, to acquire some reputation for the Society even among other Catholic schools, I am quite persuaded that it will be enormously valuable to publish as textbooks the orators, historians, and the poets, partly in octavo format, and partly in quarto. In order that these be in the end more useful and more pleasing both for teachers and for students and for all buyers, and so that they may become more marketable, we should make sure that the paper is of good quality, the type appealing and the typesetting accurate—the printer is responsible for these three features but we would have the opportunity to make additional corrections—and it seems worthwhile to scatter through-out prefaces, prolegomena, annotations, and such enticements; in this, if I am thought to be of any help, I am ready to volunteer my efforts.

3. Of the books to be printed: those held by the colleges as separate items or ones that can be removed without inconvenience, after being read and well prepared, will be sent to the printer, who will provide newly printed versions in return. Other books will be copied at the printer's expense but by a learned copyist that we engage, one whose handwriting will not slow down a composi-tor who lacks sufficient learning. And I should be given liberty to borrow from the colleges whatever books I think necessary in this whole business.

4. Certain books should be entirely reprinted, and from others selections, as will be clear from the catalog that I attach below as an example. But the judgment of the matter should more reliably rest with those who are not strangers to Greek literature. I know of none such beyond Father Gret-scher.[25] But what will be selected will be the most useful and most delightful things, and as far as possible, they will be thoroughly decent in every respect.

5. There is no reason why anyone should oppose the Roman *Ratio*—First, because the matter seems to have fallen back to nothing—Second, it will propose the same books that we ourselves have been endeavoring to pub-lish, and these have already at one time been named in the rules for classes, both in earlier years and in the *Ratio* sent to us. Nor would reverend father general not allow us to expound freely books that are good and helpful for as long as copies are being sold, even though they are not mentioned in the *Ratio*. And even though we do not think it necessary, nevertheless to do all things in a safer way, this advice of ours can be written out for Rome, and moreover these very chapters can be sent there, if perhaps they themselves wish either to make some useful instructions or to consult it. But still, we should press on with what we have started.

---

25 The complete edition of the works of Jakob Gretser (1562–1625) appeared in seventeen folios in Ratisbon in the middle of the eighteenth century.

6. We can start with Cleynaerts's *Grammatica* as arranged and edited by Cre-spin.[26] The *Syntax* of Varenne can be made shorter,[27] and the book on the eight parts of speech can be improved. A brief prosody should also be produced.

7. We also need Latin books. What occurs to me at the moment is Aemilius, Probus, Pliny, *De viris illustribus*, the *Tusculans*. Different ones will occur to different people. But the matter should be handled carefully in the Latin works so that the printer does not suffer a financial loss; for Latin books are being published in many places.

8. The printer should be entirely clear about assured yearly sales of those books. We have to take care to tell the colleges that they should not buy other editions, and, as far as is possible, that they should all expound the same authors in the same year. All of them do Demosthenes, all Euripides. In humanities, all do the *Ad Nicocles*.[28]

9. Even though I understand how much work I am undertaking, I would nev-ertheless undertake it for its general utility and for the common goal of the Society, as long as the decision is made on these chapters of proposals that I have made here, and as long as the entire matter is organized as fully and plainly and definitely as possible.

Rough Catalog of Books to Be Printed

In their entirety: Homer except for the hymns. Herodianus, Theognis.

In part: A single volume: selections from Euripides, Sophocles, Aeschylus.

Individual books: Selections from Xenophon, Plato, Isocrates, Demosthenes; especially from the holy fathers Chrysostom, Basil, Gregory of Nyssa; from the *Epigrams*, Lucian, Plutarch's *Moralia*, the first book of Hesiod, speeches of the old orators.

When this matter gets underway I will, with the colleague I have named above, diligently work through this catalog, give it clear sections and punctuation, and submit it to the fathers for review.

---

26 *Institutiones absolutissime in Graecam linguam, annotationes suis quaeque praeceptis accommo-datae, investigatio thematum, seu de verbis anomalis, de accentibus, de syntaxi partium oratio-nis, Nicolao Clenardo authore* was published by Jean Crespin (*c*.1520–72) in Geneva in 1567.

27 The *Syntaxis linguae Graecae* of Jean de Varenne (Joannes Varennius, 1462–1536) was first pub-lished in Leuven (1532) by Bartholomeus van Grave (Bartholomaeus Gravius, active 1530–81).

28 A speech by Isocrates.

FIGURE 8   A portrait of the great Jesuit mathematician Christopher Clavius (1538–1612) by the engraver Esme de Boulonois (b.1645).

Courtesy of John J. Burns Library, Boston College

CHAPTER 26

Teaching Mathematics in Jesuit Colleges
(c.1581 and 1594)

Christopher Clavius

Christopher Clavius (1538–1612) wrote various documents about the teaching of mathematics in Jesuit colleges. As one of the most famous mathematicians of his time, his endorsement of this discipline was particularly significant, and yet he struggled to communicate adequately to the Society how important this subject was for secular society, especially in European royal courts. The first document (c.1581) was most likely addressed to the rector of the Roman College, where he had been teaching since 1567. The report sketched three different formulations for mathematical programs, proportioned according to the amount of coverage desired. The basic course lasted at least two years. The second document (1582) was a report Clavius wrote to the superior general of the Society (Acquaviva, 1543–1615), who had started to collect from the professors of the Roman College suggestions for the commission drafting the Ratio studiorum. *The third document (1593) recorded Clavius's response to Acquaviva's request for a promotional device for mathematics in Jesuit colleges. The last piece (1594) was probably a speech that Clavius gave at the Fifth General Congregation of the Society of Jesus (1593–94), which took up questions concerning Jesuit curricula.*

Christopher Clavius (born March 25, 1538, Bamberg in Bavaria, Germany— entered the Society in February 1555, Rome—died February 6, 1612, Rome). Clavius attended the classes of Pedro Nunes (1502–1578), renowned cosmographer, in Coimbra. In 1563, he was called to take the chair of mathematics previously held by Baltasar de Torres (1518–61) at the Roman College. He edited Euclid's Elements, *commented on the* Sphere *of John of Holywood (c.1195–c.1256), and published a number of mathematical studies that made his reputation. Working on the commission for the reform of the calendar, he successfully defended that project from the attacks of prominent intellectuals. Some of his works were translated into Chinese by Matteo Ricci (1552–1610), a former student of his, and spread among the intellectual circles of the Celestial Empire.*

Source: *Monumenta paedagogica*, nova editio, 7:109–21 (original: Latin)

CHRISTOPHORI
CLAVII BAMBERGENSIS
EX SOCIETATE IESV

IN SPHÆRAM IOANNIS
DE SACRO BOSCO

COMMENTARIVS

Nunc tertio ab ipfo Auctore recognitus,& plerifque
in locis locupletatus.

PERMISSV SVPERIORVM.

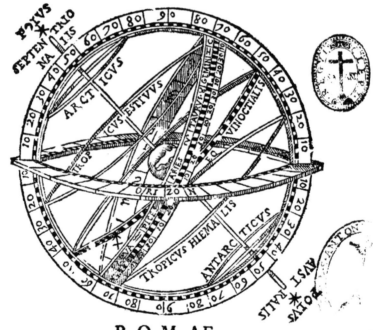

ROMAE,
Ex Officina Dominici Bafæ.   MDLXXXV.

FIGURE 9   The front page of Clavius's commentary on John of Holywood's *De sphaera*, from *Christophori Clavii Bambergensis [...] In* Sphaeram *Ioannis de Sacro Bosco commentarius*...[Christopher Clavius of Bamberg, A Commentary on the sphere of John of Holywood] (Rome: Victorius Helianus, 1570).

Courtesy of John J. Burns Library, Boston College

I

The Order to Follow to Attain Proficiency in the Mathematical Disciplines (*c.*1581)

1. The first four books of Euclid.
    Following my commentary, leaving out unnecessary explanatory comments.[1]

2. The more necessary rules for arithmetic operations, like addition, subtraction, multiplication, and division of whole numbers and fractions. Also a very brief treatment of proportions, proportionalities, and progressions, along with the golden rule of proportions, which is known as the Rule of Three, and the extraction of roots.[2]

    I will soon compose a brief treatment of this matter.[3] In the meantime, the *Practical Arithmetic* of Jemme Reinerszoon can still be read, or rather, the rules listed here can be extracted from the first book of the *Arithmetic* of Michael Stifel, who treats them extensively though with great brevity.[4]

3. The *Sphere* as briefly as possible or rather any other introduction to astronomy.[5] The more important rules regarding ecclesiastical calendrical reckoning can be added to this.

    I will also put out a brief treatment. Meanwhile, my commentary on John of Holywood's *Sphere* will suffice, leaving out operations on curves, the treatise on isoperimetrics, and so forth since these will be treated below.[6]

---

1   Clavius refers to his commentary, *Euclidis* Elementorum *libri XV: Accessit XVI de solidorum regularium comparatione—Omnes perspicuis demonstrationibus, accuratisque scholiis illustrati* [Fifteen books of Euclid's *Elements*, to which is added a sixteenth one about the comparison of regular solids—All explained with demonstrations and carefully elaborated notes] (Rome: Vincentius Accoltus, 1574).

2   The "Regula de tri" or "Regula trium" is cross-multiplication in two equal fractions to find an unknown. If $a/b=c/x$, then $x=(b^*c)/a$.

3   Clavius devoted three chapters (17–19) of his *Epitome arithmeticae practicae* [Summary of practical arithmetic] (Rome: Domenico Basa, 1583) to this subject. The section is entitled "Regula trium quae alio nomine regula aurea, sive regula proportionum dici solet" [The rule of three, also commonly called the golden rule or the rule of proportions].

4   Jemme Reinerszoon (Gemma Frisius, 1508–55) was a Dutch intellectual, a mathematician, and a globe-maker. One of his works was *Arithmeticae practicae methodus facilis* [An easy method for practical mathematics] (Antwerp: G. Bonte, 1540). Michael Stifel (Michael Stiphelius, 1487–1567) was an algebraist who published *Arithmetica integra* [A complete arithmetic] in 1544 (Nuremberg: Johann Petreius).

5   *De sphaera mundi* [On the sphere of the world], often called simply *De sphaera* or *Tractatus de sphaera*, is an elementary introduction to astronomy written around 1230 by John of Holywood (Johannes de Sacrobosco, *c.*1195–*c.*1256).

6   Clavius's text is *In Sphaeram Ioannis de Sacro Bosco commentarius* [Commentary on the *Sphere* of John of Holywood] (Rome: Victorius Helianus, 1570).

4. Books 5 and 6 of Euclid.
    From my commentary, as earlier.

5. The uses of the geometer's square, the astronomer's quadrant, and also, if it
    seems good, other instruments employed in making measurements, such as
    the rod or staff of Jacob, the torquetum, and so forth.[7]

    I will compose a little work on this subject. Meanwhile, such uses can
    be excerpted from Oronce Finé or any other like him, such as Jemme Rein-
    erszoon in his *Universal Astrolabe*, or Peuerbach, and so forth.[8]

6. The next four books of Euclid, namely 7, 8, 9, and 10. Or rather in place of
    the first three, Giordano's *Arithmetic*, or that of Gaspar Lax, where more is
    contained than in the arithmetic written by Euclid; add to these Maurolico's
    Arithmetic.[9]

    On account of mathematical music theory, I would choose out of all of
    these, Giordano's *Arithmetic*. Still, if time is too short, all this can be left out
    or put off to the very end, together with algebra; especially if we should want
    only those things that bear on astronomy and geography and are reduced to
    them, like the description of clocks, perspective, and so forth.[10]

7. Algebra, along with the arts that are necessary for its use, such as the algo-
    rithm of proportionally designated numbers, roots, binomials, and so on.
    Indeed, the algorithm of roots and binomials cannot be understood and
    demonstrated before book 10 of Euclid.

    I will put this out. In the meantime, however, Stifel's *Algebra* can be
    employed, or that of Johann Seubel or the one of Peletier.[11] Otherwise this

---

7   The staff of Jacob, also called a "cross-staff," is a pole with horizontal sticks used in naviga-
    tion to measure angles in order to help determine the latitude. The torquetum is a medieval
    computational device for determining various positional coordinates.

8   Oronce Finé (Orontius Finaeus, 1494–1555) was the French author of *De mundi sphaera*
    [On the sphere of the universe] (Paris: Simon de Colines, 1542). Jemme Reinerszoon wrote
    De astrolabio catholico [The universal astrolabe] (Antwerp: Joann. Seelsius, 1556). Georg
    von Peuerbach (Purbachius, 1423–61) wrote *Theoricae novae planetarum* [A new theory of
    the planets] (1454); he was also known as a mathematician and an instrument-maker.

9   Giordano of Nemi (Jordanus Nemorarius or Jordanus de Nemore, *fl.* thirteenth century)
    wrote *De elementis arithmeticae artis* [On the basics of arithmetic]. Gaspar Lax (1487–1560)
    wrote *Arithmetica speculativa* [Speculative arithmetic] (Paris: Hémon le Fevre, Nicolas de
    La Barre, 1515), and Francesco Maurolico (1494–1575) was the author of *Arithmeticorum
    libri duo* (Two books of arithmetic) (Venice: Francisco Francisco Senensis, 1575).

10 Clavius's *Compendium brevissimum describendorum horologiorum* [A very short abstract on
    designing sundials] (Rome: A. Zannetto, 1603).

11 Michael Stifel (1487–1567), *Arithmetica integra* [A complete arithmetic] (Nuremberg:
    Johann Petreius, 1544); Johann Scheubel (Ioannes Scheubelius, 1494–1570), *Algebrae com-
    pendiosa facilisque descriptio* [A brief and easy outline of algebra] (Paris: Benoît Prévost
    apud Guillaume Cavellat, 1551); Jacques Peletier du Mans (Iacobus Peletarius, 1517–82),

art, which it is not altogether necessary, can be postponed, as was said of the preceding four books of Euclid.

8. The last five books of Euclid, namely, 11, 12, 13, and 15, along with 16, which I have added from Candale.[12]

   From my edition, as previously. Under time limitations, books 11 and 12 can still be read and the rest postponed to a more convenient time for the reason offered in number 6. Yet it does not seem that book 13, proposition 10 should be left out, and the conversion of proposition 9 of the same book, and the note on proposition 10. For these are necessary to understand the science of curves. I have divided all of Euclid's books into four prescribed classes, not because they cannot all be understood immediately from the start, but in order that so many geometrical demonstrations that have to be learned together and in succession do not bore the students.

9. The treatise on curves, together with the use of the table of curves; also on the use of curves without tables, but only by straight lines.

   I will work this up, but still taking the table from Peter Apian or Johann Müller von Königsberg, which is extended by the individual minutes of degrees.[13]

10. *Spherical Elements* of Theodosius.[14]

    From what Maurolico has given.[15]

11. A brief treatment of spherical triangles. For Menelaus, Johann Müller von Königsberg, and Maurolico have written too verbosely about them.[16] Relevant to this are some parts of Apollonius's *Conical Elements*.[17] Such are the

---

De occulta parte numerorum quam algebram vocant [On the secret aspect of numbers known as algebra] (Paris: Guillaume Cavellat, 1560).

12 François de Foix, bishop of Aire-sur-l'Adour (Franciscus Flussates Candalla, 1512–94) edited and added to Euclid's *Elements* (Paris: Murhard, 1566).

13 Peter Apian (Petrus Apianus, 1495–1552), German humanist, mathematician, astronomer, and cartographer, wrote the *Cosmographicus liber* [Cosmography] (Landshut: Peter Apian, Johann Weißenburger, 1524). Johann Müller von Königsberg (Regiomontanus, 1436–76) was a German mathematician, astronomer, astrologer, translator, instrument-maker, and a Catholic bishop.

14 Theodosius of Bithynia (*c.*160–*c.*90 BCE), Greek astronomer and mathematician, was the author of the *Sphaerics*, a book on spherical geometry (*Theodosii Tripolitani Sphaericorum libri tres* [...] *Item eiusdem* [...] *Sinus, lineae, tangentes et secantes, triangula rectilinea atque sphaerica* [Three books of Theodosius of Tripolis (...) also of the same (...) curves, lines tangent and intersecting, right triangles, and spherics]) (Rome: Basa, 1586).

15 Francesco Maurolico, also called Francesco da Messina (1494–1575). He was a Benedictine monk and priest, a mathematician and a teacher at the Jesuit college in Messina.

16 Menelaus (Hellenistic, first century) wrote *Sphaerica*.

17 Apollonius of Perga (also Apollonius Pergeus, *c.*262–*c.*190 BCE) was a Greek geometer and astronomer famous for his treatment of conic sections in *Conicorum libri quatuor* [Four books of conics] (Bologna: Alessandro Benacci, 1566).

first 14 propositions, which are very valuable for understanding what has to be said about the construction of the astrolabe and about the shadows of pointers on sundials. For the rest seem more interesting than necessary, even though they are the most delightful and ingenious speculations.

I will complete this, and I will have printed at the same time in one volume, the *Curves* and the *Spherical Elements* of Theodosius. And also this brief treatment together with Apollonius's earlier propositions.

12. Demonstration of the structure of the astrolabe, together with its use. The second half concerning the altimetric scale should be omitted, however, since it repeats what has already been explained in the use of the geometer's square, and so on. This should be taught at the same time as the use of the material sphere or globe.

I will compose this, with the help of a certain brief treatment by Maurolico, and I will insert the use of the globe or material sphere.

13. The description of sundials of every type. Also at this point, if time allows, there can be an account of the method for marking off the dials, using Ptolemy's *Analemmate*.

I will finish this in a short while, together with an account of marking off dials from Ptolemy's *Analemmate*, and a short summary of marking off dials.[18]

14. Geography.
I will compose this. Meanwhile, however, Jemme Reinerszoon's *On the Separate Parts of the World* can be read, and so can others.[19]

15. Rules for measuring the areas of all shapes, both two- and three-dimensional. To these there can be added treatises on isoperimetric shapes if first there is a consideration of Archimedes's essay *On the Measurement of the Circle*, [and/or?] the *Divisions of Surfaces* taken from Machometo or Federico Commandino.[20]

I will deliver these too. But in the meantime, Oronce Finé can be read. Isoperimetric shapes are covered in my commentaries on the *Sphere*. A treatise on the divisions of surfaces has been printed by Federico of Pesaro.[21]

---

18 Claudius Ptolemy (*c.*90–*c.*168) worked in Alexandria in the field of mathematics, geography, astronomy, and astrology. *Liber de analemmate: De horologiorum descriptione* [On the analemma: Concerning the layout of sundials] (Rome: Paolo Manuzio, 1562).

19 *De orbis divisione et insulis, rebusque nuper inventis opusculum* [An essay on the distribution of the earth and the islands and on recent discoveries] (Douai: Louis de Winde, 1576).

20 The Italian Federico Commandino (1509–75) published the works of Archimedes and others, including a Euclidian text that was attributed to a certain Machometo Bagdadino or "Mahomet of Baghdad," a name that may refer to Muhammad ibn Musa al-Khwarizmi (*c.*780–*c.*850), the man long considered the inventor of algebra.

21 That is, Federico Commandino.

16. Perspective together with *The Burning Glass*.
    I will write this up. Oronce Finé has published *The Burning Glass*.[22] They also say that he published Archimedes or Ptolemy, but I have not seen them.

17. Various astronomical phenomena and problems comprising the entire doctrine of the *primum mobile*.[23] To these can be added the short work by Pedro Nunes on the twilight.[24]
    I will also look briefly into twilight as well. But the other things that Pedro Nunes's book covers I will attach to the treatment of problems.

18. Treatment on the motions of the planets and of the eighth sphere, along with the use of Alfonso's *Tables*, or those of others.[25] But [take this up only] after a brief consideration of the algorithm of astronomical fractions.
    I will publish this. But this treatment will correspond to the remaining eleven books of Ptolemy's *Almagest*.[26] I will also write very concise and clear rules for the *Tables*. But perhaps there will be greater authority if we would compose commentaries on the *Epitome* by Johann Müller von Königsberg.

19. The speculative music of Jacques Lefèvre d'Étaples, but Giordano's *Arithmetica* will precede it if not studied earlier.[27]
    This has been delivered by Jacques Lefèvre d'Étaples.

20. Some works of Archimedes, along with the discovery of the mean proportional to two lines, and the doubling of a cube, and also the closest approximation to the squaring of the circle.
    I will write commentaries to explain some of these.

---

22 *De speculo ustorio ignem ad propositam distantiam generante liber unicus* [The single book on the burning glass (or mirror) producing fire at a set distance] (Paris: Michel de Vascosan, 1551).

23 The *primum mobile* [first movable] in Ptolemaic cosmology was the outer heavenly sphere that moved all the inner spheres together with it.

24 Pedro Nunes (Portuguese, 1502–78) published *De crepusculis* [On twilight] (Lisbon: Ludovicus Rodericus, 1542). He was from a new Christian family and he had taught Clavius at Coimbra.

25 Alfonso X of Castile "the Wise" (1221–84) was a king of Castile, León, and Galicia, who supported the production of certain tabulations of data ("Alfonsine tables") that aided defining locations of the sun, the moon, and planets in relation to the stars.

26 The *Almagest* was a widely influential geocentric description of celestial movements.

27 Jacques Lefèvre d'Étaples (Faber Stapulensis, *c*.1455–1536), author of *Musica libris demonstrata quattuor* [Music explained in four books], which was published in 1496 with Giordano of Nemi's *Arithmetica decem libris demonstrata* [Arithmetic explained in ten books] (Paris: Johannes Higman and Wolfgang Hopyl, 1496). He was a French priest, theologian and humanist.

21. Mechanical questions of Hero, Pappus, and Aristotle, and so on.[28] Perhaps I will put out some short summary of these.

22. Also add some propositions from Serenus on the section of the cylinder, demonstrating in its second proposition also the proportion of a cylinder having of course elliptical bases.[29]

A Second, Shorter Order for Those Who Are Not Interested in Acquiring a Completely Thorough Understanding of Mathematics

1. The first four books of Euclid.
     From my edition.

2. The rules for practical arithmetic concerning addition, subtraction, and so on, both of whole numbers and of fractions, along with a brief treatment of proportions and proportionalities and progressions; immediately following this, the golden rule of proportions and the extraction of roots.
     My treatment or that of Michael Stifel.

3. The *Sphere* and ecclesiastical calendrical reckoning in very brief fashion.
     John of Holywood with my commentaries.

4. Books 5 and 6 of Euclid.
     From my editions.

5. The use of the geometer's square and the astronomer's quadrant.
     My presentation, or that of Oronce Finé, Jemme Reinerszoon, and so on.

6. Books 11 and 12 of Euclid together with the tenth proposition of book 13 with its comment, and also the conversion of the ninth proposition of the same book. For all these things are needed for understanding the science of curves.
     From my edition.

7. Treatise on curves as earlier.
     Mine.

8. The *Spherical Elements* of Theodosius.

9. A brief treatment of spherical triangles together with the first fourteen propositions of Apollonius on conical elements.

---

28 Hero of Alexandria (*c*.10–*c*.70), mathematician and engineer. Pappus of Alexandria (*c*.290–*c*.350), author of a compendium of mathematics called *Synagôgê* [Collection], and of a hexagon theorem.

29 Serenus of Antinouplis (*c*.300–*c*.360) was a Greek mathematician.

10. The structure and use of the astrolabe, leaving aside the last part on measurements, since these have been provided in the use of the geometer's square.
    My treatment.

11. A demonstrative description of sundials.
    My treatment.

12. Geography.
    My treatment, or Jemme Reinerszoon's *On the Separate Parts of the World*.

13. Rules for measuring shapes in two and three dimensions. Along with my treatise on isoperimetric figures and *Divisions of Surfaces* from Federico Commandino.
    Mine, or that of Oronce Finé.

14. Perspective, together with Oronce Finé's *Burning Glass*.
    Mine or the common one.

15. The more important astronomical phenomena and problems concerning the *primum mobile*, along with reckoning of the twilight hours.
    Mine.

16. Treatment of the movements of the planets and the eighth sphere, along with the use of Alfonso's *Tables*, and so forth. But, before these tables, the algorithm of astronomical fractions.
    Mine, or the *Epitome* of Johann Müller von Königsberg on Ptolemy's *Almagest*.

17. The measurement of the circle, from Archimedes, along with the discovery of a mean proportional to two lines [Euclid, *Elements*, book 6, proposition 13], and the doubling of the cube, and also the closest squaring of the circle.
    From my editions.

18. The *Speculative Arithmetics* of Giordano and music from Jacques Lefèvre d'Étaples.
    From the edition by Jacques Lefèvre d.Étaples.

19. The *Rule of Algebra*, together with practice of those things needed for it, without the demonstrations that depend on Euclid's tenth book. But what is derived from book 2 can be employed.[30]
    My treatment, or that of Peletier or Johann Seubel.

---

30 The *Rule of Algebra* was an Arabic treatise translated into Italian in the late Middle Ages.

A Third Order of Greatest Brevity and Adapted for a Mathematics Course That Ought to Be Finished in Two Years

First Year

1. First four books of Euclid.

   These two can be read from the beginning of studies up to the end of January.

2. Practical arithmetic as above.

3. The *Sphere* and ecclesiastical calendrical reckoning, very concisely.

   These can be finished off by Easter.

4. Books 5 and 6 of Euclid.

5. The use of the geometer's square and the astronomer's quadrant.

   These two will be treated up to Pentecost.

6. Perspective.

7. A brief treatment of sundials without demonstrations.

   These two will be read up until the end of the year.

Second Year

8. Books 11 and 12 of Euclid together with the tenth proposition of the thirteenth book and its comment; also the conversion of the ninth proposition of the same book.

   These will be completed from the reopening of studies up to Christmas.

9. The treatise on curves, along with their use regarding different phenomena and problems relating to the *primum mobile*, without the demonstrations. There can be some demonstrations from the sixth book of Euclid by straight lines, as on determining the length of daylight and the hour from the height of the sun and the reverse, and so forth.

10. Geography.

    These two will be taught up to Lent.

11. The structure of the astrolabe and its use, leaving aside the last part, as above. Still, the first five propositions of Apollonius on conic elements ought to come first.

12. Speculations on the planets, using some demonstrations, along with the use of the Alfonsine tables, very concisely.

    These two can be expeditiously presented up to the feast of St. John the Baptist [June 24].

13. The measurement of the circle from Archimedes and its squaring in near-
    est approximation, along with the discovery of the mean proportional to
    two lines from Eratosthenes, Diocles, and Nicomedes; and the doubling of
    the cube.[31]

14. The *Rule of Algebra*, along with exercise in those things that are required
    for it, applying only those demonstrations that depend on the second book
    of Euclid.

15. Rules for measuring shapes, as earlier.
    These three will be finished by the end of the year.
    Still, the students should be encouraged to read on their own, after
    books 11 and 12 of Euclid, the *Spherical Elements* of Theodosius and some-
    thing from the speculative arithmetic.

I approve the second scheme more than this one if it were possible to finish in two years. But it would be possible if the students are capable and eager
to learn.

Nevertheless, the first scheme is the most fully finished of all.

II

A Method by Which Mathematical Disciplines Could Be Promoted in the Schools of the Society

First, you will have to select a teacher of uncommon learning and authority. If
either quality is missing, the students, as experience teaches, do not seem capable
of being attracted to the mathematical disciplines. For a teacher to have greater
authority with the students, and for the mathematical disciplines to be more highly
valued, and for the students to realize their usefulness and necessity, the teacher will
have to be invited to the more important acts, at which doctors are appointed and
public disputations are held; and there, if it is suitable, he should also occasionally
propose arguments and assist those who are engaged in the discussion. This way,
it will easily happen that, seeing that the professor of mathematics is in attendance
with the rest of the faculty at such acts and that he sometimes even engages in the
disputation, the students will be persuaded that philosophy and the mathematical
sciences are linked, as they truly are; especially since up to now students seem generally to have scorned these sciences solely on the basis of the idea that they are not
valued, and indeed, consider them useless since the one who teaches them is never
called to the public acts with the rest of the faculty.

Also it seems necessary that the instructor should have a certain inclination
and attraction to teaching these sciences, and he should not be distracted by

31 Eratosthenes of Cyrene (*c.*276–*c.*195/94 BCE), Diocles (*c.*240–*c.*180 BCE), and Nicomedes
(*c.*280–*c.*210 BCE) were Greek mathematicians.

many other occupations; otherwise he will hardly be able to help the students. But so that the Society always has suitable professors for these sciences, twelve suitable people would have to be chosen to take on this service and they would be instructed in a private academy in different mathematical matters. Otherwise it does not seem possible that these studies should long remain in the Society, to say nothing of being developed, or that these sciences would be a great enhancement for the Society, being very frequently brought up in conversation in talks and meetings of princes when those individuals realize that our members are not ignorant of mathematics. This is why it happens that our men necessarily fall silent in such meetings, not without considerable embarrassment and dishonor. Those to whom this has happened have often related it. I leave out the fact that natural philosophy without the mathematical disciplines is truncated and incomplete, as I will illustrate shortly.

This is what should be said about the teacher of the mathematical disciplines. Now let me add a few things about the students.

So in the second place, it is necessary that the students realize that these sciences are useful and necessary for correctly understanding the rest of philosophy, and at the same time they greatly enhance all other arts in anyone's attainment of a perfectly finished education. And indeed, so great is the mutual affinity of these sciences and natural philosophy that unless they aid one another, they can in no way maintain their own stature. For this to happen, it will first be necessary that students of natural science study mathematics at the same time. This has always been the practice in Jesuit schools up to now. If mathematical sciences were studied at another time, the students of philosophy would think, and not without reason, that they were in no way necessary for natural science, to the point that very few would want to understand them. Since the experts agree that natural science cannot be rightly perceived without mathematics, especially the parts that bear on the number and motion of celestial orbs; the great number of intelligences; the effects of stars that depend on various conjunctions, oppositions, and the distances left among them; the infinite division of a continuous quantity; the ebb and flow of sea tides; the winds; the comets; the rainbow; the halo [around the sun and the moon] and other meteorological events; and the relationship of movements, qualities, actions, passions, and reactions, and so forth, about which calculators write many things. I am leaving out innumerable examples in Aristotle, Plato, and their renowned interpreters, examples that can in no way be understood without an intermediate understanding of the mathematical sciences. Indeed, on account of their ignorance, some professors of philosophy have very often committed many errors, and very bad ones at that; and what is worse, they have even committed them to writing. It would not be difficult to expose some of these.

By the same token, instructors of philosophy ought to be proficient in the mathematical disciplines, at least to an intermediate degree, so that they do not founder on similar reefs to the great loss and dishonor of the reputation that the Society has in letters.

I am not mentioning how the teachers will through this means win great authority with their students, when they understand how to treat according to their merits the passages of Aristotle and other philosophers that bear on the mathematical disciplines. From this, the students will arrive at a deeper understanding of the necessity of these sciences. It will be a considerable contribution to this end if the instructors of philosophy stay away from those debates that are not very helpful for understanding natural phenomena and that very much detract from the authority of the mathematical disciplines in the students' eyes, for example, that the mathematical sciences are not sciences, that they do not have demonstrations, that they are distractions from metaphysics, and so forth. For experience teaches that this is a stumbling block for the students, one that is entirely unprofitable, especially because the instructors can hardly teach them without ridiculing these sciences (as has been gathered more than once from the reports of others).

It would also help for teachers to encourage their students in private conversations to learn these sciences very well by stressing their usefulness and not to take the contrary position and lead them away from studying them, as many have in earlier years. This way they will remove all the disagreement that others think exists among our members when such teaching is given in our classes.

Furthermore, the scholastics will get the greatest encouragement to pursue these studies if every month all the philosophers convene in some particular place and one of the students presents a brief recommendation of the mathematical disciplines; then, with one student or another he should explain a problem in geometry or astronomy which is both interesting to the audience and useful in human affairs; very many such problems can be found; or he should explain some mathematical passage from Aristotle or Plato (and passages of this kind are not scarce in their works); or he should even introduce new demonstrations of certain propositions of Euclid that he has thought out on his own. Praise can be given there to those who have solved in a better way a problem that has been proposed or who have committed fewer errors, which not infrequently arise in the discovery of new demonstrations. In this way, they will start to have a burning desire for these studies when they see that this glory is set before them; and at the same time they would realize the excellence of these same studies and make greater progress in them through this exercise.

One morning or afternoon class period a month could be devoted to this exercise, and this would not inconvenience the philosophy instructors, since it would come up only seven or eight times at most in a year; or the morning time of one vacation day or certainly in that hour when they typically have math class.

Finally, around the end of the philosophy course of studies, those who want to graduate with a master's or doctorate would have to be examined in math in the manner of certain other academic pursuits. At their exam, the mathematics professor should be present along with the rest of the professors of philosophy.

III

Structural Arrangements for Mathematics

Last year action was taken to promote in our Society the mathematical studies that had already almost fallen into neglect: those who were going to be teaching this science were exempted from teaching grammar with the idea that they would study it more fully at home for the first year after completing the course in philosophy; then they would teach it publicly for one or two years.[32] This certainly promised to be a convenient arrangement. It has partially gotten underway, and it is going to be most useful not only for fostering that discipline but also for enhancing and extending the others. And finally this has been demonstrated and everyone will confess that.

There seems to be one difficulty with this arrangement: usually all the brightest and those who ought to be selected for such a ministry for the greater service of Our Lord and the greater good of the Society finish philosophy when they are still very young and in most cases when they go on, they are hardly twenty-four years old at the most; and not even to them does it seem helpful that they should spend that year teaching, since that ministry demands a period of an hour or two and the rest is at their own judgment, as they judge best; nor does this work for the school's advantage, since it is downgraded and devalued when the teachers are almost boys; nor does it favor the esteem of the Society to employ such individuals constantly to teach the more serious disciplines.

For this reason, it would perhaps help those who are selected for these ministries, after finishing the philosophical course of studies, to take classes at home for an entire year in those things they are then going to be teaching, as has earlier been decided; then they should study theology and next teach mathematics for the period originally planned for teaching. For, beyond the fact that men already of mature age and priests and theologians rather honor the chair than devalue it, they can also be more safely trusted to themselves in how they spend their free time. There would also be some uncommon advantages:

First: They would be able to attend the monthly and the private philosophical disputations, and by replying, they would both be helped and become more interested themselves and they would also help others. And if they study mathematics before they are theologians, while mere philosophers, even if superlatively gifted, it cannot happen that they would find it hard to contribute anything

---

32 "At home" means within the ambit of residential life, as opposed to the "public" setting of school classrooms and halls.

worthy of the disputation or that perhaps it would be a burden to the teachers of philosophy to deal with their challenges and arguments.

Second: Because they have already studied theology, they would employ the time left over from the effort of teaching much more usefully in reviewing philosophy and understanding the text of Aristotle than if they had devoted themselves previously even most diligently to that study. For their very age brings an increase in judgment, and the study of theology sharpens and spurs intellectual ability in a marvelous way. But it seems more in conformity with the Society for the glory of Our Lord that, as much as possible, our scholastics should progress in their studies especially at this stage of formation.

Third: They will also sometimes be able to preside over the reviews of philosophy at home and to lighten the load of the teachers who are now weighed down in other respects with a heavier burden than before, so that this will be a great assistance to them.

Fourth: This is a much better arrangement for learning mathematics well. Since they have already taken classes on the first six books, they will be able to go from the start of book 7 to book 12 inclusive; then they can add the *Spherical Elements* of Theodosius and something from the *Conics* of Apollonius.[33] This could be done handily enough in one year if they take two classes a day (which is something that should be happening). Then in the four-year period given to theology, just as the future grammar teachers do academic work at home when there is free time after the noon meal, they should also spend an hour after the noon meal (until their teaching is finished) studying the theories of planetary movements, the art of sundials, the astrolabe, something from Archimedes and some algebra, with the material being divided up evenly; and in this way they should be better prepared when they take up teaching. This would be an enhancement and a help for the rest of their studies.

But it would be important to make a special selection of those who, all other things being equal, are superior to all the others in intellectual ability, diligence, and a liking for these sciences and the way they are taught, not those who surpass others in grace; and a judgment on this should be seriously sought from those who manage them in this kind of study. Sometimes it happens that some who are either not thus inclined or not naturally equipped for that study do well enough in their other studies but are unsuitable for mathematics.

There seems to be a difficulty for this scheme in that, since we are in need of mathematics teachers, whose training is the object of all these efforts, we do not seem to have a supply of people to teach in the meantime, while the future math teachers are finishing their own studies. But not even this is an obstacle. This

---

33 The "first six books" refer to Euclid's *Elementorum libri XV*.

year, the theologians finish their studies; among them are those who have never taught and who would gladly study mathematics so that others who are able to fill the position in the meantime may teach. And to avoid having one uselessly wasting time while the other one teaches, they can review their own studies in the meantime, according to the order of studies and our *Constitutions*.

IV

Father Christopher Clavius's reflection on the manner and method by which the Society for the greater honor of God and progress of souls may be able to enlarge what people think of it and shatter in a very quick and easy way all esteem for the heretics in their educational work by which they are making great advances.

1. The great esteem that the Society of Jesus enjoys in foreign and distant regions has arisen almost entirely from its education. Any belief in someone's special moral uprightness goes generally unnoticed unless it is witnessed by those who are very near, and it is considered something held in common with other religious. But the distinction of a finer learning when the other religious orders are considered uneducated is granted the Society in the highest degree by a consensus prevailing even among its enemies. By this one thing alone it has acquired so much authority among many people living in the remotest locations that either it has kept in the Catholic faith those who are doubtful or it has called back those who have drifted into heresy, using argument alone to persuade them, because they are of the opinion that ignorance of the truth could not exist among so many men who are so learned and who hold such a strong consensus in the assertions that they are making.

2. Therefore, the Society needs to protect and amplify by all means the perception and opinion of learning that some are trying to diminish with the thought that it is characteristic of the Society to have a good number of individuals with a decent education but no one preeminent in that respect. Beyond philosophy and Scholastic theology, which the heretics scorn, calling the first a hodge-podge of opinions and the second the sophistry of Scotus and Thomas, they vigorously contend that the Society is inferior to them in what they call the more refined arts and in the knowledge of different languages; and they justify their claim by adducing from their number Tremellius in Hebrew, Wolf in Greek, Sturm in oratory, and Melanchthon in every kind of history, a superlatively well-versed individual. In their judgment, the Society has no one that it can set against these as equals.[34]

---

34 Immanuel Tremellius (Italian, *c*.1510–80), author of *Grammatica Chaldaea et Syra* [Chaldean and Syriac Grammar] (Geneva: Henri II Estienne, 1569) a convert from Judaism to Catholicism and, ultimately, to Calvinism; Hieronymus Wolf (German, 1516–80); Johannes

3. And actually, though the heretics make their boasts emptily and perhaps falsely, we must nevertheless honestly confess, because it is true, that when we leave the fields of philosophy and Scholastic theology, in which the Society has highly trained men—and these sciences are no doubt the most important and highest ranking ones although many today do not give them their just due— yet in the rest, such as mathematics and oratory and also philological expertise in Greek and Hebrew (used in almost every show put on for the public these days), although the Society does not yield to any heretics, it still has to yield to many Catholics among whom we usually find in each of these areas individuals more eminent than those found in the Society.

4. The reason for this is obvious. In the secular sphere, particular individuals often expend their efforts on particular subjects, so inevitably they are going to end up as highly learned scholars in their specialties. But in the Society everyone follows the same academic plan and course. After a slender but adequate survey of humane letters, they give three years to philosophy, four to Scholastic theology with the kind of steady application that does not make it possible or permissible for them to turn their eyes to anything else in that course. But after these years are completed, everyone is sent immediately to an assignment where they are so pressed by constant business that there is not the leisure to get into the other sciences later, except quite superficially. That is why, although many and practically all of the men of the Society attain an average understanding of many subjects, very few reach an advanced familiarity with even a single one. I always make an exception of theology. Furthermore, I make an exception of some individuals who have done outstanding work in certain subjects before joining the Society.

5. So then there is no one who fails to see how important it is to every intention of the Society to have some truly preeminent scholars in these lesser studies that people are now making so much of, scholars who may in surpassing the rest spread the reputation of the Society widely, win over the hearts of the noble youth, check the boasting of the heretics in these arts, and raise up the offspring of the Society itself to every excellence in these matters. This can be perceived most clearly of all from the fact that a single person occasionally wins on the basis of such achievement honor for the entire nation, such as (to leave aside the ancients) Manuzio was in our time: by the elegance of his Latin, he stirred up such a high regard for himself among foreign nations that I know many were ready to come from the furthest regions to Rome to hear him if he was going to speak.[35] In the Society, Perpinyá started to become

---

Sturm (1507–89), famous founder and educator of the Strasbourg Gymnasium; Philipp Melanchthon (Schwarzerdt, 1497–1560).

35 Aldo Manuzio (1547–97), son of the famous humanist printer and publisher of the same name (who lived 1449–1515), was a prodigy in Latin. He ran the Vatican press under Clement VIII (r.1592–1605).

this kind of figure, raising very high expectations in the world with very few compositions.[36] I think his fame spread more broadly than any other Jesuit's even while many members of the Society were considered more learned than he was. But nature has arranged things, I think, so that an eminence in any area, even the smallest, attracts everyone's attention to itself. This is the source of that veneration of the ancient kings for outstanding painters and sculptors. This is the reason why in our times many Catholics have delivered their own children to the heretics to be instructed and corrupted, thinking of their reputation for more excellent education. The Scottish chiefs have sent their own boy-king to the poet Buchanan, the French noblemen their sons to Pierre de la Ramée, and the Germans today to Wolf, a wicked heretic but most expert in Greek letters.[37] Indeed, if the pagan Demosthenes and the ungodly Aeschines were lecturing at Rome now, who would not join in the throng from all parts of Christendom to hear such excellent orators, even though they disagree with us in religion and morality?

6. Since therefore it is now clear that eminence in any matter gets the greatest notice from humanity since it reaches the ears of the remotest people and captures everyone's attention, let us see what the easiest way to that eminence might be, and why it is so hedged in by such difficulties that very few attain it over the centuries. Different reasons arise in different ways for this situation. Some, since they are following their own lights, that is, since they are free and under no one's command, and since their mind enjoys a variety of content, cannot bear the study of a single subject but they turn to everything that strikes their senses until they finally feel the weight of Seneca's maxim: "One who is everywhere is nowhere."[38] Others, since they are pursuing their advantage and their profit, do not press on with those studies to which they are especially suited but rather those that they trust will be of greatest use to them. Many also lack either the intellectual talent or health or leisure or money. Finally, there are those who have every other support, but who are not able to get suitable teachers through whom they may aspire to such an eminence of this kind. It is only the Society that is able to achieve this eminence very quickly and very easily. It has the diverse and very fine intellectual talents of young people, it has the free time, it has the teachers and the authority to compel its members to that kind of study for which they are most apt. This means it is able to have with no trouble, at no extraordinary expense, in the shortest time, in all these subjects that I have mentioned (certainly eloquence, mathematics, Greek and Hebrew) very famous and preeminent men who, spreading out through different

---

36 Pedro Juan Perpinyá (1530–66), represented in Chapters 19 and 24 of this Reader.
37 George Buchanan (Scottish, 1506–82). Pierre de la Ramée (French, 1515–72).
38 Lucius Annaeus Seneca (the younger, 4 BCE–65 CE), *Epistulae morales* [Moral epistles], 1.2.

nations and kingdoms like gleaming gems, are going to be a great honor to the Society and an overwhelming terror to all enemies, and an unbelievable inspiration to the younger generation, which will flock to us from every part of the world. This could be one way of doing this.

7. In four large colleges, such as Rome, Milan, Coimbra, and Paris, four academies can be established: one for [Latin] eloquence, a second for Greek, a third for Hebrew, and a fourth for mathematics. For each of these, there could be chosen ten young men from different provinces, according to each one's inclination, and they could be placed under a particular suitable teacher who privately trains them for four straight years more or less, after the philosophy course is over and apart from all other studies; in the space of this time, if they have the talent, if they have the inclination to those studies, if they have already grasped the basics (and I would only want such to be selected for these academies), and finally if they are well trained by an expert instructor in reading, writing, and speaking (for which enterprise they all ought to live together), I do not see why they should not turn out completely fluent in Hebrew, for example, or in any other language that is typically learned thoroughly in less time than four years. It would enhance the Society to no end to have ten men divided up among ten provinces, who understood, wrote, and spoke Hebrew so accurately that no Jew or other Christian would be judged their equal. Likewise, it could have ten Hellenists, ten mathematicians, and ten Latin orators who would be so distinguished that even by the judgment of our enemies they would stand out above the rest of the entire Christian community. And not to have such men by chance and only in some generations, as Pagnino appeared in the Dominican community, Teseo Ambrogio among the canons regular, different individuals in different religious orders, and many in different times in the Society; but this way offspring are steadily being produced so that they never disappear.[39]

8. Bearing very much on this endeavor is maintaining a perpetual and careful system of replacement, so that if anyone is removed by a special mission or by death, another person fills his place without delay. Next it is of the utmost importance that no one is pulled out of the course of studies for any business that threatens to interrupt it (and this is a very frequent occurrence in the Society), unless the full finish that we are looking for has already been achieved. Finally, if anyone is found unsuited for such excellence on account of either health or weakness of intellect or a change of heart, it is important that he be reassigned immediately because we are not content with what is average in this area.

---

39 Santes Pagnino (Italian, 1470–1541), Dominican philologist and biblical scholar. Ambrogio Teseo (Italian, 1469–1540), expert linguist and a canon at the Lateran basilica in Rome.

9. But these four academies, since as a whole they require only forty individ-
    uals, could not be hard to support or a burden for the Society that has so
    many members; especially since those individuals would not be useless or
    unprepared for other services of the Society. They might still be able to
    acquire as much Scholastic theology as is adequate, even though they do
    this more quickly than the rest. And they could do this either after the four
    years that have been allotted for these studies, which we at times see others
    expend on teaching humane letters; or they will be able to section off within
    the academies themselves particular hours for this purpose in the last two
    years. But they will become much better prepared for sermons from these
    studies, since each in the language he is studying, reading many authors,
    will accumulate copious material that he may then be able to use for many
    other purposes. The one who reads all the rabbinical authors in Hebrew
    and who reads the fathers, poets, and histories in Greek and Latin, if he has
    gotten a bit of an understanding of theology, cannot fail to have material
    for elegantly explaining or discoursing on any subject. Some preachers who
    know only Scholastic theology, lacking a variety of material, speak from the
    pulpit with slender results. They are compelled to discuss the dry subtleties
    of the schools or only to seize upon the particles and terms, or to serve up
    commonplace or popular ideas, to the great boredom of both themselves
    and their audiences.

To attain greater breadth and depth of knowledge, therefore, it seems most
expedient that the instructor of these young men in the academies not detain
them in an ongoing series of classes; but rather, after an adequate introduction,
especially in the languages, he should allow them to pursue different digressions into various authors, relying on their own abilities. But he, like a steers-
man, should lend assistance, directing the journey if they veer off-course in
any way, and taking care that they do not get entangled in irrelevant studies
but that instead they are carried to the port of destination with full power
and with all sails to the winds. And this way, doubtless within a very few years,
they would each become very learned men in their own profession; and by
their help and the tremendous esteem that they will have throughout the entire
world, the name of the Society would be marvelously amplified and the audac-
ity of the heretics seriously weakened; its education would grow and develop
more fully. And what matters to me even more, because it will be of greater
interest to Christendom, is that every merit of excellent education, snatched
from miscreants and gathered into the embrace of the Society, as it were, would
attract to it the entire younger generation, would strip the heretics of their
accustomed plunder, and would gain a limitless throng of souls for Christ the
Lord and Teacher of everyone. Let it be done.

CHAPTER 27

Teaching Hebrew (1593)

Michael Leder

The trial Ratio studiorum *of 1591 recommended that the teaching of Hebrew be entrusted to the professor of scripture and that the language be required of all students in the second year of theology. The professor had to be acquainted with Chaldaic and Syriac languages and know Greek well enough to read the Septuagint without any difficulty. Despite these directives, Jesuit teachers of Hebrew had trouble getting their subject appreciated by colleagues and students. In 1593, with the subject still faltering, Michael Leder, a professor of Hebrew at the college of Ingolstadt, saw the urgent need for Catholic apologists to match the linguistic abilities of Protestant scholars. Some of the latter were routinely demonstrating the philological weaknesses in Catholic readings of scripture. Leder therefore wrote this document to describe and remedy the main difficulties encountered in the acquisition of Hebrew. His focus was the lack of reliable textbooks and materials, but the topic also involved him in pedagogical issues. His criticism of the grammar of Robert Bellarmine (1542–1621), widely used up to then despite its typographical errors, well illustrates how exacting Jesuits could be about didactic issues.*

Michael Leder (born c.1562, Sankt Pölten, Austria—entered the Society c.1582, Ingolstadt?—died December 6, 1641, Munich, Bavaria, Germany). Leder completed the entire course of studies and attained the title of master of philosophy. At the college in Ingolstadt, he taught grammar for two years before being appointed to the chair of Hebrew, which he held for thirteen years. He was a renowned preacher and confessor.

Source: *Monumenta paedagogica*, nova editio, 7:105–8 (original: Latin)

Ingolstadt, July 3, 1593

Suggested Changes and Additions to the Grammar
Observations on Compiling a Hebrew Lexicon

From the certainly brief but very careful prescriptions for Hebrew in the new plan of studies, it is easy to see what great care not for just Latin and Greek but for that language as well the Roman fathers have undertaken in the name of our entire Society. After such an important judgment and witness of the whole Society, it would no longer be right for any of our members to have any more doubt about the usefulness or necessity of knowing this holy language; rather, everyone should make an effort in proportion to his ability so that day by day the study of Hebrew might flourish more and more for the greater glory of God and for assistance to sacred theology along with the other kinds of sciences and languages. Indeed, I would also suggest that not the last reason for learning Hebrew is to keep the heretics from any longer arrogating in their insufferable boasting such knowledge as their own special possession and insolently throwing in our faces, in their writings and in their direct talks, our ignorance of the same.

But since there are in Hebrew, just as there have been up to now in Greek, many difficulties or bumps that slow down the entire course of learning, I will survey (since our reverend father rector has ordered this of me) only four impediments and append to each a manner and plan by which I think they can be entirely eliminated. There will be another occasion to speak about all the inconveniences concerning the time or the teaching schedule. And clearly the first two impediments are of the sort that if they are not removed all the work of learning and teaching would have to look quite useless. Proving this requires very little argument, since the very matter and the experience of so many years past make it quite plain that many people, even though they may be endowed with great intellectual talent, stand thoroughly shaken, to put it mildly, before this one language, seeing how it is entangled in the greatest difficulties.

1. The first and foremost impediment, then, to learning this holy language is the lack of a suitable grammar. Yes, Father Bellarmine's *Institutiones linguae hebraicae* [Instructions in the Hebrew language] is expounded in schools, but this work is marred by so many and such awful typographical errors that I would not think that the author himself would recognize it, and it is quite a shame that so faulty a book is marked with the name of such a man.[1] And I think this especially applies to the Cologne edition; for the third Roman edition is a little freer of errors, although the printer also often made many bad mistakes. What will the attitude of beginners be, tell me, when they realize that they are going to have to use such error-filled books extensively to learn a language that is otherwise intrinsically difficult from the start, one having no relationship either with Greek or Latin? Will they not all abandon their intention to learn it, no matter how great their previous inclination? Will they not despair of getting anything at all from their labor? In addition, in Father Bellarmine's book not a few things have been omitted perhaps for the sake of brevity, items that not just the students but the instructors themselves rightly called for, if in fact they want to teach others. For you will have

---

1   The *Institutiones linguae Hebraicae* was first published in 1578 by the Roman publisher Zanetti (who also produced other editions). The original full title of this work was *Institutiones linguae Hebraicae ex optimo quoque auctore collectae; et ad quantam maximam fieri potuit brevitatem, perspicuitatem, atque ordinem revocatae, a Roberto Bellarmino Societatis Iesu* [Instructions in the Hebrew language, gathered from all the best authors and reproduced with the greatest possible conciseness, clarity, and order]. Leder is probably referring to Birckmann's edition (Cologne, 1580).

explained hardly one part of some biblical chapter before you have to send the students to other grammars because of defective or quiescent verbs or some other reason, with great bother (especially for those who do not have the other books) and a grievous waste of time. This is what motivated me to jot down certain points in this paper.

This impediment may easily be removed if, keeping the universally renowned name of Father Bellarmine and the essential matter of the instructional content itself, we add from Pagnino, Chevallier, including the little grammar from the King's Bible, and other outstanding authors of the kind of material that the experience and practice of teaching itself tells us is missing.[2] But this business of reprinting the grammar cannot not be put off longer without great damage, since there are no more copies of the editions from Rome or Cologne, and if any do exist, students get very little from them.

2. The second impediment. We have to add to the knowledge of the rules of grammar the presentation of a suitable author. But there is no doubt that also in this matter the students of this language have struggled along with the greatest difficulty. Up to now, we have expounded the Psalms, which for many reasons are nevertheless considered not very suitable for this instruction. Even the Roman fathers no doubt noticed this, since in the third rule for the Hebrew teacher they expressly mandated that some lucid historical author should be presented; and certainly no one would put the Psalms into this category. I think that the reason that the Psalms have been expounded up to now almost everywhere among Catholics is that no other book of the Hebrew Bible was considered so easy to manage as an individual publication. No other parts are easily sold by booksellers without other contents, and if they include anything besides the Psalms, they usually attach a heretical person's translation.

But also to say something about removing this second impediment: for these purposes, I consider nothing better than the book of Genesis, excellent both in style and in its pleasing variety of content. But it will have to be printed in such a way that on one page there is the clean Hebrew text with the more difficult roots added in the margins, and on the other Pagnino's version (which has been inserted in the King's Bible and approved by the universities of Paris and Leuven), in a word-for-word translation should be put directly opposite. And also, if the superiors think well of the idea, the Vulgate edition should be put above or below. In this way, the students will not always be hanging on the instructor's oral Latin exposition of the Hebrew text, but they themselves, when supplied with an average knowledge

---

2 Santes Pagnino (1470–1541), a famous Dominican scripture scholar and Bible translator. Antoine Rodolphe Chevallier (1523–72), a Protestant and also a scripture scholar and an author of a Hebrew grammar. The King's Bible (*Biblia regia*) was a polyglot Bible in Hebrew, Greek, and Latin, printed between 1568 and 1573 in Antwerp.

of the grammar, will successfully and comfortably make greater progress on their own than they had expected. Over the course of time, the same can be provided for the other historical books of the Hebrew Bible, such as Joshua, Judges, and Kings.

Now there follow two points, which also (even though they might seem to certain people less important than the previous ones) still seriously dampen the enthusiasm and slow down the progress of learners. But if they are removed at the direction of superiors (as I quite expect they will be), no doubt the holy language will consequently be honored in our Society in coming days no less than Greek is.

3. The third impediment. A Hebrew–Latin lexicon is needed; a person interested in the holy language cannot be without it. Pagnino's volume printed at Lyons in folio is too expensive, and it is not really suitable for beginners. But his epitome printed by Plantin is not at all adequate on account of its excessive brevity.[3] Therefore the task should be given to one from the Society to at long last put together such a lexicon (which father general is also said to have wanted for a long time), one that is as suitable as possible for the uses of Jesuits and non-Jesuits alike.[4] For the rest, the points that have occurred to me about its design and entire structure, as it were, I have added at the end of this paper, and to these, others more experienced in this language can attach additional comments or better ones.

4. The fourth impediment. Finally, as Latin and Greek are not limited to the knowledge of the rules and the explication of an author but they necessarily demand exercise in composition as well, so Hebrew will never be able to be learned well and appropriately for the Society's purpose without some practice of composition. For a single composition sets firmer roots in the mind than three readings would have.

But the students completely lack the help of books that are necessary or useful for this purpose, and this has come about certainly through no fault at all of the holy language. For although it does not supply "building blocks" as abundantly as Greek does, it still provides what is necessary for almost all words and phrases, provided that someone has undertaken the work of gathering them. And so we have to write out the listing of words and phrases with indexes, following John Posselius's Greek *Calligraphia*, in my judgment the best of all models to imitate most closely.[5] But to increase the learners' interest and to extend a little more broadly their use of the holy language itself (for it is not

---

3 Christophe Plantin (Christoffel Plantijn, 1520–89) was a Dutch printer and publisher whose most significant achievement was the printing of the King's Bible (*Biblia regia*), also called "the Plantin Polyglot."

4 The superior general was Claudio Acquaviva.

5 *Calligraphia oratoria linguae Graecae* (Frankfurt: Andreas Wechel, 1585) was written by the Greek teacher Johann Possel (Johannes Posselius the Elder, 1528–91).

as narrow as many have become convinced), a really workable plan ought to be undertaken or rather fully carried out concerning the translation into Hebrew of the Gospels and the Epistles that are typically read in church on Sundays and the feast days of the saints, preserving exactly the truth of the Vulgate edition, from which Münster deviated in his Matthew, as the others similarly did in their own Gospels, tainted by heresy or certainly serious errors.[6] This is indeed going to be a new kind of labor, but not so difficult, especially if the writer knows how to use the Syriac edition of the New Testament. We can go on from there to the remaining books, and to other books of this type, which, when placed in the hands of the students, will bring forth good results and a fuller knowledge of the holy language. That is enough on this topic.

On printing: It remains for me to say a few things about choosing a suitable printer. David Sartorius of Ingolstadt has affirmed to me that he is not inexperienced in such work.[7] But he has neither the right kind of Hebrew type nor will he acquire it before he sees a definite and almost certain hope of selling copies; how great a hope there can possibly be in Germany is certainly not clear. For at this time the holy language is taught in few Catholic schools; and the heretics themselves are not at all about to buy such a grammar since they already have their own authors of this kind and they are not bad at all. So we have to look for help in Rome: where an appealing type can more easily be found and where there will be less difficulty in retailing the copies since books of every kind are typically marketed there for different Catholic regions. But since Hebrew books, on account of the great number and variety of pointings and diacritical marks, demand much more care both by printers and copy editors than any Greek books do, we really have to be as diligent as we can be to ensure that everything is published in as corrected a form as possible, otherwise the error-filled copies will increase the difficulty of learning, rather than diminish it.

Suggestions for Changes and Additions to Reverend Father Bellarmine's Grammar

I will advise the following generally before I get into the particular parts of the *Instructions* and their chapters: namely we should add to each expression a mark made using this common sign "/" and a gloss of the Hebrew verbs, except for where it would be plainly superfluous. For the former is entirely necessary for the correct pronunciation (and it is quite important to become accustomed to it

---

6   *Tôrat ham-Māšîaḥ: Evangelium secundum Matthaeum in lingua Hebraica, cum versione Latina atq[ue] succinctis annotationibus Sebastiani Munsteri* [Tôrat ham-Māšîaḥ: Gospel according to Matthew in the Hebrew language, with a Latin version and brief annotations by Sebastian Münster] (Basel: Henricus Petrus, 1537). Sebastian Münster (1488–52) was a Hebrew scholar, a cartographer, and a cosmographer.

7   David Sartorius was a printer for the Society's university in Ingolstadt from 1572 to 1596.

from the start), and the latter is just as necessary for the easier understanding of the paradigms and usage. What I am saying about verbs here I would like to say likewise about all the other Hebrew expressions.

First Part

1. Here there can be a bit more compact presentation than certain other authors provide of what bears on the pronunciation of the letters, their name and spacing, and their numerical significance, so that more space will be left for those things that should be added in later chapters.

[…].

6. Since we should avoid letting the proposed lexicon grow into a large volume, we should leave out supplementary examples (as much in nouns as in verbs and expressions) indicating government of cases, tenses, persons, moods, formative letters, and all other things that students will have no difficulty in understanding from the grammar. Otherwise, a judgment has to be made about what deviates from the shared norm.

7. In the same way, what has already been explained in the grammar should in no way be repeated in the lexicon. It will be enough to refer to the passage in the grammar by means of a number.

8. Since all the heretics use every ploy to assail our Vulgate edition of the Bible, if ever the occasion presents itself and the brevity of our scheduled task does not prevent it, we should take care to show the truth of our version and on the other hand, the deceit or ignorance of theirs.

9. At the beginning or end of the book there should be added an index of all the Latin expressions that cover the meaning of the roots. This way, the Hebrew–Latin lexicon will provide the beginners interested in practicing composition with a lexical Latin–Hebrew section, which is likewise something that they need. On an index of heemantic nouns and so forth I say nothing since everyone realizes that it cannot be left out.

These are generally, Reverend Father in Christ, what I have decided to write at the advice and urging of our reverend father rector about removing the main impediments to this holy language, about the revision of Fr. Bellarmine's grammar book, and about making a new lexicon.[8] May God bring it about that the study of that language in our Society is seriously spurred on and developed. In our province, Reverend Father Balthasar Hagel will give better and more learned points; everyone rightly credits him greatly both for his precise understanding of different languages and for his extended teaching experience.[9]

---

8   The rector was Richard Haller (1550–1612).

9   Balthasar Hagel (1551–1616) entered the Society in 1572. He taught philosophy in Ingolstadt and Dillingen, then casuistry in Ingolstadt.

CHAPTER 28

Studying Philosophy (1549)

Diego Laínez

László Lukács, the editor of the Monumenta paedagogica, *ascribes to Diego Laínez the following letter answering the Paduan scholastics' request for advice on studying philosophy. Written in the very earliest days of Jesuit involvement in schooling, this document was not addressed to teachers (as many later documents were) but to scholastics who had to adapt to the pedagogy that they were experiencing at a non-Jesuit institution. Although this document applies to an academic setting outside of the Society's direct control, and although Laínez admits that he had not taught this subject himself, the letter nevertheless exhibits some noteworthy Jesuit pedagogical traits: selectivity in commentaries on Aristotle, attention to academic exercises, and, above all, the cultivation of close relationships between teachers and students to facilitate learning. Laínez wanted the teacher of philosophy to be an educator rather than merely a lecturer dictating texts from the podium. It is interesting that he recommended consulting with the older student, Fulvio Cardulo (1529–91), as someone who might give them great assistance "at home." Using the residence for group academic pursuits suggests how even a purely residential college could incorporate guided learning activities.*

Diego Laínez (born 1512, Almazán, in Soria, Spain—co-founder of the Society in 1540, Rome—died January 19, 1565, Rome). One of the original founders of the Society and its second superior general, Laínez was sent as a theologian at the Council of Trent (1545–63). Though he himself never taught in a Jesuit school, he made a historic contribution to Jesuit education by establishing a period of teaching as a standard part of the formation of all scholastics. In a letter written to Ignatius in 1553, he sketched a plan of studies that helped shape the particulars of the programs and structures of the Society's schools. By 1560, he was presenting the educational ministry as the most important one undertaken by the Society. During his generalate (1558–65), the number of Jesuit schools grew from forty-six to about ninety.

Source: *Monumenta paedagogica*, nova editio, 1:45–50 (original: Italian)

IHS

Concerning the method and plan for studying logic and other liberal arts, I would prefer that someone else with more expertise in such studies help you with them. Yet, since you have requested that I do this, I will say what occurs to me at this moment, and I hope, in short, that with God's help and bidden by holy obedience, I will go further at another time and we will be able to have a more extensive discussion about the whole matter.

There are mainly five things that can help in your studies: first, the lessons that you attend publicly or privately; second, your own day-by-day study in reviewing and reading commentaries and reflecting on them; third, conferring, disputing, and all other scholastic exercises of this nature; fourth, what you write in your notes after doing these three things as the fruit you gather from those efforts; and fifth, reviewing the entire course of logic after you have studied it section by section.

1. Concerning the classes you are attending, I have nothing else to tell you than to pick out what you find more to the purpose, to write in your notes what the teacher will notice, and to get to know the teacher or teachers, so that you might ask them about what you do not understand on your own.

2. Concerning your own study, when you are reviewing alone or with a class-mate, you should note any doubts that arise in order to review and deal with them later; and also because you will understand more when you read the commentaries. On the first reading, such commentaries should not be numerous but they should be the best ones, according to what the teachers will recommend for you; and you should familiarize yourself with one of them, even though you might glance at others if the first one does not satisfy you. Thinking about the whole subject seems to require mastering the contents. Let a good understanding of Aristotle be your main focus at this stage.

3. Concerning conferences at home with Master Fulvio (with whom I am talking when I talk to you about this stage of your studies) or outside with others, I will only say that I consider this exercise of disputing and responding, or rather of participating in formal disputations, a very important thing, and it ought to be done every day;[1] though some will be done more solemnly, as your rules have it, and this will become clearer when you see the college's constitutions.[2]

4. Concerning writing, at the start you can get a notebook for taking down both the solutions that you hear from the teacher and the more noteworthy things you get from books and your meditations, following the order of Aristotle's books and chapters. And so from what you have learned at one time and what you have gathered and absorbed with effort, you will be constructing a written memory to refresh your natural one, even though there will likely be many notes that you will later want to change or shorten, and so forth.

5. Concerning the review of the entire course of logic (by which I mean, after going through all Aristotle's books pertaining to this subject with the same diligence that I touched upon in the four points above), in order to better grasp

1   Fulvio Cardulo, who was studying philosophy in Padua at that time.
2   The reference is to the college constitutions that Juan Alfonso de Polanco (1517–76) was starting to draft.

it and possess it all together—since you have already dealt with each section of the body of logic—it will be very expedient to repeat everything from the beginning, and you will find more light and clarity than before. Then, you will be able to extend your scope by looking at more commentaries and you will be able to make a new and more articulate excerpt, one that is ready to use later. This excerpt will be both more learned and brief, so that after you have moved on to the other sciences and forgotten many such things, you can fall back on it.

What I have said about logic I also mean for the other academic work, but I defer to what experience will show you to be better, or to the advice of those who are more familiar [with the subject].

CHAPTER 29

Teaching Philosophy (1564)

Benet Perera

Benet Perera started teaching philosophy at the Roman College in 1559. The prefect of studies, Diego de Ledesma (1524–75), had differences with him about his teaching methodology, but in 1564 he asked Perera for his suggestions on curricular reform. Fully aware of the divergence of their views, Perera boldly and perhaps provocatively praised Arabic and Greek commentators, citing Averroes and other controversial scholars whom Ledesma disdained. This text suggests Jesuit philosophers' desire for greater interpretive freedom with Aristotle and Aquinas, the authorities prescribed in the Jesuit Constitutions. *Didactically, two points stand out: (1) the need for a careful choice of course content (textbooks and topics), and (2) the stress on exercise over reading. For Perera, learning philosophy should be based more on classroom discussion than on textual analysis.*

Benet Perera (born 1535, Ruzafa, Valencia, Spain—entered the Society in March 1551, Valencia—died March 6, 1610, Rome). An acclaimed philosopher and theologian of the Society of Jesus, Perera spent all his Jesuit life teaching at the Roman College, where he began to give classes of physics in 1559. Despite a difficult controversy with Diego Ledesma and Achille Gagliardi, who accused him of supporting Averroism, he was never removed from his office. In fact, he enjoyed great renown in his theological career and published an outstanding tract on natural philosophy (De communibus omnium rerum naturalium principiis et affectionibus *[On the first principles common to all natural realities and conditions], 1567).*

Source: *Monumenta paedagogica*, nova editio, 2:664–69 (original: Italian)

The Way to Teach the Course in Philosophy
A Short Instruction on the Manner of Teaching the Course

Scheduling

[1] The course ought to last at least three years.[1] In the first year, logic should be completed, omitting many metaphysical questions from the *Categories*, and skimming through *On Interpretation* and the *First Analytics*.[2] Of these, only the first seven chapters need be read, no more. The same can be done with the *Topics*.

---

1 The *Constitutions* prescribe the same scheduling, adding six months in order to let students prepare themselves for their final examinations.

2 Aristotle's *De interpretatione* is also known as the *Peri hermeneias*.

2. If the *Summaries of Logic* are taken up, they should be finished at the lat-est within two months.[3] In the second year, the eight books of the *Physics* should be read, and at least the first two books of *On the Heavens*, and some books of the *Meteorology*; so that for the third year there remain only the books of the *On the Generation of Animals*, *On the Soul*, and the *Metaphysics*. The teacher should provide for a division of the three-year course, or at least for one of the current year, in accordance with the classes he has to give. This will let him see how much he can take up from each book and each work, and it will help ensure that taking up less significant material does not lose the time needed for what is more important. Reading all the books of the *Metaphysics* is distasteful and useless; it would suffice to start with the sev-enth book, touching on the others only in the introductory exposition.[4]

[The Teacher]

[1] The professor who must teach in a renowned university ought to have already taught before, or at least he should be such that through his gifts of mind and good health there is good hope of success, with study and diligence.

[2] In the first course, instead of the Greek commentaries—which are very long and obscure—he can read Themistius and Vicomercati.[5] Reading Averroes is very useful, both because of his doctrine and because of the reputation he has in Italy.[6] And to be able to understand Averroes's doctrine, he will read his followers, such as John of Jandun, Burleigh, Paolo Veneto, Zimara, and Nifo.[7] He should have the catalog of the best commentaries available, on all the areas of philosophy, the way it is done in Rome. And even though the teacher ought to follow the main authors such as, among the Greeks, Alexander, Simplicius, and Themistius; among the Arabs, Averroes; and among the Latins, Thomas Aquinas and Albert;[8] nevertheless, he must not be a disciple, especially of those Latin authors who disagree with the ancients. He must be modest in refuting

---

3   The *Summulae logicales* [Little summaries of logic] of Peter of Spain (*fl.* thirteenth cen-tury), the standard textbook on logic since the thirteenth century.

4   The seventh book is the first that deals with the problem of substance.

5   The commentaries of Themistius (317–88) were reprinted in Venice in 1534. Francesco Vicomercati (1474–1570) was a philosopher from Milan who wrote renowned commen-taries on physics. By Greek commentaries, Perera means mostly those of Alexander of Aph-rodisia (*fl.* 200), John Philoponus (*c.*490–*c.*570), and Simplicius (*c.*490–*c.*560).

6   At the University of Padua, natural philosophers traditionally commented on Averroes and Alexander of Aphrodisias. The Averroistic and Alexandrist scholarship was fueled and renewed by the teaching of Pietro Pomponazzi (1462–1525) at the beginning of the six-teenth century.

7   John of Jandun (*c.*1285–1323), Walter Burleigh (1275–1343), Paolo Veneto (*c.*1372–1429), Marco Antonio Zimara (1460–1532), and Agostino Nifo (*c.*1473–1538/45) were considered supporters of Averroism, though the label of "Averroist" was very common at Perera's time as a synonym of unorthodoxy.

8   Albert the Great (1200–80).

the opinions he criticizes, particularly if they are those of important authors, although he has to take a firm stance in what he teaches, not doubtful nor puzzled; nevertheless, he must not be rash, but thoughtful in his judgments. It is very important to be clear and orderly, as it is important that the students hold him in great esteem and affection for his virtues and doctrine. In treating questions, reciting many opinions, and raising many arguments, examples, and responses, even though this helps bring credit to the professor at the start, it is simply not useful for the students. Nor should he recite a wide range of opinions in his exposition of the text; rather he should be content to mention two or three of the most important ones. He should be careful about what he teaches, so that he does not fall into or get caught in a contradiction, or find himself forced to change his opinion. Yet, if his opinion differs from what others have said, he should not pretend otherwise. He should also write some things regarding each subject, at least to highlight some fine ideas or conclusions, whether they are his or someone else's. Also he should write down some passages and leading references, either from Aristotle or other ancients: these might provide support on another occasion. He should not be so text-bound as to neglect questions or so keen on questions as to depreciate the text; but when he explains an Aristotelian maxim he will take up the questions that arise in connection with it.

[3] He should not be an enthusiast for new ideas that occur to him, but he should stay with the old maxims held in common. He should keep away from sophisms in his doctrine, and follow what is authentic and solid.

[4] An eagerness to criticize Aristotle in matters that do not contradict the faith and are commonly approved by everyone is a sign of superficiality and ignorance.

Students

1. He should not so much desire to have a great number of students as some who are prepared for the course; and so when he sees someone who is not succeeding or who is not going to succeed, he ought to report it to the superior in order to put that student in another position; if that student is an external one, the teacher should politely counsel him and direct him towards something better suited to him.

2. He should take care of everyone to the extent his position requires, and he should have and show all his students a positive disposition, even praying individually for them every day. And yet, with those who have the talent to become great individuals, he is bound by the law of charity to pay particular attention to them and be especially helpful to them.

3. He should take care to have conversations with his students often, knowing their inclinations and the progress they are making. Instructing all of them with charity and patience, he should act so that any of them with questions

or other concerns about their studies can freely talk with him. In the middle
or at the end of the first year, he will be able to separate the students into
three classes: into the first class he will put the best students, into the second
the average ones, and into the third the poorest ones. And as he ought to
have special care for the best ones, so he should also encourage the weaker
ones and show them he is mindful of them and is taking them into account.
He must see to it that the respect that is due to the teacher and the modesty that is observed in the Society's schools are also kept by the external
students. He should show courtesy to them and be approachable in talking
about their concerns, exhorting them and inviting them to engage in the
same exercises that our students do.

4.   Although it is good that the students follow and embrace their teacher's doctrine, he still ought not allow them to hear or speak ill of other teachers'
opinions, mocking or criticizing them without restraint, particularly if they
are teachers of the Society.

5.   He will give his students the commentaries he thinks are most suited to each,
not allowing them to waste their time reading other books; he should show
them the order and method of studying, and he should see to it that they are
doing what he has told them. He should notice who needs to be reined in
and who needs to be spurred on; who is spending too much time on study to
the neglect of devotion or bodily health; or, on the other hand, who is com-
mitting too much time to devotional or other exercises to the impairment of
his academic progress. He will report on all of this to the rector.

6.   To encourage the external students more and draw them into our exercises,
some of our most learned and edifying students ought to be introduced to
them so they can review and discuss together. When it is time for the main
feasts of the year, exhort them to make their confession and participate in
the devotional activities of that feast day.

7.   He should take care not to be caught in either levity or a desire for praise and
glory, since these things greatly diminish the teacher's authority.

On Exercises

[1.] Insofar as exercise helps more than any other thing in philosophy, we ought
to make very diligent use of it. In the after-class reviews, the text should be
briefly repeated along with the questions. The *repetitores* should be divided
into groups of three. Two of them should be about equal, the third weaker.
And each of them should repeat from memory, using his notes as little as
possible, so that they can all help each other.

2.   In the reviews that are made at home, they should review the class material, but they should do this briefly, touching only the main points of the
text or the questions so that there is time for the disputations. In disputing,
the teacher should divide up his students into pairs, so one may set forth a

proposition and the other may respond. They should be about equal to be able to help each other.

3. Hold disputations only on the current lesson, and ensure that the argument is characterized by brevity, clarity, and due modesty, with a distaste for all impertinence, such as mocking and disparagement and the like, which do not impact the argument positively or negatively.

4. The teacher must not allow students to get accustomed to making sophisms. They should rather look to raising questions and giving answers that are substantial and solid. In citing Aristotle or the other authors, the teacher should have them always cite the passage or the text, so they are diligent in anticipating this.

5. Since some are more capable in arguing, others in responding, and others in other things, the teacher should exercise each one mainly according to his talent. In short, he should have his students devote themselves more to consideration of the material and to disputation than to extensive reading or writing. Every week or two, they should defend conclusions in class. And where there are more philosophy teachers, every other month the defenses should be public, the way it is done in Rome and at the end of the whole school year, when only external teachers are supposed to have disputations. At the end of the third year, in the beginning of summer when vacation begins, those approved for the master's degree should start to participate in the acts, insofar as it does not seem suitable to make all of them teachers indiscriminately if there are no particular reasons to do so in the rector's judgment.

6. Those who can hear a lecture without writing anything down will exercise their intellect, judgment, and memory more; but if this is impossible, the teacher should have students write down only enough of the headings to be able to review. And outside of class they should write just the main things that either they have noted or that the teacher has dictated so they have time to read their commentaries and think about their lessons.

In the highly reputed universities of the Society, there should be an additional class beyond the three courses: the *Ethics*, for the students of the third year; the *Meteorology* or the *Little Physical Treatises* [*Parva naturalia*] for those of the fourth. This class ought to be given by an additional teacher of some standing. He can be one who has finished the course the previous year.

CHAPTER 30

Teaching Theology (*c.*1573)

Juan Maldonado

According to the reconstruction of László Lukács, the editor of the Monumenta paedagogica, *in 1573, Everard Mercurian (in office 1573–80) asked Juan Maldonado (1533–83), one of the most famous theologians who helped establish the Society's college in Paris, to draft some guidelines for teaching theology. Two aspects in Maldonado's response are particularly noteworthy: Maldonado's attitude towards the authority of Thomas Aquinas, which differed so radically from the attitude taken by Diego Ledesma ([1519–75] who wrote to Mercurian only few months later on the same issue); and Maldonado's skillful usage of the technical terms that were being employed in debates over probabilism and probabiliorism. Maldonado's preference for professorial freedom differs radically from the disposition of Claudio Acquaviva (in office 1581–1615), who sought greater uniformity and restriction in teaching, but it nevertheless coheres with the open attitudes of both Mercurian and his secretary, Antonio Possevino (1533–1611). In terms of pedagogic method, Maldonado's document helps distinguish different branches of theology, considered "Queen of Sciences" in the university's hierarchy of disciplines up to the sixteenth century.*

Juan Maldonado (born 1533, Casas de Reina, Badajoz, Spain—entered the Society August 10, 1562, Rome—died January 5, 1583, Rome). One of the most renowned theologians of the Society of Jesus, Juan Maldonado entered the Society after having completed the full course of studies in Salamanca. Once in Rome, he started to teach philosophy, but he was soon sent to Paris, where his teaching of theology gained him an outstanding reputation. Despite his standing, in 1574, some of the professors of the Sorbonne accused him of denying the doctrine of the Immaculate Conception. Pope Gregory XIII (r.1572–85) eventually exonerated him from that charge. His mastery of all the branches of theology was enhanced by a knowledge of the ancient languages that informed his own distinctive theological interpretations in the light of his scripture.

Source: *Monumenta paedagogica*, nova editio, 4:186–95 (original: Latin)

[I] The Study of Theology

The *Constitutions* say that a three-fold theology should be taught in the Society: Scholastic, scriptural, and moral, which is called "positive."[1] There is not, however,

---

1 "The scholastics should acquire a good grounding in Latin before they attend lectures on arts: and in the arts, before they pass on to Scholastic theology; and in it before they study

one standard of teaching for all of these, but each one has its own appropriate standard. The different modes of theology demand different instructors, different authors, different lengths of time, different teaching methods, different exercises, and finally different students.

[1] The Instructor of Scholastic Theology
The instructor of Scholastic theology ought to be by nature intellectually talented, keen, clear-sighted, sober in judgment, not at all reckless, but high-minded, stable, understanding, and competent in Latin, Greek, and Hebrew, so he does not speak either poorly or ridiculously or so that his linguistic ignorance does not hamper him too much in his efforts against the heretics, who are usually quite well equipped with those languages. He should be well versed in all divisions of philosophy so that either he has taught philosophy at some time (and this is greatly preferred) or he is certainly able to teach it in a very creditable way. But it is far more necessary that he is well exercised in all parts of theology; first, certainly, in sacred scripture, which is the source of all theology, so that he can refute heretics with scripture; then for the same reason, in the decrees of the councils and the books of the doctors of long ago, in church dogmas, in sacred history, from which arguments must often be sought out; and lastly, he should be so thoroughly familiar with the Scholastic authors that he knows all their opinions or the opinions of very many of them regarding each topic; but he should be so thoroughly acquainted with some one of them, such as Saint Thomas, that he knows him completely.

[2] Authors
It seems best that in our classes we expound on Saint Thomas most of all, because our *Constitutions* prescribe this and because he is the most outstanding of all the Scholastics and because the church approves his doctrine more than that of others.[2] But it does not seem good to follow him in a way that allows for no difference with him in some matters.

[3] Time
The *Constitutions* call for six years as the time period during which theology should be taught; and it seems good that this in no way be abridged but rather extended.[3] Our reverend father general should not allow anyone, Jesuit or not, to become a teacher in a shorter time in our schools, nor any Jesuit to be professed

---

positive theology. Scripture may be studied either concomitantly or later on." Padberg, *Constitutions*, 154.
2   Ibid., 182.
3   "The curriculum in theology will be one of six years. In the first four years all the matter which must be lectured on will be expounded. In the remaining two, in addition to the reviewing, the acts customary for a doctorate will be performed by those who are to receive it." Ibid., 184.

unless he has taken theology diligently and productively for four years, and has already undergone the exercises that are prescribed in the *Constitutions*.

In full colleges, two classes of Scholastic theology a day seem to be necessary:[4] one for an hour in the morning, and the second in the evening for another hour, in addition to an hour apart for review, so that students spend three hours a day in class. But instructors will be able to divide up the material among themselves and trim it down when necessary so that in four years they can finish the entire course of theology, the way the *Constitutions* lay down.

[4] The Way to Teach

The best way to teach seems to be the one that is best adapted to achieve the goal of theology. But the goal of Scholastic theology is to defend religion, refute heresies, form good character, correct bad character, give answers to those who ask about divine and ecclesiastical law, preach, and hear confessions. Therefore the instructor will teach theology best if he has as his first concern those matters that are necessary for the preservation of religion and the refutation of heresies, and if he treats those matters very diligently, learnedly, and thoroughly. His second concern should be that of character; his third should be for his students as preachers and confessors; his fourth should be that he make them fit and wise for giving good advice; the fifth concern should be for those questions which, even though they seem minimally helpful for achieving this goal, still contain some doctrine and usefully exercise one's talent. But he should entirely skip over those questions that are either plainly foreign to theology or that satisfy curiosity more than they supply some advantage. Finally, to each subject the instructor ought to devote as much care, as much interest, as much effort, and as much time as its worth and usefulness demand. Once the content has been chosen, he ought to do all he can not to leave the minds of the students doubtful about the issues considered because the arguments are so numerous or because there is such a confused variety of opinion. In all matters, he should exercise a sure judgment, one that is firm and well considered, and one that the students are able to follow; and indeed he should employ his judgment like a scale giving each thing its own just weight: when the important elements of the arguments are weighed, he should declare his judgment on the judgments—what is the faith, what is opinion, what pertains to faith and what pertains more nearly to opinion, what is a heretical proposition, what smacks of heresy, what rings false, what is reckless, what is dangerous, what is strange, what is likely, what is true. Whoever excels in this sort of judgment is a true teacher. In more difficult matters, he ought to read out the different opinions and their arguments (for one dimension of learning is knowing what each person thought about each subject); then he ought to confirm

---

4   That is, the colleges where the Society offered the entire plan of studies, from grammar to theology.

what he has judged to be the most probable opinion, after refuting all the rest.[5] But he will do this selectively and to an extent sufficient for the proposed goal. He will not dodge difficult subjects; he will rather explain them with even more care, eloquence, and clarity, and with more numerous examples. But the material will be divided in an orderly manner and he will treat it in such a methodical manner that the students get an intelligent grasp of the entire body of theology and its individual members down to the smallest parts. When explaining essential matters, he will employ, as much as he is able, the greatest eloquence, clarity, and keenness; these three things especially tend to catch and hold the students' attention. He should take care not to go on too long, especially in non-essential matters; or be too slow or somber in teaching, so that he does not perhaps put the students off; but he should be lively, cheerful, and vigorous so that he keeps the students' minds attentive and ready.

If he is going to explain Saint Thomas, he will not give any dictation from the texts of Saint Thomas or Cajetan except for whatever seems good to explain with a brief remark.[6] He will dictate briefly the testimonies of sacred scripture and ancient authors, the opinions of other Scholastics, and recent arguments, if there are any beside those that are in Saint Thomas and Cajetan, that serve for proof or refutation. He will notice from the expressions of the students whether those that have some intellectual talent seem to have understood what he is saying; and he should not go on before they have a good grasp of the material. He should move his students well to religious devotion and to those opinions which will be more connected with it; then also to Saint Thomas whom he will be explaining to them. Finally, he will form in the minds of the students that judgment which we have said ought to be in the instructor himself. For this is the greatest result that issues from taking classes: that the student is able to be a teacher. He will accomplish this at the point at which he has a judgment that is well formed and mature; for it is especially this that distinguishes a teacher from students.

[5] Exercises

The more numerous and useful the exercises are the more learned they will make the students. Seven things seem essential: First, that they review the lesson just finished and still fresh, either right at school or elsewhere, up to the point that they understand everything and have committed it to memory. Second, that they review it again at some other hour on the same day and talk about it in the presence of their teacher. Third, that for two hours on Saturday or on feast days they have disputations in class or elsewhere, under the supervision of the instructor. Fourth, that every month they hold disputations with larger audiences for half a day, where not only the students, but the instructors themselves take part in the

---

5   For Acquaviva's prohibition on this issue, see Chapter 22n5.
6   The commentary of Thomas de Vio Cajetan ([1469–1534] also called Cajetanus or Caetanus) on Aquinas's *Summa* was generally the most important reference work at Maldonado's time.

disputations. Fifth, that also every year before the opening of the school year that they keep these disputations going for one or two days with as large an audience as possible. Sixth, that they sometimes privately have lessons at home so that they might be shaped, little by little, into instructors. Seventh, that they treat some question in writing and turn it in to the instructor to be corrected, so that they learn to write when they need to.

[6] The Students
The theology students first ought to have keen intellectual talent and judgment; then they ought to be philosophers; in the third place, they should not be distracted by other concerns; fourth, they should be assiduous and steady as it should be harder to pass the fourth year of theology than the third of philosophy, to the extent that theology is more necessary and covers a wider range than philosophy does. Finally, they ought to attend class diligently and perform those seven kinds of exercises that have been listed above.

[II] Scripture

In the person who teaches sacred literature, there ought to be all those things that we have required in the teacher of Scholastic theology, and in fact, these elements should be fuller, richer, and more excellent. In addition, there should be not just an average knowledge of the three languages, as in that Scholastic theologian, but a complete knowledge of them and a greater luster in presentation and charm in speaking, a knowledge of geography and secular history as well, and also experience in understanding secular authors and in translating. There should be a certain great and natural keenness of intellect for making the most subtle conjectures, on which the understanding of many passages often depends; supreme diligence, and an almost incredible patience in comparing passage to passage, word to word, syllable to syllable, diacritical mark to diacritical mark. Also, it is extremely important that although his tongue can handle Greek and Hebrew, he should have Latin in his mind; that is, he should not be a devotee of Greek and Hebrew materials. For as some typically go astray by not knowing those languages, so others do the same out of too much admiration for them in commenting on the scriptures.

[1] The Authors
Where there are two teaching scripture, one should comment on the Old, the other the New Testament. But where there is only one, he can expound the Old Testament one year and the New Testament in the next one. In the New Testament, everything should be covered, but from the Old Testament, Genesis, Job, Psalms, Proverbs, Ecclesiastes, the Song of Songs, and the Prophets. The person who teaches the Hebrew language can comment on the other books of the Old Testament.

[2] The Time

The time for learning scripture should come to a close with the end of one's life. But the right amount of class-time for studying it seems not less than four years, so that for two years the Old Testament can be taken and an equal amount of time given to the New Testament. But getting a knowledge of the scriptures is not adequate; they should learn the method of studying and interpreting it. An hour each day should be given to the scripture lesson, and at least half an hour to a review of that lesson.

[3] On the Method

In the first place, the one who comments on scripture ought to discuss the reading if it is different from the translation or in need of correction. In this matter, he will always support the authority of our translation, and he will teach how our translator seems to have read the Hebrew or the Greek: so that if he reads Wisdom 4:19, "He will break apart those who are puffed up without a sound," he will say that our translator did not read *prenous*, as it is now, but *presous*; nor did he read *aphronous*, as it is now in Greek editions, but *aphonous*. Next, if the translation has been corrupted, he will amend sometimes from the sources, and sometimes from other Latin editions. So that if he comes upon Wisdom 5:22, "Like reins by a curved rainbow," he will say that it ought to be read as it is in Greek, *kai hos apo eukyklou tozou [ton] ephon*; and this is how it reads in other, better corrected Latin texts and as the meaning requires: "As if from a well curved rainbow." Third, only for the more difficult passages will he cover all the literal interpretations from all the authors and the points to be made about them. Fourth, he will interpret the literal meaning according to our translation, and he will show that our translator has rendered the sense better than others have. Fifth, using all the powers of his judgment, considering first the Catholic faith, then consulting the Hebrew and Greek texts, comparing other similar passages in scripture, and always reading the best commentaries, he will explain the true meaning. Sixth, he will see whether any church dogma can be confirmed from that passage, and he will do this scrupulously, citing other passages of scripture on that same subject. Seventh, he ought to know whether the heretics typically misuse that passage to prove some error of theirs, and he will diligently refute their interpretation, their reading, and their translation. Eighth, he will apply the meaning of the scripture to the moral life, occasionally using short, very well-chosen allegories, ones that have arisen in a certain way right from the literal meaning. Ninth, he should take care that when he is tracing out the literal meaning, he does not give too much weight to the Hebrew pointings or to rabbinical interpretations, and disregarding the pointings, he should try to see how our translator, or the Septuagint, or other ancient translators read when there were no pointings. Tenth, he should avoid the common faults of wandering off into preaching or in search of allegories and Scholastic subtleties, but he should always stick with the passage and with the literal meaning, once it has been discovered, and he should nicely sprinkle in some allegory if he wishes. Eleventh, as Saint Augustine teaches, he will explain the Old Testament by the New and the New by the Old as far as this can be done. Twelfth, if he wishes to give any dictation, he will do it using a very few, very clear words.

[4] Exercises
The first one ought to be listening; the second, review, and it should be very frequent; the third, to commit some books, like the Psalms and Proverbs, to memory; the fourth, to engage in disputation, especially on those passages the church uses to prove its dogma or that heretics use to assert their errors; the fifth is lessons privately given; the sixth, writing.

[5] The Students
The students ought to be more apt for coursework in scripture than in Scholastic theology. For it is essential that they have better judgment and that they be older and more versed in Scholastic theology, and that they have a better grasp of the languages and other matters.

[III] Cases of Conscience

The instructor who is going to teach cases of conscience ought to have strong judgment and prudence above all, and his mind should not be restless, wandering, or skeptical. Then he should be quite well versed in the moral area of theology and in the essential summaries that have been written about it; and if it is possible, he should be experienced not just in books but in practical affairs as well. He should be one who has thoughtfully and deliberately decided at his leisure all those doubtful matters that come up in confessions, what should be held, what said, and what given as a response.

[1] The Authors
Either no author ought to be expounded or only one who is extremely brief or very clear, such as Bartholomaeus Fumus.[7]

[2] The Time
The time for teaching seems to be all the feast days where this is possible; but if not, some day during the week, when the students can most conveniently assemble.

---

7   Bartolomeo Fumo (d.1555) was a Dominican theologian and inquisitor who wrote the *Summa, quae* Aurea Armilla *inscribitur* [A summary, which is entitled "The Golden Bracelet"] (Piacenza: Muzio and Locheta, 1549), a handbook in which Fumo listed 504 directives for priests' daily care of souls.

[3] The Method
The teaching should be brief and clear, and it should pass on the general rules by which not only the proposed question but many other similar ones can be resolved. Different opinions should not be cited except rarely; not every argument should be used when proving the main idea, but only those that are foundational and basic. Distinctions that are very clear and full should be employed to ground an understanding of everything that can occur. Examples should not be constructed as in other disputations, but they should be taken from what often happens in real life. A lesson ought to be reviewed again and again by the instructor and by the students. There should be no dictation for the students' notes, for this science ought to be kept in the memory, not in writing, although the students can jot down some notes to help them remember.

[4] The Exercises
The first will be as much review as possible; the second, reading the authors on the issue often, almost to the point of learning them by heart; the third, frequently hearing confessions; the fourth, putting the students together, some to ask questions and others to answer them.

[5] The Students
The students ought to be all the priests, all the theologians, and all who are going to be priests within two years.

Index